THE LITERARY GUIDE AND COMPANION TO NORTHERN ENGLAND

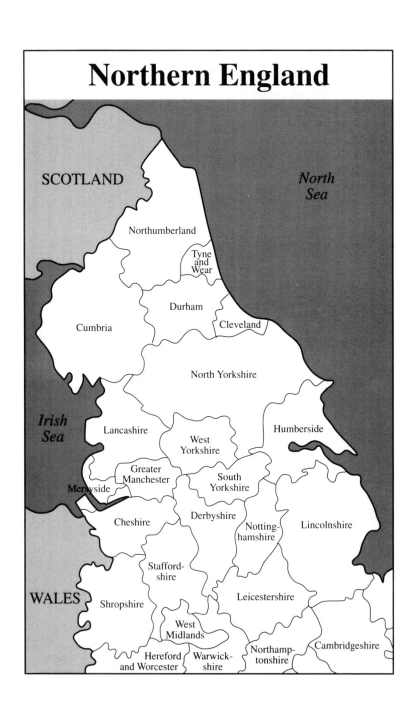

Northern England

SCOTLAND

North Sea

Northumberland

Tyne and Wear

Durham

Cumbria

Cleveland

North Yorkshire

Irish Sea

Lancashire

West Yorkshire

Humberside

Greater Manchester

South Yorkshire

Merseyside

Cheshire

Derbyshire

Nottinghamshire

Lincolnshire

WALES

Stafford-shire

Shropshire

Leicestershire

West Midlands

Hereford and Worcester

Warwick-shire

Northamptonshire

Cambridgeshire

THE LITERARY GUIDE AND COMPANION TO NORTHERN ENGLAND

ROBERT M. COOPER

OHIO UNIVERSITY PRESS
ATHENS

Ohio University Press, Athens, Ohio 45701
© 1995 by Polly Cooper
Printed in the United States of America
All rights reserved

99 98 97 96 95   5 4 3 2 1

Ohio University Press books are printed on acid-free paper ∞

Library of Congress Cataloging-in-Publication Data

Cooper, Robert M.
   The literary guide and companion to Northern England / by
Robert M. Cooper.
      p.   cm.
   Includes index.
   ISBN 0-8214-1095-4 (cloth); 0-8214-1096-2(pbk.)
   1. Literary landmarks—England, Northern—Guidebooks.   2.
Authors, English—Homes and haunts—England, Northern—
Guidebooks.   3. English literature—England, Northern—History
and criticism.   4. England, Northern—In literature—Guidebooks.
I. Title.
PR110.N67C66   1994
820.9'9427—dc20   94-21981
                                                         CIP

FOR

Rob and Pam
Ellen and Brig
and for
Rebecca, because she wasn't here last time

CONTENTS

Maps   xi
Acknowledgments   xiii
Preface   xv

I. FROM SHROPSHIRE TO THE WASH
1. THE WEST
Shropshire
    Shrewsbury and Battlefield   9
    Hodnet, Wem, and Oswestry   13
    Housman's Shropshire: Ludlow, Clun,
        the Wenlocks, and Hughley   15
    Bridgnorth, Shifnal, and Tong   23

Staffordshire
    Stafford and Shallowford   30
    Stoke-on-Trent   33
    Lichfield   36
    Edial   47
    Uttoxeter   47
    Ellastone and Wootton, and Mayfield   49
    Ilam   50

Derbyshire
    Dovedale: Ashbourne, Ilam and the Manifold,
        and Thor's Cave   55
    Walton's Dovedale: Hartington to Thorpe Cloud   60
    Wirksworth and Middleton   62
    Chatsworth and Edensor   63
    Hathersage and Renishaw   67
    Derby and Kedleston Hall   69

2. THE EAST
Nottinghamshire
    Nottingham   78
    Newstead Abbey   82

Annesley Hall	87
Eastwood	88
Welbeck Abbey	93
Southwell and Newark upon Trent	94

Lincolnshire

Lincoln	102
Gainsborough, Grantham, and Boston	105
Horncastle	109
Harrington Hall, Langton, and Somersby	110
Louth, Mablethorpe and Skegness, and Tealby	115

II. THE NORTHEAST

1. THE YORKSHIRES AND HUMBERSIDE

West Yorkshire

Leads, Bradford, and Thornton	129
Haworth	131
Roe Head, Birstall, and Gomersal	137
Halifax	139
Wakefield and Pontefract	140

South Yorkshire

Sheffield, and Barnsley and Rotherham	145
Conisbrough Castle	146

Humberside

Epworth	151
Kingston upon Hull	152
Bridlington	153
Beverley	154

North Yorkshire

York	159
Sutton-on-the-Forest, Stillington, and Skelton	167
Coxwold	170
Appleton Roebuck and Monk Fryston	173
Harrogate	176
Wordsworth's Yorkshire (1):	
Thirsk, Rievaulx Abbey, and Brompton	178
Wordsworth's Yorkshire (2):	
Rylstone and Bolton Abbey	182
Croft-on-Tees	185

Richmond	190
Castle Howard	191
Scarborough and Whitby	193

2. DURHAM TO THE BORDER

County Durham and Cleveland

Durham	205
Kelloe, Brancepeth, and Bishop Auckland	207
Binchester, Barnard Castle, Bowes, and Greta Bridge	210
Darlington, Stockton on Tees, and Hartlepool	213
Seaham	214

Northumberland and Tyne and Wear

Newcastle upon Tyne	219
Jarrow, Whitburn, and Sunderland	221
Hexham	223
Capheaton, and Wallington Hall and Cambo	224
Felton, Bamburgh, and Holy Island and Norham Castle	226

III. THE NORTHWEST

1. CHESHIRE TO LANCASHIRE

Cheshire

Chester	237
Broxton, Hawarden, Parkgate, and Winnington Hall	245
Knutsford	249
Tatton Park	257
Daresbury	258

Merseyside

Liverpool	263
Knowsley Park, Rock Ferry, and Southport	273

2. GREATER MANCHESTER AND LANCASHIRE

Greater Manchester

The City of Manchester	285
Wigan	295

Lancashire

Preston	300
Whalley, Hurstwood, and Stonyhurst College	300
Silverdale, and Cowan Bridge	302

3. CUMBRIA: THE LAKE DISTRICT

The South Lakes: Newby Bridge to Hawkshead
Newby Bridge and Near Sawrey and Esthwaite Water   313
Brantwood, Coniston, and Hawkshead   314

Between the Lakes: Windermere to Grasmere
Lake Windermere   321
Ambleside   323
Grasmere and Environs   328

Northern Cumbria
Keswick and Greta Hall   341
Windebrowe, Borrowdale, and Mirehouse   344
Egremont and Cockermouth   346
In and Around Penrith   348
Caldbeck   351
Carlisle   352
Bowness-on-Solway and Solway Firth   353

Index   355

MAPS

Shropshire   6
Staffordshire   28
     Lichfield   44
Derbyshire   52
Nottinghamshire   74
     Eastwood   92
Lincolnshire   100
West Yorkshire   126
South Yorkshire   194
Humberside   150
North Yorkshire   156
     York   160
Durham and Cleveland   204
Northumberland and Tyne and Wear   218
Cheshire   236
     Chester   244
     Knutsford   256
Merseyside   262
Greater Manchester   284
Lancashire   298
Cumbria   306

A NOTE ABOUT THE AUTHOR

Robert M. Cooper was Professor Emeritus of English Literature at Rhodes College, Memphis, Tennessee. The first of his three literary guides, *The Literary Guide and Companion to Southern England*, was published by Ohio University Press in 1986. *The Literary Guide and Companion to Middle England*, published in 1992, and *The Literary Guide and Companion to Northern England* were readied for publication by his widow, Polly Cooper.

ACKNOWLEDGMENTS

Charles Wilkinson of Rhodes College's Department of English has again proven himself invaluable as advisor, critic, scholar and friend. And Loretta Martin is again responsible for the painstakingly prepared maps. These literary travel companions—and our lives—have been enriched by *our* favorite travel companions, Pat and Leo Bent of Knutsford, Cheshire. Their alert eyes and ears and love and knowledge of their homeland have enhanced many of our experiences—and made them much more fun! And this last volume has been especially helped by the expert knowledge of Northern England of their (and now my) friend Frank O'Ryan. To all of them—and to the invariably kind and helpful people at Tourist Information Centres all over Northern England—my endless thanks.

Maps by Loretta Martin
Jacket photograph by Murray Riss

PREFACE

Before his death my husband had completed the writing of all three volumes of this series of literary guides to England. I am grateful that he was able to see at least one of them—*The Literary Guide and Companion to Southern England*—in print. He had completed the preface and started the indexing of *The Literary Guide to Middle England*, and had done the research and writing for this book, but had not done the preface, maps, or indices. I have tried to finish these tasks for him. I hope I have done a job that would meet his demanding standards. But any errors that may remain are mine.

I think I can do no better for this preface than to follow the form he set forth in the other two volumes—and so, I begin as he did in both of them with:

This book was written for the person who unabashedly loves travel, loves England, and loves English literature. In short, for somebody remarkably like the person I was when I began to plan my first trip to Britain and looked for just such a book.

To prepare the best possible itinerary before I got there, and to best use my time and enrich each moment after my arrival, I wanted answers in particular to six specific questions. But I found no answers.

Since then, he continues, a number of books on literary England have appeared, some of real value. But each has its own different purpose, and so, as with Southern England and Middle England, the initial questions remain unanswered:

1. **If I go to such-and-such, what else is there of interest nearby?**
It's very probable that if you are in Northern England, and are interested in literature as well as scenery, you'll get to the Lake District. And while there, of course, you'll almost certainly go to Wordsworth's Dove Cottage. But do you know that in practically no time you can see his final home, Rydal Mount? And, in between, is Nab Cottage where Thomas De Quincey lived. And, some ten or fifteen miles up the road is Keswick with much of literary interest including Southey's "ant hill," Greta Hall. Not only will this book get you there, but also you'll find out why Southey called it an ant hill.

2. **What's the most interesting route to take from such-and-such to so-and-so?** If, for instance, you are heading from Nottingham to York, you can use this book and its maps to plan interesting little side trips not far off whatever major highway you may be taking. On the way, perhaps, you might want to see Byron's Newstead Abbey or Lord Tennyson's Somersby. Or the Wakefield of the Vicar and of the famous play cycle. And, if the Methodist Church interests you, you'll surely want to stop by Epworth, the birthplace of the two hymn-writing brothers who are credited with starting it.

3. **I know the usual things about it, but is there anything else of literary interest connected with this place (this street, this house, this room) I'm in?** You might stop by Renishaw Hall in Derbyshire, for instance, family seat of that trio of writing siblings, the Sitwells. But did you know that the hall was the model for Lady Chatterley's home in the novel about her and her lover? And did you know that the story was a true one, based on a tale told to D. H. Lawrence by the hall's then-owner, Sir George Sitwell?

4. **Once you arrive in a town, or the general area of a place, how do you find the place itself?** Insofar as possible, precise directions are given both in text and on maps to get you just where you want to go. It would be easy to get lost, for instance, trying to find John Ruskin's home on Coniston Water unless you know that the thing to do is to take a tiny little unnumbered road off the B 5285. And you can also see it from the lake, aboard a *gondola!*

5. **What is the best way—i.e., the shortest, quickest, most comprehensive way—to cover a town with a number of literary sites?** For every town of such description, there is a suggested walking tour, and often an accompanying map.

6. **Are there any places of literary interest where I can get a meal, a pint of half and half, or even stay overnight?** Lots! In Lichfield you can stay at The George where George Farquhar set the first act of *The Beaux's Stratagem* or at The Swan where Dr. Johnson sent Mrs. Thrale back upstairs to change into something "more gay and splendid looking" when the Thrales were his guests there and he wanted his friends to make a good impression in his old home town. Or, you might want to have lunch at Betty's Cafe and Tea Shop in Harrogate where James Herriot and his wife met friends weekly for years. There's a special index at the back of the book to help you find literary locations for food, drink, and lodgings, if you wish.

Just as I felt there was no better way to begin this preface than to repeat what my husband had written in the two preceding volumes, so I feel there is no better way to end it:

> I hope you will find this book fun in the best sense of the word—fun to plan your trip with, fun to use at the various stops along the way while you're there, and fun to recollect with after you're back home.

It certainly was fun to write.

Polly Cooper

From Shropshire to the Wash

I

THE WEST

1

Shropshire

Shropshire

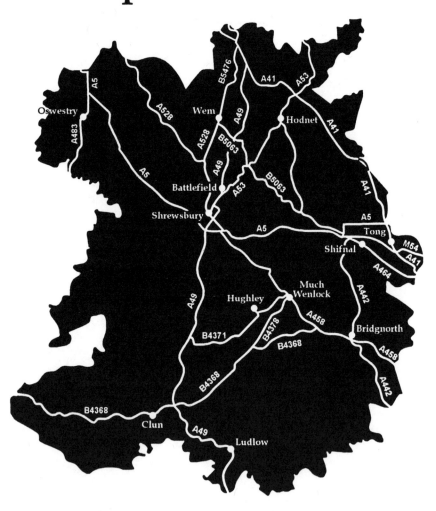

I never knew such pleasant walking as in the old streets like those of Shrewsbury. . . . There was a delightful want of plan in the laying out of these ancient towns. In fact, they were never laid out at all, but grew naturally, with streets as eccentric as the pathway of a young child toddling about the floor.

Nathaniel Hawthorne, *Our Old Home*

Shrewsbury—unspoilt and alive: a city with vigour still adjusted to its beautiful frame. Poetry—or luck—in every inch of it . . . I want to write A. E. Housman.

E. M. Forster's diary on a walking tour, 1907

Clunton and Clunbury
Clungunford and Clun,
Are the quietest places
Under the sun.

A. E. Housman, *A Shropshire Lad*

When E. M. Forster made his walking tour of Shropshire in 1907, he carried a copy of Housman's *A Shropshire Lad* in his pocket, as who wouldn't while strolling through Housman country. Except, of course, that Shropshire wasn't really Housman country at all.

The fact is, the author of the slim little volume of verses that made the county known throughout the world was never a Shropshire lad himself—or, for that matter, even a Shropshire man. He never lived there, even briefly. He was born and raised in Worcestershire. From age twenty-three to fifty-two he was a London man, first working at the Patent Office, then teaching at University College. The last twenty-five years of his life, from 1911 until his death in 1936, he was a professor of

Latin and a fellow at Trinity College, Cambridge. Only after death could Shropshire claim him for its own: Housman died at Cambridge, but is buried in the Ludlow churchyard.

He admitted that his knowledge of Shropshire was somewhat skimpy. "Very little in the book is autobiographical," he said. "I know Ludlow and Wenlock, but my topographical details—Hughley, Abdon-under-Clee— are sometimes quite wrong." The Hughley steeple he celebrated as a "far known sign," he acknowledged after finally seeing it, "actually couldn't have been much of a steeple." The town is hidden in a valley. But, he said, "as I had already composed the poem and could not invent another name that sounded so nice, I let it stand."

Even the name of the book wasn't Housman's own. He originally called it *The Poems of Terence Hearsay*. It was a friend, Alfred William Pollard, biographer and Shakespearian and Chaucer scholar, who suggested *A Shropshire Lad*. Why then did the poems feature Shropshire rather than his own native Worcester? Nostalgia for his boyhood, he explained: "I had a sentimental feeling for Shropshire, because its hills were our western horizon." At fifteen, his favorite exercise was to walk up Mount Pisgah behind his Fockbury home to see the distant Shropshire hills.

Those hills, among the loveliest in England, are in the county's lower half. In the north the land is flat. But to the south are lofty rises such as Wenlock Edge, and deep wooded valleys dotted with delightful little lakes called "meres," and delectable villages with names Housman loved, Clun and Clunbury and Abdon-under-Clee.

If Housman was no true Shropshire lad, there are writers who were. William Wycherly and Charles Darwin and Wilfred Owen, certainly—they were born there. And Sir Philip Sidney and William Hazlitt in a sense: Sidney was a schoolboy in Shrewsbury; Hazlitt was the son of Wem's Unitarian minister. Thanks to Hazlitt's father, Samuel Coleridge almost became a Shropshire minister himself. Both the "Hudibras" Butler and the "Erewhon" Butler had Shropshire connections, Milton's *Comus* had a Shropshire premiere, and Hotspur and Little Nell a Shropshire end.

To visit the literary sites of Shropshire, you couldn't choose a better headquarters than the county seat and largest town, Shrewsbury. From it highways reach out to all corners of the county, none more than thirty miles away. And as both Nathaniel Hawthorne and E. M. Forster avowed, Shrewsbury is a delightful stop in itself, beautifully located in a loop of the Severn, and with its own assortment of literary attractions.

9

SHREWSBURY AND BATTLEFIELD

Toward the end of *Henry IV, Part I* Shakespeare depicts the lord of Westmoreland and Hal, prince of Wales, hurrying toward Shrewsbury to help Hal's father, Henry IV, crush Hotspur and his rebellious friends. Almost there, they run into Sir John Falstaff heading with his rag tag troops toward the same place, but a good deal less eagerly. However, Falstaff puts up a brave front:

> Falstaff: What, Hal? how now, mad wag? What a devil doest thou in Warwickshire? My good Lord of Westmoreland, I cry you mercy! I thought your honour had already been at Shrewsbury.
>
> Westmoreland (dourly): Faith, Sir John, 'tis more than time that I were there, and you too.

And so, Falstaff follows them to Shrewsbury, but with all deliberate speed. After all, a man could get hurt in battle.

Shrewsbury   Shrewsbury has been called the gateway to Wales, a scant ten miles to the west. But it's the gateway to so much else as well. On the east is Samuel Johnson's Staffordshire, leading to Derbyshire, Nottinghamshire, and the Lincolnshire coasts of the Wash and the North Sea. Immediately to the north lie Cheshire and, beyond that, the Lake District. To the south is Hereford and Worcester, with the roads leading to Bath and the West Country. London itself is only 150 miles away, with Stratford-upon-Avon and Oxford almost directly en route.

Puzzling to many a visitor (and not only those from abroad, mind you) to Shropshire is just why in the world the natives call themselves Salopians and their county Salop. Well, Shrewsbury makes this all perfectly clear.

The Saxons of the eighth century, you see, called the town "Scobesbyrig," pronounced SHO-bes-berrig, a "scobes" (wooded) "byrig" (settlement). The more proper of their descendants, following normal linguistic patterns, softened the pronunciation through centuries to SHROPESberry ("burg"), then simply SHRO'S-berry ("bury"), changing the spelling as they went.[1] So to this day, Shrewsbury is pronounced SHROZE-

---

[1] The changes in "byrig" are no great puzzle in any event. The last two syllables of Edin*burgh*, Gains*borough*, and Canter*bury* all came from the same word.

berry. Less restrained descendants, however, let their tongues run away with them. In their mouths the name slurred to SLOPES-berry," then 'SALOP'S-berry. Et voila: Salop and Salopian.

By any name, the town is lovely to look upon. Housman wrote:

> High the vanes of Shrewsbury gleam
> Islanded in the Severn stream;
> The bridges from the steepled crest
> Cross the water east and west.

And "islanded" Shrewsbury is, as Forster said in the diary entry for his stop there in 1907, "gloriously piled on a curve of the Severn, . . . which two fine bridges traverse—the English and the Welsh, and against which laps the Quarry with a magnificent avenue of limes."

Despite some clutter of industrial and housing estates, unavoidable in a modern community of 60,000 people, Shrewsbury still largely deserves Forster's encomium, "unspoilt." Narrow streets wander off from the two main thoroughfares, with a collection of well-kept Tudor black-and-white half-timbered houses that rank among England's finest. Parts of the castle go back to the thirteenth century and even earlier, and some of the old town wall survives, including a thirteenth-century tower.

As for Shrewsbury's literary associations, there are a number, including several connected with the old Shrewsbury Grammar School. The school was founded by Henry VIII's short-lived son, Edward VI, in 1552 near the castle, on the spot where the Free Library and Museum now stand. Among its early students were Sir Philip Sidney and Sir Fulke Greville (later Lord Brooke). They entered on the same day—October 17, 1564—and became life-long friends, serving together in the court of Elizabeth I.

Although his writings never attained the stature of Sidney's *Arcadia* (1590) or *Astrophel and Stella* (1591), Greville wrote a colorful biography of Sidney, acceptable plays such as *Mustapha* (1609), and some better than average sonnets and songs.

In the nineteenth century, the school became famous for scholarship, attracting among others Charles Darwin, Samuel "Erewhon" Butler, Frederick William Faber, and Stanley John Weyman. Director of this rise to academic excellence was Butler's grandfather, Samuel Butler, who took over as headmaster in 1798. He also edited an edition of Aeschylus, was author of *A Sketch of Modern and Ancient Geography* (1813), and ultimately became bishop of Lichfield.

The younger Butler is best known for his satirical romance, *Erewhon* (1872), and the novel, *The Way of All Flesh,* published in 1903 after his death. But he also wrote some pieces of curious interest: attacks on his fellow Shrewsbury alumnus Charles Darwin such as *The Deadlock in Darwinism* (1887) and an article titled "The Authoress of The Odyssey" (1893) in which he insisted Homer was a woman.

Faber, friend of Coleridge and Cardinal Newman, was the author of a number of devotional works, but is remembered now for his hymns, notably "Pilgrims of the Night" and "The Land Beyond the Sea." Weyman wrote some good historical novels, *A Gentleman of France* (1893), for instance, and *Count Hannibal* (1901).

The young dramatist George Farquhar was a visitor to Shrewsbury in 1704 when he stayed at the Raven Inn while writing *The Recruiting Officer.* In the play, Shrewsbury serves as model for a lively picture of the problems of a recruiter trying to go about his business in a country town. Farquhar's solution is to have his hero, Captain Plume, woo its young ladies in order to snare their boyfriends as recruits.

Samuel Taylor Coleridge came to Shrewsbury in 1798 as a candidate for the pulpit of its Unitarian church. Trudging through ten miles of frozen mud to hear him was twenty-year-old William Hazlitt, living with his Unitarian minister father in nearby Wem. "Never," wrote Hazlitt years later, "the longest day I have to live, shall I have such another walk as this cold, raw, comfortless one." But, "A poet and a philosopher getting into a Unitarian pulpit to preach the gospel, was a romance in these degenerate days . . . which was not to be resisted."

Coleridge preached "like an eagle dallying in the wind," Hazlitt said. "I could not have been more delighted if I had heard the music of the spheres." But Coleridge turned the position down when offered instead an annuity of £150 a year by his friend, Thomas Wedgwood, if he would spend all his time on poetry and philosophy.

On his visit to Shrewsbury in 1855, Nathaniel Hawthorne stayed at the Lion Hotel, and walked around to the Raven for a look at the window of the room where Farquhar had written *The Recruiting Officer.* But the hostlers currying their horses in the inn yard stared at the American intruder so curiously that he slunk off after only the merest glimpse.

Forster's visit in 1907 after a tour of Wales was partly in celebration of the completion of *The Longest Journey,* just published. The reviews were mixed, some enthusiastic, some not. *The Outlook* called it "frankly the most impossible book we have read for many years." As the already-quoted excerpts from Forster's diary indicate, Forster was enchanted with Shrewsbury. His summation: "The more said, the better."

If you plan to stay over in Shrewsbury for an extra day or two, there are plenty of places to put you up. Of special interest is the three-star Lion on Wyle Cop, where Hawthorne stayed in 1855. Next door is the old house that harbored Henry of Richmond in 1485 the night before the Battle of Bosworth Field, in which he defeated Richard III, ended the Wars of the Roses, and made himself Henry VII.

In the middle of the Lion's three-section front is the original little fifteenth-century timber-framed structure, rebuilt in the eighteenth century. Among noted guests in the two hundred years since then are the real Madame Tussaud, who gave an exhibition of her wax figures in the hotel's assembly room in 1830; the famous violinist Paganini, who played there in 1831; and Charles Dickens, who was there both in 1836 with his illustrator, Hablôt Browne, and on one of his reading tours twenty years later.

Hanging in the hall of the Lion is a letter on hotel stationery attesting that Benjamin Disraeli was there in 1841, keeping count of the local election returns for his party's leader and then Prime Minister Sir Robert Peele. The returns were good. Says Disraeli's letter, addressed to Peele:

> The State of the Poll at Shrewsbury this day permits me to renew my fealty to my Chief.

As suggested, Shrewsbury would be an excellent headquarters for a tour of Shropshire. To begin your trip, Battlefield, where Hal slew Hotspur, is just four miles to the north up the A 49.

Battlefield   Today the place called Battlefield is a considerable community of more than 5,000 people. On July 21, 1403, it was simply an empty field beneath a "bosky" (bushy) hill four miles above Shrewsbury where the rival forces of King Henry IV and the powerful Percy family of Northumberland met to settle once and for all their bitter struggle for power.

Out of this came Shakespeare's *Henry IV, Part I.* The playwright builds his drama around a trio. There is the king himself, old but doughty. And his chief opponent, Henry Percy, son of the earl of Northumberland, scarcely out of his teens but so fiery and headstrong his enemies dubbed him "Hotspur." And, finally, there's the king's son, Henry "Hal," young as Hotspur, but addicted to roistering rather than battle, egged on by his old, fat, dissolute, but utterly irresistible chum, Falstaff.

When the chips are down, of course, Hal redeems himself, as all good prodigals should. He goes to his father's aid, slays Hotspur in hand-to-hand combat, then pays noble tribute to his fallen foe, "brave Percy":

> Fare thee well, great heart . . .
> Adieu, and take thy praise with thee to Heaven!

Remarkable and touching, isn't it? Equally remarkable is what Shakespeare has done to the facts of history. You almost forget that the real King Henry was thirty-six, "young" Hotspur thirty-nine, and Hal sixteen. Hal did perform valiantly in the battle. But far from dying heroically in a man-to-man duel with him, Hotspur was struck down by unknown hands as he tried to sneak off when his troops fled. Cruelest of all, the winners showed nothing like the magnanimity of Shakespeare's Hal. Hotspur's body was hanged, drawn and quartered, then the head cut off and sent to be displayed on a gate in York.

Today's visitor to Battlefield can see the church built by Henry IV to commemorate the battle.

HODNET—WEM—AND OSWESTRY

Also above Shrewsbury within easy reach are Hodnet, Wem, and Oswestry. Hodnet is twelve miles to the northeast on the A 53, Wem ten miles due north on the B 5063, and Oswestry sixteen miles northwest on the A 483.

Hodnet   Hodnet makes a pleasant little stop if only for its Church of St. Luke and the fine black-and-white half-timbers that cluster about it. Built of sandstone in the fourteenth century, St. Luke's has a tower that is octagonal from top to bottom—the only such structure in all Shropshire—as well as literary treasures such as a Nuremberg Bible printed in 1479 and a copy of the Erasmus New Testament of 1522.

Moreover, the vicar of St. Luke's from 1807 until he became bishop of Calcutta in 1823 was Reginald Heber. Heber was only twenty-four when he came to St. Luke's, but winning the post wasn't all that great a tribute to his precocity; his family owned the right of appointment.

While in India, he wrote *A Narrative of a Journey* (1824) which is agreeable enough, and edited the works of Jeremy Taylor. But he will be remembered probably for all time for some of the best-known hymns in the English language, among them "The Son of God Goes Forth to War," "From Greenland's Icy Mountain," and "Holy, Holy, Holy, Lord God Almighty." Heber is memorialized in Hodnet by a tile in the church chancel and a lamp post in town.

His family, the Heber-Percy's, remains one of Shropshire's prominent families and owns Hodnet Hall, built in Elizabethan style in 1870. Open to the public every afternoon from April through September, the estate boasts sixty acres of landscaped gardens, pools, and lakes. If you need a bracing end to your day, there are tea rooms with a unique collection of big game trophies.

Wem   After Coleridge finished the first sermon of his tryout for the Unitarian ministry of Shrewsbury, he paid a courtesy visit to a Rev. Mr. Hazlitt, who held the same post in Wem. Although the host and his guest couldn't have been more different, they got on famously. Mr. Hazlitt's essayist son, William, wrote years later that his father wouldn't have been more delighted "if our visitor had worn wings."

Young Hazlitt was equally delighted. Coleridge, he wrote, "seemed to have taken considerable notice of me." Indeed he did, listening with all due gravity to opinions delivered with the assurance only a twenty-year-old could have mustered in such august company. And when the poet left the next morning, he called for a pen and a bit of card. On it he wrote, "Mr. Coleridge, Nether-Stowey, Somerset," saying not only would he be glad to have the boy visit him there, but he would come halfway to meet him.

No wonder that twenty-five years after the event, William Hazlitt was able to recall Coleridge's visit to Wem down to its tiniest detail, even to the meal his mother had served:

> I remember the leg of Welsh mutton and the turnips on the table that day had the finest flavor imaginable.

Oswestry   Oswestry's candidate for "the" Shropshire poet was Wilfred Owen, and had he lived, he might have been a great one. But war cut him down at twenty-five. And even the years he knew, save for the very last, were far from promising.

He was born in 1893 at Plas Wilmot, the home his parents and maternal grandparents shared. While his father struggled to make a living in the railway service, young Wilfred got such education as he could, grammar school in Liverpool, then the technical school in Shrewsbury after his family settled there. He did manage to enroll at London University, but couldn't afford to stay. The years he should have been at college were spent as a lay assistant to an Oxfordshire vicar and as an English tutor in France. In 1915 he returned home to enlist in the army.

Ironically, it was the war that gave him the impetus and opportunity for intellectual maturity and development, and then ended it abruptly, all within three years. He was wounded in action soon after his enlistment. In the fifteen months of hospitalization that followed, he experienced an almost miraculous creative outburst.

Encouraged by Robert Graves and Osbert Sitwell, and especially by Siegfried Sassoon, a fellow patient at his Edinburgh hospital, he began writing grimly realistic war poetry at the farthest remove from such traditional nonsense as Tennyson's "Charge of the Light Brigade." For him, battle was never heroic. "My Subject is War, and the pity of War," he wrote in the preface for his planned collection of poems.

Owen never completed the project. In late summer of 1918 he was recalled to duty. On November 4 he died in action. Seven days later the war ended.

The poems, published by Sassoon in 1920, were to have great influence on later poets such as C. Day-Lewis, W. H. Auden, Stephen Spender, and Dylan Thomas, and have grown steadily in critical acclaim. One can but mourn for Wilfred Owen, the Shropshire lad who might have been.

HOUSMAN'S SHROPSHIRE: LUDLOW—CLUN—THE WENLOCKS—AND HUGHLEY

When Housman said he didn't know Shropshire well, he added, "except in parts," for there is an area that he came to know, at least in later life, that may in a sense be called Housman's Shropshire. He strictly delimits this area and the degree of his familiarity in the very letter that contains his confession of ignorance, written in 1934 almost forty years after the poems were published:

The Wrekin is wooded, and Wenlock Edge along the western side, but the Clees and most of the other hills are grass or heather. In the south half of the county, to which I have confined myself, the hills are generally long ridges running from north to south, with valleys, broad or narrow, between. The northern half is part of the great Cheshire plain. The Wrekin is isolated.

As you see, Housman's Shropshire wasn't all that extensive. The Wrekin, a rocky outcropping that rises to 1,334 feet, is just outside Shrewsbury. Clee Hill overlooks Ludlow. Shrewsbury and Ludlow are at most twenty-five miles apart.

From Shrewsbury, the easiest way to cover all Housman's Shropshire is to go straight down the A 49 to Ludlow, see Ludlow itself, then begin to fan out from there. Clun is a dozen miles to the west on the B 4368. The upthrust of Wenlock Edge and the town of Much Wenlock, north and northeast above Ludlow, are reached via the B 4368 and the A 458. Hughley is off the B 4371 a couple of miles below Much Wenlock.

Ludlow   Ludlow, a town of much charm, has links to Sir Philip Sidney, John Milton, Samuel "Hudibras" Butler, The American Henry Adams, Stanley John Weyman, and E. M. Forster, as well as to Housman.

Looking down on the town from its cliff above the Teme and Corve rivers are the ruins of a once mighty red-stone fortress, Ludlow Castle. Begun as early as 1090, it was one of thirty-two strongholds built to protect the border regions between England and Wales, called the Marches. Those thirty-two fortresses represent nearly twenty percent of all the castles in England.[2] In 1559 Queen Elizabeth appointed as her president of the marches and master of Ludlow Castle a Sir Henry Sidney. Thus it was that his son, that poet and dazzling Renaissance-man-to-be, Sir Philip Sidney, spent his boyhood at Ludlow and prepared for Oxford at Shrewsbury School.

The appointment of another governor of the castle brought Milton to Ludlow and occasioned his writing of *Comus*. The year was 1634, the new governor, John Egerton, earl of Bridgewater, named lord president of Wales by Charles I. To celebrate the earl's formal installation, his music master and tutor to his children, Henry Lawes, decided to stage an elaborate masque, and asked his friend, John Milton, to write one. Milton, then only twenty-six and not long out of college, was flattered and eagerly accepted.

---

[2] Purists in such things recognize a total of 186 strongholds as formidable enough to be called castles.

It was no easy task. In masques the music, dances, and spectacular stage effects predominate, putting the writer at a disadvantage. And Ben Jonson, who had brought the form to a peak earlier in the century, had made it ribald and licentious, hardly characteristics congenial to a man of Milton's temperament. In his *Pleasure reconciled to Vertue* (1618), which served as Milton's model, Jonson has Comus—the god of revelry— come on stage huge-bellied and naked, pulled in a low chariot by three naked attendants.

To make it worse, Lawes's three principal actors for such a piece would be the earl's own daughter, barely fifteen, and her even younger brothers. Somehow, Milton managed to pull it off. Critics have hailed *Comus* as the lightest, most joyous of all his works.

It was yet another lord president of Wales who brought the seventeenth-century Samuel Butler to Ludlow Castle. Richard Vaughan, earl of Carbery, made Butler his steward in 1661. While there, the satirist worked on *Hudibras,* publishing Part I in 1663. It was greeted with wide enthusiasm but there were those who found it resistible. Samuel Pepys wrote in his *Diary:*

> . . . falling into a discourse of a new book of drollery in verse called Hudebras [sic], I would needs go find it out, and met with it at The Temple; cost me 2s.6d. But when I came to read it, it is so silly an abuse of the Presbyter Knight going to the warrs, that I am ashamed of it; and by and by meeting at Mr. Townsend's at dinner, I sold it to him for 18d.

But His Majesty Charles II enjoyed the poem, made Butler a present of £300, and followed that up with a pension of £100 a year.

In the nineteenth century, Southern Shropshire was a favorite haunt of Henry Adams, who served as a personal secretary when his father was America's ambassador to England. In *The Education of Henry Adams* (1907) he wrote of a vacation in 1867, referring to himself in the third person as he customarily did:

> Whether he rode about the Wrekin, or all the historical haunts from Ludlow Castle and Stokesay to Boscobel and Uriconium; or followed the Roman road or scratched in the Abbey ruins, all was amusing and carried a flavor of its own.

One of Ludlow's greatest charms is Broad Street, where the intermingling of Tudor half-timbers and Georgian brick make it one of the handsomest streets in England. Number 54 Broad Street, not far from the picturesque old Angel Hotel, was the birthplace in 1855 of Stanley

John Weyman, the historical novelist who attended Shrewsbury School. Though it was not one of his best, *The New Rector* (1891) is of interest here for its reflection of the Ludlow of yesteryear.

Finally, there is Ludlow and Housman. Of all the places in Housman's Shropshire, surely none comes to mind more vividly. Number LXII of *A Shropshire Lad* opens with the saucy attack on Terence, their reputed author, and the poems themselves:

> Terence, this is stupid stuff,
> You eat your victuals fast enough
> There can't be much amiss, 'tis clear
> To see the rate you drink your beer.
> But oh, good Lord, the verse you make
> It gives a chap the belly-ache.

But Terence points out that beer brings no solution to the woes of life:

> Oh I have been to Ludlow fair
> And left my necktie God knows where.
> And carried half-way home, or near.
> Pints and quarts of Ludlow beer.

But when he awoke next morning, the glow was gone:

> The world, it was the old world yet,
> I was I, my things were wet,
> And nothing now remained to do
> But begin the game anew.

Therefore, Terence concludes (though now he sounds more like Housman with his tie back on):

> 'Tis true, the stuff I bring for sale
> Is not so brisk a brew as ale . . .
> But take it: if the smack is sour,
> The better for the embittered hour. . . .
> And I will friend you, if I may.
> In the dark and cloudy day.

How fitting it is that Housman should be buried in Ludlow. He died in 1936, age seventy-seven, at a Cambridge nursing home, gallant to the last. Shortly before the end, his doctor told him a bawdy joke. "Yes, that's a good one," said Housman. "And tomorrow I shall be telling it again on the Golden Floor."

Those were his last recorded words. After a memorial service in Cambridge, his ashes were buried outside the door of the Ludlow church, with a cherry tree planted near the grave and a bronze tablet in the church wall above it.

If you do stop over in Ludlow, there are two hotels of historic interest. The Broad Street Angel, said to be the oldest licensed premises in Ludlow, is small but picturesque. Refurbished a few years ago, it's rated two-star. Lord Nelson was made a burgess of the borough at the Angel in 1802. And E. M. Forster was more than happy to put in at The Angel on his walking tour of 1907. He had just walked over the Wrekin from Wellington in a driving rain, and arrived soaking wet.

Even older than the Angel is the three-star Feathers in Bull Ring. Architecturally, it is striking. The half-timber front consists of three storeys, with bays overhanging the street and above them triple gables, so that the whole facade seems about to come toppling down on you. It's been standing there since 1603, however, so it probably won't.

A parting word about one or two of Ludlow's sights-to-see. If you visit Housman's grave at the Church of St. Laurence, take a minute to look at the carved stalls and misericords inside. Also, at the Butter Cross nearby on King Street, built in 1743, there's a display tracing Ludlow's history. As for Ludlow Castle, the ruins are open to the public every day April to September, weekdays only October to March.

Clun   As you might guess, Housman's Clun—along with Clungunford, Clunton, and Clunbury—lies along the River Clun, which meanders in a sort of absent-minded way west of Ludlow. Housman based his poem on an old local jingle, and those who live in Clun have been known now and then to revert to earlier versions, where "quietest places under the sun" were instead "drunkenest" or "wickedest," but they've got to be joking.

Clun has had its lively times, however. Its castle ruins above the river are remnants of one of those thirty-two fortresses the Normans built to ward off invaders from Wales. And long before that, more than nineteen hundred years ago in fact, the ancient British chieftain Caractacus is said to have fought his last battle against the Romans in 50 A.D. He was captured and packed off to Rome, but the emperor Claudius thought he was such a fine fellow he was set free.

An oval earthwork with twenty-five-foot high ramparts southeast of the village marks Caractacus's campsite. The Jacobeans Beaumont and

Fletcher tell his story in their play *Bonduca* (1614). So does Thomas Gray's friend, William Mason, in his less than illustrious drama, *Caractacus* (1759). In the twentieth century Sir Edward William Elgar wrote a cantata called *Caractacus*.

Little Clun has other literary connections, too, in addition to Housman: Sir Walter Scott, D. H. Lawrence, Mary Webb, and E. M. Forster. Scott was in Clun in the 1820s to gather material for *The Betrothed* (1825), which is set in the Welsh Marches during the reign of Henry II. Clun's castle served as a model for the book's Garde Douloureuse, home of its heroine, Eveline.

In 1923 D. H. Lawrence came to the hills of the border area, too, to gather material for *St. Mawr,* and all of Mary Webb's novels have a Shropshire setting. Best Known for *Gone to Earth* (1917) and *Precious Bane* (1924), she was a Salopian through and through, although she lived in Weston-super-Mare, then in Somerset after her marriage in 1912. She was born in Leighton within sight of the Wrekin in 1881, lived for a time at Much Wenlock, and was buried in Shrewsbury. In her books she calls Clun "Dysgwlfas-on-the-Wild-Moors."

In *Howards End* (1910) Forster calls Clun "Oniton," where:

> Day and night the river flows down into England, day after day the sun retreats into the Welsh mountains, and the tower chimes "See the Conquering Hero."

Forster tenderly presents the town through the eyes of the departing Margaret Schlegel as, toward the end of the novel, she watches it fade behind her:

> Besides the Grange and the Castle Keep, she could now pick out the church and the black-and-white gables of the George . . . the bridge, the river nibbling its green peninsula. . . . She never saw it again.

If you go to Clun you can still see Forster's bridge and the nibbling river. But you won't see much of Scott's castle. It was in ruins even in his day. You can stop by the Buffalo Inn where he stayed, however. It's tucked into a corner of Market Square. Or have a bit of something at the Sun on the High Street. A small Tudor hostelry, it was well into its third century by the time Sir Walter got there.

The Wenlocks   Wenlock Edge is one of those long ridges Housman wrote about in the letter explaining the limits of his knowledge of

Shropshire. Some seventeen miles in all, the Edge runs in a northeasterly direction from just above Ludlow, rises to a height of 1,200 feet, and affords some lovely views. It was from the Edge that Housman first saw Hughley Village down below, and realized how wrong he had been about its church steeple. Henry Adams said that, of all his delights in Shropshire, "perhaps he liked best to ramble over the Edge on a summer afternoon and look across the Marches to the mountains of Wales." The village of Much Wenlock lies at the northeastern extreme of Wenlock Edge. Despite its name, with fewer than 2,500 people, it's not all that much. But it does have some good old half-timber houses, and the beautiful ruins of a thirteenth-century Cluniac abbey with an adjoining fifteenth-century Prior's Lodge.

Both Wenlock Edge and Wenlock appear in several of Housman's poems, among them No. XXXIX of *A Shropshire Lad,* that begins

> 'Tis time, I think, by Wenlock town
> The golden broom should blow . . . .

and ends

> Oh tarnish late on Wenlock Edge
> Gold that I never see;
> Lie long, high snowdrifts in the hedge
> That will not shower on me.

But Housman admits the poem wasn't really written about Wenlock. Originally the first line read: "'Tis time, I think, by Stourbridge town. . . ." Stourbridge was in Worcestershire near his home in Fockbury.

More directly tied to Shropshire is No. XXXI, for it not only mentions Wenlock Edge, but also the Wrekin, the Severn, and Uricon— Uricon being "Uriconium" (now Wroxeter), a fortress built five miles east of Shrewsbury by Roman legionnaires in 47–65 A.D. for defense against Welsh tribesmen. Here the locale is inseparable from the poem's theme: that today, yesterday, 2,000 years ago, man and his woes never change,

> Then 'twas the Roman, now 'tis I.

It was that old abbey at Much Wenlock that indirectly brought Henry Adams to Shropshire and taught him to love it. He tells the story in his autobiographical *The Education of Henry Adams:*

In the year 1857, Mr. James Milnes Gaskell, who sat for thirty years in Parliament as one of the Members for the borough of Wenlock in Shropshire, bought Wenlock Abbey and the estate that included the old monastic buildings. This new, or old, plaything amused Mrs. Milnes Gaskell. The Prior's house, a charming specimen of fifteenth-century architecture, had been long left to decay as a farmhouse. She put it in order, and went there to spend a part of the autumn of 1864. Young Adams was one of her first guests, and drove about Wenlock Edge and the Wrekin with her, learning the loveliness of this exquisite country and its stores of curious antiquity.

Adams returned to Wenlock several times. On a visit in 1870 he reports he got a flattering offer from his alma mater, Harvard:

> While at Wenlock, he received a letter from President Eliot inviting him to take an Assistant Professorship of History, to be created shortly at Harvard College. After waiting ten or a dozen years for some one to show consciousness of his existence, even a *Terebratula* [a mollusk] would be pleased and grateful for a compliment which implied that the new President of Harvard College wanted his help; but Adams knew nothing about history, and much less about teaching, while he knew more than enough about Harvard College, and wrote at once to thank President Eliot, with much regret that the honor should be above his powers.

It would be splendid to end the story on this note of high-minded independence. But the truth is otherwise. On his return to the States later in the year, Adams continues:

> Henry went out to Cambridge and had a few words with President Eliot . . .
> "Mr. President," urged Adams, "I know nothing about Medieval History."
> Mr. Eliot mildly but firmly replied,
> "If you will point out to me any one who knows more, Mr. Adams, I will appoint him."

But Adams couldn't—so he took the job.

Hughley   Hughley, whose name Housman loved so much he wouldn't give it up even to correct the error about its church steeple, is the tiniest of villages, but venerable. The church's tower dates from 1701, its fine screen is fifteenth-century, and the altar stone thirteenth-century.

Interestingly enough, before Housman saw the steeple error for himself while peering down at it from Wenlock Edge, he already knew that he was wrong. His brother, Laurence, author of *Victoria Regina,* had written him about this after *A Shropshire Lad* was published in 1896.

Laurence Housman also pointed out an even more amusing mistake. In the poem—No. LXI—his brother misplaces his corpses, too. In the sunny south portion of the graveyard the poet puts Hughley's elite, the proper, and the well-behaved. The steeple-shadowed north he reserves for those worst of sinners, the "slayers of themselves." But in fact the people buried to the north of the church tower aren't "suicides" at all, Laurence said with no little glee. Actually they're mostly church wardens and vicars' wives.

Bridgnorth—Shifnal—and Tong

With Bridgnorth, Shifnal, and Tong you reach the eastern limits of a literary trek through Shropshire. Bridgnorth, on the A 442 eight miles southeast of Much Wenlock, rates mention for a trio of writing clerics; Shifnal and Tong for Charles Dickens and *The Old Curiosity Shop.* Shifnal is eight miles north of Bridgnorth on the A 464, and Tong, only a brief stroll to the east from Shifnal, is on the A 41.

Bridgnorth   Bridgnorth (there is no "e") is more interesting for its non-literary attractions than its writers. A community of more than 11,000 people, it's divided in two by the Severn with High Town atop a cliff, Low Town down below, and the river running between. Linking the two are a six-arched bridge and a short railway with perhaps the steepest gradient in all England.

Other oddities include the ruins of a Norman castle that lean at an angle three times greater than the Tower of Pisa and caves cut into the sandstone cliff along the riverside that were used as dwellings as late as Victorian times. For railway buffs there's the Railwaymans Arms, a platform-side pub with two rooms furnished in old-fashioned station style, including the ancient twin-bell telephone that kept Bridgnorth in touch with stops along the line. Steam trains run to Bewdley daily during the summer.

St. Leonard's Church in the High Town has connections with all of Bridgnorth's literary figures. Housman visited Bridgnorth once "to gain local color," but stayed only a few hours. He did go to St. Leonard's, however, and reported:

In the churchyard there, I remember having heard our mother describe it and the steps up to it, which I had absolutely forgotten.

Richard Baxter came to St. Leonard's Church in 1641 as assistant rector and stayed for two years before moving on to Kidderminster. The little black-and-white half-timber in which he lived can still be seen near St. Leonard's. Baxter wrote *The Saint's Everlasting Rest* (1650)—beloved of Mrs. Glegg in *The Mill on the Floss*—in Kidderminster, but dedicated the book to his Bridgnorth parishioners.

Thomas Percy, bishop of Dromore and author of *Reliques of Ancient English Poetry* (1765), was born in Bridgnorth in 1729 and baptized at St. Leonard's. His birthplace, now called Bishop Percy's House, is the oldest house in town. It stands on Cartway, which runs from the High Street down to the river, and has those housedweller caves along its sides.

St. Leonard's has a tie to Bishop Reginald Heber, too. Heber was Hodnet's vicar from 1807 to 1823, so Hodnet claims as its own the author of "Holy, Holy, Holy," "From Greenland's Icy Mountains," and those other famous hymns. But St. Leonard's vestry has the chair he sat in while he wrote them.

Shifnal   The *Reliques* of Bishop Percy, which so influenced Sir Walter Scott and the Romantic poets, is owed to the alertness and forthright action of a Mr. Humphrey Pitt, eighteenth-century master of Shifnal's Prior's Lee Hall. Noticing that his housemaid was about to start the fire with the pages of a handwritten manuscript of quite some bulk, Pitt snatched it from her hands and discovered that it contained a considerable number of ancient poems of varying lengths, styles, and periods.

When his friend Thomas Percy came to Bridgnorth on a visit, Pitt gave him the manuscript. Now in the British Museum and called the Percy Folio, it was the most important source of the collection of ballads, historical songs, and metrical romances that Percy edited and published in 1765.

Shifnal has a fairly respectable right to identify itself as the town described by Dickens in *The Old Curiosity Shop* as having a "large number of old houses built of a kind of earth or plaster," the doors "arched and low," the windows "latticed in little diamond panes." Here Little Nell and her grandfather, shepherded by the kindly schoolmaster, make one of their last stops on the long flight from that monstrous dwarf, Daniel Quilp.

Tong   What little Nell and her guardians are heading for is Tong. The book doesn't say so, but Dickens did. Here was

> The village street—if street that could be called which was an irregular cluster of poor cottages of many heights and ages, some with their fronts, some with their backs, and some with gable ends toward the road.

And here, too, was the little parsonage by the old church tower, clad in its "ghostly garb of pure cold white," where, past midnight, Nell's rescuers come too late:

> She was dead. Dear, gentle, patient, noble Nell was dead. Her little bird—a poor slight thing the pressure of a finger would have crushed—was stirring nimbly in its cage; and the strong heart of its child-mistress was mute and motionless for ever.

Pathetic? Dickens himself wept, even as he wrote it.[3]

*****

Tong is indeed at the end of Shropshire. The M 54 roars right past it. The borders of Staffordshire, the land of Dr. Johnson, lie not two miles away.

---

[3]Oscar Wilde's reaction was a bit different. Said Wilde: Only a man with a heart of stone could read the death of Little Nell without laughing.

STAFFORDSHIRE

Staffordshire

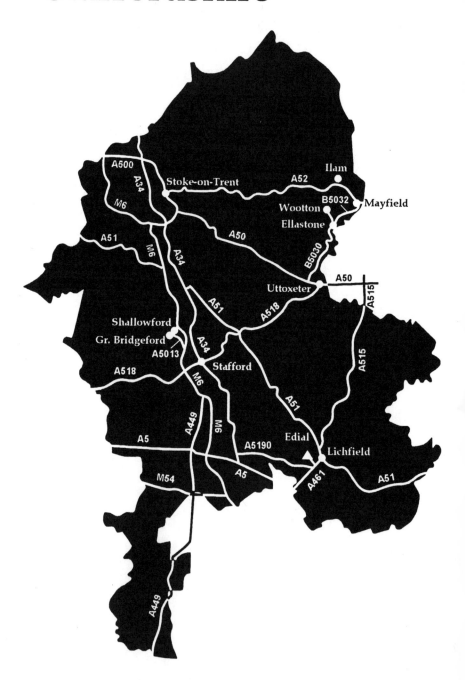

Very little business appeared to be going forward in Lichfield . . . upon the whole, the busy hand of industry seemed
to be quite slackened. "Surely, Sir, (said I), you are an idle set
of people." "Sir, (said Johnson) we are a city of philosophers,
we work with our heads, and make the boobies of Birmingham
work for us with their hands."

James Boswell, Esq., *The Life of Samuel Johnson*, L.L.D

Hanley and Burslem are about the most dreadful places I
have seen. Labyrinths of tiny blackened houses and among
them the pot-banks like monstrous burgundy bottles half
buried in the soil, belching forth smoke. Signs of poverty
everywhere.

George Orwell, in his diary of a journey to Wigan Pier

Although two hundred years separate Dr. Samuel Johnson from George
Orwell, their sharply differing remarks both hold true for the Staffordshire
of today. It does and does not sit back in bucolic serenity; the busy hand
of industry is slackened. It has and has not escaped the blight of belching
smokestacks. It depends on where in Staffordshire you happen to be.

For much of the county Dr. Johnson's comment pertains as ever it
did. Almost at the southern border with West Midlands and Birmingham
and not seven miles from where Johnson was born, the cows of Staffordshire still stroll past farmhouse doors to their evening milking, and
housewives still make their "egg money" selling eggs.

Up there in the northwest corner near Cheshire, however, the scars
of Orwell's pot-banks and blackened houses persist in Stoke-on-Trent,
the six-town conglomerate that includes Hanley and Burslem.

The Staffordshire between the extremes of Birmingham and Stoke-
on-Trent—at most thirty-five miles wide, fifty-five long—can be lovely
as well as rural. Dovedale Valley, forming the borderline with Derbyshire
in the northeast, and the Manifold with its underground rivers are idyllic.
Cannock Chase, thirty-thousand acres of wild parkland between Lichfield
and Stafford, provides open heaths and wooded areas. The Trent River,

third largest in Britain, has its moments of magic as it twists and turns clear across the county on its way to Humberside and the North Sea.

Stafford, which is the county seat, will serve you well as a base for exploration. Of much interest in itself, it is within sixteen miles of all the other major literary stops as well. And it couldn't be easier to get in and out of. If you're coming from the west—Shrewsbury or Tong, say— the A 5 links with the A 449 to deliver you directly. For Ashbourne in Derbyshire and all the east, it's the A 518. And if you insist, the M 6 at Stafford's back door offers the ghastly prospect of zipping north all the way to Scotland, or south as far as London or the West Country without once leaving a motorway.

STAFFORD AND SHALLOWFORD

Stafford   With 60,000 people or so, Stafford is the county's only sizeable town other than the megalopolis of Stoke-on-Trent/Newcastle-under-Lyme. Its central street pattern remains as it was in medieval days, encircling the ancient market square and with one dominant artery, Greengate, cutting through the heart of it.

Happily, the four places of major literary interest are not only all on Greengate, but practically touching each other. The eighteenth-century Chetwynd House stands on the corner of Mill Bank and Greengate, and only a couple of blocks up, at Martin and Greengate, is the twelfth-to-fifteenth-century Church of St. Mary. In between are the High House and the Swan Hotel.

High House is a wonderful half-timber affair of the fifteenth–seventeenth centuries, with a bay that peers precariously down at the street and a plethora of gables at the top. In 1642 after the Great Rebellion broke out, High House sheltered Charles I for several nights, along with his nephew, Prince Rupert, count palatine of the Rhine, who had dashed over from exile in Holland to help his uncle.

St. Mary's medieval stone and wood were sacrificed to a Victorian "restoration" program, but it still has the curiously wrought Norman font in which Izaac Walton was baptized, and his bust in the north aisle to commemorate the event. England's most famous angler was born at Number 62 in nearby Eastgate Street, where a plaque marks the site.

Dramatist Richard Brinsley Sheridan lived at Chetwynd House, a fine specimen of Georgian architecture, while serving as a member of Parliament for Stafford. Not that he was a Stafford man. Far from it. He was born in Dublin and as early as age twenty-three had begun his glittering London career with *The Rivals* (1775), followed quickly by *The Duenna* and part-ownership of the Drury Lane Theatre in 1776, and the writing of other stage hits like *The School for Scandal* (1777) and *The Critic* (1779).

Sheridan got that seat in Parliament because his price was right; he paid Stafford's burgesses a handsome five guineas apiece for their support. All the same he went on to win acclaim as one of the greatest orators the House of Commons had ever known, especially during the historic debates over the impeachment of Warren Hastings and the war with the American colonies.

You'll have no trouble discovering that Chetwynd House was where Sheridan stayed while M.P. for Stafford. A medallion on the wall tells you so. And you'll have no trouble getting in to see it. It now serves as Stafford's post office.

Three other writers associated with Stafford have left records of the accommodations they found: George Borrow, Charles Dickens, and George Orwell. Their reports are graphic, but not necessarily flattering.

The first two were both at the Swan, Borrow in 1825, Dickens only twenty years later. The hotel, only a few steps from Chetwynd House, looked pretty much as it does now, with a typically Georgian facade, clean-cut and uncluttered, adorned only with bow-windows. But under the eighteenth-century skin there lurked, as it still does, a Jacobean town house. Built some time after 1600 as a private dwelling, it wasn't converted to an inn until the early eighteenth century. The Georgian look didn't come about until 1770.

Borrow was only twenty-two when the Swan hired him to oversee its stables. In *The Romany Rye* (1857) he describes what a thriving coaching inn of the early nineteenth century was like:

> The swan was a place of infinite bustle . . . an army of servants of one description or another was kept, waiters, chambermaids, grooms, postilions, shoe blacks, cooks, scullions and what not. . . . There was running up and down stairs and along galleries, slamming of doors, of "Coming Sir" and "Please to step this way, ma'am" during eighteen hours of the four and twenty.

But Borrow left within the year when he realized "there was little poetry in keeping an account of the corn, hay and straw which came in, and was given out, and I was fond of poetry."

Charles Dickens, stranded in Stafford between trains, found little to like at the Swan, equating it with the extinct dodo in a piece for *Household Words:*

> It provides me with a trackless desert of a sitting room, with a chair for every day in the year, a table for every month, and a waste of sideboard where a lonely China vase pines in a corner for its mate long departed . . . . The Dodo has nothing in its larder . . . . The Dodo is narrow-minded as to towels, and expects me to wash on a freemason's apron without the trimming . . . the Dodo has seen better days.

Today's Swan is back to somewhat better times. It's owned by a chain, and rates two stars.

George Orwell, who stopped overnight in Stafford in 1936 during his walk to Wigan, makes Dickens's quarters sound like a suite at the Ritz. Orwell put up at something called the Temperance Hotel. He says in his Wigan diary:

> . . . thinking this would be cheap, but bed and breakfast 5/1. The usual dreadful room and twill sheets, greyish and smelly as usual. Went to bathroom and found commercial traveller developing snapshots in bath. Persuaded him to remove them and had bath, after which I find myself very footsore.

Orwell still had sixty weary miles to go. First thing next morning, sore feet and all, he couldn't wait to leave Stafford behind.

Shallowford   Izaak Walton left Stafford before he was twenty to become an ironmonger's apprentice in London, but he never lost his love for his native town and county. In 1644 he bought some property in Shallowford, a tiny village five miles northwest of Stafford. And though he was elsewhere much of the time, he lived there off and on during the rest of his long life.

The first part of his paean to fishing and the contemplative life, *The Compleat Angler,* was published in 1653. In his own leisurely way, he added to it in various editions for the next twenty years. By the time the fifth edition appeared in 1676, the original thirteen chapters had grown to twenty-one, to the delight of as devoted a band of readers as any writer has ever enjoyed.

As one might guess from the book, Walton was a sweet and gentle man. When he died in 1683 at age ninety, he bequeathed his Shallowford property to the poor of Stafford.

Lovingly restored, his Shallowford cottage is now a museum dedicated to his life and works. It's not open every day of the week, though, so you'd better inquire in advance about the hours. To get there, take the A 5013 out of Stafford and turn right at Great Bridgeford.

STOKE-ON-TRENT

The best that can be said for today's Stoke-on-Trent, excoriated so by George Orwell in 1936, is that it's better than it was then. Celebrated for fine china since the days of Josiah Wedgwood and known widely as "The Potteries," its ceramics are shipped to more than 140 markets throughout the world. But as with most industrial cities, the price of success has been high.

Now a city of well over a quarter of a million people, Stoke-on-Trent was created in 1910 by the amalgamation of six towns: Langton, Fenton, Stoke, Hanley, Burslem, and Tunstall. Native son Arnold Bennett, who reduced the six to the "Five Towns"—he omitted Fenton—of *The Old Wives Tale* (1908) and the *Clayhanger* trilogy (1910–16) is unsparing in describing them:

> They are mean and forbidding of aspect—sombre, hard-featured, uncouth; and the vaporous poison of their ovens and chimneys has soiled and shrivelled the surrounding country till there is no village lane within a league but what offers a gaunt and ludicrous travesty of rural charms.

A mere sixteen miles from the charm of Stafford via the A 34, only five miles from the greening Cheshire border on the A 52, Stoke's urban ugliness still takes a bit of adjusting to as you enter it. But it has made progress.

Thanks to electric firing and legal restrictions, Stoke's vast modern factories have relegated the belching pot-banks of Orwell's day to pottery museums. Great civic enterprise has established refreshing oases here and there—Forest Park near Hanley Centre, for instance, the "Greenways" on abandoned railway lines for pedestrians and horsemen, and the "Blueways" of the old canals.

Just outside the city, too, are retreats to which people have escaped for weekends and holidays since long before the time of Bennett. Two of them have literary notes of their own: Trentham Gardens on the southern outskirts of town, and Rudyard Reservoir, six miles to the northeast.

The Gardens, which come in every possible variety, were originally laid out on mile-long Trentham Lake by the great eighteenth-century landscape artist, "Capability" Brown. Also on the 700-acre tract are parklands and facilities for picnicking, swimming, fishing, and boating. Still visible are the ruins of the mansion, Trentham Hall, used by Disraeli in *Lothair* (1870) for the great ducal estate he called "Brentham."

Rudyard Reservoir was built on a two-mile lake in 1797. Ruggedly handsome with steep wooded banks, it remains a favorite for fishing and boating. Two Victorian visitors who came from afar in the early 1860s were John Lockwood Kipling and his wife, on leave from his post as architectural sculptor at the Bombay School of Arts. They were so enchanted that even after their return to India they never forgot their visit. When their son was born in Bombay in 1865 they called him Rudyard.

Bennett aside, Stoke has few other literary connections. Best known is Dinah Maria Mulock Craik, who was born there in 1826 and lived from 1831 on in adjacent Newcastle-under-Lyme. Vera Brittain, born in Newcastle in 1896, also knew both towns well. Mrs. Craik is now remembered for *John Halifax, Gentleman* (1857), Ms. Brittain for the autobiographical *Testament of Youth* (1933).

Stoke's literary credentials, then, obviously depend largely on Arnold Bennett, and even he was not often there after he departed for London at age twenty-two to seek something more exciting than his father's law firm.

When Bennett was born in 1867 his father, Enoch Bennett, was a hard-grubbing tradesman, and their house on the corner of Hope and Hanover streets in Hanley doubled as pawnbroker-draper's shop. But the elder Bennett didn't intend to remain a tradesman. The model for the Darius Clayhanger of his son's novels, he was as hard-driving as his fictional counterpart, with the same characteristics: "bad temper, discipline, ambition, indigestion."

Enoch's efforts finally paid off in 1878 when, after years of night classes, he was able to win a solicitor's license and build a home of his own at No. 205 Waterloo Road in Burslem. He made sure that people would notice the new house. There were three storeys and two huge cellars, six bedrooms and two bay-windowed front rooms. Ornate stained glass adorned the window-tops, flowery tiles the fireplace.

Meanwhile young Arnold (he was christened Enoch Arnold Bennett) went to the Burslem Endowed School and then the middle school in Newcastle-under-Lyme. His favorite haunt during these years was his maternal grandfather's shop in St. John's Square, Burslem. It was the "only comfortable place" he knew in his early years, he said later, the sole refuge from the dreary surroundings of his Hanley birthplace.

In 1885, at the age of eighteen, he went into his father's law firm. Four years later it was off to London and a job with *Woman* magazine. By 1896 he was its editor. His first attempt at a novel, *A Man From the North,* in 1898 was on the shaky side. But with *The Old Wives Tale* in 1908 he hit his stride. Thereafter came a deluge of novels, short stories, plays, and critical pieces. His earnings were enormous, his spending spectacular, with no little of the ostentation that had marked his father's building of the house on Waterloo Road.

That may be why, in part at least, it has always been somewhat fashionable to sneer at Arnold Bennett as artist. He made too much money too easily and was too brazen about writing as a commercial venture, setting even friends like John Galsworthy and H. G. Wells on edge. Hugh Walpole confided, though only to his diary, that Arnold Bennett was a "guttersnipe." Perhaps so. But there is no gainsaying the true artistry of *The Old Wives Tale,* the first *Clayhanger* novel, and *Riceyman Steps.*

Even Stoke-on-Trent itself seems to ignore Arnold Bennett. There are no streets, buildings, or parks named after him. Go to the Information Centre and ask what to see, and all they'll give you are reams of folders and brochures about the potteries.

There *is* an Arnold Bennett Literary Society with the Lord Mayor as patron, but it seems to be struggling for existence. Its one-time Arnold Bennett Museum at 205 Waterloo Road has dwindled to one pathetic little wall case in a hallway of the City Museum and Art Gallery in Hanley. But you can, if you're determined, take a sort of Arnold Bennett tour of your own.

The City Museum and Art Gallery is as good a place to start as any. It's on Hanley's Bethesda Street, and you'll find the little wall case with Bennett mementoes in a passageway outside the "Spitfire Room." Now *that's* an exhibit to see—the Spitfire Room, that is. Reginald Mitchell, designer of the Spitfire, went to Hanley High School and taught in Fenton, and the room has a real-for-true, life-size sample of the plane that saved England during the Battle of Britain.

Anyway, in the Bennett wall case are his spirit flask, his fountain pen, a walking stick, and a boots-and-glove stretcher. There's his railway reading lamp, too, the "lamp" being actually a small box holding the stub of a candle. There are no manuscripts, alas, but among copies of his published books is *The Old Wives Tale* open to Chapter VII, headed "Success," with the author's own hand-written revisions above the printed words.

A few blocks to the northwest of the City Museum is the junction of Hope and Hanover streets, and you may want to pause there a moment to see the plaque that marks where Bennett was born before you push on along what is actually the A 50 up to Burslem.

No. 205 Waterloo Road in Burslem, that grand house Enoch Bennett built to signal his becoming a solicitor, will be on your right immediately after you pass Rushton Road. In *Clayhanger* Bennett calls Waterloo Road "Trafalgar Road," (Burslem is "Bursley"), and describes the house as "palatial," which it is not. Sandwiched in a row of similar red-brick buildings, it now looks somewhat run-down, but was obviously substantial enough when the Bennetts first moved in.

Next, where Waterloo Street turns into Swan Square, turn right on Queen Street and go down to St. John's Square. While on Queen Street, notice the building on the right with the ceramic exterior. It's now the public library, but in Bennett's childhood housed the endowed school he attended from 1877 to 1889. Both St. John's Square itself ("St. Luke's Square" in the novels), and the three-storey building that included his grandfather's Longson's shop are fortunately little changed since the days when young Arnold found them so inviting.

Burslem Cemetery, reached by turning right up Market Place (it soon becomes Moorland Road), makes a fitting last stop for your tour. Here, even in death, Bennett received less than his due. After his death and cremation in London in 1931 the author's brother, Frank, bore the ashes to Burslem by train—in a third-class carriage. There Bennett was buried in the nondescript family grave, beneath a cheerless granite obelisk that at best can be called unattractive. And, final indignity, whoever did the inscription got the date wrong.

LICHFIELD

Should you go to Lichfield directly from Stoke-on-Trent, you're in for the most delightful of contrasts. Even if you drive the sixteen miles down from Stafford, you're in for a treat. Either way, you'll be coming in on the A 51, and as you see the three enchanting spires of Lichfield Cathedral suddenly rising before your eyes on the horizon, your heart will skip a beat and you'll find yourself murmuring, "No wonder Samuel Johnson loved it."

It is true that today Lichfield's industry is not quite so slackened as it was when Johnson showed the city off to Boswell in 1776. Those "boobies of Birmingham" have prevailed upon Lichfield to accept some spill-over of manufacturing, and even to provide housing for some of the boobies themselves. But Lichfield's guardian angels have managed to restrict the more untidy signs of these concessions largely to the northern outskirts, and the inner core retains its charm.

Long before Dr. Johnson, Lichfield was ancient. Its cathedral was already six hundred years old when he was born in 1709, and the little church from which the cathedral grew was started more than four hundred years before the cathedral, near the ruins of a fort the Romans had built yet another five hundred years before *that!* The Romans called their settlement Letocetum, whence comes the "Lich" of the modern name. Nathaniel Hawthorne, on the other hand, claims in his account of a visit he made in the 1850s that the name means "Field of Dead Bodies," referring to the graves of two sons of an early Mercian king martyred for accepting Christianity.

Lichfield had its literary figures before Johnson, too, as well as after, and in surprising numbers. Elias Ashmole, the antiquarian, for instance, was born there in 1617 and went to its grammar school. The donation of his collection of curiosities to Oxford was the nucleus of the university's famed Ashmolean Museum, the first such institution in England.

Toward the end of the seventeenth century Joseph Addison, whose essays sparkled in *The Tatler* (1709-11) and *The Spectator* (1711-12), was a pupil at that same school. He was born in Wiltshire in 1672, but grew up in Lichfield after his father became dean of the cathedral.

George Farquhar, the dramatist, came to Lichfield in 1705 to recruit soldiers for the duke of Marlborough. He used Lichfield as a setting for his pleasant comedy, *The Beaux's Stratagem,* and placed the first scene in the hotel where he stayed, The George on Bird Street.

Two writers who lived in Lichfield in Johnson's own day won acclaim, more indeed than either deserved: Anna Seward and Erasmus Darwin. Johnson knew them both. Anna Seward, who somehow acquired the title of "The Swan of Lichfield," was the daughter of Canon Thomas Seward and lived with him in the cathedral close at the bishop's palace. She and Johnson shared a vast antipathy for each other. Her grandfather, John Hunter, a brutal man, had been Johnson's schoolmaster, and Johnson once told a friend that Anna looked so like her grandfather he "could tremble at the sight of her." For her part, the strong-willed Miss Seward simply didn't like Johnson. Nevertheless, she gave Boswell many details for his biography.

The Cambridge History of English Literature sums up her poetry in one neat phrase: "the Swan of Lichfield . . . sang so much and so long before her death that she has been entirely inaudible since." Sir Walter Scott admired her, though, and visited her in Lichfield. She bequeathed him her poetry, which he—showing more loyalty than judgment—published in 1810.

Erasmus Darwin settled in Lichfield in 1757 as a physician. He lived in a big two-storey house near the cathedral and became friendly with the canon's young daughter whom he saw frolicking about the close. Soon he was encouraging her to write poetry. That's right: she was Anna Seward. But he made amends of sorts. His own *The Botanic Garden* (1789, 1791), a two-part eruption of heroic couplets, was irrefutable proof that with enough effort one could write poetry even worse than hers.

Dr. Darwin fancied himself a scientific writer, too, and the publication of *Zoonomia* (1794–96) made him well-known. His more famous grandson, Charles Darwin, was to damn the work, a treatise on generation, with the faintest of praise. "It anticipated the views of other early evolutionists," said the grandson, and "the erroneous grounds of their opinions."

Erasmus Darwin seemed to attract off-beat ideas and talents. In 1766 a young Irishman named Richard Lovell Edgeworth went to Lichfield just to see him and was captivated both by his host and by the social and intellectual stimulation Lichfield provided. When Edgeworth's wife died in 1773 he married a Lichfield girl within four months and moved there with his five-year-old daughter, Maria.

His strongest tie with Erasmus Darwin had been their mutual interest in education. Out of this followed Edgeworth's revolutionary experiments in the raising and schooling of children, which resulted in a spate of related books, both fiction and non-fiction, by a trio of authors, including Richard Edgeworth himself, his friend Thomas Day, and the most famous of the three, Richard's daughter, Maria.

Edgeworth's inspiration was the French philosopher Jean-Jacques Rousseau, especially his *Emile* (1762). Rousseau's theory that sin was the product of society itself was put to the test in Edgeworth's own home, using poor Maria and the other children as guinea pigs. Together with his new wife, Edgeworth then wrote the fictional *Harry and Lucy* (1778) to promote realistic and useful education for all children, especially those of the working class. It was he who first proposed a nation-wide system of "secondary schools." Indeed, he invented the term himself. Thomas Day, barrister, sometime social reformer and writer, and full-time eccentric, had been Edgeworth's friend in college. At twenty-one Day took over the education of two young orphan girls with the purpose of making one of them his wife. He married a rich heiress instead. But he did write the three-volume *History of Sandford and Merton* (1783–89) to further his ideas. Though it's not much of a novel, it enjoyed much success. And why not? After all, Tommy Merton is rich, and therefore obnoxious; Harry Sandford is only a farmer's son and so, of course, virtuous; and virtue in the end, praise the Lord, has its reward.

In contrast to both her father and Thomas Day, Maria Edgeworth was a true novelist. Her books may be tinged by the admonitions of purpose and morality forced upon her by her father, but *Belinda* (1801), *The Absentee* (1812), and *Ormond* (1817) are works of high order, and Sir Walter Scott paid tribute to the influence of her *Castle Rockrent* (1800).

A late nineteenth-century entry in Lichfield's roster of writers is Richard Garnett, born there in 1835. His father, then the cathedral's priest-vicar, went on to become keeper of the books at the British Museum. The young Garnett made the museum's library his career, too, while at the same time writing a prodigious number of books of all sorts. Among these were biographies of Milton, Coleridge, Carlyle, and Emerson; volumes of poems; fresh and imaginative fairy tales; and a still-valued collection of sardonic little stories called *The Twilight of the Gods* (1888).

Towering above all these authors, needless to say, is Samuel Johnson, born September 18, 1709, in a bedroom over his father's bookstore by the Market Place. The baby's prospects were hardly promising. His father was fifty-two and about to begin what proved to be a steady decline into poverty. At forty his mother, Sarah, was also too old for a first child, which made her labor difficult and dangerous.

Fearful that their son might not live, the parents had him christened that very day and put him out to a wet nurse whose milk proved tubercular. After ten weeks, Johnson related later, he was brought home "a poor, diseased infant, almost blind." He added that, when he was still a child, his own aunt had told him "she would not have picked such a poor creature up in the street."

At four the boy was sent to Dame Oliver's School on Dam Street, which proved to be a happy experience. Fourteen years would pass before he would go off to Oxford. But Mrs. Oliver remembered him. She came to bid him goodbye, brought him some gingerbread, and called him "the best scholar she ever had." From age seven through fifteen he attended the same Lichfield Grammar School in St. John's Street where Elias Ashmole and Joseph Addison had been students. Its lower school teacher was Humphrey Hawkins, a kindly man. "I was indulged and caressed," Johnson said, but the master of the Upper School, Anna Seward's grandfather, John Hunter, was something else. He would flog the boys unmercifully for not knowing the Latin equivalent of such outlandish words as candlestick, saying all the while, "this I do to save you from the gallows."

In 1725, then just sixteen, Johnson was rescued from this by his cousin Cornelius Ford, a dazzling and well-to-do thirty-one-year-old who had already retired from his "tedious" post as a fellow at Cambridge. Cornelius took young Samuel off to the Ford family's Warwickshire home outside Stourbridge, introduced him to the local high society, and managed to tone down somewhat his all too rustic manners and speech.

Between the ages of sixteen and eighteen, Johnson worked at his father's bookstore and made two enduring and vital friendships: those with Gilbert Walmesley and David Garrick. Walmesley was forty-seven, a prosperous lawyer who lived at the bishop's palace, which he had leased. David Garrick was a precocious ten-year-old student at the grammar school with a great gift of mimicry. His parents lived on Beacon Street across from the close.

Walmesley, whom Anna Seward called "the finest gentleman in Lichfield and its environs," delighted in having both the youngsters, Samuel and David, to dinner at the palace as often as two or three times a week. It was an unusual friendship, as Johnson said:

He was of an advanced age, and I was only a boy; yet he never received my notions with contempt. . . . I honoured him, and he endured me.

Fifty years later Johnson could say:

Such was his amplitude of learning and such his copiousness of communication that it may be doubted whether a day now passes in which I have not some advantage from his friendship.

Garrick's influence was life-long, too. While still a boy he was one of the three original pupils in Johnson's ill-fated attempt to open a school of his own; as a youth he accompanied Johnson to London to seek their fortunes in 1737; and as a man and the nation's greatest actor, his loyalty and support had no limits.

The rest of Johnson's early days in Lichfield can be quickly told. At twenty poverty forced him from Oxford after a single year. He spent the next two years mainly in aimless drifting, helping now and then at his father's shop. Next came in turn four months as undermaster at a school in Market Bosworth, Leicester; a bit of journalism and more drifting in Birmingham; and finally his marriage in 1735 to Elizabeth "Tetty" Porter, twenty years his senior.

That fall he opened the school of his own at Edial, three miles southwest of Lichfield, only to close it fifteen months later in January 1737 for lack of pupils.[1] In March of that same year, penniless, twenty-six, and without prospects, he was on his way to London with the twenty-year-old Garrick. In 1739 he did come back home for some months while trying to win the headmastership of a school at Appleby, nearby in Leicester. When that failed he returned to London. It was twenty-two years before he saw Lichfield again.

When he did at last go back toward the end of 1761—now fifty-three, his monumental *Dictionary* finally published, his fame assured as the "Great Lexicographer"—he was dismayed. In a letter to a friend he wrote:

> Last winter I went down to my native town, where I found the streets much narrower and shorter than I thought I had left them, inhabited by a new race of people, to whom I was very little known. My play-fellows were grown old, and forced me to suspect that I was no longer young. . . . I wandered about for five days, and took the first convenient opportunity of returning [to London].

The letter has an eerie tone to the readers of *Rasselas,* which Johnson had written two years before to pay for his mother's funeral. In the novel, the philosopher Imlac returns after a long absence, as Johnson was to do. Says Imlac:

> I now expected the caresses of my kinsmen, and the congratulations of my friends, and was not without hope that my father . . . would own with gladness and pride a son who was able to add to the felicity and honour of the nation. But [my] father had been dead fourteen years . . . of my companions the greater part was in the grave, of the rest some could with dif-

[1] For details, see p. 47.

ficulty remember me, and some considered me as one corrupted by foreign manners.

Despite this, Johnson became a regular visitor to Lichfield, especially to see his stepdaughter, Lucy Porter, before going on to visit his old friend, John Taylor, in Ashbourne, Derbyshire. Excursions to Lichfield in 1774 with his long-time friends, Henry and Hester Thrale, and in 1776 with James Boswell, were particularly pleasant. Johnson delighted in the company of the few intimates who were left: Lucy Porter, David Garrick's brother Peter, and some relatives of Gilbert Walmesley, and enjoyed breakfasting with acquaintances such as Erasmus Darwin.

He never lost his pride in Lichfield, either. Says Boswell in his account of their visit:

> He expatiated in praise of Lichfield and its inhabitants, who, he said, were "the most sober, decent people in England, the genteelest in proportion to their wealth, and spoke the purest English."

Regarding that boast about the purest English, however. Boswell impishly adds:

> I doubted as to the last article of this eulogy: for they had several provincial sounds; as there, pronounced like fear instead of like fair; once pronounced woonse, instead of wunse or wonse. Johnson himself never got entirely free of those provincial accents. Garrick sometimes used to take him off, squeezing a lemon into a punch-bowl, with uncouth gesticulations, looking around the company, and calling out, "Who's for poonsh?"

Even in the last years of his life, when ill health made travelling itself a torture, Johnson continued his trips home. He wrote from Ashbourne in July of 1784, when he was seventy-five, "I staid five days at Lichfield, but being unable to walk, had no great pleasure." The weather was bad, he said, "but how low is he sunk whose strength depends on the weather!"

The Ashbourne visit over, he returned to Lichfield, surely knowing he would never see it again. But a spark of the indomitable Johnson remained. To while away the time, he translated one of Horace's odes into English. The poem's theme was that unlike the autumn of nature, with its promise of spring and rebirth to come, the autumn of man's life is final. In Johnson's words:

> The changing year's successive plan
> Proclaims mortality to man.

So be it, says Horace soberly, but maybe the gods will allow us one more tomorrow before then. Johnson's version is practically jaunty:

> Who knows if Jove who counts the score
> Will toss us in one morning more?

Johnson left Lichfield on November 20. He died in London on December 13.

For the visitor, Johnson's presence remains in Lichfield. When Nathaniel Hawthorne came in the 1850s he was thwarted in his efforts to get into Johnson's house, then a private dwelling. But he says in *Our Old Home* (1863), the great man was still there:

> It is mortifying to be so balked in one's little enthusiasms; but looking around in quest of somebody to make inquiries of, I was a good deal consoled by the sight of Dr. Johnson himself, who happened, just at that moment, to be sitting at his ease nearly in the middle of St. Mary's Square, with his face turned toward his father's house.
>
> Of course . . . the intelligent reader will at once comprehend that he was marble in substance, and seated in a marble chair, on an elevated stone pedestal. In short, it was a statue, sculpted by Lucas, and placed there in 1838.

Today, such reminders of Johnson and Lichfield's other literary notables are abundant and highly visible. In one easy walk of no more than two hours you can see them all. And such a lovely walk it is.

A Suggested Tour

It would be best to begin at **Johnson's Birthplace** (1) off the Market Place, contenting yourself with simply a view of the outside, saving the inside for a more leisurely inspection later. The house, built by Michael Johnson in 1707, looks bigger than it is. There are three storeys plus attic and basement, and it's five windows wide as you face it from Breadmarket Street. But it's shallow, with only two fair-sized or three tiny rooms per floor.

Across the way in the Market Place are the **Johnson and Boswell Statues** (2). One of the bas reliefs at the base of Johnson's statue depicts

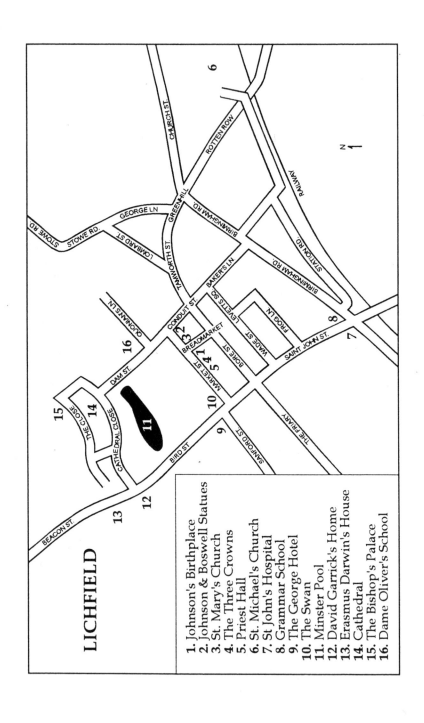

LICHFIELD

1. Johnson's Birthplace
2. Johnson & Boswell Statues
3. St. Mary's Church
4. The Three Crowns
5. Priest Hall
6. St. Michael's Church
7. St John's Hospital
8. Grammar School
9. The George Hotel
10. The Swan
11. Minster Pool
12. David Garrick's Home
13. Erasmus Darwin's House
14. Cathedral
15. The Bishop's Palace
16. Dame Oliver's School

him as an old man standing in the rain at Uttoxeter, doing penance for refusing to go there as a youth to aid his ailing father who kept a bookstall in the square. **St. Mary's Church** (3) is right below the Market Place. The present building was built in 1870, replacing the one in which Johnson worshipped, but has the register of his birth.

Back across the street, a plaque on the building below the birthplace marks what was **The Three Crowns** (4) inn. Says the plaque:

DR. JOHNSON FREQUENTLY STAYED HERE
DURING HIS MANY VISITS TO LICHFIELD
IN 1776 HE WAS ACCOMPANIED BY
BOSWELL, WHO DESCRIBED HIM AS
"NOW MONARCHISING WITH NO FEWER
THAN THREE CROWNS
OVER HIS ROYAL BROW."

Next door is **Priest's Hall** (5), once the living quarters for St. Mary's clergy. In 1617 it was the birthplace of Elias Ashmole.

You don't have to, but if you just love steep hills and are wild about graves, you can now turn east and toil up Tamworth Street to Greenhill and **St. Michael's Church** (6), where Johnson's father, mother, and brother Nathaniel are buried. The Latin epitaph he wrote for them on his final visit to Lichfield is inscribed by the chancel steps.

At the southern end of St. John Street where it runs into Birmingham Road, **St. John's Hospital** (7) on the west side and the old **Grammar School** (8) on the east face each other across the street. The only surviving building from the various times when Addison and Johnson were pupils is the seventeenth-century master's house, now council offices. The hospital building, as a plaque explains, was used as a place of worship as early as 1135, and the Grammar School originated there in 1495. In Johnson's day, the students still marched across the street to attend chapel services at St. John's.

Going back up St. John Street to where its name changes to Bird Street, you'll pass **The George Hotel** (9) then **The Swan** (10). The George is the hotel connected with Farquhar, The Swan the place where Johnson stayed with the Thrales in 1774.

Above The Swan, after Bird becomes Beacon Street, you'll see on the right the entrancing little **Minster Pool** (11). It was man-made in the eighteenth century from what had become scarcely more than a silted-up puddle. In 1771 the bottom was dredged, the south bank cut back, and the excavated earth added to the other side from a graceful curve. Who was the leader in all this? None other than Anna Seward. She'd been to London and thought Lichfield ought to have a Serpentine of its own.

Still on Beacon Street, just past the close, come in order the site of **David Garrick's home** (12), now marked by a plaque, and the fine big house that was **Erasmus Darwin's** (13), also with a plaque.

In the **cathedral** (14) behind them, you'll find busts of Johnson and Garrick, and memorials to Anna Seward, Gilbert Walmesley, Erasmus Darwin, and Lady Mary Wortley Montagu. Lady Mary, an eighteenth-century beauty, is remembered now not only for having been pilloried by Alexander Pope in poems like "Epistle to Dr. Arbuthnot," but also for introducing vaccination to England.

The Bishop's Palace (15), where both Gilbert Walmesley and Anna Seward had lived, is just north of the cathedral, and is now St. Chad's Cathedral Choir School.

Finally, down on Dam Street on the left, shortly before you reach Quonian's Lane, a marker shows the location of **Dame Oliver's School** (16), where Johnson went as a four-year-old. Legend has it he was so near-sighted even then he had to be held by the hand all the way, lest he fall into an open sewer.

Back at the Birthplace Museum, you'll probably want to linger a long time. It's beautifully done, with each well-stocked room illustrating a different stage of Johnson's life and career.

There is indeed so much to see here and elsewhere in Lichfield, that you might well want to stay over a day or so. If you do stay, you have your choice of not just two, but three hotels of literary interest, all on the same street. Up near the cathedral, where it's called Beacon Street, there's the Georgian Angel Croft (two star) which Erasmus Darwin knew well, since he lived across from it. Further down, where the name changes to Bird Street, are Farquhar's George (three-star) and Johnson's Swan (two-star).

If you should decide on The Swan, you don't have to follow Samuel Johnson's dictum about dress. When he had the Thrales there as guests, he was eager to show them off. When Mrs. Thrale came down to break-fast the first morning in casual clothes, he sent her right back upstairs with the order: "Change your apparel for one more gay and splendid."

EDIAL

If ever a project was destined to fail, it was Samuel Johnson's attempt in 1735, at age twenty-six, to open a school of his own. To begin with, as his stint three years earlier as an undermaster in Market Bosworth had shown—it only lasted four months—he wasn't cut out for the classroom. His ungainly appearance and awkward mannerisms made students titter, and he didn't like teaching anyway. Without any college degree, not even a B.A., it would have been hard to attract pupils on his own. And if he located anywhere near Lichfield, he'd face the stiff competition of its grammar school.

On the other hand, what else was there for him to do? He had no skills or experience fitting him for any other profession. And now, having married Tetty Porter in July, he had a wife to support. Besides, Tetty herself was all for it.

Tetty supplied the money from the limited estate left her by Harry Porter. Faithful old Gilbert Walmesley lent moral support and suggested a location, a vacant house in the little village of Edial (EDGE-all), three miles west of Lichfield. Called Edial Hall, it was an odd-looking building, with a roof like a flat-topped pyramid and a chimney shaped like an Egyptian obelisk. But it was roomy and the rent was cheap.[2]

Walmesley got their first pupils for them, too, the son of a friend with a year to go before entering Cambridge, plus eighteen-year-old David Garrick and his twelve-year-old brother, George. But these original three never increased beyond eight. By the following fall, enrollment was down to two, David and George Garrick.

Next January the school closed. Ahead for Johnson lay London and a new start. It's easy to grieve for him and the pain this failure must have brought. But in terms of literary history, at least, it could have been worse. Suppose Edial had succeeded?

UTTOXETER

From Lichfield, Hawthorne went directly to Uttoxeter, he said, "on one of the few purely sentimental pilgrimages that I ever undertook."

---

[2] It's been much whittled down, but the basic structure still stands on what is now the B 5012.

His purpose was precisely what yours may be: to see the spot where Dr. Johnson stood as an old man of seventy-two in penance for disobeying his father a full fifty years before.

Uttoxeter ("you-TOX-eter") is an easy jaunt from Lichfield, a mere twenty miles via the A 515 and A 50. It's even shorter from Stafford, fourteen miles straight up the A 518. Your destination, in the very heart of town, is the irregularly shaped square where the people of Uttoxeter still hold their weekly market. They've been doing so ever since 1251, when Henry III gave them his royal permission.

For some years Johnson's father operated a small bookstall at this very market, riding up from his own shop in Lichfield every week. One day in 1731, seventy-five years old and too ill to get out of bed, he asked his son to go in his stead. Boswell gives us the story in Johnson's own words. Generally, Johnson says, he was not an undutiful son, but

> Once, indeed, I was disobedient; I refused to attend my father to Uttoxeter-market. Pride was the source of that refusal, and the remembrance of it was painful. A few years ago I desired to atone for this fault. I went to Uttoxeter in very bad weather, and stood for a considerable time bareheaded in the rain, on the spot where my father's stall used to stand. In contrition I stood, and I hope the penance was expiatory.

Hawthorne was indignant that there was no monument to mark the site where this took place. Worse yet, he discovered, the inhabitants knew nothing about the penance and cared nothing for the scene of it. As he waited at the station for his train, he asked a boy near him—"an intelligent and gentlemanly lad twelve or thirteen years old"—if he had ever heard the story of Dr. Johnson:

> The boy stared and answered—
> "No."
> "Were you born in Uttoxeter?"
> "Yes."

The reply left Hawthorne shocked, but hardly speechless.[3] "Just think of the absurd little town," he wrote in *Our Old Home* (1863), "knowing nothing of the only memorable incident which ever happened within its boundaries since the Britons built it."

---

[3]But then, Reception at the White Hart Hotel in that same Market Place told me she'd never heard of Nathaniel Hawthorne—or *The Scarlet Letter* either.

There is a memorial now in the market place, erected about a dozen years after Hawthorne wrote. It's a stone kiosk of typical overwrought Victorian design with an incongruous little dome on top, and has served as a candy and newspaper stand. But it does have a replica of the bas relief on the statue of Johnson in Lichfield, showing Johnson aged and bareheaded, stooping against the driving rain while market-goers, young and old, stand and stare.

And today's inhabitants do care about the event. Every year on the Monday following Johnson's birthday (September 18), the mayor lays a wreath on the memorial.

Ironically, there's still some dispute as to exactly where in town Johnson's father sold his wares. A short way down the street from the market is St. Mary's Church and it was outside the church gate, many think, that Michael Johnson actually had his stall. Opposite St. Mary's, at any rate, was the Red Lion Inn, one of the public houses whose abundance so impressed Hawthorne, "one at every step or two: Red Lions, White Harts, Bull's Heads, Mitres, Cross Keys, and I know not what besides." Michael Johnson stored his stock of books at the Red Lion between market days. It's still standing, now known as the Red Lion Buildings and no longer an inn. Also standing, and still operating as a hotel, is the White Hart on Carter Street across from the memorial.

ELLASTONE AND WOOTTON—AND MAYFIELD

From Uttoxeter, the B 5030 and B 5032 go northwest for nine miles, skirting Staffordshire's boundary with Derbyshire all the way to Mayfield. There the A 52 takes you the remaining mile or so east into Ashbourne and Derbyshire itself. Shortly before Mayfield, the B 5032 passes through Ellastone. Wootton is on an unmarked road one and a half miles northwest of Ellastone.

Ellastone and Wootton   George Eliot was born in Warwickshire, but before going there in 1802, her father, Robert Evans, had worked at both Ellastone and Wootton, first as a forester, then as estate bailiff at Wootton Hall. In Eliot's *Adam Bede* (1859), Ellastone appears as "Hayslope," where Adam lives.

Wootton Hall had for a short time been the home of French exile Jean Jacques Rousseau, when he rented it in 1766 and began writing his sensational *Confessions*. But, from the first, he and the natives eyed each other suspiciously. They looked askance at his Armenian garb and muttered about "Owd Rossall" behind his back. For his part, Rousseau came to fear his own servants. Convinced they were planning to poison him, he fled.

Mayfield   Thomas Moore, poet and satirist, and great friend of Byron, lived at Mayfield Cottage (now Standcliffe Farm) in Mayfield from 1813 to 1817. In Mayfield he wrote *The Twopenny Post Bag* (1813) attacking the prince regent, and *Lallah Rookh* (1817), the work that made him known throughout Europe.

ILAM

Ilam is to the west of the Dove River, Ashbourne to the east. Ilam is a village, Ashbourne a town. Ilam is in Staffordshire, Ashbourne in Derbyshire. Two communities, two counties, two entities. Right? Well, no, not to Samuel Johnson, that man of eminent good sense.

To him they were a unit, less than four miles apart, sharing between them the beautiful valley of the Dove. They were "Dovedale," which he loved, the supposed inspiration for the "Happy Valley" of his *Rasselas* (1759). John Taylor's home might be in Ashbourne. But whenever Johnson was staying there and had a chance to show Dovedale off to other guests—the Thrales, say, in 1774, or Boswell in 1777—where did he take them? To Ilam.

It makes sense, then, to treat Ilam and Ashbourne together, as they will be at the beginning of the Derbyshire section that follows immediately. For now, let it suffice to say that not only Dr. Johnson, but also Izaac Walton, William Congreve, George Eliot, and even Gawain and the Green Knight await you there.

DERBYSHIRE

Derbyshire

There was a rocky valley between Buxton and Bakewell, once upon a time, divine as the Vale of Tempe; you might have seen the Gods there morning and evening—Apollo and all the sweet Muses of the Light—walking in fair procession on the lawns of it. . . .

You Enterprised a Railroad through the valley—you blasted its rocks away, heaped thousands of tons of shale into its lovely stream. The valley is gone, and the Gods with it; and now, every fool in Buxton can be at Bakewell in half an hour, and every fool in Bakewell at Buxton.

John Ruskin, addressing the entrepreneurs of England, in *Fors Clavigera*

. . . they were obliged to give up the Lakes, and substitute a more contracted tour; and according to the present plan, were to go no farther northward than Derbyshire. In that county there was enough to be seen to occupy the chief of their three weeks; and to Mrs. Gardiner it had a peculiarly strong attraction. The town where she had formerly passed some years of her life . . . was probably as great an object of her curiosity as all the celebrated beauties of Matlock, Chatsworth, Dovedale or the Peak.

Jane Austen, *Pride and Prejudice*

I spent inside of a week motoring about Derbyshire, which was new to me, and in parts very picturesque indeed, especially Dovedale, of which I walked the best ten miles.

A. E. Housman, in a letter to his sister

He that has seen Dovedale has no need to visit the Highlands.

Samuel Johnson

Mr. Ruskin didn't have to get *that* carried away with the Victorian railroad builders and their havoc. Since the railways began crawling across

Britain in the 1830s they have left their scars in Derbyshire as elsewhere. So, too, have the collieries of the county's south and east; and belching smoke from limestone quarries still dims the sun above some of its most famous valleys, including the vicinity of Buxton-Bakewell. Yet Derbyshire (DAR-be-shur) has suffered nothing like the ruin that Ruskin implied.

From top to bottom (West Yorkshire to Leicestershire) Derbyshire has something over one thousand square miles of space, and something under one million people to accommodate. So, since a quarter of these people live in a single town, Derby, that leaves more than ample room for all the rest. Even Ruskin's Buxton has at most 25,000 of them, and Bakewell fewer than 5,000. What's more, almost the whole upper part of the county, including the splendid Peak District, has been designated a national park, and so is forever protected.

The "celebrated beauties" of *Pride and Prejudice* remain as they were when the book was written nearly two hundred years ago: the great stately mansions of Chatsworth, Haddon, and Hardwick Halls; the Peaks of the north; the Heights of Abraham at Matlock. And many a real-life Derbyshire village today can rival the fictional Lambdon that the novel's Mrs. Gardiner remembered so fondly then: remote little Ilam in the moorlands above Bakewell, for instance, and Hathersage among the gritstone cliffs above the Derwent.

In 1665, Eyam (it's "EE'm"), isolated though it was, fell victim to the devastating plague raging in London when the village tailor shop was shipped a box of contaminated clothing. Heroically, to protect other districts, the people of Eyam barred their gates, forbidding anyone to enter or leave, though many were desperate to flee. Of the 350 inhabitants, 250 died, but the disease spread no further. Hathersage, rugged and charming, provided not only a setting and the heroine's name for Charlotte Brontë's *Jane Eyre* (1847), but also a fourteen-foot grave in its churchyard for Robin Hood's friend, Little John.[1]

For us, too, there's still the section of the Dove that, two centuries apart, drew Johnson and Housman and, long before either, Izaak Walton. You can ignore Johnson's hyperbolic "He that has seen Dovedale has no need to visit the Highlands." Why in the world not visit both? But begin with Dovedale.

---

[1]See p. 67.

DOVEDALE: ASHBOURNE—ILAM AND THE MANIFOLD—AND THOR'S CAVE

The Dove River wanders vaguely south and east for some forty-five miles as it divides Derbyshire from Staffordshire. At its source on the slopes of the Axe Edge near Buxton it is a mere trickle, "a contemptible fountain which I can cover with my hat," said Izaak Walton's friend Charles Cotton. At its end, when it flows into the Trent below Derby, it is a full-fledged stream. Dovedale and Ashbourne come almost exactly midway in its course.

Ashbourne After he got his pension from George III in 1762 and could afford the luxury of travel, Samuel Johnson visited no place, not even his native Lichfield, more faithfully than Ashbourne. He might have had some interest in the area anyway, since his father was born just five miles to the south in Great Cubley.[2] But what drew him to Ashbourne, year after year to the very last months of his life, was the hospitality and friendship of Dr. John Taylor.

Today's Ashbourne isn't all that different from the one Johnson would have known. Located at the junction of the A 52 and A 515, it now has 6,000 people or so and some light industry to bolster the agricultural marketing it has always relied on. But the 212-foot spire of St. Oswald's still soars above the church that the bishop of Coventry dedicated in 1241, and Dr. Taylor's big town house still stands next to it. Across the street from both, the original building that housed the grammar school Queen Elizabeth I chartered in 1585 still serves as a master's quarters and boarding house for students, although the campus has moved to the outskirts of town.

And what's got to be the roughest community sport in the world, called Royal Shrovetide Football, is still played every Shrove Tuesday and Ash Wednesday as it has been for centuries, with the only rule apparently being "Thou shalt not kill thy opponent."

Players, the number unlimited, are divided by Henmore Brook, a tiny tributary of the Dove, flowing through the middle of the town. Those that live north of it are the Up'ards, those south, the Down'ards. Their respective goals, out of town, are three miles apart! Play starts at 2 P.M. and continues without stop until either a goal is scored or it's ten o'clock.

---

[2]Although much altered, Michael Johnson's birthplace still stands, identified by a plaque over the door.

Quitting from exhaustion or drowning in the Henmore are considered unsporting.

In their various days and ways, Izaak Walton, Thomas Moore, Mrs. Gaskell, and George Eliot all found Ashbourne attractive. In *The Compleat Angler* (1653) Izaac Walton has Viator and Piscator stop by for a chat at the Talbot, an inn on the site of what is now the Town Hall. Thomas Moore, who lived in neighboring Mayfield, was so impressed with the chimes of St. Oswald's that he wrote "Those Evening Bells." Mrs. Gaskell used to visit her cousin who lived at Ashbourne Hall, today's county library. And George Eliot made the Oatbourne of *Adam Bede* (1859) "that pretty town within sight of the blue hills."

For Samuel Johnson, Ashbourne was more than Dr. Taylor's mansion and the ready welcome it always afforded. Called without subtlety The Mansion, the building itself was impressive, a three-storey red-brick structure with spacious living quarters, a domed octagonal music room, and a grand dining hall with crystal chandeliers. Out back, splendid gardens ran down to Henmore Brook. The hospitality provided Johnson was lavish: his own commodious apartment, attentive servants, good food, and an audience drawn from the town's elite.

Johnson was hardly indifferent to such amenities, but in his host he got something more rare than any of this. For in John Taylor, clergyman and one of Ashbourne's wealthiest men, he had a friend unique among all his friends and acquaintances.

Taylor and Johnson were men of enormous differences, seemingly bound by the slimmest of ties, the sheer accident of being thrown together in the same Lichfield schoolroom as boys. Even then they were worlds apart. Taylor was eight-and-a-half, son of a prosperous Ashbourne attorney, athletic, self-assured, but a run-of-the-mill pupil. Johnson was a year and half older, son of an impoverished Lichfield bookseller, near-sighted, moody, but already inordinately bright.

In adult life, the contrasts grew even more pronounced. Taylor was a stolid but genial man, shrewd ("acute" was Johnson's word) and practical rather than intellectual, worldly and quite at ease with the bounties life brought him. Johnson was emotional and often melancholy, prodigious of mind, stirred by sensual pleasures yet plagued by conscience and a puritan streak that over-ruled them. But the men shared perhaps the scarcest commodity of all in the relationship between any two human beings, complete honesty with each other.

Only to Taylor could Johnson, a deeply spiritual man, bare his grave doubts about religion itself. To no one else could he reveal the most intimate of personal matters, including details of his marriage with Tetty. Johnson frequently complained to him of the "wretchedness of his situation with such a wife," Taylor confided to friends after Johnson's death. Johnson once said to Mrs. Thrale, "Dr. Taylor is better acquainted with my *heart* than any man or woman now alive."

Johnson and Taylor saw each other's faults clearly and could speak about them openly. Johnson told Boswell that Taylor had "such a sort of indolence that if you should put a pebble on his chimney-piece, you would find it there, in the same state, a year afterwards." Johnson also frankly criticized his friend's behavior as too worldly for a clergyman: "His habits are by no means sufficiently clerical; this he knows that I see."

For his part, Taylor said to Boswell about Johnson with equal candor, "There is no disputing with him. He will not hear you, and having a louder voice than you, must roar you down." When Tetty died, Taylor refused to officiate at the funeral and read the sermon that Johnson himself had written. Johnson's praise of his wife was more than Taylor could stomach.

Taylor was generous about inviting various friends of Johnson to be fellow guests while Johnson was there. One such guest was Boswell, who stayed several weeks in 1777. In his *Life of Samuel Johnson* (1791), he gives a vivid account of what these visits were like. Leisurely breakfasts, afternoon teas, and long dinners with guests at home or at elegant neighbors' abroad filled many hours of the day. Between came much reading, much talk, and walks about the town and vicinity.

They inspected Taylor's farm with its prize cattle, admired the gardens of the Ashbourne School, attended services at St. Oswald's. One morning Johnson worked at trying to clear away the debris blocking an artificial waterfall Taylor had constructed behind his garden. Finally exhausted, he handed the long pole he'd been using to Boswell, saying, "Come, *you* shall take it now." Boswell did, and at last dislodged the obstacle that had defied Johnson's every effort: an enormous dead cat.

There were trips afield, too, in Dr. Taylor's post chaise, visits to great estates like Kedleston Hall down near Derby, a tour of a china manufactury in Derby itself, and especially that memorable outing to Ilam Hall and Dovedale.[3]

---

[3]See p. 59.

When you get to Ashbourne, to see much of what Boswell saw as he strolled about town, simply follow its one major street. Begin at the western end of town where the A 52 enters from Leek and Mayfield and becomes Church Street. Here, naturally enough, you'll find on your right St. Oswald's Church, almost as large as a small cathedral. To George Eliot it was "the finest mere parish church in the Kingdom," and Boswell declared it "one of the largest and most luminous that I have seen in any town of the same size." If you're lucky enough to be in Ashbourne of a late Sunday, you'll get to hear the tower ringing out Moore's "Those Evening Bells."

Next door to the church is Dr. Taylor's The Mansion, and almost directly across the street is the many-gabled building that housed the grammar school in Queen Elizabeth's day. A bit further down the name changes from Church Street to St. Johns Street. On the right is Dig Street and Compton Bridge, where you can peer down at Henmore Brook and imagine the Up'ards and Down'ards having at each other.

Straight ahead on St. Johns Street is The Green Man and Black's Head Hotel. But first you may want to take the short turn to the left through Victoria Square to the market place, where the indubitably Victorian Town Hall indicates where Izaak Walton's Talbot Hall used to be. In the old days, the Market Place was the starting point for Royal Shrovetide Football, which begins when some imported dignitary "turns up" the ball, i.e., tosses it among the waiting players.

The dignitary is still primed for his task with a gala luncheon at the Green Man, which has in its Johnson Bar an honours board naming everyone who has done the turn up since 1873. In 1928 he was H.R.H., the Prince of Wales, giving the game the right to the prefix "Royal" ever since. The hotel grew out of two inns, The Green Man and The Black's Head, and a gallows sign stretched across the street shows both the be-turbaned head of a black man on top, and a green-clad hunter and his dog below.

You can put up at The Green Man yourself if you like. It's rated two-star and comes recommended by none other than James Boswell as a "very good inn." Admittedly, he was asked to do so by its mistress, a Mrs. Killingley, "a mighty civil gentlewoman."

On the morning of his departure from Ashbourne, he picked up his post chaise there. "Curtseying very low," he recorded in his journal, she presented him with an engraving of the sign of her house, along with the following hand-written message:

M. KILLINGLEY's duty waits upon <u>Mr. Boswell</u>, is exceedingly obliged to him for this favour; whenever he comes this way, hopes for a continuance of the same. Would <u>Mr.</u> Boswell name the house to his extensive acquaintance, it would be a singular favour conferr'd on one who has it not in her power to make any other return but her most grateful thanks, and sincerest prayers for his happiness in time, and in blessed eternity.

Today The Green Man has a more tangible return for the favor. It now has a Boswell room.

Ilam and the Manifold   Ilam, where Dr. Johnson took Boswell when showing off Dovedale and where they watched the little Manifold River emerge from its mysterious four-mile passage as an underground stream, is on a by-road four miles northwest of Ashbourne. Boswell's own account of the excursion will serve admirably to describe what's there. But a preliminary word or two of explanation may be helpful.

First Boswell's unusual spellings—"Islam" and "Manyfold"—suggest how these names may have originated. Second, he's quite right that William Congreve paid a visit to his family's one-time ancestral home, Ilam Hall, when the Ports owned it, and may well be correct in saying that the playwright's first comedy, *The Old Bachelor* (1693), was written there. However, Stretton Hall in Staffordshire, where he was living with his grandfather, claims that he began the play there. Third, the point at which the Manifold goes underground is near Thor's Cave. It would have been here that the gardener inserted his corks to prove that it was the same stream that emerged at Ilam.

Here is Boswell's account:

> Dr. Johnson obligingly proposed to carry me to see Islam, a romantick scene, now belonging to a family of the name of Port, but formerly the seat of the Congreves. . . .
>
> I recollect a very fine amphitheatre, surrounded with hills covered with woods, and walks neatly formed along the side of a rocky steep, on the quarter next the house, with recesses under projections of rock, overshadowed with trees; in one of which recesses, we were told, Congreve wrote his *Old Bachelor*.
>
> We viewed a remarkable natural curiosity at Islam; two rivers bursting near each other from the rock, not from immediate springs, but after having run for many miles under ground. Plot in his "History of Staffordshire," gives an account of his curiosity; but Johnson would not believe it, though we had the attestation of the gardener, who said he had put in

corks, where the river Manyfold sinks into the ground, and had catched them in a net, placed before one of the openings where the water bursts out.

Ilam Park now belongs to the National Trust. Since the Hall is let as a Youth Hostel, the house is not open to the general public, and in any event isn't the original structure, but a Victorian replacement. But you can see the grounds and park any day all year-round, and teas are served in a building at the rear of the hall from Easter to the end of September.

Thor's Cave From Ilam, a footpath takes you to Thor's Cave. Though it is only one of several locations that have been suggested, it has as good a claim as any to being the site of Gawain's New Year's Day rendezvous with his giant adversary in the fourteenth-century classic, *Sir Gawain and the Green Knight*. Certainly the terrain about the cave, high above the Manifold, more than lives up to the menacing landscape that Gawain encounters:

> By a mountain next morning he makes his bold way,
> Deep into a forest, fearsome and wild.
> High hills bend down over dark woods below,
> Huge, hoary oak trees, an hundred or more;
> Hazel and hawthorne entangled together
> With raveling mosses, all ragged and rough.
> On bleak branches sit the shivering birds,
> Piteous their piping, their pain of the cold.

WALTON'S DOVEDALE: HARTINGTON TO THORPE CLOUD

Dovedale proper, the "Eagle Dale" of George Eliot's *Adam Bede*, is that part of the Dove, less than five miles in all, that runs from immediately below Hartington and the B 5054 to Thorpe Cloud, just above Ashbourne. Dr. Johnson wasn't the only one moved to superlatives by its enchantment. Byron wrote ecstatically to Thomas Moore, "Was you ever in Dovedale? I assure you there are things in Derbyshire as noble as in Greece or Switzerland." And in *The Compleat Angler* Izaak Walton said of the verdant meadows by the riverside:

> I thought of them as Charles the Emperor did of the City of Florence, that they were too pleasant to be looked upon but only on holy days.

Walton must have felt that the waters of the Dove were his own special preserve, shared with his favorite fishing companion, Charles Cotton. He came whenever he could as Cotton's guest, for Cotton lived in a grand house in Dovedale itself, and built a charming little "Fishing Temple" alongside the stream. Their talk, as the two fished side by side, must have been sprightly, for Charles Cotton was an accomplished fellow in his own right.

A wealthy young gentleman—he was thirty-seven years younger than Walton—Cotton wrote verses pleasant enough to win the approval of Charles Lamb, amusing burlesques of Virgil and Lucian, and an agreeable translation of Montaigne's *Essays*. In 1676 he wrote the dialogue between Piscator, the fisherman, and Viator, the traveler, that formed the second part of the fifth edition of *The Compleat Angler*. It was Cotton, not Walton, who was the expert in the intricacies of fly fishing, and Cotton who supplied the book's directions for making artificial flies, interspersed with picturesque descriptions of the rocky terrain.

At Hartington there's a footpath you can follow all the way down to Thorpe Cloud through a series of dales of surpassing beauty, but don't expect the going to be easy. First to come is Beresford Dale, with both Cotton's Fishing Temple and the site of his home. The Temple, which had murals of fishing subjects and portraits, remains in private hands, and so is off bounds to visitors. Beresford Hall, Cotton's home, stood about the Dale, but little of it is left.

Further down, at Milldale, you'll pass the bridge mentioned in *The Compleat Angler,* now called Viator Bridge. From there go on to such spectacular sights as the two caves known as Doveholes, the grand outcropping called Ilam Rock, and finally the famous stepping stones at Thorpe Cloud, which rises almost one thousand feed above them.

Also at Thorpe Cloud is The Izaak Walton, one of the two hotels that form convenient anchors to Dovedale. The other, at Hartington, is The Charles Cotton, a seventeenth-century inn with grounds bordering the Dove, is small, and at last report rated one star. The Izaak Walton, a converted eighteenth-century farmhouse, is considerably larger, has a modern wing, and is rated three stars.

If you have a yen to fish in Walton's waters yourself, you'd better plan to book into one or the other of these hotels. Guests at either have fishing privileges. All others have to gain membership into one of the local angling clubs, which isn't easy. They often have a waiting list, and there are no day tickets.

WIRKSWORTH AND MIDDLETON

Wirksworth and Middleton are about seven miles northeast of Ashbourne; Wirksworth a town of 6,000 or so on the B 5035 and B 5023, Middleton a village on the B 5023 a mile and a half above Wirksworth. By a coincidence of absolutely no consequence at all, each gave rise to a book published under a name not the author's own. Wirksworth's author was "George Eliot," really Mary Ann Evans, as just about everybody knows. Middleton's writer, "Lawrence H. Davidson" was actually—can you guess?—D. H. Lawrence.

Wirksworth   George Eliot's father, Robert Evans, had originally come from Derbyshire, and the novelist returned there from time to time to visit her Aunt Elizabeth, who lived at Wirksworth. Elizabeth Evans not only supplied her niece with the basic plot of *Adam Bede*, but also figures in the book as its Dinah Morris.

Elizabeth Evans herself was a Methodist preacher, as was Dinah, and in that capacity had heard the real-life confession of child-murder made to her by a girl she'd ministered to in prison. In the novel, Wirksworth appears as Snowfield, and the town's connection wtih *Adam Bede* is recalled by a commemorative plaque in its Ebenezer Memorial Church.

Middleton   When D. H. Lawrence arrived in Middleton in the spring of 1918 as WWI was drawing to an end, he was a forlorn figure. The war years had been brutal to him, and explained how he came to be in Middleton.

In 1915 the government had seized his novel, *The Rainbow*, successfully prosecuted it as obscene, and had it destroyed. In 1917 police had invaded his cottage at Zennor on the coast of Cornwall, accused him and his German-born wife, Frieda, of spying on the sea-lanes for the German Navy, and given them twenty-four hours to evacuate. In a letter Lawrence makes clear how desperate the situation was:

> We must leave Cornwall, and live in an unprohibited area, and report to the police. It is *very* vile. We have practically no money at all—I don't know what we shall do.

Early in 1918 his sister, Ada, who lived in Ripley twelve miles east of Ashbourne, gave such help as she could. Wanting him near her, she found Mountain Cottage for him at Middleton and offered to pay the modest rent. In May, the fugitives moved in. Although he admitted that he felt "queer and lost and exiled . . . like Ovid in Thrace," Lawrence expressed pleasure:

> I think it will be nice. It is in the darkish Midlands, on the rim of a steep valley, looking over darkish, folded hills—exactly the navel of England, and feels exactly that.

The debacle of *The Rainbow* had apparently cooled Lawrence's zest for novel writing, at least for the time being. He turned to the onerous task of reading the whole of Gibbon's *Decline and Fall of the Roman Empire* and used this research to write *Movements in European History*, an elementary textbook for schoolboys. Perhaps he found the project demeaning. Or maybe he simply didn't want to saddle it with the name of a novelist grown notorious. At any rate, when the history was published in 1921, it appeared as the work of Lawrence H. Davidson.

CHATSWORTH AND EDENSOR

Chatsworth   To call Chatsworth, fifteen miles northeast of Ashbourne on the B 6012 just above Bakewell, a stately home is paltry praise indeed. They don't come any statelier. Its park has an eleven-mile circuit and contains more than a hundred acres. Its fountains rival those of Versailles, and the Louvre would love to get its hands on its art collection. Its front lawn once accommodated an entire village. Its history goes back before the days of William the Conqueror, and so does its name. Long before 1066 an old Saxon chieftain named Chetel held forth at his court ("voerde") there—Chetel's-voerde.

The first great house on the site was begun in 1553 by Sir William Cavendish and his wife, Elizabeth. They were quite a pair. She was his third wife, he her second husband. He had become rich and knighted by helping Henry VIII loot monasteries during the Dissolution. She had made a name for herself as "Bess of Hardwick," imperious daughter of the squire of Hardwick, a dozen miles to the west. It was she who had talked Sir William into buying Chatsworth.

After Sir William's death in 1557 Elizabeth went on to become the richest woman in England by the simple expedient of adding the fortunes of two more husbands to the sizeable legacies of her first two. She also became "Building Bess of Hardwick" by completing Chatsworth and erecting two more grand mansions, Hardwick Hall and Oldcoates.

Throughout the seventeenth century, the descendants of Sir William and Bess continued to prosper, two of them having as tutor the same man who'd taught the Prince of Wales (later Charles II)—the great philosopher Thomas Hobbes, author of *The Leviathan* (1651). In the reign of William and Mary, the pair's great-great-grandson, also a William Cavendish, capped the family's climb by acquiring one of the great titles of the realm. He was sensible enough to be one of the seven signers of the original document that invited William of Orange and his wife, Mary, to come back to England as successors to the ousted James II. The new monarchs showed their gratitude by making Cavendish duke of Devonshire, a title the Cavendishes have owned, along with Chatsworth, ever since.

It was this first duke of Devonshire who initiated Chatsworth's march to today's magnificence. In 1686 he had begun re-doing its Elizabethan south facade. Next came a new east front, and so on and on, all around the building. By the time he died in 1707 the original Tudor structure was gone. In its place stood a classic of Restoration Palladian architecture.

Aside from the indulgence of a personal whim here and there by the next several dukes, this was essentially the Chatsworth that Elizabeth Bennet would have seen in *Pride and Prejudice* (1813) as one of those "celebrated beauties" of Derbyshire she visited before going on to her embarrassing encounter with Mr. Darcy at Pemberley. It may even have been the model of Pemberley itself, though Jane Austen has generalized her fictional account of what Elizabeth and her friends saw:

> The park was very large, and contained great variety of ground. . . . They gradually ascended for half a mile, and then found themselves at the top of a considerable eminence, where the wood ceased, and the eye was caught by Pemberley House, situated on the opposite side of the valley, into which the road with some abruptness wound. It was a large, handsome stone building, standing well on rising ground, and backed by a ridge of high woody hills, and in front a stream of some natural importance was swelled into a greater, but without artificial appearance.

This was the Chatsworth, too, that Dr. Johnson would have known, for he was acquainted with the fifth duke of Devonshire, and when visiting Dr. Taylor at Ashbourne had gone over to see Chatsworth on several occasions. He went there, in fact, on the very last trip of his life, in 1784, when he was seventy-five and quite ailing. His report to a London friend is sad:

Do you know the Duke and Duchess of Devonshire? And have you ever seen Chatsworth? I was at Chatsworth on Monday; I had seen it before, but never when its owners were at home; I was very kindly received, and honestly pressed to stay; but I told them that a sick man is not a fit inmate for a great house. But I hope to go again sometime.

William Wordsworth visited the place when the sixth duke of Devonshire was the master of Chatsworth, and he yielded to the temptation, as he too often did on his travels, to write a sonnet:

> Chatsworth! thy stately mansion, and the pride
> Of thy domain, strange contrast do present
> To house and home in many a craggy rent
> Of the Wild Peak. . . .

Wordsworth muddles on for the rest of the fourteen lines, to come at last to the conclusion that the poor should realize that the rich aren't a bad sort, either.

Of course, if the rich aren't satisfied with things as they are, they can change them. About 1839 the same sixth duke of Devonshire decided to do for Chatsworth's setting what the first duke had done for the house. To begin with, he thought the entrance really should have a grand vista of that river down below, with a great lawn dotted with clumps of trees stretching all the way to its banks. True, the good-sized village of Edensor did stand between him and those banks. But no matter. The duke had a word with his landscaper, and the next thing the villagers knew, they were living on the other side of the river—houses, barns, churches, chicken-coops, and all.[4]

Today's Chatsworth is still the home of the Cavendish family, which maintains private quarters there. And an added contemporary literary fillip: the current duchess of Devonshire was Deborah Mitford of the writing Mitford sisters, who included Nancy, Diana, Jessica, Unity, and Pamela.

You can tour today's Chatsworth any day you like from 10:30 in the morning until 4:30 in the afternoon, from the last week in March through most of October. For a substantial fee, needless to say, for Chatsworth now is a vast enterprise. Be prepared to be overwhelmed by the rooms upon rooms, the state apartments and marble halls, the furniture, the

---

[4]Details on p. 66.

paintings, the sculpture, the jewelry and other priceless objects d'art, the etc., etc., etc.

No amount of preparation, perhaps, can get you adequately ready for the live milking demonstrations with a running commentary by the milker, staged every afternoon as part of the Farmyard and Forestry Exhibition. But you can recoup at the Stables Tea Bar, featuring homemade food and refreshments, including homemade ice cream. From those same cows, no doubt.

Edensor   Edensor ("EE-n'sor"), the village that the sixth Duke of Devonshire moved in its entirety because it blocked his view, now stands on the other side of the Derwent River, west of Chatsworth Park. The man entrusted by the duke to supervise the actual removal was his gardener, Joseph Paxton, who later won renown and a knighthood for designing the Crystal Palace for Queen Victoria's Great Exhibition of 1851.

Paxton went about his work with a generous hand and freewheeling fancy. He insisted that the villages' new houses be set well apart, and that no two be alike. With the aid of a Derby architect he ran the gamut of England's building history—plus putting in a dash of the continental. There were Tudor chimneys, Jacobean gables, and Georgian doorways; Italian windows, and Swiss-chalet roofs.

James Boswell would have sought in vain for the village he'd stayed in on his way home from Ashbourne in 1777. But the story he tells about his Edensor innkeeper in his *Life of Samuel Johnson* is worth repeating:

> I cannot omit a curious circumstance which occurred at Edensor-inn, close by Chatsworth, to survey the magnificence of which I had gone a considerable way out of my road to Scotland. The inn was then kept by a very jolly landlord whose name, I think, was Malton. He happened to mention that "the celebrated Dr. Johnson had been in his house." I enquired who this Dr. Johnson was, that I might hear my host's notion of him. "Sir, (said he), Johnson, the great writer; Oddity as they call him. He's the greatest writer in England; he writes for the ministry; he has a correspondence abroad, and lets them know what's going on."

When he heard the outlandish tale, Johnson's reaction was refreshing and characteristic. "My friend," said Boswell, "laughed a good deal at this representation of himself."

For American travelers today, Edensor has a special, poignant interest. President John F. Kennedy's sister Kathleen is buried in its churchyard. She was the wife of the tenth duke of Devonshire's eldest son, the marquis of Hartington, and had she and the marquis both lived, they would have reigned together in their turn as the next duke and duchess. But he was killed in action during WWII, and she died in an airplane accident in 1948. A commemorative stone marks President Kennedy's visit to her graveside.

HATHERSAGE AND RENISHAW

Up above Chatsworth are the villages of Hathersage and Renishaw. Each had a part in the writing of a celebrated novel.

Hathersage is seven miles to the northwest of Chatsworth on the B 6001 and, if you're driving from one to the other, you might want to stop for a look at Eyam, off to your left about halfway to Hathersage. Eyam's contribution to literature was limited, to say the least. Anna Seward, the "Swan of Lichfield" who mistook energy for poetic talent, was born there in 1774. But Eyam is where the citizens so heroically kept the plague of 1666 from spreading to other villages by forbidding anyone to enter or leave.

Renishaw is fourteen miles northeast of Chatsworth on the A 616.

Hathersage   Hathersage sits on a hillside above the Derwent Valley, surrounded by the cliffs of the Peak District. Its Church of St. Michael is notable for its graveyard, its vicarage, and some fifteenth-century commemorative brasses.

Among the graves in the churchyard is a huge one, fourteen feet long, pointed out in all earnestness as the eternal resting place of Robin Hood's stalwart companion, Little John Little. Surely only a pedant would want to suggest that there may be a bit of discrepancy—say 150 years or so—between the time Robin Hood is supposed to have flourished and the building of the church here in 1381.

As for the vicarage, Charlotte Brontë was a visitor there in 1845, guest of her friend from schooldays on, Ellen Nussey. The occasion was not without its irony. Ellen was tending the vicarage for her brother, the Rev. Henry Nussey, who had once proposed to Charlotte and been turned down. Henry, you see, was off on his honeymoon.

Charlotte put her stay to good use for all that, which is where those brasses come in. For some centuries, the area's leading family had been the Eyres, and the church abounds with their memorial brasses. Charlotte's first attempt at a novel, called *The Professor,* had been rejected by publishers, but she was already pondering another. When it appeared in 1847 its heroine's name was Jane Eyre; its village of "Morton," where Jane meets St. John Rivers, is recognizably Hathersage; and its "Moor House" is Moorseats Hall, still to be seen behind the vicarage.

Renishaw   In 1625 a George Sitwell built himself a fine house at Renishaw on the A 616, and called it Renishaw Hall. Nearly 300 years later his descendant, namesake, and owner of that same house, Sir George Sitwell, made three distinct contributions to literature without any intention of doing so. He sired a talented trio of writers, became the subject of an outstanding literary portrait himself, and gave rise to a novel that proved a landmark.

The writers he sired were Edith, Osbert, and Sacheverell Sitwell, and their combined output of poems, essays, fiction, criticism, and biography was awesome, often controversial, and sometimes dazzling. In Osbert's five-volume autobiography, beginning with *Left Hand, Right Hand* (1944–50), Sir George figures as the very embodiment of an eccentric, amusing, but difficult and domineering father.

It was while in Italy in the summer of 1926 that Sir George launched a novel without realizing it. He ran into a fellow Englishman named Lawrence and discovered that he not only had a sister who lived in Derbyshire within twenty miles of Renishaw, but who was a writer as well. Really, Sir George said to his new friend, he ought to go and meet his children when he got a chance, since they wrote a bit, too.

Soon after his return to England, D. H. Lawrence did so, borrowing his sister Ada's car and driving over to Renishaw from Wirksworth. The younger Sitwells, he found, were unfortunately away. But Lawrence was impressed with Renishaw Hall, and decided to use it as a model for the home of the titled heroine of his new book—especially since the novel was to be based on a story he'd heard from Sir George himself.

And such a story it was! Sir George, it seemed, had had a neighbor, a youth who'd shown great promise as a student at Eton and Oxford. But at twenty he was thrown from his horse and gravely injured. Though he recovered sufficiently to become a distinguished linguist and write several books, he was left both crippled and impotent. Even so, over the strenuous objections of his family he insisted on marrying a beautiful and aristocratic young lady, with predictably disastrous results. The marriage, of course, could not be consummated, and they lived out their lives in separate misery.

The novel's title, needless to say, was *Lady Chatterley's Lover.*

Renishaw Hall is now lived in by Sir Sacheverell's son, Sir Reresby, and his wife, Lady Penelope; and, in season, the magnificent gardens are open on specified days (better check first). But be forewarned: as you drive up the curving road to the house, you will see a most effective "no trespassing" notice. A largish sign reads, "Please do not tread on Mr. Sitwell's snakes."

DERBY AND KEDLESTON HALL

Derby is thirty miles southwest of Renishaw and on the A 52, the highway that takes the traveler on his eastward trek straight into the next county, Nottinghamshire. First, however, Derby itself and Kedleston on the outskirt have their own points of interest to offer.

Derby　With nearly a quarter of a million people, Derby is Derbyshire's largest town and its county seat. It is also one of England's oldest settlements and newest cities. The Romans had a fort there as early as the second century A.D. Queen Elizabeth II formally named it a city during her jubilee visit in 1977. Among its literary associations are ties to George Fox, Maria Edgeworth, Herbert Spencer, George Eliot, and especially Samuel Johnson.

Derby was one of Fox's earliest stops in a career that was to take him in and out of any number of jails throughout England, and it was the Derby imprisonment that gave the Society of Friends he founded its popular name. Brought before Derby's Justice Gervase Bennett for blasphemy and asked why his followers heeded him, Fox replied boldly, "Because I bid them, 'Tremble at the word of the Lord!'" They've been known as Quakers ever since.

Fox was author of many books and pamphlets, as well as his famous *Journal,* published in 1694 with a preface by William Penn. And while they would hardly serve as a textbook on spelling or grammar, they do display a strong narrative style and a knack for the striking phrase.

The novelist Maria Edgeworth went to a girls' school in Derby, and Herbert Spencer, who was born there in 1820, both attended and taught at the city school. George Eliot makes Derby the "Stoniton" of *Adam*

Bede, and its county hall in St. Mary's Gate serves as the scene of Hetty Sorrel's trial for the murder of her child.

Samuel Johnson visited Derby a number of times, most notably for his marriage to Mrs. Elizabeth Porter at St. Werburgh's Church in Friar Gate in 1735. The bride and bridegroom had set forth on horseback, and Johnson himself gave Boswell this account of their odd passage home after the ceremony:

> Sir, she had read the old romances, and had got into her head the fantastical notion that a woman of spirit should use her lover like a dog. So, sir, at first she told me that I rode too fast, and she could not keep up with me: and, when I rode a little slower, she passed me, and complained that I lagged behind. I was not to be made the slave of caprice; and I resolved to begin as I meant to end. I therefore pushed on briskly, till I was fairly out of her sight. The road lay between two hedges, so I was sure she could not miss it; and I contrived that she should soon come up with me. When she did, I observed her to be in tears.

As Boswell observes wryly, "This, it must be allowed, was a singular beginning of connubial felicity."

Today Derby is justly famous for its Royal Crown Derby china, but in 1777, when Boswell and Johnson were fellow guests of Dr. Taylor at Ashbourne, the industry was new and George III had just granted its originator, William Duesbury, the right to put a crown on his wares. So Johnson took Boswell over to have a look. Boswell admits he was impressed:

> I admired the ingenuity and delicate art with which a man fashioned clay into a cup, a saucer, or a tea-pot, while a boy turned round a wheel to give the mass a rotundity.

Not so Dr. Johnson, however. Boswell continues:

> The china was beautiful, but Dr. Johnson justly observed it was too dear; for that he could have vessels of silver, of the same size, as cheap as what were made of porcelain.

Kedleston Hall   It was on this same outing that Johnson stopped on the north edge of Derby to show Bosworth Kedleston Hall, owned by Lord Scarsdale, whom he knew. It was already one of England's renowned estates, had been the seat of the Curzon family since the twelfth century, and was now famous all over again for its recently rebuilt mansion. Again Boswell's account shows how he and Johnson differed in their reactions:

> I was struck with the magnificence of the building; and the extensive park, with the finest verdure, covered with deer, and cattle, and sheep, delighted me. The number of old oaks, of an immense size, filled me with a sort of respectful admiration: for one of them sixty pounds was offered.

Boswell continues,

> "One should think (said I) that the proprietor of all this *must* be happy."
> —"Nay, Sir, (said Johnson), all this excludes but one evil—poverty."

Nowadays Kedleston Hall is another of the great private homes of England that doubles as a public enterprise, though hardly on the scale of a Chatsworth. It's open Sundays from the last week in April to the last week in August, and has its requisite marble hall, state apartments, and collection of old master paintings, as well as a five hundred acre park with lakes and a bridge by the famous eighteenth-century architect, Robert Adam, who also designed the house.

True, it doesn't have Chatsworth's daily milking demonstrations with their running commentary. But then, Chatsworth doesn't have an Indian museum, because it never had a Curzon of Kedleston, George Nathaniel, First Marquess. And there may well be some who prefer the collection of oriental treasures that Lord Curzon amassed as governor-general of India even to Chatsworth's homemade ice cream.

THE EAST

NOTTINGHAMSHIRE

Nottinghamshire

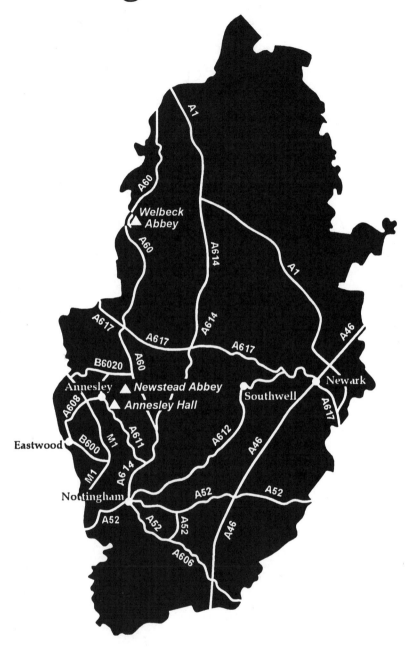

I was born nearly forty-four years ago, in Eastwood, a mining village of some three thousand souls about eight miles from Nottingham. . . . To me it seemed, and still seems, an extremely beautiful countryside, just between the red sandstone and the oak-trees of Nottingham, and the cold limestone, the ash trees, the stone fences of Derbyshire. To me, as a child and a young man, it was still the old England of the forest and agricultural past; there were no motor cars, the mines were, in a sense, an accident in the landscape, and Robin Hood and his merry men were not very far away.

D. H. Lawrence, *Phoenix*

To Norman Abbey whirl'd the noble pair,—
An old, old monastery once, and now
Still older mansion,—of a rich and rare
Mix'd Gothic, such as artists all allow
Few specimens yet left us can compare
Withal; it lies perhaps a little low,
Because the monks preferr'd a hill behind,
To shelter their devotion from the wind.

George Gordon, Lord Byron, *Don Juan*

About three Years ago, Mr. Gulliver growing weary of the Concourse of curious People coming to him at his House in Redriff, made a small Purchase of Land, with a convenient House, near Newark, in Nottinghamshire, his native Country; where he now lives retired, yet in good Esteem among his Neighbours.

Jonathan Swift, *Gulliver's Travels*

Selecting quotations from Byron and D. H. Lawrence to introduce this section was inevitable. To an unprecedented degree they constitute Nottinghamshire's gifts to literature. Iconoclasts both, they are fittingly joined by yet a third in Lemuel Gulliver. For Gulliver really is, of course, Jonathan Swift, who could have said with Byron,

77

I have not loved the World, nor the World me,—
I have not flattered its rank breath, nor bowed
To its idolatries a patient knee.

Maybe something about Nottinghamshire sparks independence, even defiance. Robin Hood was a Nottinghamshire man, sheltered by its Sherwood Forest.

Once that forest covered almost half the county's length, running northward from Nottingham, unbroken for more than twenty miles, and stretching at times to ten miles in width. Beginning in the twelfth century with Henry II, it was long a favorite hunting ground of royalty and, paradoxically, real-life outlaws who challenged Norman and Plantagenet kings alike. Today the forest has been nibbled away, but you can still drive through it for miles. At Edwinstowe there's a Sherwood Forest Visitor Centre in a 450-acre park of ancient oaks, with a Robin Hood exhibition, a film-slide show, and well-marked footpaths.

West of Nottingham is the country Lawrence describes—hilly, laced with valleys and brooks, but scarred too with the coal mines of *Sons and Lovers* (1913), where Lawrence's own father made his dreary living. Most of the rest of the county is low-lying and flat, and remains largely agricultural.

Nottingham, with more than 300,000 people, is the county seat and the only city of any size. It makes an ideal base for seeing Nottinghamshire. Roads run to and from it in all directions. The A 52, for instance, that brings you in from Derby and the west, will take you all across Lincolnshire to Boston in the east. Going north and south, you have your choice of hustling along the M 1 or enjoying the leisure of a variety of A roads. And, best of all, with only one or two exceptions, every literary site of any importance is within a radius of ten miles, including Lawrence's Eastwood and Byron's Norman Abbey-mansion looking better than it ever did when the poet lived there.

NOTTINGHAM

As boys, both Byron and Lawrence knew Nottingham. Then as now its historic past was signalled by Nottingham Castle. The original Norman fortress was built nine hundred years ago on the rock that rises precipitately 130 feet above the town, and saw a parade of royal visitors thereafter, not always with happy results.

Young King Edward III came there stealthily in 1330 to arrest his own mother and her lover, Earl Mortimer, for murder, and you can still see the hundred-yard tunnel that let him in.[1] It's called "Mortimer's Hole." Edward IV proclaimed himself king from this same castle. His were the two small princes of London Tower, murdered by Edward's brother, Richard III. Richard, in turn, used the castle as the starting point of his march to Bosworth Field in 1485, where he lost his horse, his throne, and his life.

In 1642 Charles I fled London to hoist his flag over Nottingham Castle and to rally his loyal subjects to his support. Some rally! Fewer than 300 of Nottingham's best heeded the royal appeal. After Charles's defeat and execution, Cromwell's Parliament ordered the castle destroyed. But that was not the end of its tempestuous career. William Cavendish, the 1st Duke of Devonshire, rebuilt a town mansion on the site of the ruins in 1674, but this was destroyed in 1831 when the Nottingham townspeople rioted and set fire to it during the disturbance leading to the Reform Bill of 1832. Finally, the shell was renovated by the town (1875–78) and now houses a museum and art gallery.

In its literary past, Nottingham has had an assortment of lesser lights, worth a mention before getting to Byron and Lawrence. Charles Cotton, that amiable fishing partner and collaborator of Izaak Walton, and sometime poet, was married at Nottingham's St. Mary's Church in 1656. The match inspired Richard Lovelace to write "The Triumph of Philamore and Amoret." Although not great poetry, it was the friendly thing to do.

Henry Kirk White, son of a Nottingham butcher, was born in 1785. His *Clifton Grove and Other Poems,* published in 1803 when he was barely eighteen, had enough merit to win the approval of both Byron and Robert Southey. Southey's collection of his work ran through a number of editions, but White is known today only for a hymn or two, such as "Oft in Danger, Oft in Woe."

Another native of Nottingham was Philip James Bailey, born there in 1816. Early on he became a barrister at London's Lincoln's Inn, but he much preferred writing poetry. So in 1836, at age twenty, he retired to his father's house near Nottingham and began to write his version of the Faust legend, which he called *Festus.* The trouble was he didn't know when to stop. In all he published three versions of the poem—in

---

[1]Christopher Marlowe tells their story in *Edward II* (1594).

1839, 1845, and 1889—each adding to its predecessor. By the time he was through, he had amassed over forty thousand lines!

In 1821 a young couple named William and Mary Howitt came to Nottingham as chemists and settled down in a small flat above their shop in Parliament Street before moving on to a real house in the Market Place. Like Bailey, however, they'd much rather have been writers and had already collaborated on *The Forest Minstrell and Other Poems*, published in 1823. They went on to write all sorts of things, both poetry and prose. But a quick look at their titles—William's *A Boy's Adventures in the Wilds of Australia* (1854), say, or Mary's *The Heir of Wast-Wayland* (1847)—suggests why there's not likely to be a Howitt revival any time in the near future. John Drinkwater was yet another who found himself in Nottingham toiling at something else when he'd rather be writing. Drinkwater worked for the Northern Assurance Company in Victoria Street from 1898 to 1901. But by 1913 he had managed to become the director of the Birmingham Repertory Theatre. He later won solid success with historical plays like *Abraham Lincoln* (1918) and also wrote some pleasant verse.

Byron came to Nottingham in 1789 after a transformation as amazing as anything that ever happened to his fictional Don Juan. One moment he had been simply little George Byron of Aberdeen, Scotland, the ten-year-old son of a penniless widow. The next, as heir to a great-uncle he had scarcely heard of, he was George Gordon Noel Byron, sixth Baron Byron, master of a storied estate called Newstead Abbey.

But when he and his mother hastened down to Nottinghamshire to claim their estate, they found they had inherited problems as well. The abbey was a dilapidated pile, barely habitable, stripped of furniture to pay creditors, and heavily mortgaged. While Mrs. Byron sought for solutions, they found lodgings in Nottingham, first with relatives in Pelham Street, then at No. 76 St. James Street.

Byron was never in Nottingham all that much. From 1801 on, he was away at school, and during vacations he liked to make do at the abbey and play at being a lord. And in 1803 his mother quit the town entirely for Southwell, twelve miles east of Newstead. But Byron never forgot Nottingham. His first speech after he took his seat in the House of Lords was an impassioned defense of its starving weavers who had risen up and smashed the machines that had stolen their jobs.

Nottingham was far more important to D. H. Lawrence. It gave him such education as he had and provided him with a wife. He first went there in 1898, as the recipient of a fellowship to Nottingham High School, but hardly distinguished himself. In English he finished thirteenth in a class of twenty-one. After graduation he worked for some months at a surgical appliance factory in Castle Gate before returning to Eastwood as an uncertified teacher.

After various vicissitudes, he went back to Nottingham in 1906 to spend two years at University College earning a teaching certificate. Nottingham and the college both figure in Lawrence's *The Rainbow* (1915), and neither fares well. Nottingham is a "dirty, industrial town," and, despite a good first impression, the college is "sham, spurious: spurious Gothic arches, spurious peace, spurious Latinity."

In 1912, after ill health forced him to give up teaching, Lawrence was back in Nottingham seeking the advice of his old French teacher, Ernest Weekley, as to what to do next. The professor's young wife supplied the answer. She was Frieda von Richtofen, cousin of the man who was to be the famous German flying ace of WWI. Frieda and Lawrence fell in love and within a month fled together to Germany. In 1914 they were able to get married.

A number of reminders of Nottingham's literary past, including both of Lawrence's schools, await you as you stroll about the city today. The high school, now much enlarged, is in the northern part of town, in Arboretum Street; and a quarter of a mile below it, in Shakespeare Street, Trent Polytechnic includes what used to be University college.

A bit further south come Pelham and Victoria Streets. Byron's Pelham Street house is gone, but on Victoria Street a marker shows where John Drinkwater worked for the Northern Assurance Company. Just east of Pelham and Victoria, by the way, is Goose Gate, which has no literary significance, but you may want to take a peek at it anyway. For there, around 1887, a Nottingham family opened a chemist's shop that grew into a great chain of stores known to every traveler from abroad. The family's name? Boots.

Continuing south a few more blocks you come to High Pavement, with the Unitarian Chapel that Byron attended as a boy, and in which Coleridge had once preached. St. James Street, where Byron lodged at No. 76, is a third of a mile or so due west of Pavement. The house is marked with a plaque.

Looming above everything, a little west of St. James, is the castle. Outside of the castle is a statue of Robin Hood, but none of his nemesis the Sheriff of Nottingham—possibly because the town had no sheriff unti 1449, a good 250 years after the outlaw supposedly breathed his last.

And finally, if you're a collector of pubs that are the one-and-only-for-true oldest in England, there's one at the foot of the castle that says precisely that. Down on Castle Road, big black letters take up the whole side of a modest little two-storey building to proclaim:

YE OLDE TRIP TO
JERUSALEM
AD 1189

—

THE OLDEST
INN IN ENGLAND

Step inside and they'll assure you that, during the Middle Ages, travelers would stop in for a quick fortifier on their way to crusade in the Holy Land.

NEWSTEAD ABBEY

When, as a ten-year-old, Byron first saw Newstead Abbey off the A 60 and the B 6020, "hall of my Fathers . . . gone to decay," it was already more than six hundred years old.[2] About 1170 Augustinian monks established the Priory of St. Mary at Newstead, low in the valley of the River Leen—perhaps, as Byron observed wryly in *Don Juan* (1819–24), "to shelter their devotion from the wind." Tradition has it that Henry II built it as one of his efforts to prove he was sorry for the death of Thomas à Becket. As Tennyson's *Becket* (1884) and Eliot's *Murder in the Cathedral* (1935) have shown, Henry had plenty to be sorry about. It was four of his own men who had hacked Becket to death at Canterbury.

In any event, Newstead and its monks prospered for the next 370 years. But during the Dissolution, Henry VIII seized the place and in 1540, in the words of the grant still hanging in the abbey, sold

> to our beloved servant John Byron of Colewyke . . . all the house and site, ground and soil, of the late Monastery or Priory of Newstede within the Forest of Sherwode in our said County of Notingham.

---

[2]The quotation is from Byron's early poem, "On Leaving Newstead Abbey" (1807), written while he was still a student at Cambridge.

Sir John, descended from a family that had come from France with William the Conqueror, got a bargain. For £810 he got not only the abbey and all its grounds, but also land in the adjoining parishes, for a total of seven hundred acres that brought him an income of £220 a year! He converted the main buildings into comfortable living quarters, and thereafter his successors and the abbey had their ups and downs. Several years later Sir Johns accumulated sizeable debts, sold off some of the holdings, and let Newstead itself deteriorate. But things picked up when the fifth in the line of these Sir Johns was made a baron by Charles I, and the second Baron Byron made some progress in getting the estate back in shape.

With the fifth Baron Byron, however, came disaster. He was known variously as the "Wicked Lord" and "Devil Byron," and thoroughly deserved both nicknames. First, he killed a neighboring relative, William Chaworth, in a drunken tavern duel. Next, furious at his own son for marrying the wrong woman, he set about deliberately destroying Newstead so there would be nothing left worth his inheriting. In this grotesque revenge he both succeeded and failed.

He failed because by the time he got around to dying, sixty-two years after coming into the title, there were no immediate kin left to succeed him. Both his son and his son's son were dead. The only heir surviving was that ten-year-old grandnephew in Aberdeen. Thus it was that George Gordon became Lord Byron.

But in neglecting the abbey and piling up massive debts, the bitter old man had succeeded all too well. Treasures of the centuries, fine old paintings, priceless furniture, even the venerable trees of his parkland had been sold to stave off creditors. Horace Walpole, author of *The Castle of Otranto* (1764), a visitor in 1760, was shocked at what he saw. "The present Lord has lost huge sums," he wrote a friend, "and paid part in old oaks, £5,000 worth of which have been cut near the house."

Byron's "hall of my Fathers" had gone to decay indeed.

The new young lord's first view of his inheritance, in August of 1798, was a little drama in itself:

> The coach from Aberdeen bearing Mrs. Byron, son George, and his nurse, May Gray, pulls up at the gatehouse outside.
> "What nobleman lives at this place?" demands Mrs. Byron of the woman gate-keeper.
> "It was Lord Byron, Ma'am," . . . replies the woman, "but he's dead."
> "And who is heir now?"
> "They say a little boy that lives at Aberdeen."

"This is him, God bless him!" bursts out May Gray, kissing her embarrassed young charge.
Exit coach and trio through the gate.

In many ways, the mother and son who drove through that gate were a pathetic pair. She had been Catherine Gordon of Bight, Scotland. In 1786, at age twenty-one, she was holidaying in Bath, trying uneasily to cope with its high life, when she met John Byron—"Mad Jack," they called him. Hardly the makings of a match, it would seem. She was awkward, untutored, and provincial. He was dashing and worldly. The grandson of the fourth Baron Byron and an army officer, he had run off with the wife of the Duke of Leeds and married her for her money after her divorce. But though she had obligingly died within five years, he had already gone through her considerable fortune and was in Bath for just one purpose: heiress-hunting. Catherine Gordon was an heiress, worth £23,000.

Jack Byron ran through her wealth with even more dispatch. By the time their son was born in London, on January 22, 1788, he was so pursued by creditors he dared not attend the baptism lest he be arrested for debt. When Catherine retreated to Aberdeen he followed her, took what little money remained, and escaped to France, dying there mysteriously two years later.

Their baby had been born handicapped, crippled by a clubfoot that a special shoe last and cruel exercises made worse. Now poor George was left to be raised by a mother sadly unfit for the task. She possessed neither gentility nor self-control. An outpouring of caresses and kisses could be followed by ranting and raving. Even as a child her son recognized her basic stupidity. His answer when a schoolmate said to him, "Byron, your mother is a fool," was simply, "I know it."

In all, there were only sixteen years from the first time that Byron saw Newstead and the last, in 1814. Between, he was there himself a total of perhaps seven years at most. But he was fiercely proud of both his estate and his title. Whenever he could, he came for his holidays from Harrow and Cambridge, by courtesy of a young Lord Grey, to whom it had been leased. Only after he attained his majority in 1808 was Byron able to move in and make such repairs as he could afford. They weren't much.

The abbey's east wing and all the larger rooms were uninhabitable, so he chose its northwest corner for his own living quarters, at the farthest remove from the rest of the household. "I have to walk half a mile to my Bedchamber," he complained. The grand furnishings and wallpapers he installed were ruined because he couldn't mend the roof. What had been the great hall was in such shambles he used it for pistol practice. A visitor in 1809 reported, "The old kitchen with a long range of apartments is reduced to a heap of rubbish."

Byron did have house parties amid the debris, and bizarre affairs they were. Normally, nobody would arise until one in the afternoon at least. It was well past two before breakfast was over. Then came fencing, riding, cricket, or sailing on the lake for exercise, and for more relaxing amusement, reading, playing with Byron's pet bear, or teasing his wolf. The real entertainment came after dark, according to Byron's college friend, Charles Skinner Matthews:

> Between seven and eight we dined; and our evening lasted from that time till one, two, or three in the morning. The evening diversions may be easily conceived.
>
> I must not omit the custom of handing round, after dinner, on the removal of the cloth, a human skull filled with burgundy . . . . A set of monkish dresses, which had been provided with all the proper apparatus of crosses, beads, tonsures, etc., often gave a variety to our appearance and to our pursuits.

Nathaniel Hawthorne saw the skull on a visit in 1857 and described it all too vividly:

> It has a silver rim and stand, but still the ugly skull is bare and evident, and the naked inner bone received the wine. I should think it would hold at least a quart—enough to overpower any living head into which this deaths-head should transfer its contents; and a man must be either very drunk or very thirsty, before he would taste wine out of such a goblet.

From 1809 to 1811 Byron traveled—to Spain, Portugal, Greece, and the Levant. He returned to live in London where in 1812, as he said, he awoke one morning and found himself famous. *Childe Harold* had just been published. Thereafter he was only occasionally at Newstead. His final visit in 1814 was with his half-sister Augusta Leigh, child of their father's first marriage. Two years later, rumors of an incestuous affair with Augusta drove him into self-imposed exile abroad with the bitter words, "I felt that, if what was whispered, and muttered, and murmured, was true, I was unfit for England; if false, England was unfit for me."

He sailed from Dover in April of 1816 for Italy, left Italy for Greece in 1823 to help the Greeks in their war of independence, and died there of a fever in 1824. His body was brought home for burial in the family vault at Hucknall Torkard Church, four miles south of Newstead.

In all these travels, the abbey was ever in his thoughts, recurring again and again in his poems, not only here and there in longer ones like *Childe Harold* and *Don Juan*, but in special pieces like "On Leaving Newstead Abbey," "Elegy on Newstead Abbey," "The Adieu," "Newstead Abbey," and "Poem to an Oak." He had vowed never to sell it, but in 1817, desperate for money, was forced to do so. Happily, the abbey fell into good hands.

The purchaser was Col. Thomas Wildman, an old Harrow schoolmate and a wealthy retired army man. It is largely to Wildman that we owe the Newstead that we see today. He paid the then enormous sum of £94,000 to buy it, and spent almost as much on its extensive and intelligent restoration, at one time employing upwards of a hundred men. Subsequent owners were equally sensitive in adding their own personal touches, and in 1931 a Nottingham philanthropist, Sir Julien Cahn, ensured its preservation by buying it and presenting it to the city.

One's first visit to the abbey today can be a shock, but such a pleasant one. The decayed ruins of Byron's inheritance have become in fact what he could then, in *Don Juan*, envisage only in fancy. The imagined "Huge halls, long galleries, spacious chambers join'd" of the poem stand now in magnificent reality, replete with elegant furnishings, paintings, tapestries, and sculpture. All this, and more—carved sixteenth-century overmantels, seventeenth-century Dutch plaster ceilings, a post-Restoration staircase lighted by eighteenth-century glass spiraling up to what had been the poet's bedroom.

The bedroom, the North Gallery, and the East Gallery are especially interesting to the literary traveler. It is a mark of Col. Wildman's regard for Byron that he kept the bedroom just as it was when the poet lived there, and made him promise that should he return to England, his first stop would be the abbey. The room now has the gilt four-poster bedstead the poet used at Cambridge, various personal items, and the mahogany library table on which he is said to have written *English Bards and Scotch Reviewers* (1809).

On display in the North Gallery (now the Byron Gallery) are the shoe lasts made to correct his clubfoot, his various sporting equipment, the huge wedding ring from his ill-fated marriage to Anne Isabella Milbanke, and a dashing black leather helmet he designed for his expedition to Greece. The East Gallery houses a first-rate collection of Byron's manuscripts, letters, and first editions.

Outside, the grounds are equally impressive. Spreading out from the graceful, empty west facade of what was the thirteenth-century Priory Church are three hundred acres of parkland, gardens, walks, waterfalls, and lakes. On the Upper Lake are the two turreted forts the "Wicked Lord" built so that he could play mock war with his servants. Below that are the stump of the oak tree of Byron's "Poem to an Oak," planted when he first came to Newstead, and the Stew Pond where the monks bred carp for their Lenten meals.

In front of the abbey's east wing is the poet's monument over the grave of his dog, Boatswain, defiantly placed on what he believed to be the site of the Priory's high altar. Byron missed the exact location by several hundred feet, but the epitaph he wrote for the dog's tomb says much about a sensitivity and loneliness he took great pains to hide from the world:

> To mark a Friend's remains these stones arise;
> I never knew but one,—and here he lies.

The grounds are open every day from 10:00 A.M. until dusk, while the house is open afternoons from Good Friday through September 30.

ANNESLEY HALL

Annesley Hall is an old mansion three miles southwest of Newstead Abbey. There in the summer of 1803, on vacation from Harrow, Byron was a frequent visitor. Sometimes he would ride over from Southwell, ten miles off, where his mother now lived. Sometimes he'd come from the abbey itself. The magnet was pretty Mary Chaworth, whose family owned the hall. Although she was eighteen and already engaged to be married, and he was only fifteen, he'd fallen deeply in love.

They were distant cousins, for she was the granddaughter of William Chaworth, the kinsman whom Byron's great uncle, the "Wicked Lord Byron," had killed in a drunken duel. At first Mary was amused by the boy's attentions, and sometimes even induced her parents to let him spend the night with them. But finally his persistence began to wear on her, and when she tried to cool his ardor, he grew sulky.

Things came to a head late one night when, just as he was passing her bedchamber on the way to his own, he heard her exclaiming to her maid, "Do you really think I could care anything for that lame little boy?" Crushed, Byron tore from the house and rode furiously off to Newstead.

Both the hurt and the love stayed with him, however. Two years later, preparing to leave Southwell to enroll at Cambridge, he dashed off a parody of Robert Burns's "Farewell to Ayreshire," beginning with a grand take-off of his model's sentimental "hills of Ayreshire":

> Hills of Annesley, Bleak and Barren,
> Where my thoughtless Childhood stray'd.
> How the northern Tempests, warring,
> Howl above thy tufted Shade!

But then Byron's tone changed abruptly. He continued:

> Now no more, the Hours beguiling,
> Former favourite Haunts I see;
> Now no more my Mary smiling
> Makes ye seem a Heaven to me.

And among the exhibits in the North Gallery at Newstead Abbey, alongside the great gold wedding ring from his marriage to Annabella Milbanke, is a lovely little miniature—of Mary Chaworth.

EASTWOOD

D. H. Lawrence's Eastwood and Byron's Newstead Abbey and Annesley practically run into each other, Eastwood southwest of the other two on the B 600 and B 608. Eastwood is the "Bestwood" of *Sons and Lovers*, (1913), and in his essay "Return to Bestwood," Lawrence describes the setting:

> one looks across at the amphitheatre of hills, which I still find beautiful, though there are new patches of reddish houses and a darkening of smoke. Crich is still on the sky line to the west, and the woods of Annesley to the north.

After 1912 Lawrence rarely saw Eastwood, and the few times he did return he had to confess, "it always depresses me." Now four times as large as the village of some three thousand souls that Lawrence knew, Eastwood is still a bit on the grim side, though the three hundred coal pits that surrounded it in his day have dwindled to a mere two dozen, and many of its townsfolk now commute to the offices and factories of Nottingham, Derby, and Mansfield.

The youngest of four children—three boys and a girl—Lawrence was born at No. 8 Victoria Street on September 11, 1885, and christened David Herbert Richards Lawrence. The house was tiny, a narrow two-storey red brick building with an attic in which the boys slept. Mrs. Lawrence made the cramped quarters even more limited by using the front room and its street-side window as a shop for laces, linens, and baby clothes. It was a gallant venture. The Lawrences needed the extra income badly. But the house sits below Nottingham Road, the town's main street, and Victoria itself runs steeply down from it to disappear into nothing within two blocks. You can't help wondering how in the world she ever expected anyone to wander down to see her wares.

Two years later the family moved to what is now 28 Garden Road in an area called The Breach. They were to stay here for the next four years, and the house, its setting, and the life he lived there were to affect Lawrence profoundly. The Breach, called "The Bottoms" in the novel, sets the opening tone of *Sons and Lovers:*

> The Bottoms consisted of six blocks of miners' dwellings, two rows of three, like the dots of a blank-six domino, and twelve houses in a block. This double row of dwellings sat at the foot of the rather sharp slope from Bestwood, and looked out, from the attic windows at least, on the slow climb of the valley towards Selby.
>
> The houses themselves were substantial and very decent. One could walk all around, seeing little front gardens with auriculas and saxifrage . . . . But that was outside; that was the view on to the uninhabited parlours of all the colliers' wives. The dwelling-room, the kitchen, was at the back of the house, facing inward between the blocks, looking at a scrubby back garden, and then at the ash-pits. And between the rows, between the long lines of ash-pits, went the alley, where the children played and the women gossiped and the men smoked. So, the actual conditions of living in the Bottoms that was so well built and that looked so nice, were quite unsavoury because people must live in the kitchen, and the kitchens opened on to that nasty alley of ash-pits.

Mrs. Lawrence had the barest edge on the other tenants:

> . . . she had an end house in one of the top blocks, and thus had only one neighbor; on the other side an extra strip of garden. And, having an end house, she enjoyed a kind of aristocracy among the other women of the

"between" houses, because her rent was five shillings and sixpence instead of five shillings a week. But this superiority was not much consolation.

The truth was, Mrs. Lawrence hated it. Like Gertrude Morel of the novel, she "came of a good old burgher family" and had married beneath her. Arthur Lawrence was a miner, or more precisely a "butty," and therefore supposedly a bit above his fellows. As butty he had a stall, hired day mine workers, paid them on Fridays for their week's production, and kept the remainder. But he still had to dig in the pits himself each day.

He lived for the weekends, spending all his time and more of his money than he could afford at his pub, the Three Tuns Inn. When he'd finally go home, he and his wife would quarrel. Often he beat her. In return, she taught the children to despise him, as Paul—the hero of *Sons and Lovers,* and really the novelist himself—shows shockingly:

> Paul hated his father. As a boy he had a fervent private religion.
> "Make him stop drinking," he prayed every night. "Lord, let my father die," he prayed very often. "Let him not be killed at the pit," he prayed when, after tea, the father did not come home from work.

From Garden Road, the Lawrences moved on to No. 8 Walker Street, the house looking across the amphitheatre of hills to Annesley, in 1891, and then in 1904 to No. 97 Lynncroft. Meanwhile "Bertie," as D. H. was called—the "pale-faced, dirty-nosed frail boy" described in "Getting On"—attended the Eastwood Board School on Mill Road. Though he was apparently no great student, he was driven hard by his mother, and somehow won a scholarship to Nottingham High School in 1898.

Thereafter Eastwood saw little of him.[3] He was there in December of 1910 as his mother lay dying of cancer, and was able to show her an advance copy of his first novel, *The White Peacock.* The contrast between the sense of pride and self-fulfillment this gave her and her husband's reaction illustrates the tragic gulf between them.

After returning from his wife's funeral, Arthur Lawrence picked up the book, struggled through a few pages, shook his head, and turned to his son. The novelist tells the story himself.

> "And what dun they gi'e thee for that, lad?"
> "Fifty pounds, father."

---

[3]For a quick summary of succeeding years, see pp. 93–95.

"Fifty pounds!" He was dumbfounded, and looked at me as if I were a swindler. "Fifty pounds! An' tha's niver done a day's hard work in thy life."

Today, happily, the chief sites of Lawrence's early years remain much as they were then, and can be seen with dispatch. Begin your tour where he began, at No. 8 Victoria Street, a few steps off Nottingham Road.

A Suggested Tour

The **Birthplace Museum** (1) still has Mrs. Lawrence's shop window with a display of the kinds of linens and laces she offered for sale, as well as, just behind it, the living room and kitchen furnished as they would have been in the 1880s. Upstairs you can watch an excellent video tape, and perhaps a bedroom or two may be open for you to see.[4]

From Victoria Street, go back to Nottingham Road and turn right. At the stoplight you'll run into a street that's called Church Street to the south, and Mansfield Road to the north. The Church Street segment down below the church is the location of **cemetery** (2) where the Lawrence family—though not the author—is buried. On Mansfield Road, where it runs into Greenhills Road, are the offices of today's Barber, Walker and Company, the "new red-brick building, almost like a mansion" of *Sons and Lovers's* **Carston, Waite & Company** (3), where young Paul Morel would go, on Friday afternoon, little calico bag in his pocket, to pick up his father's earnings for the week.

A turn south off Greenhills takes you to **28 Garden Road** (4), and east of that, at the junction of Mill Road and Dovecote, is the Greasley Beauvale Infants School, in Lawrence's day the **board school** (5) he attended.

In a cluster bounded by Walker, Lynncroft, and Nottingham Road are **No. 8 Walker Street** (6), the **97 Lynncroft** (7) home, and **Three Tuns Inn** (8)—The Sun and Moon in *Sons and Lovers.*

Finally, on Nottingham Road itself is the **Eastwood Library** (9). The library has the Hopkins Collection of D. H. Lawrence books, as well as

---

[4]The Birthplace Museum is open daily at varying hours, except for Christmas week. The "Breach House" on Garden Road is supposed to keep similar hours, but you'd better check. The other Lawrence homes remain private dwellings.

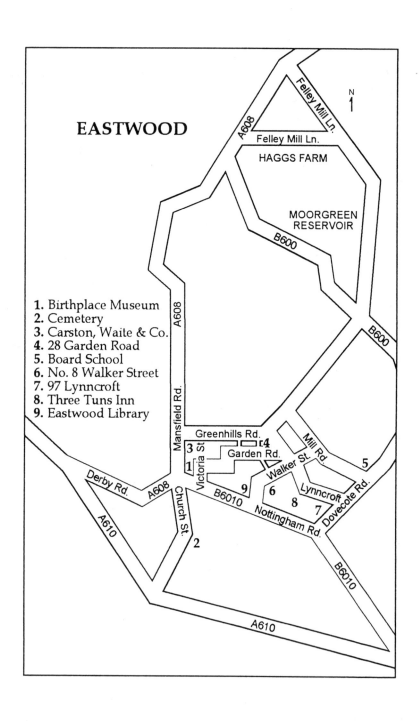

EASTWOOD

1. Birthplace Museum
2. Cemetery
3. Carston, Waite & Co.
4. 28 Garden Road
5. Board School
6. No. 8 Walker Street
7. 97 Lynncroft
8. Three Tuns Inn
9. Eastwood Library

the headstone from Lawrence's grave in Vence, France, where he died and was first buried in 1930. His body was later cremated and the ashes were brought to the ranch in New Mexico that he had shared with his wife Frieda in the 1920s. In his writing, Lawrence returns again and again to Eastwood and its countryside in poems, plays, short stories, and novels. The list is far too long to give in its entirety, but chief among the works with Eastwood connections are *The White Peacock* (1911), *Sons and Lovers* (1913), *The Rainbow* (1915), *Women in Love* (1920), *Aaron's Rod* (1922), and *Lady Chatterley's Lover* (1928).

Of the various sites outside Eastwood, near at hand are Beauvale Priory, Moorgreen Reservoir, Haggs Farm, and Felley Mill Farm, all north of town. The ruins of Beauvale, scene of "A Fragment of Stained Glass," are off the B 600 and the A 608. Haggs Farm was the home of Jessie Chambers, whom Lawrence met in 1901, and with whom he carried on a somewhat tempestuous relationship for the next dozen years. It was Jessie who encouraged him to write, and who served as the model for the "shy, wild, quiveringly sensitive lover of Paul Morel" in *Sons and Lovers*. Felley Mill Farm is the Strelley Mill of *The White Peacock*.

WELBECK ABBEY

The actual distance between Eastwood and Welbeck Abbey, off the A 60 to the northeast, is only eighteen miles. But on September 11, 1885, the day he was born, the social and economic distance between D. H. Lawrence and a twelve-year-old girl living at Welbeck was incalculable. For he was a coal miner's son, and she was Ottoline Cavendish Bentinck, offspring of two of England's great families and half-sister of the duke of Portland. The house she lived in was a grand old mansion that went back to the early seventeenth century. Shakespeare's friend Ben Jonson had once staged a masque there, *Love's Welcome* (1633), for a king, Charles I.

That Ottoline and Lawrence would ever meet, let alone become intimates, would seem on the farthest edge of improbability. Yet just thirty years after his birth she was introducing Lawrence to London's elite— Virginia Woolf, Lytton Strachey, E. M. Forster, and Bertrand Russell among them.

Ottoline had come to Welbeck at six when her half-brother, William, became duke of Portland following the death of a second cousin. The abbey must have been a fascinating place for children to explore while Ottoline was growing up. For this cousin, the fifth Duke, had been an odd one, with such a morbid a fear of contact with his fellow man that he built a network of tunnels beneath most of his estate so that he could walk about at will without running into anyone. One tunnel was over a mile long, and so wide that two carriages could pass without touching.

Ottoline went on to become one of the celebrated figures of her time. As Lady Ottoline Morrell, wife of a liberal M. P., she presided over an elegant house in London's Bedford Square and a palatial estate outside Oxford called Garsington Manor. At both she played hostess to a steady stream of literary notables.

Lawrence had begun to make himself known with *Sons and Lovers* when he was taken to one of her London evenings in August of 1914. But she had read nothing of his then, and paid him scant attention. Shortly thereafter, however, Bertrand Russell recommended Lawrence's collection of tales, *The Prussian Officer* (1914), to her, and she found them "quite wonderful." And why not? As she said in her thank-you letter to Russell, "All the Nottingham stories are very familiar to me."

Soon Lawrence became almost the center of her galaxy of stars, perhaps—once they had met at all, that is—inevitably. For when he told her of his origins, she confessed how as a girl she had been captivated by coal miners: "tall, black, and mysterious" they appeared to her, "rather fierce, and yet full of fun. . . . How I wished I could talk to these men, or share their good solid tea, and so bridge the gulf that lay between us."

Lawrence put her in *Women in Love* as Hermione Ridice, and included a touching description of her Garsington Manor. He was a rebel and often anti-establishment, true, but that was no reason why a coal miner's son should eschew the good things that Lady Ottoline's circle afforded.

"I am no democrat, save in politics," he wrote her frankly. "<u>Life itself</u> is an affair of aristocrats."

SOUTHWELL AND NEWARK UPON TRENT

It is fitting that the last two literary stops in Nottinghamshire, so dominated by Byron and D. H. Lawrence, should be Southwell ("SUTH'll") and Newark upon Trent. Southwell has associations with both, and Newark marked Byron's first appearance as a published author.

Southwell, a pleasant place with upwards of 6,000 people, is on the A 612, fourteen miles northeast of Nottingham. Newark, a town of more than 25,000, is on the A 617, seven miles east of Southwell, and only three miles from the border of Lincolnshire.

Southwell   Byron's mother left Nottingham in 1803, and for the next five years rented Burbage Manor in Southwell. It was a comfortable three-storey wooden structure with attractive garden and grounds and faced the village green. Byron spent his vacations from school there, at first as a fifteen-year-old at Harrow, and from 1805 to 1808 as a student at Cambridge.

But though he later admitted that Southwell had provided "the advantages of very genteel society without the hazard of being annoyed by mercantile affluence," he found it boring and escaped when he could to spend a day or two with the caretaker they'd hired to look after Newstead Abbey. The "crater of dullness," he once called Southwell.

Fortunately, he soon became friendly with the Pigot family, who lived just across the green, and especially with their daughter, Elizabeth. She was several years older than he, and, according to the poet's friend and biographer, Thomas Moore, at first she dismissed Byron as "a fat, bashful boy with his hair combed straight over his forehead." She grew fond of him before long, however, she told Moore, and Byron would "come in and go out at all hours, as it pleased him, and in our house considered himself perfectly at home." They spent endless hours together, and he began writing poems to her.

Even better were the times her brother, John, came home on his holidays from medical studies in Edinburgh, and they could do amateur theatricals in the assembly rooms down by the Saracen's Head Inn. A high spot was Byron's leading role as the disappointed lover, Penruddock, in Richard Cumberland's *Wheel of Fortune* (1795), for which the star wrote his own prologue.

The Southwell era came to an end in 1808, when Byron reached his majority and was able to take over Newstead Abbey. But some of those poems to Elizabeth Pigot—"Eliza," he calls her—were to find their way into *Fugitive Pieces*, his first published collection of verse.

D. H. Lawrence has Ursula and Birkin in *Sons and Lovers* come to Southwell for a tour of its "rigid, sombre, ugly cathedral" before going on to tea at the Saracen's Head. He is too harsh on the cathedral. Admittedly, it is on the severe side, and the central tower may be a bit lower than some would like. But it has some interesting features. In a chapel there's an airman's altar made of fragments of airplanes shot down in WWI. And the cathedral's brass lectern, along with two brass candlesticks, came from the Eagle Pond at Newstead Abbey. They were recovered in the eighteenth century by none other than Byron's great uncle, the "Wicked Lord Byron." The abbey monks, annoyed at Henry VIII for taking their monastery away from them, had thrown them into the pool during the Dissolution. And, no, that Lord Byron didn't give them to the cathedral. He sold them.

You can have tea at the Saracen's Head yourself. Or spend the night, if you like, quite agreeably; the inn deserves its three-star rating. The timbered entrance to the court and heavy wooden gates indicate its antiquity, and a listing in the hall attests to a long and truly royal history of hospitality. Richard I was there in 1194, twenty years before his brother, King John, put his pen to the Magna Carta. John himself was there in 1213, and his son, Henry III, visited twice, in 1223 and 1258. Edward I was a guest in 1281, Edward III in 1258.

Richard II, son of Edward III, must really have liked the place. He was there three times in four years, in 1395, 1396, and 1398. That last stopover, though, couldn't have been much fun. In his play *Richard II*, Shakespeare shows Richard weakly trying to arbitrate the feud between his cousin Bolingbroke and Thomas Mowbray, duke of Norfolk. Bolingbroke accuses Mowbray of masterminding the murder of Richard's uncle, Gloucester. Mowbray fires back:

> . . . Bolingbroke, as low as to thy heart,
> Through the false passage of thy throat, thou liest.

The year is 1398. Richard, of course, winds up sending both Mowbray and Bolingbroke into exile, and Bolingbroke winds up returning to England to seize Richard's throne.

The visit of Charles I to the Saracen's Head wasn't all that festive, either. He stopped in on the night of May 5, 1646, to put himself into the hands of the Scottish commissioners, figuring that they would protect him from the rebelling English Parliament. After all, he was a Scotsman himself. Instead, they turned him over to the parliamentarians—for £400,000.

If you have a fancy for such things, you can sleep in the very room at the Saracen's Head where poor Charles spent his last night in freedom. It is one of four refurbished new bedrooms in the oldest part of the hotel, and boasts an early seventeenth-century Jacobean wall painting discovered during the rebuilding.

Newark upon Trent   They're peripheral at best, but among Newark's literary claims are the seventeenth-century poets Richard Corbett, who describes a stay there in his engaging "Iter Boreale" (1648), and John Cleveland, who was a judge advocate at its Royalist garrison.

Of much more interest are Byron's two visits to Newark. He came in 1805 and again in 1807, staying each time at the Clinton Arms, an inn still operating in the Market Place.[5]

What brought Byron to the Clinton Arms was the publication of his first two volumes of poetry, both by a Newark printer he had hired. In 1806 it was *Fugitive Pieces,* containing a variety of his earliest efforts, including some of the "Eliza" verses he had written to Elizabeth Pigot. Some of the poems in the collection were too revealing, and others too spicy. A couple, particularly one called "To Mary," apparently based on a real-life frolic with an unidentified Southwell girl, were frankly erotic. When a furor arose, Byron called in the copies he had distributed to friends, except for four whose recipients refused to give them back.

Byron proceeded to revise them, substituting fictional names for real ones, toning down the language, and omitting a pair that even he realized were too hot. The result, titled *Poems on Various Occasions,* was correct to a fault, wondrously chaste, and distressingly juvenile.

In some ways, his *Hours of Idleness,* printed in Newark in 1807, was even worse. He eliminated a number of the poems published the year before, and replaced them with imitations and translations of Virgil and Anacreon, plus a few nostalgic new ones such as "Elegy on Newstead Abbey." He achieved a paradigm of immaturity that cried aloud for ridicule which—though the volume won some acceptance—most critics were happy to supply. Typical was a comment in the magazine *The Monthly Mirror:*

> If this was one of his lordship's *school exercises* at Harrow, and he escaped whipping, they have there either an undue respect for lords' bottoms, or they do not deserve the reputation they have acquired.

---

[5]Subsequent guests included the duke of Wellington and prime minister-to-be William Gladstone, who found its balcony a grand place for cajoling the electorate.

There was, however, a happy outcome to all this. Stung, particularly by a blistering attack in the *Edinburgh Review,* Byron struck back in the poem called *English Bards and Scotch Reviewers.* In it he flailed away in all directions, including a number of unkind cuts—some of which he later regretted—at established poets like Scott, Southey, Coleridge, and Wordsworth.

He saved his sharpest thrusts to address critics such as Francis Jeffrey, editor of the *Edinburgh Review:*

> Fear not to lie, 't will seem a sharper hit:
> Shrink not from blasphemy, 't will pass for wit;
> Care not for feeling—pass your proper jest,
> And stand a critic, hated yet caress'd.

Jeffrey and his ilk had unwittingly done Byron a favor. Byron had discovered that his true bent was for satire. The publication of *English Bards and Scotch Reviewers* in 1809, when he was just twenty-one, was indisputable proof that a new literary genius had arrived.

Lincolnshire

Lincolnshire

I used to say Alfred should never have left old Lincolnshire,
where there were not only such good seas, but also such fine
hill and dale among "The Wolds," which he was brought up
in, as people in general scarce thought on.

Edward FitzGerald,
speaking of his friend Alfred Lord Tennyson

I climb the hill: from end to end
    Of all the landscape underneath
    I find no place that does not breathe
Some gracious memory of my friend
We leave the well-beloved place
    Where first we gazed upon the sky:
    The roofs that heard our earliest cry
Will shelter one of stranger race.
I turn to go: my feet are set
    To leave the pleasant fields and farms;
    They mix in one another's arms
To one pure image of regret.

Tennyson, in *In Memoriam*, on leaving Lincolnshire at 28

If the literary history of Nottinghamshire is dominated by two writers,
that of Lincolnshire is dominated by one man alone. The man, of course,
is Alfred, Lord Tennyson.

Lincolnshire is among the country's large counties, almost seventy
miles from north to south and fifty from east to west. Even its keenest
admirers, however, would hardly call it the most scenic. Henry VIII, in
fact, called it "the most brute and beastly shire" in England. But Henry
is not being fair. Those introductory quotations from Edward FitzGerald
and Tennyson are far nearer the mark.

The county can best be described in terms of its historic three divi-
sions called ridings, from the Anglo-Saxon "thriding," meaning a third.
In Roman times, rivers and the sea made the largest of the three, Lind-

sey, practically an island. To the west was the Trent; to the north, the Humber; to the south, the Witham and marshlands, and to the east, the Wash and the North Sea. Covering just about all the northern half of the county, this is the Lincolnshire that both FitzGerald and Tennyson were talking about. The North Sea and the Wash are FitzGerald's "good seas." The undulating chalk downs, known as The Wolds, running from the northeast border with Humberside all the way down to near Somersby are his "fine hill and dale," and Somersby itself is at the center of those pleasant fields and farms Tennyson left with such regret.

Kesleven, the southwest section of Lincolnshire below the Witham, was once a great wooded area and has more the feel of middle England. The southeastern part, by far the smallest of the three and aptly named Holland, reaches to the coast of the Wash on the east and to the border with Cambridgeshire on the south. Here are marshlands and fens, and the dikes, canals, and windmills so reminiscent of its namesake.

Not the least of Lincolnshire's virtues, perhaps, is the total absence of great cities. Lincoln, the largest, with at most 80,000 people, makes a fine headquarters for touring the county. Only seventeen miles from Newark upon Trent via the A 46, it has a distinct charm, several good hotels, and literary claims of its own. A drive of thirty miles or less along the A 158 will take you to Somersby and all the land of Tennyson.

LINCOLN

Situated as it is at the northeastern edge of the fen district (where the A 15, the A 46, the A 57, and the A 158 converge), the country about Lincoln can hardly avoid being flat, even to the point of monotony. But one thing you must say: You certainly can't beat it as a backdrop for a cathedral that sits on the only hill anywhere about. You drive and drive and drive over that flat plain, and then suddenly they jump right up before you—the honey-colored towers of Lincoln Cathedral.

Lincoln and its hill rise sharply, two hundred feet or more, from the banks of the River Witham. The description Nathaniel Hawthorne gives of his visit in 1857 is no exaggeration:

> Passing through the Stone Bow, as the city gate is called, we ascended a
> street which grew steeper and narrower as we advanced, till at last it got

to be the steepest street I ever climbed,—so steep that any carriage, if left to itself, would rattle downward much faster than it could possibly be drawn up. Being almost the only hill in Lincolnshire, the inhabitants seem disposed to make the most of it. . . .

And still the street grew steeper and steeper. Certainly, the Bishop and the clergy of Lincoln ought not to be fat men, but of very spiritual, saint-like, almost angelic habit, if it be a frequent part of their ecclesiastical duty to climb this hill.

The cathedral's eminence is matched by its beauty and size; its length, area, and height rivalling those of even mighty York Minster. Its central tower rises to 271 feet and houses the famed "Great Tom of Lincoln" bell, all five and a half tons of it. The cathedral is old, too, begun about 1072 by Remigius, a close companion of William the Conqueror and the first Norman ever to be given an English bishopric.

But compared to Lincoln itself, the cathedral, for all its nine hundred-year history, is a newcomer. There was a Roman fortress on these same banks of the Witham a thousand years before William and Remigius ever left Normandy for England. By the year 100 A.D., the Romans had built a city there, calling it Lindum Colonia—shortened later by the Britons to Lindcoit, whence comes "Lincoln."

Ample testimony to the Romans' presence remains. They built the Newport Arch at the end of Bailgate. Now serving travelers heading for the A 15 and points north, it is the only Roman gateway in all Britain still handling traffic. Theirs, too, was Fosdyke Navigation, eleven miles long, connecting the Witham with the Trent. It was dug more than one thousand eight hundred years ago and is the country's oldest canal, yet boats still bob about in it.

In literature, as in everything else, the cathedral has been a center of Lincolnshire life. Its library in the Wren Gallery has over 240 manuscripts dating from before the Reformation, as well as the best of four extant copies of the Magna Carta and a magnificent illuminated Old Testament made some time before 1200 A.D.

In the twelfth century, Walter Map (or Mapes), writer of satirical verse and an early Latin version of the Sir Lancelot stories, was one of its canons. And in the twentieth century, D. H. Lawrence, in *The Rainbow* (1915), has Will and Anna visit the cathedral, giving him a chance to show off a bit of his knowledge of medieval architecture. Robert Grosseteste, author of the allegorical poem, *Chateau d'Amour,* as well as philosophical and theological translations from the Greek, and first chancellor of Oxford University, was another clergyman associated with the cathedral. He was bishop from 1235 to 1253 and is buried in its Chapel of St. Peter and St. Paul.

In the south choir aisle, not far from Grosseteste's tomb, are the remains of the shrine of Little St. Hugh of Lincoln. Born about 1246, he was supposedly murdered by a local Jew when only nine years old, and speedily went on to win both sainthood and national renown as the hero of the ballad, "Hugh of Lincoln." But the medieval masters of the cathedral may only have been trying to cash in on what was already a folk tale widespread throughout England. From the fifth century on, no fewer than twenty-seven versions of the legend appeared, many of them with a happy ending in which the murdered child is miraculously restored to life.

Among subsequent accounts of the same general story are the Prioress's Tale in Chaucer's *Canterbury Tales* (1387), the ballad of "The Jew's Daughter" in Percy's *Reliques,* and a miracle play performed at Lincoln in 1316.

Chaucer puts into the tender-hearted prioress's mouth as gory a tale as can be, artfully changing details to make it even more pathetic. Hugh is now a "litel chergeon" (choir boy), a widow's son, and only seven years old. What's more, even after he's slain and thrown into a pit, he goes right on singing the hymn, "Alma Redemptoris," until his body is found and his murderer caught and executed, so that the prioress can conclude dramatically, "Modre wol out, certeyn, it will not fail" (Murder will out, for certain, it will not fail.)

Other literary figures associated with the cathedral are Elizabeth Penrose and Ada Bayly, both of whom lived in Minster Yard. Mrs. Penrose, who is buried in the cathedral's Cloister Garth, was the Mrs. Markham who wrote school histories of England (1823) and France (1828) that were so popular they became practically required reading in classrooms throughout Victorian England. Ada Bayly, under the name Edna Lyall, wrote novels such as *Donovan* (1882) and *We Two* (1884), which were favorites in their day.

Lincoln does not slight Tennyson either. On the green at the east end of the cathedral is George Watts's heroic statue of the laureate, standing majestically in his cape, with great sombrero in one hand as he gazes solemnly down at a specimen of his "flower in a crannied wall" in the palm of the other. Down below the cathedral in Danesgate, the Usher Gallery has a room devoted to his manuscripts, letters, and personal memorabilia.

One final literary note on Lincoln concerns Charles Lamb. It has no connection with the cathedral, and, admittedly, no great significance either. But it's worth the telling anyway. It's from Lamb's "Old Benchers of the Inner Temple."

He calls his character Lovel, a "quick little fellow of incorrigible and losing honesty." He was only a servant and had to wear a uniform. But it never occurred to Lovel that this was anything but a badge of honor. His master was Mr. Samuel Salt, a gentlemen and a London lawyer, no less. Says Lamb:

> At intervals he would speak of his former life, and how he came up a little boy from Lincoln, to go to service, and how his mother cried at parting with him, and how he returned, after some years' absence, in his smart new livery, to see her, and she blessed herself at the change, and could hardly be brought to believe that it was "her own bairn."

Lovel, you see, was really Lamb's own father.

GAINSBOROUGH—GRANTHAM—AND BOSTON

Gainsborough, Grantham, and Boston are outside Lincoln, before you get to Tennyson country proper. Gainsborough, seventeen miles northwest on the A 631, is on the very western edge of Lincolnshire, where the River Trent forms the border with Nottinghamshire.

Gainsborough It was the Trent that brought George Eliot to Gainsborough in 1859. She had been working on a novel, ultimately to be called *The Mill on the Floss* (1860). Like *Scenes of Clerical Life* (1857) and *Adam Bede* (1859) before it, it would depend heavily upon memories and settings from her Warwickshire childhood. But for her climactic scene, where the heroine, Maggie Tulliver, and her brother, Tom, were to drown in a catastrophic flood by the mill, she needed a river that could provide a suitably mighty and sudden tidal wave.

Hearing of the Trent after several other possibilities had proven unsatisfactory, she went to Gainsborough to take a look for herself and found just what she wanted.

With nearly 20,000 people, today's Gainsborough won't remind you much of the "St. Ogg's" Eliot wrote about. But at certain times the Trent will still produce a tidal wave—or, as they call it, the "eagre."

Grantham   Twenty-five miles south of Lincoln on the A 52 and the A 1, Grantham boasts a highly unlikely trio of celebrated men and a pair of historic old inns. The men are Richard III, Isaac Newton, and Charles Dickens. The inns are The Angel and Royal and The George.

King Richard and The Angel, as it was originally named, figured in what may be the earliest equivalent of today's saying, "There's good news and bad news." Shakespeare coined his version in *Richard III*, calling his news "best" and "colder." Richard was staying at The Angel the night of October 19, 1483, in what has come to be known as La Chambre du Roi, when he sat down to write to his lord chancellor in London. He wanted the chancellor to send him the Great Seal so he could use it to sign the death warrant of his own kinsman, the duke of Buckingham. Buckingham, he'd just learned, had treacherously defaulted to the earl of Richmond, and Richmond was even then on his way from France to challenge Richard for the throne.

Later, en route to Milford Haven in Wales to keep Richmond from landing there with his troops, Richard gets his good news and bad news from Sir William Catesby:

> My liege, the Duke of Buckingham is taken;
> That is the best news; that the Earl of Richmond
> Is with a mighty power landed at Milford
> Is colder news, but yet they must be told.

Isaac Newton, who was born only seven miles away at Woolsthorpe in 1642, lived in the house that is now The George Hotel and attended the Grantham Grammar School. Built in the fifteenth century and today called King's School, the building still stands in Church Street and has a window ledge on which Newton carved his name.

Charles Dickens stayed at The George with his illustrator, "Phiz" (Hablôt Browne), in 1838 while on his way to visit boys' boarding schools in Yorkshire in preparation for *Nicholas Nickleby* (1838–39) Dickens liked the inn so much he put it into the novel. The newly hired Nickleby and Mr. Wackford Squeers are heading for Dotheboys Hall in Yorkshire one night when the packed coach stops briefly in a town between Stamford and Newark upon Trent. It is a bitterly cold night, and

> two of the front outside passengers, wisely availing themselves of their arrival at one of the best inns in England, turned in, for the night, at The George at Grantham.

But Nickleby is hardly that fortunate. In addition to his new young assistant, Mr. Squeers has a bevy of unlucky little new recruits for his academy in tow, and Squeers has never seen much virtue in tossing money recklessly about. His party, like the remainder of the passengers,

> wrapped themselves more closely in their coats and cloaks, and leaving the light and warmth of the town behind them, pillowed themselves against the luggage, and prepared, with many half-suppressed moans, again to encounter the piercing blast which swept across the open country.

Dickens would still like The George. It's on the High Street, and rates three stars.

The Angel and Royal Inn still flourishes, too, also on the High Street. It has entertained royalty from as far back as 1213, when King John and his retinue held court in Grantham, to 1866, when the Prince of Wales (later Edward VII) gave it the right to add "and Royal" to its ancient name, The Angel.

Boston   When Nathaniel Hawthorne wound up his visit to Lincoln, it was not surprising that he went straight on to Boston. The New England novelist grew up in the shadow of its American namesake, and no other pair of cities in the two countries have such close or ancient ties as the Boston of Lincolnshire and the Boston of Massachusetts, U.S.A.

William Brewster and the other Puritans who sailed in the Mayflower to settle Plymouth Colony in 1620 made their first attempt to flee England for religious freedom from the original Boston, and were arrested and tried there for doing so in 1607. You can still see the courtroom where the trial was held and the prison cells in which they were kept at the fifteenth-century Guildhall, now the Borough Museum. It was their subsequent flight to Holland that won them the name "Pilgrims." A second wave of emigrants from old Boston, led by John Winthrop, made it to the New World in 1630 as part of the Massachusetts Bay Company venture, and it was they who established the American Boston.

Lincolnshire's Boston, on the A 1121 and the A 16, is at the very point where the Witham River ends its winding course from Lincoln and flows at last into the Wash. Hearing that there was a steamer that regularly plied between the two towns, Hawthorne decided to take it for his trip to Boston for the sake of the river scenery. It proved a dreadful mistake.

The boat was "small, dirty, and altogether inconvenient." The scenery was non-existent:

> Unfortunately, there was nothing, or next nothing, to be seen,—the country being one unvaried level over the whole thirty miles of our voyage,—not a hill in sight either near or far, except that solitary one on the summit of which we had left Lincoln Cathedral. And the Cathedral was our landmark for four hours or more, and at last rather faded out than was hidden by any intervening object.

Hawthorne had left Lincoln at ten o'clock in the morning. It wasn't until about three o'clock that afternoon that he finally saw anything of interest—another church tower suddenly rising up from the plain. For just as Lincoln is announced and dominated by its cathedral's towers, so Boston is announced and dominated by the lantern tower of its St. Botolph's Church. Two hundred and seventy-two feet high, the tower is famed throughout England as the "Boston Stump" because that's what it looks like from a distance. And such a distance! From its top you can see a third of the entire county; on a clear day, even Lincoln itself.

Begun in the early fourteenth century, St. Botolph's is a mighty church, and a beautiful one. A. E. Housman, who saw it on a holiday excursion to South Lincolnshire in 1930, said, "Boston must be the largest and finest parish church in England: Yarmouth and St. Michael's Coventry are said to cover more ground, but they have less bulk and grandeur." It was its parish church that gave Boston its name. The place was originally known as Botolph's Town, but in Hawthorne's scornful phrase, "shortened, in the course of ages, by the quick and slovenly English pronunciation," to Bos'-town.

Neither the bulk nor the grandeur that Housman saw in its church, alas, applies to Boston's literary credentials, which are scant indeed. John Foxe, author of *The Book of Martyrs* (1563), was born there in 1516; and Jean Ingelow, known for poetry such as *The High Tide on the Coast of Lincolnshire, 1571* (1863) and children's stories such as *Tales of Orris* (1860). Jean Ingelow shares a commemorative window at St. Botolph's with Anne Bradstreet, who lived in Boston for a time. In 1630 she, her husband, and her father helped found the new Boston as part of the Massachusetts Bay Company.

Not an imposing roster of writers. But Anne Bradstreet did become not only the New World's first woman poet, but also the first American poet of either sex to be published in England.

HORNCASTLE

Horncastle is on the A 158, twenty miles east of Lincoln. By coincidence, the town and its church figure in the lives of George Borrow and Alfred Tennyson, and within a span of just eleven years. Borrow's association with Horncastle was brief and casual. He wandered by one summer day in 1825 to see its horse fair, and out of a chance visit to its church wove an amusing episode for his novel, *The Romany Rye* (1857).

Tennyson's experience at that same church in 1836, however, was momentous. There he fell in love with the woman of whom he was to say, "the peace of God came into my life before the altar when I wedded her." She was Emily Sellwood, daughter of a Horncastle solicitor. The Sellwoods were cousins of the Cracrofts of Harrington Hall, a mile or so down the road from the Somersby rectory where the Tennysons lived, and it was this connection which had first brought them together. But their initial encounter was hardly auspicious. Alfred was a giant of a man and handsome, beginning to make his mark as a third-year student at Cambridge. She was frail, shy, and only sixteen. He was barely aware of her existence.

Their next meeting, the following year, was a bit more productive, but only on her side. Alfred had brought his dearest Cambridge friend, Arthur Hallam, home for Easter, and Tennyson's sister invited Emily to the attendant festivities. When Tennyson came upon her sitting alone amid the trees, he cried out jokingly, "Are you a Dryad, or a Naiad, or what are you?" She was smitten on the spot. He remained impervious.

It took six more years and a rendezvous at the Horncastle church to bring Tennyson round. But when it happened, it came in classic fashion. He was best man, she was bridesmaid when his brother, Charles, and her sister, Louisa, were married there. Fourteen more years were to pass, often wretchedly, before Alfred and Emily would marry. Her father's misgivings about Alfred's poverty and religious views kept them apart. Sometimes Mr. Sellwood forbade their even writing each other.

But in 1859, the publication of *In Memoriam* not only established Tennyson as a great poet, but assured him of an income as well. On June

13, 1850, Alfred and Emily were married. On November 19, Queen Victoria made Tennyson poet laureate.

HARRINGTON HALL—LANGTON—AND SOMERSBY

The A 158 from Horncastle will bring you directly into the land of Tennyson—to the pleasant fields and farms, to the hills and dales and seasides that so shaped his formative years and found such loving reflection in his works. Just drive five miles or so east along the highway until you reach the village of Hagworthingham, and there you are. A left turn at Hagworthingham takes you within minutes past Stockwith Mill, the old water mill which inspired Tennyson's poem, "The Miller's Daughter," to Harrington Hall. At Harrington there's a three-way fork. The branch straight ahead leads on to the A 16; the one on the right goes two miles to Langton; the one on the left, a mile and a half to Somersby.

Harrington Hall   Harrington Hall is a Jacobean manor house of goodly size. The wing to the left of its imposing three-storey entrance tower has no fewer than fourteen windows; the one to the right, twelve. Above the entrance itself there's a sundial and a date: 1681. To Tennyson the hall was not only the place where he first met Emily Sellwood. It was also for a time the home of a woman whom, had things gone differently, he might have married in Emily's stead.

Tenant of Harrington Hall in 1832 was an Admiral Arthur Eden who had an exceedingly attractive young stepdaughter named Rosa Baring. Rosa and Tennyson's sister became fast friends, and Tennyson soon found himself visiting Rosa often, too. A birthday poem he wrote to her in 1834 is rather appalling verse, but leaves no doubt that he was enamored:

> Thy rosy lips are soft and sweet,
> Thy fairy form is so complete,
> Thy motions are so airy free,
> Love lays his armour at thy feet.

Something, however, went wrong. Possibly Tennyson realized his love was hopeless. Rosa was very wealthy, an aristocrat far above him socially. Perhaps the admiral dropped a hint that the poet's attentions were less than welcome. Or perhaps Tennyson simply saw Rosa in a new light. At any rate, by 1836 the infatuation was over, and the lines in the birthday poem had become:

> A perfect-featured face, expressionless,
> Insipid, as the Queen upon a card.

Tennyson was free to love Emily Sellwood.

But Rosa Baring lived on in his memory. In *Maud,* the dramatic poem he wrote in 1855, the moody, distraught narrator, thinking of the girl he once had loved, suddenly lashes out:

> Faultily faultless, icily regular, splendidly null,
> Dead perfection, no more.

Langton   From the time of the early Norman kings, the Langtons have been one of Lincolnshire's notable[1] families, a thirteenth-century Stephen Langton having been archbishop of Canterbury and a signer of the Magna Carta at Runnymede. Their family seat, Langton Hall, a mile or so south of Harrington, was well known to Tennyson and served perhaps as a model for his "Locksley Hall."

An eighteenth-century member of the family, Bennet Langton, was one of Samuel Johnson's closest friends despite a great disparity in age, and supplied James Boswell with many details for his *Life of Samuel Johnson.* That they ever met at all, let alone became so attached to each other, is itself a tribute to Johnson as a writer—and as a person. For Langton was only seventeen and a student at Oxford when, in 1754, he made a special trip to London just in hope of meeting the celebrated author of *The Rambler* essays he admired. He even survived the shock of the meeting when it did take place. Langton had expected, he recalled later,

> a decent, well-drest, in short, a remarkably decorous philosopher. Instead
> of which, down from his bed-chamber, about noon, came, as newly risen,
> a huge uncouth figure, with a little dark wig which scarcely covered his
> head, and his clothes hanging loose about him.

Langton—"Lanky," as Johnson came to call him—grew so devoted that he persuaded his father to offer Johnson a lucrative rectory in Lin-

---

[1]So notable in fact, that there are two Lincolnshire villages named Langton, both off the A 158 within an easy twenty or so miles of each other.

colnshire. But the writer wisely refused. As Johnson told Boswell, speaking of a clergyman they knew, "This man, Sir, fills up the duties of his life well. I approve of him, but could not imitate him."

Johnson came to Langton Hall for a visit in 1764, and Bennet Langton has left an appealing revelation of the playful, even boyish, spirit that lurked beneath Johnson's burly and intimidating exterior.

The Langtons and their guest had walked to the top of a high hill near the Hall, and Johnson, delighted with its steepness, announced that he would like to "take a roll down." His hosts did their best to dissuade him, but Johnson would not listen. No, sir, said he firmly, he would not desist: "I have not had a roll for a long time." Whereupon he emptied his pockets of purse, watch, pencil, and keys, stretched himself along the edge of the hill, and rolled himself in utter glee, over and over again, all the way to the bottom.

Somersby   The mile and a half between Harrington Hall and Somersby is a pleasant drive along what isn't much more than a country lane. About halfway there you'll pass the tiny village green and simple fifteenth-century church of Bag Enderby, one of three other church livings in the possession of Tennyson's father, in addition to Somersby itself.

The Rev. George Clayton Tennyson hadn't wished to be a clergyman at all. As the firstborn son of a rich landowner, he should have inherited his father's wealth and applied himself to a life of leisure. But his father, a rather mean-spirited man, decreed otherwise. Arbitrarily, he chose his younger son, Charles, as heir and arranged a clerical career for George. First, in 1791, he negotiated the living of Benniworth church for the older boy, though George was only thirteen at the time; added those of Somersby and Bag Enderby in 1806; and finally the vicarage of Great Grimsby in 1815.

Of course, George had to wait until he could attend university and then take Holy Orders before he could begin his ministerial chores, but in 1802 he took over at Benniworth, and in 1808 moved into the rectory at Somersby. There Alfred Tennyson, fourth of what were to be twelve children in all, was born on August 5, 1809.

The rectory was actually owned by Robert Burton, a long-time family friend, but George obviously needed more room for his fast-growing menage, and old Mr. Tennyson did pay for that. Added almost immediately were a nursery, two servants' rooms, an enlarged kitchen, and stables. Later came three more small rooms and a book-lined drawing room and, in 1820, a gothic dining room complete with stained glass windows and an oak chimney-piece carved to look like stone.

Even with all this, the quarters were hardly much beyond adequate. Once, in trying to explain his refusal to have his own sister as a house guest, George wrote their brother, Charles: "When lately she offered to come see us we had not accommodation. We are three and twenty in family, and sleep five or six in a room." In addition to all the children, the Tennysons had ten servants.

Alfred slept with his older brothers in a bedroom in the gabled attic. It had its own steep stairway by way of access, a skylight for illumination, and a great beam on which the boys practiced acrobatics.

It was an odd household at best. George Tennyson was a moody, nervous, irritable man, and a stern father. At times he could be downright brutal, at other times lethargic. He had, and passed on to his sons, what the poet was to call the Tennysons' "black blood." He suffered from epileptic seizures, and toward the end of his life he drank heavily.

Mrs. Tennyson coped with all this as best she could. She was easygoing and warm, but absentminded and feckless. Often she forgot about meals until it was nearly time for the family to sit down to eat, and she would have to send off in haste to a neighbor for two or three ducks or chickens.

But there were compensations of a sort. Dr. Tennyson—his father had negotiated an L.L.D. for George in 1813—was a bright man and had a great library of books, more than two thousand five hundred in all. He managed most of the boys' wide-ranging education on his own. He and Mrs. Tennyson loved poetry, too, and he had written some himself. Both parents encouraged their sons to attempt verse, and all three older boys did from their earliest years.

Apparently Alfred was trying his hand as early as age five but, according to reports, his first reviews were mixed. When at eight he showed his brother, Charles, a piece he had written about their garden, Charles—then all of nine—surveyed it gravely and announced, "Yes, you can write." But soon after, having read Alfred's lament on his grandmother's death, his grandfather handed the boy ten shillings with the words, "There, that is the first money you have ever earned by your poetry, and, take my word for it, it will be the last."

At fourteen, Alfred had completed a three-act blank-verse comedy with resounding lines like, "Ha! Ha! Ha! Poor man, thou summer midge." But there were some touches with the keen observation and precise detail that were to become hallmarks. By 1826 the Tennyson boys had written enough verse to publish *Poems by Two Brothers,* chiefly the work of Alfred and Charles, though Frederick also contributed several poems. The publisher paid them £20, a rather handsome reward.

Typical of their level of achievement was Alfred's "Remorse":

> Oh! 't is a fearful thing to glance
>   Back on the gloom of mis-spent years:
> What shadowy forms of guilt advance,
>   And fill me with a thousand fears!

The lines are rather remarkable nonetheless, considering that the author's total years—mis-spent and otherwise—amounted to the grand total of sixteen when he wrote them.

With *Poems, Chiefly Lyrical* in 1830, however, Tennyson indicated clearly he had the makings of a poet, and a good one. The volume contained "The Kraken," "The Poet," "The Poet's Mind," and "Mariana," and critics were generally kind.

In 1832, with a collection called simply *Poems,* came a setback. Its offerings included "The Lady of Shalott," "The Palace of Art," "Oenone," and "The Lotus Eaters." Yet the reviewers were almost unanimous in condemning it, especially *The Quarterly,* the same magazine that had been so brutal to Keats. Crushed, Tennyson never published again while at Somersby. It would be ten years before the *Poems* of 1842 appeared triumphantly with "Ulysses," "Break, Break, Break," "Lockesley Hall," "Tithonous," and others of equal luster.

By then Tennyson had long since quitted Somersby for High Beach in Epping Forest, near London. His father had died in 1831. Somersby's new young rector, son of George Tennyson's patron, Robert Burton, and owner of the rectory, had kindly let the Tennysons stay on. But in 1836 he had announced that he was getting married and would need the place for himself. Tennyson never saw Somersby again.

Somersby rectory and church are well worth a visit today. Little has changed. The sprawling old home, now called Somersby House, still stands along the narrow country lane. White-painted with oriel windows and the tall gabled roof beneath which Alfred Tennyson had slept as a boy, it is much as he left it.

Directly across the road, up a steep bank, is his father's church, a low fifteenth-century structure of green sandstone. In the southwest corner of the churchyard amid the yew trees is Dr. Tennyson's tomb, and inside the church are a bust of the poet and the ancient font in which he was baptized.

In the squat little church tower patched with brick are a pair of bells— bells he had heard as they rang on the first Christmas day after Arthur Hallam's death. The sound sadly recalled the happiness of just the year before, when Hallam had been at the rectory to celebrate the holiday with them. Tennyson wrote in *In Memoriam:*

> This year I slept and woke with pain,
> I almost wish'd no more to wake,
> And that my hold on life would break
> Before I heard those bells again.

LOUTH—MABLETHORPE AND SKEGNESS—AND TEALBY

Last stops in Lincolnshire for the literary traveler heading for the Yorkshires are Louth, Mablethorpe, Skegness, and Tealby, all with interesting associations with Tennyson. Louth, on the A 16, nine miles north of Somersby, is where he had his only formal education, a scant four years before entering Cambridge. Mablethorpe and Skegness, both on the A 52 along the coast east of Louth and Somersby, were favorite haunts of Tennyson as a boy. And Tealby, on the B 1203 within ten miles of the North Yorkshire border, provokes a teasing fantasy of the Tennyson that might have been.

Louth   It's easy to find Louth (rhymes with "south") if you're driving from Somersby on the A 16. The tower of St. James's church rises up from the plain higher than Lincoln's Cathedral or Boston's Stump. Octagonal in shape and 295 feet tall, it crowns an edifice begun not long after Chaucer's death. A twentieth-century successor to Tennyson as poet laureate, Sir John Betjeman, called St. James's "one of the last great medieval Gothic masterpieces."

Tennyson's mother had been Elizabeth Fytcher, daughter of the Louth vicar, and when Alfred was seven his parents sent him off to the King Edward VI Grammar School there. He lodged nearby at his grandmother's house—both were on Westgate—along with his brothers, Charles and Frederick, already at the school. Its headmaster was the Rev.

J. Waite, another of their mother's relatives, and it was reputed to be one of the best local schools in Lincolnshire.

But the boys often must have wished they were back home in Somersby. Alfred's teacher was as adept at ear-pulling as he was at flogging, and the poet later said he so hated the school that whenever he returned to the town he'd make a detour so he wouldn't have to pass the schoolhouse. Tennyson's grandmother was a strict disciplinarian, too. She once threw buckets of cold water on one of her sleeping young charges, a cousin of Alfred's, because he hadn't yet gotten out of bed to light the fire—a full hour before he was supposed to.

After four years the boys were brought home to Somersby, and from the age of eleven until he went to Cambridge at eighteen, Alfred was taught by his father, and he supplemented his studies by extensive reading of the great collection of books in Dr. Tennyson's library.

Louth was the scene of Tennyson's public debut as a writer. It was a bookseller there named Jackson who paid Alfred and Charles that advance of £20 for the collection of verse they called *Poems by Two Brothers,* and brought it out in April of 1827. Few copies were sold, and Alfred later dismissed it as "early rot." But at the time, he and Charles couldn't restrain themselves. On the day of publication they hired a carriage and went racing off to the beach at Mablethorpe to shout their triumph at the waves.

The grammar school still exists on Westgate, and so does the building where Jackson had his shop. Called C. Parker and Company, it's at No. 19 Market Place and has a plaque on the front announcing that "From these premises was published *Poems by Two Brothers.*" Appropriately enough, it's still a bookstore, and if you do stop by, be sure to get a copy of the little *Guide to Tennyson's Lincolnshire* they have on sale. It's a charming booklet, and has several amusing stories of the poet's youth.

Mablethorpe and Skegness   The Tennysons holidayed on the beaches of Mablethorpe at the east end of the A 1104 and Skegness all the years Alfred was growing up. At Mablethorpe they stayed at a cottage that is now the oldest in town. Tennyson describes it in his "Ode to Memory":

> . . . a lowly cottage whence we see,
> Stretch'd wide and wild, the waste enormous marsh.

Here the interminable rolling tides captured his imagination forever, as any reader of "Ulysses" or "Break, Break, Break" might guess. He remembered his first glimpse of these waves in the poem "Mablethorpe":

> Here stood the infant Ilion of my mind,
> And here the Grecian ships did seem to be.

Tennyson returned to Mablethorpe again and again. Sometimes, as in 1827, triumphantly. Sometimes in sorrow. He was there in December of 1833 brooding over the savage attacks upon his just-published *Poems,* and his description of Mablethorpe then matched his mood:

> A miserable bathing place on our bleak,
> flat Lincolnshire coast.

But he was also at Mablethorpe in the summer of 1847, reading the proofs of *The Princess,* and as late as *The Last Tournament* (1871) he could still dwell on how

> . . . the great waters break
> Whitening for half a league, and thin themselves
> Far over sands marbled with mood and cloud.

The place where the Tennysons first stayed in Skegness where the A 158 and the A 52 converge and end was small, just one room deep, but was the only house then fronting the sea. As the family grew, they turned to the Vine Hotel, which is still in business and has a bust of the poet in its cocktail bar, which is known as (what else?) Tennyson Lounge.

The Tennyson booklet mentioned earlier as for sale at Parker's in Louth has a grand anecdote about Alfred's Skegness days. Often as a youth he could stroll down the beach to a farmhouse at Gibraltar Point, where he liked to sample the housewife's jam and worry her cat. Years later, a young friend of the poet found himself at that same farmhouse door. Establishing that the old couple within had indeed known young Alfred, the visitor told them that Tennyson was not only now poet laureate and wealthy from his writing, but that Victoria had offered him a baronetcy.

"Missus," the farmer shouted to his wife, "do you hear what this young gentleman is saying about Mr. Alfred? He saays he's wurth thousands by his poetry!"

"Naay, naay, Sir, you mun be mista'en," his wife replied. "Well, I nivver! Why you know i' them daays, we thowt he wur daft. He was allus ramblin' off quite by issen, wi'out a coat on his back and wi'out a hat on his head."

Then, with a shake of her head: "Well, Well! And the Queen wants to maake him a lord, poor thing!"

Tealby   And now for Tealby and the fantasy of what might have been.

The ancestral home of the Tennysons was Bayons Manor at Tealby on the B 1203, near Market Rasen. After Charles, the younger son, inherited the estate that should have gone to the poet's father, George, Charles went on a spree. Drawing on his enormous new wealth—one property in Grimsby alone was worth £200,000—he proceeded to build both a new and baronial country seat, and a new family tree to justify it.

The new Bayons Manor covered six acres enclosed within walls, with deer and black-faced sheep roaming in the park. The manor itself boasted an oratory, stately halls, a great gallery and a two hundred-seat dining room attended by an army of footmen in blue livery and gold-laced collars. Adopting old Mr. Tennyson's fancy that they were descended from Norman aristocracy, Charles re-styled himself Charles Tennyson d'Eyencourt, complete with pedigree, arms, and crest, and filled the gallery with portraits of instant ancestors.

All this, alas, ultimately came to nought. After WWII and its use by the military had left it a decaying ruin, Bayons Manor disappeared altogether one day in the explosion of a few sticks of dynamite to make way for "progress." Its rubble was used to build a new road.

Alfred Tennyson was never fond of either his grandfather or his Uncle Charles, and went to Bayons as rarely as possible. In *Maud* he wrote scornfully of just such a new lord,

> Seeing his gewgaw castle shine,
> New as his title, built last year.

Still, the game of "what if" teases. What if Dr. George Tennyson had inherited those riches as he should have? What if his famous son had grown up at Bayons Manor? There would have been no Somersby and its lovely fields and farms. No Harrington Hall and Rosa Baring. No Horncastle and Emily Sellwood.

And no Alfred Lord Tennyson, poet laureate?

THE NORTHEAST

II

THE YORKSHIRES AND HUMBERSIDE

With regard to the rusticity of *Wuthering Heights* I admit
the charge, for I feel the quality. It is rustic all through. It is
moorish, and wild, and knotty as a root of heath. Nor was it
natural that it should be otherwise; the author being herself
a native and nursling of the moors.
Preface, by Charlotte Brontë,
to Emily Brontë's *Wuthering Heights*

A miller there was there dwelling, many a day,
Proud as any peacock, and as gay.
Round was his face, and concave was his nose
A Sheffield blade was hidden in his hose,
And in his pouch a jolly little knife,
None durst him touch, for peril of their life.
Geoffrey Caucer, *The Canterbury Tales*[1]

Had we but world enough, and time,
This coyness, lady, were no crime. . . .
Thou by the Indian Ganges' side
Shouldst rubies find; I by the tide
Of Humber would complain.
Andrew Marvell, "To His Coy Mistress"

He who holds York holds England.
Old saying

---

[1]My translation shifts the lines a bit to keep as close as possible to Chaucer's
rhyme scheme. The original, from "The Reeve's Tale," is:
A millere was ther dwellynge many a day,
As any pecok he was proud and gay. . . .
A joly poppere baar he in his pouche
There was no man, for peril, dorste him touche.
A Sheffield thwitel baar he in his hose
Round was his face, and conus was his nose.

WEST YORKSHIRE

_____

West Yorkshire

York has been held by many, over many centuries. And there has been so much of it to hold.

At the time of Christ's birth the region that came to be known as Yorkshire was ruled by a tribe called the Brigantes. In 51 A.D. the Brigantes betrayed a British chieftain called Caractacus to the legions of the Emperor Claudius, thus affirming the old saying (in the opening quotes of this section) by opening up ancient Britain to the Romans.

The new rulers speedily secured their hold, establishing a settlement at the point where the rivers Ouse and Foss came together and naming it Eboracum. For the next three hundred years, succeeding emperors felt the place so important that no fewer than four of them made the long, arduous trip from Rome in person. Hadrian came to supervise the building of his famous wall across the whole of northern England. Servius and Constantius actually died in York. And Constantius's son, Constantine the Great, was proclaimed emperor there.

After the Romans pulled out in 406 A.D. the Saxons took over and modified the name by changing "Ebor" to Eofor, and adding "wic" (i.e., dwelling): Eoforwic. Four hundred years later, marauding Vikings seized control. In their mouths, Eoforwic became Jorvik, close to what finally stuck—York.

The Saxons managed a comeback in the eleventh century, when one of their number called Harold defeated the Norsemen in 1066 at Stamford Bridge near York. But as his name and the date 1066 suggest, Harold's hold on both York and England set a record for brevity. Before the year was out William the Conqueror, a Norman, had dispatched Saxon Harold at the Battle of Hastings and claimed the country as his own. As soon as he could, he built a pair of castles at York, one on each side of the Ouse, to be his northern anchors. When the people round about rebelled, he settled the matter decisively by reducing the entire area from York to the River Tees at Durham to a wasteland. William's descendants, the Plantagenets, were to rule England for centuries to come.

The original Yorkshire that all this history embraced was enormous, its six thousand square miles covering more than twelve percent of all England. As another old saying had it, "There's more acres in Yorkshire than words in t' Bible." North to south it ran for well over one hundred miles from the Tees all the way down to Sheffield. East to west it

127

stretched 140 miles, from the shores of the North Sea to the border of Lancashire within sight of the Irish Sea.

When England's great restructuring of counties came in 1974, the one old county of Yorkshire furnished most of the makings of five new ones: West Yorkshire, South Yorkshire, North Yorkshire, Humberside, and Cleveland.

Like Lincolnshire, the original Yorkshire had been divided into three sections or ridings (i.e., "thridings," or thirds). West Riding, the largest, had included the big industrial cities of Leeds, Bradford, and Sheffield, the celebrated spa and resort of Harrogate, and in the northwest corner, part of the Pennine Peaks. Leeds and Bradford are now in what is today's West Yorkshire, Sheffield is in South Yorkshire, and Harrogate and the Pennines remain in North Yorkshire.

Old North Yorkshire, second in size, always had the rest of the Pennines as well as the steel and iron works of Middlesbrough, the Tees estuary, and North Sea resort towns like Scarborough and Whitby. Now Middlesbrough belongs to what has become Cleveland County, Scarborough and Whitby to refashioned North Yorkshire.

The one-time East Riding was ninety per cent agricultural, mainly on the undulating plateau of the chalk wolds, its chief city being that great port of Hull on the Humber. Most of East Riding went to make up the new county of Humberside.

Plainly, twentieth-century politicians had themselves a field day hacking up ancient Yorkshire. When you come to explore all this vast area for yourself today, however, you'd do best to ignore all their newfangled county lines. Both logistics and convenience suggest you simply treat the present three Yorkshires and Humberside as if they were still a single unit.

What is the West Yorkshire-South Yorkshire-Humberside area like? Moorish, wild and knotty, says Charlotte Brontë. Home of industrial giants like Sheffield, maker of world-famous cutlery like the miller's blade for six hundred years or more, says Chaucer. Land of water, says Andrew Marvell, with the mighty seaport of Hull, third largest in the nation on the Humber tide.

Oddly enough the counties—all three of them—can be all of these at once. The Humberside coast east of Hull can be rugged and remote, with stark cliffs rising hundreds of feet above the sea. South Yorkshire has moorlands of its own just outside those steel-working factories of Sheffield. And West Yorkshire has, creeping within ten miles of those lonely Brontë moors, an industrial sprawl that dwarfs even Sheffield: Bradford and Leeds together have over three quarters of a million people.

LEEDS—BRADFORD—AND THORNTON

Although neither city is of any great literary consequence in itself, the Leeds-Bradford complex makes a good starting point for a tour of the three counties. The cities are served by both the M 1 and the M 62, as well as by a number of A roads, and nothing of literary interest in West Yorkshire is more than fifteen miles from one or the other.

Leeds Leeds, like Bradford, produced woollen goods, not writers. As long as there have been sheep grazing on the nearby moors, the two cities have been busy turning fleece into cloth and clothing. Indeed, by the 1920s, Leeds boasted the largest clothing factory in the world. But its literary pretensions are built of such slim stuff as having George Orwell as a visitor now and then (his sister lived there). A trivial little incident in Leeds, though, led the three Brontë sisters to become novelists.

One day in June of 1826, the rector of nearby Haworth stepped into a Leeds toy shop to buy a set of wooden soldiers for his only son, Patrick Branwell Brontë, about to turn nine. Young Branwell, as he was called, immediately shared his gift with his sisters. The four Brontë children were close-knit, as they had to be. They were near in age; Charlotte a year older than her brother, Emily one year younger, Anne, two. Their mother was dead, and their father left them largely to their own devices. Isolated as they were at the Haworth parsonage, they entertained each other as best they could.

The toy soldiers brought a whole new dimension to their lives. Branwell let each girl choose a soldier for herself and be its guardian. Charlotte, as the oldest, took the handsomest and called him the Duke of Wellington. Soon all four children were inventing wild stories about their charges to tell the others. Under the overall rule of Charlotte's Wellington, the children's heroes set up their individual kingdoms in "The Great Glasstown Confederacy" in West Africa, peopled with ranks from prime ministers to poets, from generals to publicans, all busy with adventures and love affairs, marriages and families, conquests and defeats.

The game progressed to the production of books in which to record these momentous events—tiny home-made affairs no bigger than two to three inches high and printed in microscopic handwriting. And according to Charlotte, even then the girls had yearnings for a larger audience. After *Jane Eyre, Wuthering Heights,* and *Agnes Grey* had made all three famous, she wrote, "We had very early cherished the dream of one day becoming authors."

Bradford   Bradford's major contributions to literature were the novelist Oliver Onions and J. B. (John Boynton) Priestly.

Onions (1873–1961) was born in Bradford. He wrote *The Compleat Bachelor* (1908) as well as ghost stories and tales of the uncanny collected under the titles *Widdershins* (1911) and *Tales of a Far Riding* (1902). However, Onions's best work is probably the grimly realistic *In Accordance with the Evidence* (1912).

Priestly was born in Bradford in 1894, the son of a local schoolmaster. As critic, novelist, and playwright, he churned out more than a hundred works in all. He will probably continue to be remembered for novels such as *The Good Companions* (1929) and *Angel Pavement* (1930), and among his plays for *Time and the Conways* and *I Have Been Here Before*—both in 1937—and possibly for *Dangerous Corner* (1932), which he wrote in a single week.

Priestly once complained of himself, "I write too much." But then, he admitted, "I have always been a grumbler. I am designed for the part." He spurned a knighthood, and after Harold Wilson spent half an hour trying to persuade him to become a peer, Priestly gave the prime minister a flat "no." When he did at last agree to join the select ranks of the Order of Merit in 1977, he growled, "First, I deserve it. Second, they've been too long about giving me it."

His views on his native town were equally blunt. Once, when its local council was energetically tearing down the city centre, Priestly rose to his feet at a civic luncheon to announce, "I may not have put anything up in Bradford, but at least I can say I've never pulled anything down."

After Bradford finally got around to awarding him the freedom of the city, he accepted, but his reaction was pure Priestly: "I got nothing concrete out of it at all, not even a free ride on the buses."

Thornton   There are no qualifications whatsoever about Thornton's contributions to literature. Of the Rev. Patrick Brontë's six children, four survived to maturity, and all were born in Thornton. The survivors were: Charlotte, born in 1816; Emily, 1818; Anne, 1820; and their brother, Branwell, 1817.

Thornton is four miles to the west of Bradford on the B 6145, and is now really a part of that city's suburbs. Mr. Brontë came to Thornton as curate in 1815 after an exchange of livings with the curate of nearby Hartshead, and served the Thornton church until his move to Haworth in 1820. The unassuming red-brick house where his famous offspring were born still stands in Market Street, at a turning off the High Street, and is marked with a plaque.

HAWORTH

Haworth is seven miles northwest of Bradford, and you reach it via the B 6144. But when you visit Haworth—it's pronounced "HO-warth"— be prepared for a shock. A guidebook of the early twentieth century described it baldly as "an ugly village on the edge of bleak moors."

It's worse today. The cobbled Main Street, rising steeply to the Brontë's parsonage and church at the top, is lined with tawdry souvenir shops and the like. After Stratford-upon-Avon, Haworth is the most visited literary landmark in England. At the peak of the summer season, its Main Street is jammed curb to curb with sightseers, as if every one of the three quarters of a million people in adjacent Bradford and Leeds had all taken a notion to run over and have a look on the same day.

And yet, when you've finally reached the grey stone parsonage and stand gazing through its windows at the dark churchyard beyond, its tombstones bleak and ancient, an overwhelming tide of emotion sweeps over you, and it's all worthwhile.

The Patrick Brontë who became incumbent of Haworth's parish church in 1820 was a self-made man. He was born Patrick Brunty in 1777, of poor peasant stock, in County Down, Ireland. By age sixteen he was already a weaver and the master of a small village school. At twenty-five, he had saved enough money to begin putting himself through Cambridge with the aid of a sizarship.[2] By the time he reached Haworth at forty-three, he had acquired a wife, six children, and a new name.

---

[2] A scholarship allowance unique to Cambridge University and to Trinity College, Dublin.

His wife was Maria Branwell, a Cornish woman he had met in 1812 while curate at Hartshead. The children, who came almost yearly beginning in 1814, were in order: Maria, Elizabeth, Charlotte, Patrick Branwell (always called Branwell), Emily Jane and Anne. The new name, Brontë, their father had appropriated from his hero, Lord Nelson, who had been made duke of Brontë.

Sorrow, as it would often, came to the Brontës almost at once. Mrs. Brontë had always been frail, as all six of her children were to be. Barely eighteen months after coming to Haworth she died of cancer, leaving behind the strangest kind of household.

Ostensibly, care of the children fell to the sister who'd come from Cornwall, Elizabeth Branwell, addressed simply as Aunt Branwell. But she found it hard to be responsive, ate alone, and gave little time to her charges. They saw equally little of their father. He spent most of his waking hours in his study, even eating all his meals there except breakfast. Such attention and affection as the children had came from Tabitha ("Tabby") Aykroyd, the servant who joined the family the year Mrs. Brontë died. Tabby stayed until her own death thirty years later.

So the young Brontës made their own lives. In summer they wandered endlessly about the moors; in winter they clustered about the kitchen stove to play games of their own devising. They read constantly from among their father's books.

Most of all, they spent their time inventing lives and worlds for those toy soldiers that Mr. Brontë had brought Branwell from Leeds, filling the tiny books of their own making with wild adventures—and "filling" is the right word. Though the average size of their books rarely exceeded 2½ x 1½ inches, the children managed to get several hundred words per page in their minuscule hand printing. Their total output is beyond estimate, but more than one hundred of these manuscripts are still in existence. And these are the work of Charlotte and Branwell alone. None of Emily's or Anne's has survived.

The children's first view of a world beyond the parsonage came in 1824 when all but Branwell and Anne were sent to the Clergy Daughters' School at Cowan Bridge, in what is now Lancashire. Maria, the oldest, was then ten. Soon wretched conditions at the school alarmingly undermined the girls' health, and their father brought them home. But it was too late for Maria and Elizabeth. Within months, both were dead. Maria was eleven, Elizabeth ten.

Thereafter, Charlotte, Emily, and Anne were to leave home a number of times, first as pupils at one school or another, later as teachers or governesses here or there. Charlotte and Emily went to Brussels to study languages in preparation for a school of their own they thought of opening. But they were never away anywhere for long. Always they returned to Haworth and its parsonage. It was there that within eight scant months death swept away the rest of the Brontë family, leaving Charlotte alone with her father. Branwell died in September 1848, Emily that December, Anne the following May while on vacation with Charlotte at Scarborough. Branwell was thirty-one, Emily thirty, Anne twenty-nine. It was at the parsonage, too, that Charlotte married her father's curate, Arthur Bell Nicholls, in 1854 when Mr. Brontë finally gave his consent. And it was at the parsonage that she herself died nine months later. She was thirty-eight.

Everything the Brontës wrote was done at Haworth, too. It was natural that they should turn to writing. The child-play fiction they wrote about their toy-soldier heroes had been invaluable training and, as Charlotte had said, had raised even then "the dream of one day becoming authors." Moreover, there was the example of their own father. Mr. Brontë had written two volumes of poetry and two of fiction as a younger man, and though they were in no way outstanding, all were good enough to find publishers.

The trio's first publication was a joint effort, a little volume entitled *Poems by Currer, Ellis, and Acton Bell* printed in 1846 when Charlotte was thirty. The pen names were adopted, perhaps out of modesty, or in hopes that their masculine sound would bring wider acceptance. In any event, only two copies of the book were sold.

Charlotte meanwhile had begun work on a novel, *The Professor*, based on the attachment she'd had for Monsieur Constantin Hegar, headmaster of the school she had attended in Brussels. Publishers found it too short and its tone too bitter. It was turned down nine times in all and not published until after Charlotte's death. Undaunted, she was working on *Jane Eyre* even as the first rejection slips were coming in. Published in 1847, again under the pseudonym Currer Bell, the book was an immediate and resounding success.

Charlotte solidified her position as a novelist with *Shirley* (1849) based on the West Riding textile mills and the violent Luddite clashes between workers and owners there in 1812. Next came *Villette* (1852), a better re-telling of the basic materials of *The Professor*.

Emily published her only novel, *Wuthering Heights*, in 1847. It won little praise in her own day (she died the very next year) but is recognized now as one of the great novels of all time. Anne, for her part, brought out *Agnes Grey* (1847), drawing on her own experiences as a governess, and *The Tenant of Wildfell Hall* (1848), depicting the sorry deterioration of a gifted young man into a drunkard. The drunkard was her brother, Branwell.

Near the top of the hill, in fact, as you toil your way up Haworth's Main Street, you will pass the Black Bull Inn on the right, the pub where Branwell drank himself to his early death. As you'll see, it was all too close to the parsonage which lies a few steps further up on the left, just behind his father's church.

Built in 1778 of local stone, the parsonage as the Brontës knew it was of modest size, essentially two storeys of four rooms each. It was bought for the Brontë Society in 1928 by Sir James Roberts, a native son, and has been carefully and lovingly brought to life as the Brontë Parsonage Museum, with much of their furniture, personal belongings, and memorabilia.

On the right of the arched hallway as you enter is Mr. Brontë's study, a room he rarely left when at home. Here he read, wrote his sermons, gave Branwell lessons in Greek and Latin, talked with parishioners, and ate his solitary meals, even after only he and Charlotte were left. In the room are his pipe and tobacco jar, walking stick, stovepipe hat, spectacles, and psalter. Along one wall is Emily's piano, and on another hang Charlotte's drawings of Anne's dog, Flossie.

Across the hall to your left is the family dining room where the sisters did most of their writing. Notable are the fender where Anne liked to warm her feet, and above the marble overmantel a portrait of Charlotte's beloved duke of Wellington, for whom she named the toy-soldier hero of her childhood stories. Under a likeness of Charlotte herself is the sofa on which Emily died, indomitably refusing to the last to be confined to her bedroom.

This was the room in which Charlotte carried on alone to the end of life an eerie custom the three girls had begun when she couldn't have been more than nine, Emily seven, and Anne perhaps five. The novelist Elizabeth Gaskell, friend and biographer of Charlotte, tells the story. She had visited the parsonage in 1853, and her account comes from Martha Brown, Tabby's long-time assistant, in Martha's own words:

> For as long as I can remember—Tabby says—since they were little bairns—Miss Brontë & Miss Emily & Miss Anne used to put away their

sewing after prayers & walk all three one after the other round the table in the parlour till near eleven o'clock. Miss Emily walked as long as she could & when she died Miss Anne and Miss Brontë took it up—and now my heart aches to hear Miss Brontë walking, walking on alone.

Mrs. Gaskell had heard those footsteps for herself. Each night Charlotte would see her upstairs to her bedroom, say goodnight, then descend the stairs again. Within minutes, Mrs. Gaskell reports, it would come from the room directly beneath her—the sound of that "slow, monotonous, incessant walk."

Back of the dining room is the kitchen where Tabby reigned, and to its left the one-time store room that Charlotte converted into a study for Mr. Nicholls in 1854.

The rooms upstairs were also subject to Charlotte's alterations. On the right front is the bedroom in which Mrs. Brontë died, and which became Charlotte's room. On display are personal items of the sisters, including Charlotte's tiny shoes and dress. George Orwell visited the museum in 1936, and it was these shoes that moved him most. He wrote in his diary:

. . . was chiefly impressed by a pair of Charlotte Brontë's cloth-topped boots, very small with square toes and lacing up the sides.

The room opposite Charlotte's was Mr. Brontë's. Between their two rooms had been the nursery, later Emily's room, and on the walls you can still see some of the drawings the children scratched into the plaster. The two back rooms were Tabby's and Branwell's.

After Mr. Brontë's death (he died in 1861 at age eighty-four) his successor added a gabled north wing, which now houses exhibition rooms. In the Bonnell Room is a superb collection of Brontë manuscripts and drawings, gift of an American enthusiast, Henry Houston Bonnell of Philadelphia. Just to see its display of those tiny little books hand-fashioned by the Brontës in their childhood is, in itself, a rare privilege.

The museum is open every afternoon of the year (from 11 A.M. weekdays) except for the last three weeks in December.

Back of the parsonage stretch for miles the desolate moors where all the sisters, especially Emily, loved to roam. If you're up to a testing walk, you can do the same. Two miles or so to the southwest you'll see their favorite bridge and waterfall on the little stream called Sladen Beck. And farther afield are the sites where Emily is said to have found models for two key places in *Wuthering Heights:* Ponden Hall for the Lintons' Thrushcross Hall, and Top Withens for Wuthering Heights itself.

A little lane leads from the parsonage back to Main Street and Mr. Brontë's church. All that survives of the building the Brontës knew is the tower. The rest was replaced in 1881. But a brass plate in the new church indicates the site of the vault in which all the Brontës but Anne are buried, and the location of the family pew. Also on view is a stained-glass memorial to Charlotte from an American admirer, and the certificate of her marriage to Mr. Nicholls.

In the nicely integrated new chapel added to the church a few years ago, there's the seventeenth-century carved oak table used for the Holy Sacrament, before which the couple knelt during the ceremony. A plaque on the south wall records the dates of the births and deaths of the Brontë parents and their six children, and opposite this a small memorial tablet to Aunt Branwell.

A month after Charlotte's death, Matthew Arnold signalized his veneration for her in a poem entitled "Haworth Churchyard: April, 1855." In it he recalls being present at the first meeting of "two gifted women," Harriet Martineau and Charlotte, and he goes on to lament Charlotte's too early death with:

> Half her laurels unwon
> Dying too soon!

He thinks sadly of "the moors of Yorkshire," where

> . . . the church
> Stands on the crest of the hill,
> Lonely and bleak;—at its side
> The parsonage-house and the graves.

When Mrs. Gaskell pointed out to Arnold that the Brontë sisters weren't buried outside at all, but inside the church in the family vault beneath the pavement, the poet replied:

> It really seems to me to put the finishing touch to the strange cross-grained character of the fortunes of that ill-fated family that they should even be placed after death in the wrong, uncongenial spot.

Arnold was right. Charlotte and Emily and Anne Brontë belong in that lonely, haunting graveyard that faced them every morning from their dining room window.

ROE HEAD—BIRSTALL—AND GOMERSAL

Roe Head, Birstall, and Gomersal are all in the near vicinity of Bradford, and all were significant in the life of Charlotte Brontë. Roe Head is eight miles to the southeast just off the A 62, three miles south of Heckmondwike on Mirfield Moor. Birstall is five miles southeast on the A 62, and Gomersal five miles southeast on the A 643.

Roe Head   Charlotte, at not quite fifteen, first went to Roe Head in 1831, when it was Miss Margaret Wooler's Seminary for Young Ladies, and she stayed for eighteen months. At first she was understandably unhappy, for she was shy and reserved, ill-equipped for the hurly-burly of a girl's school. But, fortunately, she soon won the affection of three schoolmates, Ellen Nussey and Mary and Martha Taylor. Ellen and Mary were to remain warmest intimates for the rest of her life.

Charlotte came back to Roe Head as a governess in 1835 and brought Emily with her as a pupil. When Emily went back home after two months, Anne took her place and remained at the school for two years. Charlotte herself stayed this time for a total of nearly three years. So Miss Wooler's and Roe Head must have proved congenial enough. Aside from the Haworth parsonage, Charlotte spent more of her life there than at any other single place.

The old school building later became a private residence until 1959 when it was returned to its original function. Handsomely remodeled and enlarged by the Verona fathers, it now serves as part of a Roman Catholic boys' school.

Birstall   Ellen Nussey lived in an imposing house in Birstall called The Rydings, no more than four miles from Miss Wooler's school. Charlotte was at Rydings often, for Ellen became dearer to her than anyone except her sisters. Charlotte's letters to Ellen, and Ellen's intimate knowledge of Charlotte are two of the most valuable sources of what is known about the novelist.

The two visited back and forth and took trips together. Ellen was with Charlotte on that vacation in Scarborough when Charlotte's sister, Anne, so suddenly died. Ellen was bridesmaid at Charlotte's marriage to Arthur Bell Nicholls. And the Rev. Henry Nussey, often cited as the prototype of St. John Rivers in *Jane Eyre*, was Ellen's brother. Charlotte's rejection of Henry Nussey's proposal of marriage to her is a classic and reveals much about Charlotte's view of her own character:

> I am not the serious, grave, cool-headed individual you suppose; you would think me romantic and eccentric; you would say I was satirical and severe. However, I scorn deceit, and I will never, for the sake of attaining the distinction of matrimony, and escaping the stigma of an old maid, take a worthy man whom I am conscious I cannot render happy.

Also for *Jane Eyre*, the Nussey's Rydings provided both architectural details and atmosphere for Mr. Rochester's Thornfield Hall. The outside of Thornfield, like Rydings, is "gray and battlemented . . . the principal object in the vale" below the village, with "woods and dark rookery [that] rose against the west." Inside, the mansion's chambers are "well arranged and handsome," but up above, the third floor has a dark, almost menacing air that Jane feels from the beginning, the long passageway "like a corridor in some Bluebeard's castle," leading to dark and low rooms stuffed with the moldering furnishings of owners

> that for two generations had been coffin-dust. All these relics gave to the third storey of Thornfield Hall the aspect of a home of the past: a shrine of memory.

The village of Birstall became the Briarfield of Charlotte's novel *Shirley* (1849), and its sixteenth-century Oakwell Hall the Fieldhead where the book's heroine, Shirley Keeldor, lives. Both the Rydings and Oakwell still exist. The Rydings is on the grounds of a factory, but is visible from the road. Oakwell Hall is now a museum, open weekdays except Monday from 10 A.M. on, and Sunday afternoons.

Gomersal   Gomersal, less than a mile from Birstall, is where Charlotte's other school friends, Mary and Martha Taylor, lived. Their house was a spacious one, called the Red House because it went back to an original of 1660 built of red brick instead of the local stone everybody else used. Between 1831 and 1840 Charlotte spent a number of weekends there.

Charlotte was fond of her friends' parents, and once said, "the society of the Taylors is one of the most rousing I have known." The family was not gentry, but well-to-do middle class, with a thriving farm and a prosperous woolen mill. In *Shirley* Charlotte makes Joshua Taylor the thorough-going Yorkshire mill owner Hiram Yorke, and Mary and Martha appear as Rose and Jess Yorke. Red House is called Briarmains.

Red House today is a museum, open year-round on weekdays from 10 A.M. on, and Sunday afternoons. It has very little that relates directly to Charlotte, but is furnished much as it would have been when she visited there. Upstairs in an artshop display room there is a book shelf filled with books about the Brontës, however. Among them is a copy of Charlotte's *The Professor* dated 1857, with a preface by her husband and the identification, "By Currer Bell, author of *Jane Eyre* and *Shirley.*"

HALIFAX

Now a town of more than 90,000, Halifax is eight miles southwest of Bradford, reached via the A 6036. Like most of the area roundabout, its prosperity was built on the woolen industry. Its centuries-old Piece Hall is the only surviving manufacturers' hall in Britain where as many as 315 merchants at a time once bought the pieces—or lengths—of wool brought in by the weavers. It also has a reconstruction of the Halifax Gibbet, notorious from the thirteenth century on. It was the gibbet that gave rise to the saying, "From Hell, Hull, and Halifax, Good Lord, deliver us." Actually a kind of guillotine, the gibbet was used to execute cloth stealers.

Also like most of the area roundabout, Halifax has its Brontë connections. In 1837 Emily became a governess at Miss Patchett's School at Law Hill, just southeast of town, and stayed for two years. For what it is worth, one of her colleagues was named Earnshaw. And nearby Shibden Hall, a fifteenth-century mansion, may have supplied a touch or two to the description of Thrushcross Grange in Emily's *Wuthering Heights.*

The Brontë's brother Branwell was also once in the neighborhood of Halifax, but briefly. In 1841, when twenty-four, he came as a railway clerk to Luddenden Foot, three-and-a-half miles to the west, but lost his job the next year when his accounts showed £11 to be missing. Branwell did furnish one of Luddenden's pubs with a literary tie of a sort. Its Lord Nelson Inn was the site of drinking bouts that Branwell himself described as "malignant debauchery."

Halifax also has associations with Daniel Defoe, Laurence Sterne, William and Dorothy Wordsworth, and Phyllis Bentley. Defoe is supposed to have written parts of *Robinson Crusoe* (1719) at the Rose and Crown Inn on Black Lane. Sterne went to school at Halifax for a year or two at age eight. And Wordsworth at seven was separated from his sister when their mother died in 1778 and Dorothy was sent to Halifax to live with relatives. It would be nine years before they saw each other again. This prolonged separation may explain in part the more than ordinary attachment the two had for one another.

Phyllis Bentley, novelist, essayist, and biographer of the Brontës, was born in Halifax in 1894. "A very hilly, bleak, and windy place," she called it, but she loved the region, and used it often in her fiction. Her very first novel, *Environment* (1922), she freely admitted, was "the story—need it be said—of a Yorkshire girl rather like myself." So, too was its sequel, *Cat-in-the-Manger* (1923). And in *Sleep in Peace* (1938), she used a frightening incident that occurred shortly after her own birth, when the chimney of the room in which she had been born blew down and its stones, mingled with the flaming coals, rolled out of the hearth and across the floor.

WAKEFIELD AND PONTEFRACT

Wakefield, nine miles south of Leeds on the A 61, and A 642, now incorporates Pontefract, a bit east of Wakefield proper on the A 639. Together, the two form a city of more than 60,000 people. And together they furnish some interesting literary sidelights: Wakefield with Oliver Goldsmith, George Gissing, and one of the Middle Age's four great cycles of mystery plays; Pontefract with Sir John Betjeman, Richard Monckton Milnes, and Shakespeare's *Richard II.*

Wakefield On a building at No. 30 Westgate in Wakefield's market place there's a plaque to indicate that novelist George Gissing was born upstairs in 1857. The downstairs was his father's chemist shop. Gissing used Wakefield as the heroine's home town in *A Life's Morning* (1888).

More likely to come to mind when Wakefield is mentioned, however, is Oliver Goldsmith's *The Vicar of Wakefield* (1766). This is ironic, of course, since the place barely figures in the novel. In Chapter I there is the mere mention of its name. In Chapter II we learn that it is known for its three "wants": the parson wants pride, the young men want wives, and the ale house wants customers. And in Chapter III the vicar and his family leave Wakefield for a distant neighborhood. And that's it. The book might better be called "The Vicar *From* Wakefield."

Wakefield's real gift to literature was what well deserves to rate as the first good play to be written in the English language. Popular in medieval times were dramatic representations of Bible stories called miracles or mysteries. Fostered by the church, they were designed to teach laymen the mysteries of Christ's redemption of man, since ordinary people then could neither read nor write, and in any case couldn't have read the Scriptures for themselves if they'd wanted to: there was no translation of the Bible into English.

Towns came to take great pride in putting on these plays. As many as forty-eight individual plays would be combined into a series, or "cycle," to tell the whole Christian story from the Creation through the Crucifixion and even to the Day of Judgment. Four complete cycles survive to this day, the best being the one produced in Wakefield.[3]

Best of the Wakefield cycle itself is "The Second Shepherd's Play," one of two that treat of the Nativity. It's a skillful blend of a serious telling of the birth of Christ and a comic subplot, and the latter is very funny indeed. While the shepherds are busy watching their flocks by night, a scamp named Mak steals one of their sheep, takes it home, and has his wife hide it in a cradle, pretending it's their newborn baby.

Soon the shepherds arrive, sure that Mak is the thief. Mak offers them a drink, but instead they demand to see what's in the cradle.

Mak: Nay, do way! He sleeps.
Shepherd: Methinks he peeps.
Mak: When he wakens, he weeps.
    I pray you go hence.
Shepherd: Give me leave him to kiss, and lift up the clout. [lifts the cover]
    What the devil is this? He has a long snout.
Mak: I tell you sirs, hark—his nose was broken.

The shepherds force Mak to confess, but instead of meting out real punishment, they content themselves with merely tossing Mak in a blanket, and go off to see the real babe in a manger. It is, after all, a season for rejoicing and mercy.

Wakefield's mystery plays have been performed in the city now for more than six hundred years. The "Second Shepherd's Play" was written by some unknown author about 1385. The cycle may even have given the place its name: i.e., the field of the wakeplay, for wake originally meant "to sit up late for pleasure or revelry."

---

[3]The other three are those of York, Coventry, and Chester.

Pontefract   The connection of Richard Monckton Milnes, Lord Houghton, with Pontefract was political: he was its member of Parliament from 1837 to 1863. Biographer of Keats, friend of Tennyson, Thackeray, and Emerson, and among the first to champion Swinburne, Houghton lived just twelve miles away at Monk Fryston Hall.[4]

John Betjeman's association with Pontefract had to do with one of its best known products, licorice lozenges. His "The Licorice Fields at Pontefract" (1954) is an entertaining love poem of a sort and includes a description of the town.

Shakespeare's connection—he uses the old form of the name, Pomfret—is historical. After Richard II's submission to Henry IV, Richard is imprisoned in Pomfret Castle, and Shakespeare makes this the final scene of his play, *Richard II*.

> I have been studying how I may compare
> This prison where I live unto the world. . . .

Suddenly Exton, Henry's emissary, breaks in with hired assassins and strikes him down, but not before Richard has valorously killed two of the murderers himself. It is Richard's finest moment in the play.

---

[4] See pp. 175-76.

SOUTH YORKSHIRE

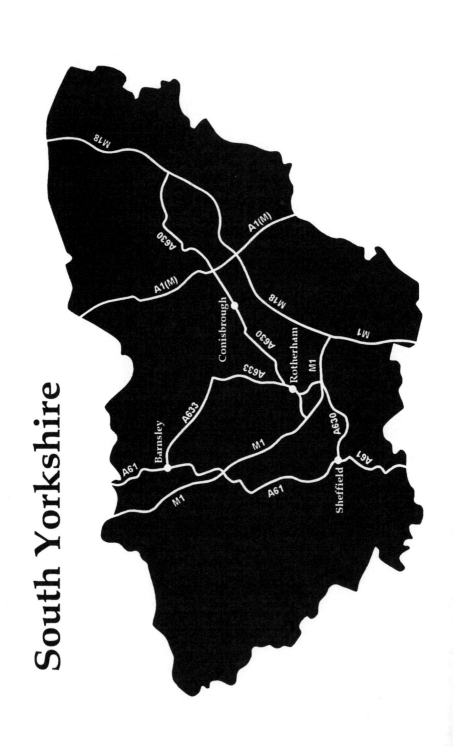

South Yorkshire

Although South Yorkshire and Humberside of today, taken together, account for almost twenty percent of the vast territory that was the original Yorkshire, their literary heritage is scant. Of chief interest in South Yorkshire are the Sheffield-Barnsley-Rotherham area and Conisbrough Castle. Sheffield is on the A 61, twenty miles south of Wakefield; Barnsley, also on the A 61, twelve miles above Sheffield; and Rotherham on the A 633, seven miles northeast of Sheffield. Conisbrough is eight miles northeast of Rotherham on the A 630.

SHEFFIELD AND BARNSLEY AND ROTHERHAM

Sheffield   Sheffield remains unabashedly what it has been since the Middle Ages, a manufacturing town turning out cutlery and other steel products such as the keen-edged knife or "thwitel" that Chaucer's Miller kept hidden in his hose. To this day the office of master cutter ranks second only to that of Sheffield's lord mayor.

In consequence, Sheffield also has been a rather unlovely town, especially after the Industrial Revolution brought in its belching factories, although in recent years the citizens have worked nobly to clean things up. The eighteenth-century novelist Horace Walpole, contrasting its attractive location on the Rivers Sheaf and Don with what industry had done to the surroundings, called it "one of the foulest towns in England in the most charming situation."

Aside from Chaucer, writers with ties to Sheffield are hardly literary bywords. A fellow named James Montgomery, for instance, was editor of the *Sheffield Iris,* got himself imprisoned for libelous essays, and composed poems like "The Wanderer of Switzerland" (1806), yet he remains this side of immortality. Some of his hymns, however, such as "Songs of Praise the Angels Sang" and "Forever with the Lord" are still sung.

A bit better was the early Victorian, Ebenezer Elliot. He was a master founder and owner of an ironworks, but won considerable literary attention as the "Corn-Law Rhymer." Vehemently opposed to the tax on bread, he voiced his wrath in his *Corn-Law Rhymes* (1828). Among his other long poems were "The Village Patriarch" and "Love." He also wrote some lyrics that were well above average, and won the praise of Robert Southey, then poet laureate. The workers of Sheffield certainly liked him. They showed their appreciation by erecting in his honor a bronze statue, now on view in Weston Park.

John Ruskin came to Sheffield in 1876 in one of his quixotic attempts to stem the tide of mechanical progress. He bought thirteen acres there to establish a rural Elysium, and roundly declared, "We will have no steam engines upon it, and no railroads." Ironically, quite the reverse has occurred. On the site today is the Abbeydale Industrial Hamlet, devoted to heralding the very Industrial Revolution Ruskin fought. On display are a complete eighteenth-century water-powered steel works, workmen's cottages, and coach house, plus a depiction of the entire process of producing steel goods.

Barnsley and Rotherham   Although the three towns are not contiguous, Barnsley and Rotherham seem in a way to be extensions of Sheffield. Barnsley's coal pits sustained it for five hundred years before closing not too long ago. Rotherham shared Sheffield's dependence upon iron and steel plants.

None of this endeared them to George Orwell. He came to Sheffield in 1936 on his walking tour from Coventry to gather material for what became *The Road to Wigan Pier* (1937), and extended his explorations to Barnsley and Rotherham. But after some weeks, he decided he'd had enough. In a comment approximating that of Walpole two hundred years earlier, Orwell confided to his journal, "I have been in these barbarous regions for about two months"—and got back on the road to Wigan.

CONISBROUGH CASTLE

Sir Walter Scott was wrong when in *Ivanhoe* he called his Conisbrough Castle a "Saxon" fortress. True, there had been earthen defense works there far back in Saxon times. The name comes from the Saxon Cyninges-burgh—the King's "burgh" or stronghold. But the great stone battlements that Scott wrote about weren't begun until after 1160, the work of Henry II's illegitimate half-brother, Hamelin Plantagenet.

Scott sets his novel at a time when this Norman castle was brand new, during the reign of Richard the Lion-Hearted, 1189–1199. Ivanhoe is the stout supporter of Richard in his struggles with his brother, John. Ivanhoe's beloved is the Lady Rowena, the intended of Athelstane of Conisbrough.

By the time Scott got around to using Conisbrough Castle, it was already pretty much the ruin it is today. But if you like, it's yours for the viewing, open daily the year-round, the hours varying with the season.

Humberside

Humberside

Humberside's major points of literary interest are Epworth, Kingston upon Hull, Bridlington, and Beverley. Epworth is tucked away in the county's southwest corner, on the A 161 near the South Yorkshire border. The other three are in the east and northeast: Kingston upon Hull (often simply called Hull) on the A 63 at the mouth of the Humber; Bridlington, twenty-five miles northeast of Hull on the A 165; and Beverley, seven miles north of Hull on the A 164.

EPWORTH

The village of Epworth is known to the world for contributing the founders of the Methodist Church, but John and Charles Wesley barely made it past early childhood. In 1709 the Epworth rectory in which they lived burned to the ground, and they were literally snatched from the flames by their nurse. John was then just six, Charles only a baby of two.

Their father, Samuel, was the descendant of a well-known noncon-formist family and had gone to Epworth as rector in 1697. Before either of his two famous sons were born, he had achieved some recognition as an author himself, chiefly for his *Life of Christ in Verse* (1693) and *History of the Old and New Testament in Verse* (1701). In all, he sired nineteen children. John was No. 15, born in 1703, Charles No. 18, born in 1707.

John grew up to be the organizer of the two, promoting the spread of Methodism with tireless energy, travelling as much as five thousand miles a year by horse or afoot and giving up to fifteen sermons a week. As author, he published twenty-three collections of hymns, many of them translations. In addition, he wrote a *Journal* that is a literary work of high order, remarkable for its humor, pathos, and shrewd insights.

The real hymn writer, however, was Charles, and Charles was unwit-tingly responsible for their church's name. While a student at Oxford in 1727, he had—as brother, John, put it—"awoke out of his lethargy" and begun to meet regularly with two or three friends in their rooms at Christ College. When a fellow student, struck by their almost abrasive piety and no-nonsense study of the Bible, sneered, "Here is a new set of methodists sprung up," the name stuck. Thus was a movement born.

In all, Charles wrote more than 6,500 hymns; "Jesus, Lover of my

Soul," "O for a Heart to Praise my God," "Jesus Christ is Risen Today," and "Hark, the Herald Angels Sing" are his.

KINGSTON UPON HULL

Kingston upon Hull, or Hull, began as a seaport. In the twelfth century, Cistercian monks from nearby Meaux Abbey established a base there, where the River Hull flows into the Humber, in order to ship their wool to the continent. Hence the name Hull. But in 1293 Edward I took it over, laid out a new town, and called it, well, King's-town.

As early as the fourteenth century, Chaucer knew of it as one of the country's major ports. In the Prologue to the *Canterbury Tales,* in fact, when groping for an English equivalent to Carthage with which to impress us with the shipman's awesome knowledge of his trade, he chose Hull:

> But of his craft, to reckon well his tydes,
> The streams and dangers that he faced besides,
> His navigation, ports and pilotage
> There was none such from Hulle unto Cartage[5]

This same need for an effective comparison moved Andrew Marvell, too, when he came to write "To His Coy Mistress" in 1647. What Marvell needed was an English river mighty as the Ganges in India, but half the globe away, so that he could dramatize to his beloved that she and he didn't have eternity and a whole world in which to play hard-to-get.

> Had we but world enough, and time,
> This coyness, lady, were no crime
> Thou by the Indian Ganges' side
> Shouldst rubies find; I by the tide
> Of Humber would complain.

Marvell, however, also had strong personal reasons for choosing the Humber. He was born in 1621 near Hull within five miles of the Humber estuary, at Winestead, where his father was vicar. Three years later the family moved to Hull itself, where Mr. Marvell filled the dual posts of vicar and master of the grammar school his son attended. And by a

---

[5]Slightly modernized to avoid one or two now-obsolete words like "lodemenage," which means pilotage anyway.

strange twist of fate, the poet's father was to drown in the River Humber before Marvell was twenty. From 1659 until his own death in 1678 the poet represented Hull in Parliament, and served vigorously. The result was a series of sharp satires and pamphlets, written first to attack opposing ministers, but ultimately zeroing in on Charles II himself.

The Humber also caught the attention of John Taylor, the rollicking Jacobean boat-hand known as the Water Poet. Taylor stopped by Hull on one of those madcap "merry-wherry-ferry" voyages of his that made him the toast of London. (He once essayed rowing from London to Queensbrough in a brown-paper boat, and barely escaped with his life.)

In the eighteenth century a fictional sailor, even better known than Chaucer's shipman, sailed down the Humber on an adventure known today throughout the world. A bronze plaque in Queen's Gardens now reminds us that when Daniel Defoe sent Robinson Crusoe off for his celebrated rendezvous with Friday, he had him leave from Hull.

On a more sober note, a stately house at 25 High Street today serves as a museum honoring the one man most responsible for the total abolition of slavery in Britain. William Wilberforce was born in that house in 1757, and as philanthropist, M.P. for Yorkshire, and writer, devoted his life to this cause. His *A Practical View of the Prevailing Religious System of Professed Christians* (1797) must rank as one of the most influential political works ever written. He died in 1833, just weeks after word reached him that the second reading of Parliament's bill abolishing slavery had passed.

The Wilberforce Museum is fascinating, if not a little disturbing. Among its shocking relics of the slave trade is a model of a slave ship Wilberforce used in his lectures to Parliament that had slaves "laid out like sacks of corn in every inch of the hold."

BRIDLINGTON

Charlotte Brontë visited Bridlington with Ellen Nussey several times, staying with the Hudsons, friends of Henry Nussey, at Easton Farm. On her first stay in September of 1839, Charlotte, who had never seen the ocean before, was so entranced that she burst into tears. Her second visit in June 1849 was a painful one. Her sister, Anne, had just died while they were vacationing at Scarborough, only five months after Emily Brontë's death. Devastated as she was, however, Charlotte somehow managed to keep working on *Shirley,* the novel she had begun following the success of *Jane Eyre.*

BEVERLEY

For a final note on Humberside, Beverley provides an interesting cast of characters: Hotspur, Lewis Carroll, Anthony Trollope, and Dick Turpin.

Beverley has two outstanding churches. One is Beverley Minster whose twin western towers dominate the surrounding terrain. And dominating the minster itself is the ornate fourteenth-century tomb of the Percys, one of the most powerful families of medieval England. Hotspur, fiery challenger of Prince Hal and Henry IV himself in Shakespeare's *Henry IV Part 1,* was a Percy.

Lewis Carroll may well have found his White Rabbit at Beverley's other great church, the parish church of St. Mary. Carroll had friends who lived outside Beverley, and spent several vacations with them. On the door in the north side of St. Mary's is an ancient carving of a hare with a remarkable resemblance to the one Carroll had illustrator Sir John Tenniel draw for *Alice in Wonderland.*

Trollope's brush with Beverley was costly. In 1868, for some reason, he took the notion that he'd like to be Beverley's member of Parliament, although he lived at Waltham Cross in Hertfordshire. He spent months on the effort and wore himself out. He not only lost—he found himself £2,000 the poorer, and that, added to the other unexpected expenses, forced him to give up the cherished country estate he had worked so hard to acquire.

If nothing else, Dick Turpin gives you a good excuse to have a refreshing drink at the seventeenth-century inn called The Beverley Arms at North Bar Within. Fabled in many a story and legend, especially in William Harrison Ainsworth's *Rookwood* (1834), the famed highwayman lost his freedom and ultimately his life doing that very thing.

In 1737, after shooting a man in London, Turpin fled to what was then Yorkshire's East Riding and set himself up as a horse dealer named Palmer. But thirst overtook him one day and he was spotted riding a stolen horse in the yard of the Beverley pub, then known as the Blue Bell. Inquiries led to the revelation of his true identity, and he was hanged in York on April 10, 1739.

North Yorkshire

North Yorkshire

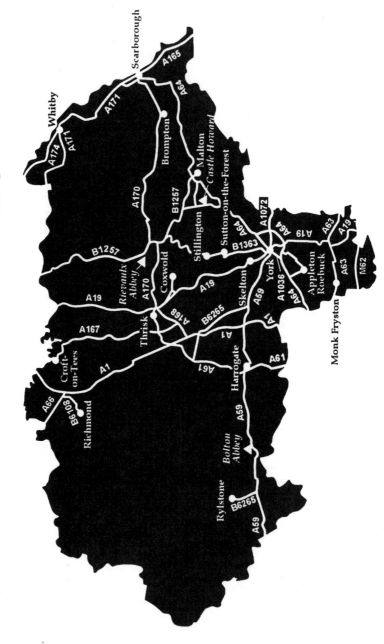

> My Yorkshire starts in the Pennines in the west and runs
> east across the Yorkshire Dales and the North Yorkshire
> Moors to the enchanting villages and towns on the coast of
> the North Sea . . . I know there are other glories in this,
> the biggest county in England. There are several entirely dif-
> ferent Yorkshires, but this is mine.
>
> James Herriot, *James Herriot's Yorkshire*

The heart of Mr. Herriot's Yorkshire, land of *All Creatures Great and Small* and the rest, is the high country, with "wilderness and solitude breathing from the bare fens, yet a hint of softness where the river wound along the valley floor. And in all the green miles . . . not another human being to be seen."

But Herriot is right. There are several entirely different Yorkshires, and other writers had their own Yorkshires. Laurence Sterne's was the home of good living. In the midst of writing *Tristram Shandy,* he pushed aside his manuscript one day in 1767 to exult to a friend:

> I wish you could see in how princely a manner I live—'tis a land of
> plenty. I sit down to venison, fish and wildfowl, or a couple of fowls or
> ducks, with curds, and strawberries, and cream, and all the simple plenty
> which a rich valley under the Hambleton Hills can produce.

Wordsworth's is the Yorkshire of history and legend, a solitary steeple rising above the ruins of Bolton Abbey, ravaged by Henry VIII. Here, Wordsworth tells us, in *The White Doe of Rylstone* (1807), the people still came to worship decades later, in a chapel that happy chance had spared:

> From Bolton's old monastic tower
> The bells ring loud with gladsome power;
> The sun shines bright; the fields are gay
> With people in their best array . . . .
> And thither young and old repair,
> This Sabbath-day, for praise and prayer.

To Bram Stoker, it is the Yorkshire he puts into the early chapters of *Dracula*. This Yorkshire is made up of his recollections of a vacation there in 1890—of the rugged North Sea coastline just outside his window and a phantom ship fleeing the fury of a great storm:

> It was now nearly the hour of high tide, but the waves were so great that in their troughs the shallows of the shore were almost visible. The wind suddenly shifted and then, between the piers, leaping from wave to wave as it rushed at headlong speed, swept the strange schooner before the blast with all sails set and gained the safety of the harbour.

And for Charles Dickens and Daniel Defoe, it is particularly the Yorkshire of York itself. Defoe not only gives a good account of the city in his *Tour through the Whole Island of Great Britain* (1724-7), but has his famous hero Robinson Crusoe open his story with "I was born . . . in York of a good family, though not of that country."

Dickens goes out of his way to drag York into *Nicholas Nickleby* as he strands Nicholas and Mr. Squeers at a rundown Yorkshire inn just so they (and we) can listen to the grey-haired gentleman spin his tender—and absolutely fictional—tale of York's Minster and the magnificent Five Sisters Window. Seven centuries have passed, the gentleman explains, since the first of the sisters died and the others had the window made with a flat, broad stone beneath it to mark where, one by one, thereafter, each would be buried in turn.

As he concludes, the gentleman might almost be talking to us:

> That stone has worn away and been replaced by others, and many generations have come and gone since then. Time has softened down the colours, but the same stream of light still falls upon the forgotten tomb, of which no trace remains; and, to this day, the stranger is shown, in York Cathedral, an old window called the Five Sisters.

An archbishop of Canterbury once wrote, "It is the bounden duty of every English-speaking man and woman to visit Canterbury at least twice in their lives." In reply, the archbishop of York might well scoff: "Only twice? Enough for Canterbury, perhaps—but hardly for York, Sir."

For York is utterly beguiling. Situated almost in the center of the county, fed by any number of fine highways, the A 19, the A 64, the A 59, and the 1036 for starters the city has only one drawback as the beginning of your tour of Yorkshire. You may never want to leave it to go elsewhere.

YORK

"York's streets have developed from the original Roman street plan," say modern guidebooks brightly. Well, yes and no. Those legions of the first century A.D. laid out their settlement in their usual way, all right—a rectangle with two main streets intersecting at its center. The two even survive in today's York as Stonegate and Petergate. But the pattern of streets that has evolved since then is chaotic. They're tortuous, narrow, helter-skelter.

Within a mere one thousand yards a single thoroughfare can be called Bootham, High Petergate, Low Petergate, Colliergate, Fossgate, and Walmgate. And even these names aren't what they seem. On reporting his 1857 visit in *Our Old Home,* Nathaniel Hawthorne blithely assured his Yankee readers there were many streets "bearing the name of the particular gate in the old walls of the city to which they lead."

Not at all! "Gate" is a leftover from the Vikings who occupied the city after the Romans, coming from the Scandinavian word "gatan" and simply meaning street. What the people of York do call their gates is "bars," because they barred entry to the city. Notable among those remaining are Micklegate Bar, with a grand Norman archway, and Bootham Bar, built in the eleventh century on the very spot where the Romans had built a gate a full thousand years before.

All this is preparation for a simple injunction: Don't plan on using your car to explore York. Besides, you don't have to. Yes, there is much to see—very much. King George VI once said, "The history of York is the history of England." But fortunately the area involved—from top to bottom, from York's Minster to Clifford's Tower, the old castle keep by the river—is a scant half mile. Moreover, if you do it right, it's downhill most of the way. If need be, depend on public transportation to get you there and back.

Start your tour at **York Minster** (1), and then just amble your way downward at your own pace. If it's a pleasant day, before you do enter the minster, stroll atop the section of the medieval city wall that lies behind it. Dating from the thirteenth century and now wonderfully restored, the walls cover three miles in all and provide a breath-taking overview of the city. For your sampling, ascend at **Bootham Bar** (2) and go along to **Monk Bar** (3) at Goodramgate. The views of the minster are spectacular.

Now you are ready for the minster itself. Officially it's called the

YORK

1. York Minster
2. Bootham Bar
3. Monk Bar
4. St. Mary's Abbey
5. Assembly Rooms
6. Shambles
7. No. 20 Coney
8. Micklegate Bar
9. Holy Trinity Church
10. Clifford's Tower
11. Castle Museum

BOOTHAM

GILLYGATE

LORD MAYOR'S WALK

MONKGATE

MARYGATE

ST. LEONARDS

HIGH PETERGATE

DEANGATE

GOODRAMGATE

ALDWARK

4

2

1

3

BLAKE ST.

STONEGATE

LOW PETERGATE

SWINEGATE

ST. ANDREWGATE

SPEN LN.

LENDAL

MUSEUM ST.

DAYGATE

CHURCH ST.

JUBBERGATE

SHAMBLES

COLLIERGATE

ST. SAVIOURGATE

5

LEEMAN RD.

WELLINGTON ROW

NEW ST.

CONEY ST.

PARLIAMENT ST.

PAVEMENT

FOSSGATE

6

STATION RD.

ROUGIER ST.

NORTH ST.

7

HIGH OUSEGATE

COPPERGATE

PICADILLY

TANNER ROW

B1225

OUSE BRIDGE

KING ST.

CASTLEGATE

RIVER FOSS

TOFT GREEN

MICKLEGATE

TRINITY ST.

FETTER LN.

CLIFFORD ST.

9

PRIORY ST.

BISHOPHILL JR.

RIVER OUSE

10

DEWSBURY

LOWER PRIORY

BISHOPHILL SENIOR

SKELDERGATE

TOWER ST.

8

11

NUNNERY LN.

NEWTON TER

PRICE'S LN.

BRIDGEGATE

TERRY AVE.

N

Metropolitical and Cathedral Church of St. Peter, and it's both a cathedral and a minster. It's a minster because it's the mission center of Christian teaching and ministering. It's a cathedral because it houses the throne (i.e., "cathedra" or chair) of the Archbishop of York, primate of all north England.

In age, size, history, and accoutrements, York Minster is awesome. York actually had a Christian bishop in Roman times. After a lapse, the region returned to the faith in 627 when its pagan King Edwin was tricked into it by his Kentish wife, who'd been converted. She persuaded Edwin, about to do battle with the West Saxons, that he'd have better luck if he prayed to her Christian God rather than his own. He did so, and he won. Poor Edwin. Grown man though he was, and no doubt feeling more than a bit foolish, there was nothing he could do but keep his promise and suffer himself to be baptized.

The structure that you see today, 524 feet long and England's largest gothic church, was begun about 1220 and completed about 1480—some 250 years in all. How long is 250 years? Well, if its builders had begun in the reign of Elizabeth, say, they'd have still been toiling away when Victoria came to the throne. If they had started on the day that George Washington was inaugurated as first president of the United States of America, they would have been at it through every presidency the country has ever had in all its history—and still have fifty years to go.

Mr. Matthew Bramble, who visited York in Tobias Smollett's *Humphry Clinker* (1771), didn't like the minster:

> The external appearance of an old cathedral cannot be but displeasing to the eye of every man who has any idea of propriety of proportion, even though he may be ignorant of architecture as a science; and the long slender spire puts one in mind of a criminal impaled, with a sharp stake rising up through his shoulder.

Nathaniel Hawthorne wasn't exactly swept away by it either:

> There is a great, cold bareness and bleakness about the interior; for there are very few monuments, and those seem chiefly to be of ecclesiastical people. I saw no armed knights asleep on the tops of their tombs.

Hawthorne is quite right about the minster's lack of illustrious dead. In all that vast space, the only royal tomb is that of Prince William of Hatfield, second son of Edward III—and William was only a boy of eight when he died. Hawthorne, however, does have the grace to conclude: "What nonsense to try to write about a cathedral!"

What the minster does have in abundance is stained glass, the greatest single concentration of medieval glass in the country: 128 windows, with several more than eight hundred years old, thanks to the conscience of a local man, Lord Thomas Fairfax. He was the parliamentary general when York's royalists surrendered to Cromwell's troops on condition their churches be spared pillage. Fairfax insisted the promise be kept.

York's great East Window is the largest sheet of medieval glazing in the kingdom; at 78 x 31 feet, it's bigger than a tennis court. The five giant lancets of Dickens's beloved Five Sisters Window are each more than fifty feet tall and five feet wide.

An early literary figure associated with the minster was Alcuin (Ealhwine), poet and author of numerous religious and philosophical works. Born in York in 735, he was educated at the cloister school, went on to become its headmaster, and became so renowned he drew students from all over Europe. In 781 he met the Emperor Charlemagne, who talked him into settling on the continent. Alcuin ultimately became abbot of Tours and more famous abroad than at home.

In the seventeenth century Laurence Sterne's great-grandfather, Dr. Richard Sterne, was archbishop of York for twenty years before his death in 1683. He wasn't much of a writer, his most engaging effort being something called *3,600 Faults in Our Printed Bibles*. But he did leave his famous descendant a legacy of sorts. Dr. Sterne established six scholarships at Cambridge, and his great-grandson took advantage of one, even though they were supposed to be for natives of Yorkshire and Nottinghamshire only. Laurence was born in Ireland, but he had several direct ties to York Minster. He served as its prebend in 1740 when his uncle was the canon residentiary, and was married there in 1741.

And, in a fictional event at another time, Ivanhoe and Rowena, with the blessings of Richard the Lionhearted, are united at the minster in Scott's *Ivanhoe*.

Four hundred yards or so southwest of the minster, at Marygate, are the ruins of **St. Mary's Abbey (4)**, where what might be called the longest theatrical run in history still goes on, well past its 650th year. Here every three or four years York stages its series of the medieval religious dramas called mystery plays—like Wakefield's putting biblical stories into popular form. In the beginning, about 1330, they were performed by various local guilds as part of the festival of Corpus Christi in June. Each guild had its own play, staged on its own huge wagon which stopped at a dozen key points about the city to entertain the waiting crowds.

Today one or two of the plays are still put on this way, but the remainder take place on a great outdoor stage at St. Mary's nightly for about three weeks in June. As always, the cast is primarily town citizens, but is now seasoned with a few professionals.

Midway between the minster and St. Mary's, at the point where Blake and Museum Streets come together, are the **Assembly Rooms** (5). Built between 1732 and 1736, they were the social center of all north England in the Georgian era, rivalling Bath and London itself. The rooms impressed even Smollett's Matthew Bramble. In *Humphry Clinker,* Mr. Bramble scoffs at Bath's Circus as "Vasparian's amphitheatre turned outside in," but says of the York showpiece:

> There is nothing of this Arabic architecture in the Assembly Room, which seems to me to have been built upon a design of Palladio, and might be converted into an elegant place of worship.

There's a mural in the rotunda showing the Emperor Constantine's grand entry into York in the fourth century. If his face looks suspiciously English it has every right to: It's the face of Richard Boyle, third Earl of Burlington, who designed the building.

York's famous version of a **Shambles** (6) lies directly below the minster, running King's Square down to Pavement. It's as fine a medieval street as you'll find in all Europe. It's so narrow and the houses lean so far over it that you expect the people in the upper rooms on either side to lean out their windows and shake hands.

The street was originally called Fleshammels, "shambles" itself coming from Middle English *schamel,* meaning a bench or stool. First it applied to stalls where meat was displayed for sale, and ultimately to where the animals were slaughtered. A pretty messy business obviously, hence today's meaning. In York the overhang of the buildings was a decided plus; the meat on the hooks above the shop windows was in the cool shade most of the day.

From the bottom of the Shambles, Pavement (now called High Ousegate and then Low Ousegate) goes west past Coney to cross the river and continue on to Micklegate and Micklegate Bar, in all a distance of about half a mile.

In Coney Street one of the more bizarre episodes in Shelley's life occurred—if to use the word bizarre for anything that happened to Shelley isn't redundant. The sketchiest outline of the circumstances that brought Shelley to York has in it the stuff of an entire novel.

In March of 1811 Shelley, then eighteen, published a little pamphlet setting forth the religious views he shared with his dearest friend and fellow student at Oxford, Thomas Jefferson Hogg. Within days it turned the poet's world upside down. The pamphlet's very title tells why: *The Necessity of Atheism.* The university expelled him. His father cut off his allowance. When he went home, as he wrote Hogg, he found his mother almost equally unyielding:

> I sometimes exchange a word with my mother on the
> subject of the weather, upon which she is irresistibly
> eloquent; otherwise all is deep silence!

In response, Shelley ran off to Edinburgh with sixteen-year-old Harriet Westbrook and married her despite his strong anti-matrimonial convictions. In October he took her to York to join Hogg, who was now in legal training there. The lodgings the Shelleys found at **No. 20 Coney** (7)—now Torq Limited, a jewelers' shop—were dingy at best, but all that they could afford. The plan, Shelley explained to Harriet, was simple: They would stay a year while Hogg finished his training; then it was off to London for all three—"forever."

But things were never simple for Shelley. He took a quick trip back home in a vain effort to gain some financial support, leaving Harriet in Hogg's care. He returned to find that Hogg had declared himself madly in love with Harriet and had pursued her relentlessly. Even for Shelley this was too much. He wrote a friend:

> I told him I pardoned him freely, fully, completely pardoned, that not the
> least anger against him possessed me. His vices and not himself were the
> objects of my horror and my hatred.

But the idyll of York was over. On November 1, when Hogg stopped in at No. 20 Coney, he found only a curt note. Shelley and Harriet had gone to the Lake District.

Micklegate Bar (8) was the chief of York's original four great city gates. Through it kings arrived on their ceremonial visits, and on it traitors had their severed heads displayed. For all Prince Hal's resounding rhetoric over his fallen rival's body in Shakespeare's *Henry IV,* Hotspur's head wound up on a pole above Micklegate Bar.

On Micklegate itself is **Holy Trinity Church** (9).[1] From 1089 to 1426

---

[1]Somewhat confusingly, there's another church of the same name on Goodramgate.

this was part of the great church of the Benedictine Priory of the Holy Trinity, and remnants of its original Norman central tower piers are still visible. Holy Trinity was also the first and major stop on the medieval mystery plays' wagon tour of the city. On the south wall of the church chancel there's a memorial to the York historian, Dr. John Burton. He served as model for Dr. Slop in *Tristram Shandy,* one of a number of townsfolk Sterne used, and the way he emerges in the novel suggests why its reception in York was somewhat less than enthusiastic:

> Imagine to yourself a little squat, uncourtly figure of a Dr. Slop, of about four feet and a half perpendicular height, with a breadth of back, and a sesquipedality of belly, which might have done honour to a sergeant in the horse-guards.

In *Ivanhoe,* Isaac the Jew, father of the beautiful Rebecca, lives in Castlegate, a street that runs off Coppergate below the Shambles. Interestingly enough, at **No. 20 Castlegate**—now the offices of estate agents—was the book-publishing firm of William Alexander, friend of Walter Scott. Mr. Alexander was a Quaker, and when Scott offered him *Ivanhoe* for publication, he replied, "Walter Scott, I esteem thy friendship, but I fear thy books are too worldly for me to print."

Also on Castlegate was the **Blue Boar Inn,** also no longer in existence, where Dick Turpin, the notorious eighteenth-century highwayman portrayed in a romantic light in William Harrison Ainsworth's *Rockwood* (1834), had a brief stay—after his death. Following his hanging at York for horse stealing, Turpin's corpse was brought to the Blue Boar Inn before burial in St. George's churchyard.[2]

At the end of your literary ramble down York's streets from the minster, at the point where the Ouse and Foss rivers come together, you'll come to one of the most fascinating museums in the world. Off Tower Street and at what's left of the thirteenth-century castle keep called **Clifford's Tower** (10) are the two buildings of **Castle Museum** (11). Once you step inside you may never want to leave, for with a little imagination you can bring a whole world of literature to life.

For instance, there's a full-size Victorian parlor,—red plush, claw-

---

[2]Even after death, Turpin was hardly peaceful. Buried in St. George's, his body was exhumed, probably destined for dissection, and spent a night in a surgeon's back garden. The following day, a mob of Turpin's cronies retrieved the body and reburied it in St. Georges—this time covering it with unslaked lime to render it unfit for the dissecting room.

footed horsehair sofa, velvet throw and all—where you can almost see Sir Florian's widow in Anthony Trollope's *The Eustace Diamonds* (1873) sitting and fingering the priceless necklace her husband left her. And right across the hall there's the 1810 kitchen of just such a Yorkshire farmer as Hiram Yorke in Charlotte Brontë's *Shirley.*

The museum was converted from a one-time prison, and you can see the actual cell in which not only Dick Turpin spent his last hours, but also where the Aram of Bulwer Lytton's *Eugene Aram* (1832) scratched his initials before his execution in 1759. Outside the building, a real-life water mill, re-erected, stone by stone, on the banks of the Foss, grinds out its flour, conjuring up a picture of Maggie Tulliver's brother, Tom, in George Eliot's *Mill on the Floss* (1860) at the mill moments before the tidal wave sweeps them both to their deaths.

Then, with the leap of a mere hundred years, you can stand before a World War I trench and recall the words of war poets such as Siegfried Sassoon in "Aftermath" (1918):

> Do you remember the dark months you held the sector at
> > Mametz—
> The nights you watched and wired and dug and piled sand-
> > bags on parapets?
> Do you remember the rats; the stench
> Of the corpses rotting in front of the front-line trench . . . .
> *Have you forgotten yet?*
> *Look up and swear by the green of the spring that you'll*
> > *never forget.*

And, incredibly, there's Kirkgate, a whole Victorian street built inside what used to be the prison exercise yard. It's roofed over, but you'd swear you were walking along the real thing as you peer into shop windows ranging from a sweet shop to a general store, from a pawnbroker to a bank, a fire station to a tallow-candle factory. On the cobbled street outside are the hansom cab, top-hatted driver, and horse, waiting for Sherlock Holmes to come striding from the tobacconist's and go dashing off in mad pursuit of the evil Professor Moriarty.

In Half Moon Court, the Edwardian equivalent of Kirkgate, stare into the chemist's and you can almost see H. G. Wells's George Ponderevo watching his uncle mixing up the wondrous elixir of Tono-Bungay in the novel of that name. At the draper's it could be poor young Arthur Kipps, hero of that same author's *Kipps* (1905), as he begins another thirteen-hour day of slavery, unaware that he has just inherited a fortune.

Yes, you may never want to leave the Castle Museum—or York itself—
but much more beckons.

SUTTON-ON-THE-FOREST—STILLINGTON—AND SKELTON

Sutton-on-the-Forest   Sutton is a small village eight miles north
of York, on the B 1363, celebrated today because its vicar for thirty years
was Laurence Sterne, now best remembered as the author of *Tristram
Shandy*. Sterne received the post in 1738 immediately following his or-
dination as a priest, but it was three years before the parishioners saw
much of their new shepherd. It was an age when many a clergyman saw
no need to get too involved with pastoral duties. Why, a man might get
so tied down with them there'd be no time left for life itself, let alone
being free enough to add another parish or two to his collection should
the opportunity present itself.

Sterne heartily agreed with this philosophy. Besides, York was a much
more attractive place to live. Sutton was isolated, more woodlands than
farms (hence its name), and therefore sparsely populated. What's more,
York was where church preferment lay, especially if your uncle happened
to be Dr. Jaques Sterne, influential canon of York Minster and archdeacon of Cleveland. Uncle Jaques was a sterling example of what an ambitious young cleric might do if he put his mind to it; he owned a dozen or
more different church parishes himself.

So, from 1738 to 1741 Laurence was more than happy to leave Sutton
largely to its own devices except for conducting the Sunday service. But
in 1741 he got married. Still only twenty-seven, he had already acquired
three ecclesiastical offices, and in all could count on an income of more
than £200 a year. But now he needed a house. And besides, the money
would provide more princely living in the country.

The move was not without its problems. In the first place, being stuck
in a little village with a wife like Elizabeth Lumley could hardly have
been entrancing. Sterne was social, witty, and warm-blooded, to say the
least. Elizabeth was practical, stolid of mind, and less than amiable. Her
own cousin called her a "fretful porcupine." The letters Sterne wrote her
before their marriage, looking forward to their life together, don't sound
like those of a young man swept away by passion:

> We will learn of Nature how to live,—she shall be our alchymist [sic]
> to mingle all the good life into one salubrious draught,—The gloomy fam-

ily of care and distrust shall be banished from our dwelling, guarded by thy kind and tutelary deity.

The parsonage they moved into was no bargain, either. The chimneys smoked, the floors sagged, the plaster fell. Sterne groused about the expenses required to make it liveable, "shaping the rooms, plastering, underdrawing, and jobbing, God knows how much!" His attempts at farming there were equally unhappy. Looking back years later, after the success of *Tristram Shandy,* he wrote a friend:

> Curse on farming (said I), I will try if the pen will not succeed better than the spade. The following-up of that affair (I mean farming) made me lose my temper: a cart-load of turnips was (I thought) very dear at two hundred pounds.

One thing Elizabeth Lumley did bring Sterne was another parish to add to his string. Her friend Lord Fairfax had promised that, if she married a Yorkshire clergyman, he would give her the living of Stillington, which was in his control. Soon after the couple moved to Sutton his lordship kept his promise.

Stillington   Only a couple of miles north of Sutton, Stillington, also on the B 1363, proved a multiple blessing. Sterne could stroll over there on Sunday afternoons after his morning service at Sutton, fulfill his only regular obligation, the weekly sermon, and be back home for tea if he liked. And not only did Stillington bring him another £40 a year, it provided him an escape from Elizabeth, and a friend and stimulus he sorely needed.

The escape grew ever more essential as Sterne worked his way through a succession of mistresses. The friend and stimulus was Stephen Croft, who had grown wealthy in the wine business before inheriting Stillington Hall and moving there to live. Croft and Sterne became great friends, and the clergyman was often at the hall as a dinner guest.

It was to the Crofts that Sterne read the first chapters of a novel he began writing some years later, *The Life and Opinions of Tristram Shandy, Gentleman.* There is even a report that, when he finished the reading Sterne, thinking they didn't like it very much, tossed the manuscript into the fireplace, and Croft rescued it just in time. True or not, it does make a good story.

Stillington offers some lively details of Sterne's style as a country parson. He was inordinately fond of hunting, and it is said that, one afternoon while he was walking through the fields on his way to his afternoon sermon, his dog flushed out a covey of partridges. Sterne turned on his heels and went straight back home to Sutton for his gun, leaving his Stillington congregation waiting in vain. But maybe they didn't wait very long. Sterne was no great orator, and often enough, it seems, while he was in mid-stream, listeners would get up and leave the church.

Sterne wasn't particularly popular with his Stillington flock, for that matter. A contemporary account has it that, once, when he was skating on the pond in Stillington Commons, the ice gave way, leaving him thrashing about in the water and crying aloud to bystanders for help. Nobody bothered to respond.

Skelton   Sterne found even more escape from Sutton in freewheeling visits to Skelton,[3] fifteen miles to the west on the A 19. Master of Skelton Castle was John Hall-Stevenson, whose reputation and way of living would have given almost any eighteenth-century gentleman let alone a clergyman, pause. But not so Sterne.

An old university friend, Hall-Stevenson furnished the very things Sterne relished: a keen and witty mind, a love of the eccentric, excellent company, and high living. Moreover, he was a writer of some talent, author of acceptable occasional verse, amusing little satires, and a collection of droll pieces called *Crazy Tales* (1762).

The castle itself was as wonderfully romantic as the author of *Tristram Shandy* could have wished, a mass of gothic-tale battlements with dark dungeons below and forbidding turret above, surrounded by the stagnant, weed-choked waters of a moat. Hall-Stevenson did the place full justice. After inheriting it from his father, he renamed it Crazy Castle and made it headquarters for a group of fellow bon vivants who dubbed themselves the Demoniacs. Their revels were legendary, marked by good food and fine wines, loose and bawdy talk, and—rumor had it—behavior to match.

No wonder Sterne visited as often as he could. If there was more than a touch of notoriety attached to Crazy Castle and its master, so much the better.

---

[3]As the unwary traveller finds from time to time in England, counties sometimes allow themselves two villages or towns with the same name. North Yorkshire is one of these counties and has *two* Skeltons—quite near to each other. The one you *don't* want for the purposes of this book is some twenty miles northwest of York off the A 1.

COXWOLD

Coxwold is a lovely village set among high hills eight miles northwest of Sutton, near the A 19. Old houses of honey-colored stone line the broad street that climbs past St. Michael's Church, with its octagonal tower going back to 1450 and an old gabled house that was once its parsonage. It was to this parsonage and to St. Michael's that Lawrence Sterne came as new vicar in 1760, still glowing from a London trip and as heady a triumph as ever greeted a newborn author.

He had gone to London in March quite unexpectedly, after running into Stephen Croft in York. Croft was off to London, and would pay all expenses if Sterne would come too. Sterne did and, within twenty-four hours of arriving, discovered that he was a literary sensation. The first two volumes of *Tristram Shandy* had just been published, and their humor and bawdiness had taken London by storm. The book was completely sold out. Lords and ladies clamored for his attention. The great actor David Garrick took him in tow. The duke of York himself, whose brother was on the verge of becoming George III, invited him to dinner. Sterne's publisher gave him a brand new contract for the incredible sum of £650—£270 for further rights to the first two volumes of *Tristram Shandy,* and £380 for volumes III and IV to come.

And to top it off, the vicarage of Coxwold had just become vacant. It was a post that Sterne had coveted for years. Moreover, it was in the gift of Lord Fauconberg, a long-time friend. When Sterne was nominated, he accepted with alacrity. It was a far different man, then, from the simple country parson who had left Sutton just three months earlier who entered the gates of the Coxwold parsonage that summer day in 1760, driving a handsome new carriage and resplendent in new London clothes.

With vast content, Sterne settled down into what he termed "sweet retirement," calling his new home Shandy Hall. It was an inviting place, long and low with three gables and steep tiled roofs. Inside were wainscotted walls and space for bedrooms, drawing room, small study, dining room, and a kitchen with a great fireplace from which came the succulent roasts, fish, and wildfowl that made Sterne "happy as a prince." Out back were the trees and shrubs and garden where he turned to "pruning or digging or trenching or hacking up old roots" when respite from writing was needed.

He began to write in earnest. The new parish yielded him £160 a year, more than his other three combined. Now he could afford to pay a curate to take over his duties at Sutton and Stillington and to devote himself to Coxwold and writing—and still clear an additional £70 a year.

He had already arranged to bring out a collection of his sermons. Enamored of the "fellow of infinite jest" in Shakespeare's *Hamlet*, Sterne had called his "witty, sensible and heedless" parson Yorick in *Tristram Shandy*. Now he capitalized on this, calling the collection *The Sermons of Mr. Yorick* and claiming that their publication had been spurred by the one he had written for the novel:

> The sermon which gave rise to the publication of these, having been offer'd to the world as a sermon of Yorick's, I hope the most serious reader will find nothing to offend him, in my continuing these two volumes under the same title.

To be safe, however, he had added a second title page:

Sermons by Laurence Sterne, A. M. Prebendary
of York, and Vicar of Sutton on the Forest,
and of Stillington near York.

Sterne's first concern at Coxwold was the continuation of *Tristram Shandy*. The study he wrote in was tiny, with just enough room for his books, desk, and double-knobbed chair, but cozy, and he could work uninterrupted. By the end of 1762 he had published four more volumes of the novel, although by this time Dr. Johnson, Oliver Goldsmith, Samuel Richardson, and Horace Walpole had joined a rising tide of criticism against its literary quality and ribaldry.

Sterne managed to publish the rest of *Tristram Shandy*—Volumes VII and VIII in 1765, Volume IX in 1767—as well as the first two volumes of *A Sentimental Journey* in 1768 before his death. But by then his world had crumbled about him.

After several separations, his wife had broken with him completely, taking with her their only daughter, Lydia, whom he adored. The financial arrangements he made for them both were generous, adding to the debts that were beginning to mount. Then, through the carelessness of his curate, the Sutton parsonage burned to the ground, leaving Sterne with the cost of replacing it.

Finally, Sterne's always fragile lungs gave way and he began to hemorrhage. On March 18, 1768, while on a trip to London, he died—alone, far from his beloved Coxwold and Shandy Hall, and bordering on insolvency.

What followed was grotesque. Soon after his burial in London's Bayswater area, the rumor spread that graverobbers had stolen the body and sold it to a physician for dissection. Friends abandoned plans for a tombstone with an epitaph by Garrick. The grave went unmarked for twenty years. And when finally a stone was set in place, both his age and date of birth were wrong.

Today you can visit Shandy Hall thanks to the efforts of a gifted and tireless pair of Sterne enthusiasts, Julia and Kenneth Monkman. The hall had ended its days as a farmhouse, but still had a trace of the literary. The final tenants were a Mr. and Mrs. Charles Smedley, and for thirty years the veterinarian who came regularly to lamb their ewes and treat their calves and sit in their warm kitchen drinking tea was James Herriot. Somewhere in the pages of *All Creatures Great and Small* (1972) or *All Things Bright and Beautiful* (1974), hiding behind fictional names, the Smedleys may live on yet.

But the years had not been kind to Shandy Hall. When the Monkmans came upon it, in 1963, they realized that within a few years it would be beyond retrieve. So they gave up their London careers to dedicate themselves to its rescue, spearheading the foundation of the Laurence Sterne Trust and what has turned out to be a stunning restoration of the house. It is now open to view Wednesday afternoons from June to September, and at other times by arrangement with the curator.

At St. Michael's Church you can see the pulpit from which Sterne preached and the box-pews that, an agent at the time wrote Lord Fauconberg, were designed "on a new Scheem [sic] of Mr. Sterne's [to] give a better Sound and a better light, and," he added, to avoid disputes about who would get the best seats, "they will all face the Parson alike."

Startlingly enough, you also can see Sterne's gravestone with the famous inscription, "Alas poor Yorick." The Sterne Trust brought it and Sterne's bones to Coxwold after learning that the Bayswater cemetery was about to be cleared away by developers.

On the outskirts of Coxwold, about a mile south of Shandy Hall, is Newburgh Priory, established by Augustinian monks in 1145. It was a favorite spot of Sterne's, and he was sometimes a dinner guest there. In a letter he wrote about it, we get a glimpse of the Sterne family in happier times:

'Tis a very agreeable ride out in the chaise I purchased for my wife. Lyd [his daughter] has a poney [sic] which she delights in. While they take these diversions, I am scribbling away at my Tristram. . . . My Lydia helps to copy for me, and my wife knits and listens as I read her chapters.

One owner of Newburgh was an earlier Lord Fauconberg who married Oliver Cromwell's daughter, Mary, and it is thought the lord protector's bones were secretly hidden in a sarcophagus in the priory's roof. A later owner was a Sir George Wombell who took part in the Charge of the Light Brigade during the Crimean War of 1854, a disastrous bit of military derring-do that profited nobody. Except, of course, Alfred Tennyson who made a mighty good thing out of it.

Just before St. Michael's Church there's a fine old stone inn that would be worth a stop if you were only passing through the village; it's that attractive. But it's more than that. Now called the Fauconberg Arms after Sterne's benefactor, in his own day it was the Belasyse Arms, run by a man named Barwick, and Sterne knew it well. Barwick attended the sale of parsonage furnishings following the writer's death and bought one of Sterne's tables. Given to the Laurence Sterne Trust by a descendant of Barwick's, it is now on display at Shandy Hall.

APPLETON ROEBUCK AND MONK FRYSTON

The villages of Appleton Roebuck and Monk Fryston are just below York, Appleton Roebuck being five miles to the southwest on a small road between the A 64 and the A 19, Monk Fryston fifteen miles southwest on the A 63. Both have connections with major literary figures— Appleton Roebuck with Marvell, Milton and Dryden; Monk Fryston with Victorians ranging from Tennyson to Swinburne and Charles Kingsley.

Appleton Roebuck   Nun Appleton House at Appleton Roebuck was originally a nunnery, but at the Dissolution under Henry VIII it passed into the possession of the Fairfax family, who rebuilt it as a fashionable Tudor mansion. Here in the seventeenth century lived the great parliamentary general, Lord Thomas Fairfax, whose victories over the Royalists at Marston Moor in 1644 and Naseby in 1645 were two of the decisive battles in the war against Charles I. He was the same General Fairfax who had saved York Minster's priceless stained glass from destruction by his own troops.

In 1650, Andrew Marvell, then twenty-nine, came to Nun Appleton House to tutor Fairfax's daughter, Mary, and spent what he called the two happiest years of his life. He wrote some of the best poems of his life there, too, but they were unknown to his contemporaries. The bulk of Marvell's verse wasn't published until 1681, three years after his death, by a woman who claimed to be his widow, but in fact was just a house-keeper. A number of graceful lyrics—among them "The Garden," "The Mower," and of course, "Upon Appleton House, To my Lord Fairfax"—relate directly to Nun Appleton and the poet's delight in its loveliness. There, he says,

> Thus I, easy philosopher,
> Among the birds and trees confer.

An easy philosopher, maybe, but not without the wry wit you'd expect from the author of "To His Coy Mistress." Yes, he says in "The Garden," Nun Appleton's trees and shrubs and flowers are truly paradise, Eden itself, but Eden as it was before Eve came along, and for the same reason:

> Such was the happy garden-state
> While man there walked without a mate.

Lord Fairfax had an even closer tie with John Milton. They served together in Cromwell's cause, in which the poet's pen was as powerful as the soldier's sword. Milton paid high tribute to Fairfax, "whose name in arms through Europe rings" in a sonnet, "On the Lord General Fairfax at the Siege of Colchester," hailing his climactic victory there.

It was through Lord Fairfax that Marvell was appointed Milton's assistant when Milton was Latin secretary of the commonwealth. Marvell more than repaid the favor. When the Restoration swept away the commonwealth and Milton was in grave peril, it was largely Marvell's efforts that saved Milton from prison and possible execution.

Yet another Fairfax connection with literature was through Marvell's pupil, the general's daughter, Mary. She married George Villiers, second duke of Buckingham. This was the Buckingham who not only wrote the comedy *The Rehearsal* (1671), but was himself the subject of one of the wittiest and most devastating pen-portraits ever written. He was the "Zimri" of John Dryden's *Absolem and Achitophel* (1681).

There is even a nineteenth-century footnote to Nun Appleton House. The poet, Sir Francis Hastings Doyle, author of "The Red Thread of Honour" and "The Loss of the Birkenhead," and professor of poetry at Oxford after Matthew Arnold, was born at Nun Appleton in 1810. In his *Reminiscences and Opinions* (1886) Doyle has a curt comment on what Marvell's Eden had become after extensive improvements made by later owners: "An ugly place."

Monk Fryston   Monk Fryston's grand manor, Monk Fryston Hall, goes back to medieval days. In the nineteenth century it attracted a galaxy of literary figures, for its owner was Richard Monckton Milnes, first Baron Houghton, and Lord Houghton was a remarkable man. At Cambridge he was the fellow student and intimate of Thackeray, Tennyson, and Hallam, and, like Hallam and Tennyson, a member of that small group of university elite known as The Apostles. As versatile as he was wealthy and gifted, he won success as politician, writer, and, above all, discoverer and champion of literary greatness in others.

As a politician, he served for years as M.P. for Pontefract in what is now West Yorkshire. He was author of a number of pieces on political and critical subjects, wrote songs and poems, and published his *Poetic Works* in 1876, including "The Brookside" and "Strangers Yet." And the list of writers that he discovered and helped push to prominence would be hard to equal in number or importance.

He joined with Alexander Gilchrist and the Rossettis in rescuing William Blake from oblivion, and was a pioneer in promoting Tennyson, Swinburne, the American Ralph Waldo Emerson, and John Keats. Houghton was not only the first to publicly pronounce Keats a great poet, but his *Life of Keats* (1848) was a landmark and remains invaluable today.

The American historian and man of letters, Henry Adams, was a guest at Monk Fryston in 1862, and left vivid impressions of the hall and its master in his famous autobiography, *The Education of Henry Adams* (1907). Adams himself might almost be called a Houghton discovery, for at the time of his visit he was only twenty-four, the totally unknown secretary to his father, America's ambassador to England.

Of the hall, Adams says:

> Fryston was one of a class of houses that no one sought for its natural beauties, and the winter mists of Yorkshire rather more evident for the absence of the hostess on account of them.

Of Lord Houghton, Adams says, "Milnes made it his business to be kind"; he was a man who was "never like anybody, and his country parties served his purpose of mixing strange elements." Adams could hardly have been more flattering:

> Milnes required a knowledge of society and literature that only himself possessed, if one were to try to keep pace with him. He had sought contact with everybody and everything that Europe could offer. He knew it all from several points of view, and chiefly as humorous.

A fellow guest of Adams was Algernon Swinburne, only twenty-five and also totally unknown, though he had just published *The Queen Mother. Rosamund. Two Plays* (1860). Swinburne, Adams wrote, resembled

> a tropical bird, high-crested, long-beaked, quick-moving, with rapid utterance and screams of humor, quite unlike any English lark or nightingale.

Houghton introduced Swinburne to the other guests as a man who had written "some poetry, not yet published, of really extraordinary merit." From then on, Swinburne held forth well into the night, reading unpublished poems like "Faustine" and "The Ballad of Burdens." Both were included in *Poems and Ballads* (1866), the book that scandalized the Victorians and launched Swinburne on a career that lasted nearly half a century.

Another of Houghton's guests during Adams's stay was Laurence Oliphant, later to become known as author of the satirical novel *Piccadilly* (1865). Oliphant, Adams reported, was a man "with a certain grace and gentle charm, a pleasant smile, and an interesting story." Then in the diplomatic service, he was just back from Japan, his arm in a sling from fanatics' attacks on the British legation.

Adams was in no way exaggerating when he said the purpose of Houghton's Fryston Hall parties was "mixing strange elements." Another writer who found his way there was Charles Kingsley, a straight-laced clergyman, reformer, and author of novels like *Alton Locke* (1850) and *Westward Ho!* (1855). It never occurred, but one wonders what might have happened had the Reverend Kingsley and, say, Algernon Swinburne been guests at the same time. Or even more fascinating, Kingsley and another Houghton favorite, Richard Burton, master of erotica and translator of the first complete and unexpurgated edition of the splendidly wicked *Arabian Nights* (1855–88).

Lord Houghton's mansion is now the Monk Fryston Hall Hotel. It's a good one—three stars—and set amidst its own spacious grounds and handsome gardens.

HARROGATE

Despite upwards of 70,000 people, Harrogate—twenty-two miles west of York on the A 59—rightly calls itself "the town in a garden." Trees, lawns, and flowers seem to be everywhere. Circling the town are two hundred acres of parkland called The Stay, protected by an act of Parliament passed in 1770.

Harrogate's atmosphere now is distinctly Victorian and it thrives mainly as a conference and exhibition center. But its mineral springs long made it one of England's most celebrated health spas. At its peak, the Royal Pump Room alone served more than one thousand glasses of sulphur water in a single morning as people—from Tobias Smollett in the eighteenth century to E. M. Forster in the twentieth—flocked in from everywhere.

In *Humphry Clinker* (1771), Smollett has Mr. Bramble and his party stop at Harrogate on their trip north. Mr. Bramble is not impressed with the waters:

> As for the water, which is said to have effected so many surprising cures, I have drank [sic] it once, and the first draught has cured me of all desire to repeat the medicine. As for the smell, if I may be allowed to judge from my own organs, it is exactly that of bilge-water.

Forster brought his mother to Harrogate in September of 1913, hoping the springs would help her rheumatism, and while there a novel sprang almost full-blown into his head—plot, main character, happy ending, and all. He plunged at once into the writing of it, without the lengthy pondering and planning and replanning that were his habit.

By the following June it was practically finished. But he had no intention of publishing it, or even sharing it with his closest friends. For the novel dealt far too explicitly for its day with homosexual love. It must not appear, Forster said darkly, "until my death or England's." Nor did it. Called *Maurice,* it wasn't published until 1971. Forster died on June 7, 1970.

In his delightful book on Yorkshire, James Herriot admits that Harrogate is actually his fictional "Brawton," and explains why he loves the town so:

> I had a half day off every week, and when you are a country vet living on the job, it is no good spending that leisure time at home. Your clients will undoubtedly come and winkle you out and you can find yourself using up the precious afternoon in calving or lambing. You need a refuge, a hideaway, and mine has been Harrogate for nearly forty years.

A chance encounter with a stranger provided an even greater reason for these weekly visits to Harrogate. The Herriots were lunching as usual at Betty's Cafe and Tea Shop (still in business on Parliament Street) when the man at the next table suddenly came over to ask in a Scottish accent thick as Herriot's own, "Are you George Donaldson?"

No, said Mr. Herriot, he wasn't.

"Well, you look just like George Donaldson," the man persisted. "He was at school with me at Strathallan."

Sorry, said Mr. Herriot. He didn't know anyone from Strathallan, though he had heard a lot about a chap from Strathallan School named Gordon Rae, a veterinarian up at Boroughbridge.

"Gordon Rae?" the man laughed. "That's me!" The Raes, it seemed, had come down to Harrogate for the same precious once-a-week escape as the Herriots.

Thus began the two couples' weekly rendezvous in Harrogate, kept without fail. Even after Mr. Rae's death, thirty years later, the remaining three continued their ritual: meeting at Betty's, then shopping and the cinema, and finally a late meal together.

"Nobody," says Mr. Herriot, "took better advantage of a half-day than we did, because we knew—wives as well as husbands—that another week's hard slog lay ahead."

WORDSWORTH'S YORKSHIRE (1):
THIRSK—RIEVAULX ABBEY—AND BROMPTON

Yorkshire was familiar country to William Wordsworth long before the 1807 visit to Bolton Abbey that produced *The White Doe of Rylstone* later that year. His sister Dorothy had been sent to Halifax (now in West Yorkshire) to live with relatives when she was seven years old, and William had visited her as a teenager. And during their twenties William and Dorothy made several trips into Yorkshire to visit their dearest friends, Sarah and Mary Hutchinson.

Their relationship went back to early childhood. While the Hutchinson sisters and their brother, Thomas, were growing up in Penrith in the Lake District, the young Wordsworth came to stay with their grandfather, a Penrith linen draper. The children all attended the same Penrith dame school and soon became inseparable. In 1787 Dorothy Wordsworth returned to live with her Penrith kin, and the intimacy was renewed, especially when William was there on student holidays from Cambridge.

Even after the Hutchinsons moved to Yorkshire, and Dorothy and

William to Dorset and then to Alfoxden in Somerset, the friendship persisted. When the Wordsworths came back to the Lake District in 1799 to settle into Dove Cottage at Grasmere, it grew warmer than ever, and visits between the two households, separated though they were, became a regular thing.

In 1799, too, Dorothy and William had visited Thomas Hutchinson, who now had a farm at Sockburn on the Yorkshire-Durham border. There Coleridge had joined them on what must have been a heady occasion. The two poets' recently published *Lyrical Ballads* had England's critics in tumult.

Thus, when William and Dorothy set forth one day in early October of 1802 for Brompton,[4] a village near Scarborough and the Yorkshire coast, they weren't exploring new territory. This trip was hardly routine. Mary Hutchinson was housekeeper for her uncle in Brompton, and William had at last decided to marry her.

The route, via Thirsk past Rievaulx Abbey and the Hambleton Hills, was a familiar one, largely along what are now the A 684 and A 170. Dorothy and William had even walked it several times, though the distance was over a hundred miles. For the Wordsworths were prodigious walkers. On just such a ramble in 1797 with Coleridge, the two poets had created the basic framework of *The Rime of the Ancient Mariner* (1798) while they walked and talked. On a similar outing with Dorothy in 1798, while strolling from the abbey ruins in Wales down to Bristol, William had composed the whole of his incomparable "Tintern Abbey" in his head—"not a line of it was altered," he maintained, "and not any part of it was written down till I reached Bristol."

For this trip to Brompton, however, Wordsworth treated himself to the luxury of a coach.

Thirsk   Seventy-five miles or so from Grasmere (and twenty-four miles northwest of York) on today's A 170, Thirsk has still much of the charm and loveliness that William and Dorothy saw when they stopped there. The Market Place has the same venerable cobbles. The same narrow little lanes have the same old houses of mellowed brick with undulating tile roofs.

Still overlooking the Market Place and awaiting you, too, are a pair of

---

[4]Once again North Yorkshire tests your mettle—this time with two Bromptons. The one you don't want is just above North Allerton on the A 167.

old inns that the Wordsworths knew well, the Three Tuns and the Golden Fleece. William and Dorothy had breakfasted at the Three Tuns on their trek to Brompton the summer before William's marriage to Mary Hutchinson in the Brompton Chapel on October 4, 1802. It was at the Three Tuns on that earlier trip that they had an altercation with the hostess. For that time they were walking, not riding, which didn't set well with the mistress of the region's leading coaching inn. Dorothy's account in her *Journal* is brisk:

> We were well treated but when the Landlady understood that we were going to walk off and leave our luggage behind she threw out some saucy words in our hearing.

Rievaulx Abbey   From Thirsk, the A 170 climbs eastward through the Hambleton Hills where, ten miles out, off on a side road, are the ruins of twelfth-century Rievaulx Abbey. Even in a Yorkshire remarkable for its old abbeys, Rievaulx (pronounced either "Rivers" or "reevo") is special. The setting alone is breath-taking. You follow a lane beside a little river skipping over ancient rocks, push past a thick framework of trees, and suddenly there they are: the great soaring arches of the choir!

The Wordsworths found Rievaulx irresistible. They had stopped there on their walk to Brompton that July preceding the wedding. Dorothy's *Journal* paints a lovely picture:

> . . . thrushes were singing, cattle feeding among green grown hillocks among the Ruins. These hillocks were scattered over with grovelets of wild roses and other shrubs, and covered with wild flowers.

Now in October, hurrying to the wedding itself, they stopped the coach and were even more profoundly moved. The hour was late, and the magic of dusk was settling about them. Wrote Dorothy:

> . . . far far off us, in the western sky, we saw Shapes of Castles, Ruins among groves, a great, spreading wood, rocks and single trees, a minster with its tower unusually distinct, minarets in another quarter, and a round Grecian Temple.

Next day at Brompton, wedding or no, William found time to write one of his better travel sonnets.[5] He begins:

> Dark and more dark the shades of evening fell. . . .

[5]"Composed After a Journey Across the Hambleton Hills, Yorkshire."

and continues, echoing his sister's words as he does throughout:[6]

> Yet did the glowing west with marvelous power
> Salute us; there stood Indian citadel,
> Temples of Greece, and minster with its tower
> Substantially expressed.

Brompton   From Rievaulx Abbey, Brompton is another twenty-five miles east along the A 170, so the Wordsworths couldn't have reached it until well into the night of October 3, 1802. Since William's marriage to Mary Hutchinson at the Brompton church took place early the next morning, he couldn't have found time to write his sonnet about the abbey until after the ceremony. Excusing oneself from a bride you'd just married to go off and write a poem isn't quite what you'd expect from an ordinary young man. But there was little about Wordsworth's marriage to Mary Hutchinson—the match, the wedding, or the aftermath—that was ordinary.

Mary's family took a dark view of the proceedings from the start, as well they might have. Wordsworth was a man of no prospects, a vagabond who had wandered from place to place for all the ten years since he'd graduated from Cambridge. He had held no regular job nor seemed likely to. He went nowhere without a wild-eyed sister who was overly possessive, even obsessive about him. And the two were just back from a trip to France where they had made provisions for an illegitimate daughter William had sired while there in 1791.

The wedding itself wasn't precisely conventional, either. First, even before they left for the church that morning, William and Dorothy had gone through a little ritual with the wedding ring as if they were the two getting married rather than William and Mary. Then Dorothy got so overwrought with emotion she couldn't even make it to the ceremony, but took to her bed. When the celebrants returned from the church, Dorothy roused herself sufficiently to take over William again, leaving poor Mary to fend for herself.

Eventually things settled down enough so that William could get to writing his sonnet and Dorothy could record the events of the day in her *Journal:*

> At a little after 8 o'clock I saw them go down the avenue to the church.
> William had parted from me upstairs. I gave him the wedding ring—with

---

[6]For another example of brother following sister see p. 349.

how deep a blessing! I took it from my fore finger where I had worn it the whole of the night before—he slipped it again onto my finger and blessed me fervently.

I kept myself as quiet as I could but when I saw the two men running up the walk, coming to tell us it was over, I could stand it no longer and threw myself on the bed where I lay in stillness neither hearing or seeing anything, till Sarah [Mary's sister] came upstairs to me and said, "They are coming." This forced me from the bed where I lay and I moved faster than my strength could carry me till I met my Beloved William and fell upon his bosom.

Next day it was off to Grasmere and Dove Cottage and the honeymoon—for William, and Mary, and, of course, Dorothy.

Back in London, the essayist Charles Lamb, devoted friend of both Wordsworth and Coleridge, added a last fitting touch with a sly announcement that he somehow managed to have inserted in *The Morning Post:*

> Monday last, W. Wordsworth, Esq., was married to Miss Hutchinson of Wykeham, near Scarborough, and proceeded immediately, with wife and sister, for his charming cottage in the little Paradise Vale of Grasmere.
>
> His neighbour, Mr. Coleridge, resides in the Vale of Keswick, 13 miles from Grasmere. His house (situated on a low hill at the foot of Skiddaw, with the Derwent Lake in front and the romantic River Greta winding round the hill) commands perhaps the most various and interesting prospects of any house in the island. It is a perfect panorama of that wonderful vale, with its two lakes, and its complete circle, or rather ellipse of mountains.

WORDSWORTH'S YORKSHIRE (2): RYLSTONE AND BOLTON ABBEY

Rylstone and Bolton Abbey are in North Yorkshire's southwest corner, almost at its border with present day Lancashire, Bolton being about forty miles west of York adjacent to the A 59, and Rylstone another five miles west on the B 6265. The two also are only twenty miles or so south of the A 684, along the route William Wordsworth took so often both before and after his marriage to Mary Hutchinson, when he journeyed to see Mary's kin in the Scarborough area or her brother, Thomas, up at Sockburn-on-Tees.

But it wasn't until 1807 that he actually visited Rylstone and the abbey. There he found a bonanza: a setting that stimulated him, and a trio of romantic stories. Two poems resulted, one being *The White Doe of Rylstone*, which ran over 1,980 lines and was his most ambitious attempt to match the reigning king of the historical ballad, Sir Walter Scott.

He came to the region especially to see Bolton Abbey. Actually a priory rather than an abbey,[7] and correctly called such in *The White Doe of Rylstone*, the Augustinian monastery was originally established by the de Romilly family about 1120 at Embsay, a few miles away. But in 1151, in memory of a son drowned in the River Wharf, the founder's daughter, Lady Alice de Romilly, had the priory re-established on a bend of the river at Bolton. In Lady Alice, Wordsworth found story Number One, and uses it in both "The Force of Prayer" and *The White Doe.*

Stories Two and Three came from events connected with Henry VIII's destruction of the monasteries during the Dissolution of 1536-1539. Henry was particularly harsh on Yorkshire. Because the monks there defied him he reduced some of their monasteries to rubble.

Bolton Priory was more fortunate. Henry spared its chapel, for it had served as the area's parish church since 1170 and the king allowed the people to keep it for that purpose. The happy accident of the chapel's survival is central in stories Two and Three, both based on putative history.

Early in the reign of Henry's daughter, Elizabeth I, Richard Norton, lord of Rylstone Hall near the chapel, took part in the Catholic rebellion against Elizabeth. All his sons but the eldest, Francis, joined him—and all perished in the vain endeavor. Nor was Francis spared. Enemies hunted him down and killed him at Rylstone. When faithful retainers came upon his body, they buried it at Bolton Priory.

Wordsworth found this story in a collection of old poems called *Reliques of Ancient English Poetry*, published by Bishop Thomas Percy in 1765, and *The White Doe* tells it in considerable detail. Story Number Three is really a continuation of the Norton story, based on a local legend. After Francis's burial, so the tale goes, his sister, Lady Emily, came regularly to mourn at his graveside at Bolton Priory, accompanied always by a white doe that had been her pet in happier days.

Even after Lady Emily's own death, the doe maintains the vigil, coming over on her own from Rylstone each Sunday, in the words of Wordsworth's poem, to the

---

[7]A priory was the lesser of the two, the off-shoot of an abbey and usually dependent upon it.

> . . . Chapel, like a wild-bird's nest,
> Closely embowered and trimly drest;

where

> . . . Thither young and old repair,
> This Sabbath-day, for praise and prayer.

While the people worship in the chapel, the doe

> Beside the ridge of a grassy grave
> In quietness she lays her down.

Then, the service over, the people go their several ways and the doe goes promptly back to Rylstone, all to wait the coming of next Sunday.

Wordsworth weaves into *The White Doe* the story of Lady Alice de Romilly (Aäliza in the poem) and her unremitting grief for her drowned son:

> When Lady Aäliza mourned
> Her son and felt in her despair
> The pang of unavailing prayer.

But the poet gives a fuller treatment of her story in "The Force of Prayer," also written in 1807. It's a good story, and he tells it well enough, although perhaps a bit too melodramatically. The tragedy occurred at a point above Bolton Priory where the Wharf river narrows to go boiling through a steep, rocky chasm, four to six feet wide, called in Yorkshire, a strid. Here's Wordsworth's version:

> Young Romilly through Barden Woods
> Is ranging high and low:
> And holds a greyhound in a leash,
> To let slip upon buck or doe.

> The pair have reached that fearful chasm,
> How tempting to bestride!
> For lordly Wharf is there pent in
> With rocks on either side.

> The striding place is called THE STRID.
> A name which it took of yore:
> A thousand years hath it borne that name,
> And shall a thousand more.

And hither is young Romilly come,
And what may now forbid,
That he, perhaps for the hundredth time,
Shall bound across THE STRID?

He sprang in glee,—for what cared he
That the river was strong, and the rocks were steep?—
But the greyhound in the leash hung back,
And checked him in his leap.

The Boy is in the arms of Wharf,
And strangled by a merciless force;
For never more was young Romilly seen
Till he rose as a lifeless corse.

Nowadays the nave of the Bolton Priory is open during the summer, and services, open to the public, are still held there regularly on Sunday year-round. There is also a set walk up the river to the Strid. If you take it, don't let the apparent narrowness of the chasm fool you into emulating young de Romilly. The gap is not only a bit wider than it looks, but the rocks can be mighty slippery when wet.

****

After leaving Bolton the Wordsworths went on to visit Mary Wordsworth's kin in the Scarborough area and then her brother, Thomas Hutchinson, in Sockburn, where most of *The White Doe* was written.

CROFT-ON-TEES

In the reign of Queen Victoria, there was a Charles Ludwidge Dodgson, a lecturer in mathematics at Oxford who liked to wear somber black clothing. He wrote learned works like *Euclid and his Modern Rivals* (1879), known only to the academic elite.

At the very same time there was a Lewis Carroll, a writer who likewise lived at Oxford. But he was warm and outgoing, especially in the company of his "child-friends," mainly young girls. "I am fond of children (except boys)," he wrote one of them, "and have more child-friends than I could possibly count on my fingers, even if I were a centipede."

Carroll would don bright holiday clothes to take his child-friends on outings, where he would spin wildly imaginative tales that he would publish later in books such as *Alice's Adventures in Wonderland* (1865) and that were to become known world-over by millions. Carroll also was a gifted photographer, capturing subjects like the Tennysons, the Rossettis, Holman Hunt, Ellen Terry, and John Ruskin.

Dodgson and Carroll, of course, were the same person, though the lecturer in mathematics tried desperately to conceal the fact that he was indeed the author of *Alice*.[8]

Behind these two identities, however, was a third, perhaps the truest to the real person that lay hidden beneath the other two: the Yorkshire lad who grew up in Croft-on-Tees, son and namesake of the village vicar, the Rev. Charles Dodgson.

This Charles was shy, but affectionate as well. He foreshadowed both the disciplined mathematician who wrote *Euclid* and the unbridled humorist who created *Alice*. By the time he reached Richmond Grammar School in 1844 at the age of twelve, he was not only already a skilled user of logarithms but also the author of comic plays written for his brothers and sisters to act out, and saucy verses like "Rules and Regulations," in which he poked fun at his parents' admonitions, including those about the speech impediment he was to suffer all his life:

> Shut doors behind you,
> (Don't slam them, mind you.)
> Write well and neatly,
> And sing most sweetly.
> Learn well your grammar
>
> And never stammer,
> Eat bread with butter.
> Once more, don't stutter.

In 1843, at the age of eleven, Charles had come to Croft from Daresbury in Cheshire, his birthplace. Croft was then much as it is now, a pleasant little village on the A 167 and Tees River, just below Darlington in Durham and forty-five miles northwest of York. Croft Bridge

---

[8]The two names are transparently the same, the pseudonym a play on the given names Charles Ludwidge: Lewis is the English equivalent of the German Ludwig, Carroll the Latin equivalent of Charles.

across the Tees, in fact, marks today's boundary between the counties of Durham and North Yorkshire.

For the Dodgsons, the move was more than propitious. The Daresbury living had provided the barest of incomes and cramped quarters. Now, as archdeacon of Richmond and residentiary canon of Ripon as well as vicar of Croft, Rev. Dodgson had the grand total of £900 a year. And the Croft rectory was charming and roomy. They needed every room; in all there were eleven Dodgson children, four boys and seven girls.

Their house, right across the road from the church, was a three-storey brick structure of simple design, with many windows to keep it light and airy. The grounds were a delight. Tall trees framed the house, flowers and shrubs adorned the front lawn, along with a colorful acacia that was the children's favorite. Out back stretched great gardens, with rambling pathways that Charles used as roadbeds for the toy railway he built.

The railway was but one product of the wide-ranging and unfettered imagination and creativity that Charles possessed from childhood. When he was only twelve and in his first term at Richmond, his teacher saw in him "a very uncommon share of genius," and wrote in the boy's progress report, "He is capable of acquirements and knowledge far beyond his years."

Devoted to his mother, Charles did all he could to lighten her burden by entertaining the other children. He built a puppet theater for them, stocked it with marionettes of his own design, and wrote his own little plays for it, including *The Tragedy of King John* and a ballad-opera spoof of *Bradshaw's Railway Guide* he called *La Guida di Bragia.*

He was fascinated with trains, which were new not only to Yorkshire, but to Britain itself. He spent endless hours constructing his own engine and cars of barrels and a wheelbarrow, laying out his railway along those paths in the back gardens, and building stations, ticket offices, and refreshment rooms. Of all the diversions he invented to keep his brothers and sisters occupied, none could equal the Railway Game he made up, complete with such whimsical rules as: To qualify as injured, you had to be run over at least three times.[9]

For the household's further amusement, Charles began to produce a series of little magazines with his own poems, stories, and drawings. It

[9]The rule book is now at Harvard's Widener Library.

was in the first of these, done shortly after the Dodgsons moved to Croft, and titled *Useful and Instructive Poetry,* that those impish lines about stuttering appeared.

Another of these magazines, *The Rectory Umbrella,* reflects the happiness he always felt when at Croft with his large and loving family. There, after graduating from Rugby, he spent 1850 preparing for Oxford. A poem in the *Umbrella*—a parody of Macauley's *Lays of Ancient Rome* he called *Lays of Sorrow*— depicts the lightsome mood:

> Fair stands the ancient Rectory,
>   The Rectory of Croft,
> The sun shines bright upon it
>   The breezes whisper soft.
>
> From all the house and garden
>   Its inhabitants come forth,
> And muster in the road without,
> And pace in twos and threes about,
>   The children of the North.

Yet another of these magazines, *The Mischmasch,* produced the summer of 1855 while Charles was vacationing in Croft after his graduation from Oxford, included what are perhaps the most profound four lines of English poetry ever written:

> 'Twas brillig and the slithy toves
> Did gyre and gimble in the wabe
> All mimsy were the borogoves
> And the mome rathes outgrabe.

The whole of "Jabberwocky," though, was not published until it appeared in *Through the Looking Glass* in 1872. Alice complains, "It's very pretty, but rather hard to understand." Humpty Dumpty soon sets her right: "Brillig" means four o'clock, "slithy" obviously means slimy and lithe, and anyone who knows a gyroscope and a gimlet can figure out "gyre" and "gimble."

The rectory the Dodgsons knew (now the Old Rectory) still stands, little changed on the outside, but divided into separate dwellings inside. And the children's beloved acacia remains on the lawn out front, thanks to a sort of born-again miracle that gave it a new trunk not many years ago, just when people began to think it was dying. Much of the splendid gardens in the back, though, have given way to new houses.

Across the street from Rev. Dodgson's Church of St. Peter's, protected by an iron fence is the grave the archdeacon shares with his wife.[10] Inside the church there's a bronze tablet in his son's honor and the hourglass that young Charles used to gaze at longingly during his father's often interminable sermons. If you'd like to take a peek you can arrange (on a weekday), in advance, to get the key from the verger who lives nearby.

Also inside the church is the enormous, red-curtained pew of the Milbanke family. Towering almost to the ceiling and reached only by a winding flight of stairs, it overwhelms the whole north side of the nave.

Here Lord Byron worshipped—if you can use the word worship for an activity of Byron's—while honeymooning with Annabella Milbanke at Halnaby Hall in 1815. Halnaby (pronounced "Hannaby") is two miles off the highway that passes through Croft (the A 167), on the Middleton-Tyas Road. The hall has vanished, but its two sets of gates, situated a mile apart from each other, remain, and the gatehouses are lived in.

Back on the highway, on the corner where the Middleton-Tyas Road begins, a solitary building boldly proclaims itself to be the Croft Spa Hotel. And a good thing it does. It's the only notice of any size that indicates where you are. Without it, the village is so small you could roar right through it and never know you'd been to Croft.

Long past its days of glory, the hotel was well-known to both young Charles Dodgson and his father, and is still there to bid you a warm welcome. In its heyday the Croft Spa Hotel thrived on visitors who came from everywhere for the restorative waters of its sulphur springs, and was one of the north's notable coaching inns.

Charles loved Croft, and during his dual careers as mathematician and whimsical writer he returned to it again and again until his father died in 1868 and the rectory passed into other hands. "Solitude," a poem he wrote in 1853, tells why:

> I'd give all wealth that years have piled
> The slow result of Life's decay,
> To be once more a little child
> For one bright summer-day.

---

[10]"Lewis Carroll" is buried in Guildford, Surrey, where he died in 1898.

RICHMOND

It was natural that the Charles Ludwidge Dodgson, who was to become famous as Lewis Carroll, should get his first education at Richmond Grammar School. After all, it was not only close to his home at Croft, but his father was archdeacon of Richmond as well as vicar of Croft. Charles went there at twelve, in 1844, and stayed for eighteen months in all, leaving at Christmas of 1845 to go on to Rugby.

For Charles, Richmond was a happy place. His teachers recognized his "uncommon share of genius" from the start. The school provided outlets for both sides of his genius, the logical, structured mind that would lead him to become lecturer in mathematics at Oxford and author of mathematical treatises, and the abandoned master of whimsy that led to *Alice in Wonderland* and *Through the Looking Glass*. His headmaster reported at the end of the first term at Richmond: "He has passed an excellent examination now in mathematics, exhibiting at times an illustration of that love of precise argument, which seems to him natural." And the school magazine gave an outlet for his first published fiction, a sensational mystery story called "The Unknown."

You'll be happy in Richmond, too. A grand old market town of 8,000, on the A 6108, ten miles southwest of Croft, forty-five miles northwest of York, it's Yorkshire at its best. On its hilltop stand the ruins of the massive castle the Normans built in the eleventh century to guard the Swayle River twining at its feet.

The heart of the town is its grand cobbled Market Place. And the Market Place itself is a most fitting location for Holy Trinity Church. Holy Trinity is unique among English churches in having stores actually built into its walls. Adding to Richmond's distinctiveness are the twisting alleys and streets called wynds, some narrow enough to dare even the smallest car to get through, some steep enough to test the stoutest walker.

Richmond's castle has its own version of the many legends that have caused Arthur to be called "the once and future king." Local tradition has it that he and his knights still sleep there in some hidden chamber, ready to rise again at the trumpet call should England need them.

Richmond Grammar School and Holy Trinity Church together furnished one of the poets of the so-called "Graveyard School" that began in the eighteenth century with Robert Blair and Edward Young. Herbert Knowles attended the grammar school, and in 1816 wrote "The Three

Tabernacles," better known as "Stanzas in Richmond Churchyard." Robert Southey, then poet laureate, thought enough of it to help young Knowles get a scholarship to Cambridge.

The town also is celebrated in one of the best-known ditties of the eighteenth century, "The Sweet Lass of Richmond Hill." The lass was Frances l'Anson, who lived at Hill House (now flats) and married the composer, Leonard McNally, in 1787.

Veterinarian James Herriot, author of the books and television series that began with *All Creatures Great and Small,* thought Richmond "just about the most romantic and charming town in the country." An anecdote in *James Herriot's Yorkshire* (1979) goes even further in its praise:

Having duly finished his stint on earth, a native applies at the pearly gates for admission.

"Where are you from?" asks St. Peter.

"From Richmond," says the man.

"Ah well," murmurs St. Peter sadly, "I'm afraid you'll not be satisfied with what we have to offer."

CASTLE HOWARD

The lure of Castle Howard, a tourist attraction since the eighteenth century, was enhanced all the more when it served as the setting for the television version of Evelyn Waugh's *Brideshead Revisited* (1945) in 1981. Since then visitors have delighted in coming upon a room, a patio, a fountain that they remember from the film.

Located just off the A 64, four and a half miles southwest of Malton and fifteen miles northeast of York, the castle rises from magnificent parklands and is visible for miles. It has belonged to the Howard family since 1571.[11] The palatial structure you see now, however, was begun in 1699 by Charles Howard, third earl of Carlisle, to replace the one severely damaged by fire in 1693. Today's edifice isn't really a castle at all, but a mansion designed by Sir John Vanbrugh, the dramatist-architect who fellow architects wished had stuck to writing plays like *The Provok'd Wife* (1697).

---

[11]A far-flung family prominent throughout English history, the Howards were originally pig farmers, "hog-wards," a term which developed into "Howard."

The novelist Horace Walpole, who visited it a few years after its completion, described what Vanbrugh had wrought:

> At one view, one sees a palace . . . town . . . fortified city . . . temples . . . woods . . . and the noblest lawn in the world fenced in by half the horizon.

The mausoleum, moreover, said Walpole, would "tempt one to be buried alive."

The fifth earl of Carlisle, Frederick Howard, was a diplomat of stature. Lord North dispatched him before the American Revolution to try to effect reconciliation with the colonists, and from 1780 to 1782 Howard served with distinction as viceroy to India. He was a writer, too, and a good one. A number of his poems and two tragedies *The Father's Revenge* [1793] and *The Stepmother* [1806] won high praise from his contemporaries, among them Walpole and Dr. Johnson.

This Lord Carlisle is remembered today even more importantly as one of the major victims of Byron's wrath in *English Bards and Scotch Reviewers* (1809). Carlisle's mother had been the daughter of the fourth Lord Byron, and when the poet became the sixth Lord Byron while yet a boy, Carlisle was named his chancery guardian.

After Byron's half-sister, Augusta, paid a visit to Castle Howard in 1804, the poet wrote her:

> I am glad to hear . . . you like Castle Howard so well . . . and that Lord Carlisle is much more amiable than he has been represented to me.

The truth is, however, that Byron could not stand his guardian or his literary pretensions. His attack on Carlisle in *English Bards* is scathing:

> No muse will cheer, with renovating smile
> The paralytic puling of CARLISLE
> The puny schoolboy and his early lay
> Men pardon if his follies pass away;
> But who forgives the Senior's ceaseless verse,
> Whose hairs grow hoary as his rhymes grow worse?

Castle Howard is open to the public, Easter to October, for a goodly fee, and ranks high among the stately homes that have practically become an industry. On view are the expected great halls, magnificent rooms, fine paintings, furniture, and furnishings. In addition, there's an impressive collection of historic costumes and other attractions that can keep you all day—if you want to be kept, that is.

SCARBOROUGH AND WHITBY

For a fitting finale to your tour of North Yorkshire, you couldn't do better than have a look at its eastern coast. Fronting the North Sea and stretching forty-five miles or more—from Filey in the south near the border with Humberside to Staithes at the gateway to Cleveland—its towns and villages offer a wide range of interests.

Chief among these between Filey and Staithes are Scarborough, Robin Hood's Bay, and Whitby. Filey has six miles of sandy beach, and is the terminal of the Cleveland Way Walk, second largest in Britain, originating at Helmsley and taking you through the heart of the glorious North Yorkshire moors.

Scarborough is one of the largest seaside resorts on the whole eastern coast. Much smaller Robin Hood's Bay has ageless charm and a main street that seems to plunge right into the sea. It got its name, some say, because the outlaw once kept a couple of boats there in case he required a quick getaway by water. Why he would need to do so that far from the clutches of the sheriff of Nottingham, however, remains a mystery.

Whitby still smacks of the great whaling center it once was. And Staithes is what you dream an old seaside village should be: a tiny harbor enfolded by cliffs, picturesque fishermen's houses clinging to their steep sides, and little fishing boats bobbing below almost at their doorsteps.

Scarborough and Whitby have considerable literary interest, too. Scarborough—forty miles northeast of York on the A 165 among other highways—has associations with Tobias Smollett, Richard Brinsley Sheridan, the Brontës, George Eliot, all three Sitwells, and the modern playwright, Alan Ayckbourne. Whitby, twenty miles north of Scarborough, where the A 171 meets the A 174 can boast of Mrs. Gaskell, Charles Dickens, Leo Walmsley, George du Maurier, and Bram Stoker.

Scarborough   Today Scarborough is a bit on the tawdry side, the victim of its success in attracting tourists. It's too big (45,000) and too crowded with visitors jostling for position on the beach in hopes of getting enough sunbathing to convince their friends back home they've had a wonderful two weeks' holiday at the shore. But the setting is memorable with its two bays separated by the bold, rocky upthrust of its headland, atop which sit the remains of a great twelfth-century Norman castle.

In the seventeenth and eighteenth centuries Scarborough flourished as a spa, and in *Humphry Clinker,* Smollett's Mr. Bramble, stopping by to inspect the magical waters, suddenly finds himself naked and in need of rescue. The playwright Sheridan stopped by, too, and used some local color in his adaptation of John VanBrugh's *The Relapse* (1697), which Sheridan called *A Trip to Scarborough* (1781).

Anne Brontë went to Scarborough as a last wish before dying. She, Charlotte, and a friend took rooms at Wood's Lodging on St. Nicholas Cliff, an area now completely covered by the Grand Hotel, and there she died of consumption on May 28, 1849. She is buried in the churchyard of Scarborough's St. Mary's Church.

The waters also drew George Eliot to Scarborough, seeking to improve the health of her longtime companion—and later, husband—George Lewes. They came in 1864 and were charmed. "Even the sands of Tunby," the novelist wrote a friend, "are not so fine as these."

All three of the twentieth century's most celebrated trio of writing siblings—Sir Osbert, Sir Sacheverell, and Dame Edith Sitwell—grew up in Scarborough. Their summer home, on the Crescent, called Woodland, is now the Natural History Museum.

As for Alan Ayckbourne, he must like Scarborough. He lives there. James Herriot likes it, too, even though he was stationed there as an airman during WWII at a Grand Hotel stripped of all its splendor and most of its comfort. After the war Herriot took particular glee in going back to the hotel to dine in glass-plated elegance in a room that in his day had been only an empty terrace on which troops were trained to use an Aldis lamp.

Whitby   Anyone who has been there at twilight and seen the gaunt silhouette of its abbey ruins high on its rocky cliff and etched against the darkening sky will never forget Whitby. It's old, the Abbey is, having looked down at the harbor and the River Esk since the thirteenth century. But harbor and town are far older.

As early as 657 A.D., St. Hilda founded a monastery there, one of whose members, Caedmon, became the very first English Christian poet. Bede, the renowned Anglo-Saxon cleric, tells in his *Ecclesiastical History of the English People* (731) how Caedmon came to be a poet. As a Northumbrian layman, Caedmon had felt utterly incapable at feast-time celebrations when guests would pass the harp from hand to hand, each singing a song for the others as it came to him. So Caedmon would always find some excuse to leave the table in advance.

But one night in a dream he heard a voice saying, "Caedmon, sing me some." Caedmon demurred and sought to excuse himself, but the voice persisted: "Caedmon, sing me of the creation." So Caedmon did, and what's more, remembered the song in its entirety when he awoke. Bede gives us the *Hymn* that resulted. Written in the West Saxon dialect, it begins:

> Nu sculon herigrean heanfrices weard
> (Now must we praise heaven's warden)
>
> Meotodes Meahte and his modgethank
> (The Maker's might and his mind-thoughts.)

Whitby is much smaller (14,000 people) and more picturesque than Scarborough. It's really two towns in one on their separate cliffs. The old part is on the abbey's East Cliff, redolent of the past, with narrow streets, steep alleys and red-tiled old cottages. It's "across t'watter," as natives used to say, from the modern seaside resort on the West Cliff.

The eastern part was the site of Whitby's great fishing days. James Cook served nine years there as apprentice and sailed away in Whitby-built ships in the eighteenth century to explore the world. During the eighteenth and nineteenth centuries Whitby was one of the great whaling centers of the world, sending as many as fifty ships forth from that single harbor. If no Whitby man ever ran into Captain Ahab and his "Pequod" of *Moby Dick* while cruising the South Seas, he might well have encountered the book's author, for in 1841 Herman Melville was a seaman aboard the whaler "Acushnet" in those very waters.

Whitby has always attracted visitors. Alfred Tennyson, who loved the sea, came to both Whitby and Scarborough in the summer of 1852 and found the sea air helped his hay fever wonderfully. Mrs. Gaskell arrived in Whitby in 1858 to do research for an upcoming novel, staying in Abbey Terrace. She found just what she wanted, and made Whitby the Monkhaven of *Sylvia's Lovers* (1863-4) a novel set in a whaling port at the end of the eighteenth century.

Charles Dickens visited Whitby in 1844, staying at nearby Mulgrave Castle, and when his friend and some-time collaborator Wilkie Collins went there in 1861, he sympathized with him about the awful stage coach trip required to get there.

The novelist Mary Linskill was born in Whitby in 1840, and though her name may no longer be widely remembered, her *Haven under the Hill* (1886) was a Victorian best-seller.

Much better known today, of course, is Bram Stoker's *Dracula* (1897), which Whitby brought into being. George du Maurier, author of *Trilby* (1894) and grandfather of *Rebecca's* Daphne du Maurier, was a Whitby enthusiast and suggested it as an ideal place for his friend, Bram Stoker, to take his family on holiday. The summer of 1890 Stoker did so, taking apartments at No. 6 Royal Crescent.

Stoker fell in love with the town, and wrote glowingly:

> This is a lovely place. The little river, the Esk, runs through a deep valley which broadens out as it comes near the harbour. . . . The houses of the old town—the side away from us—are all red-roofed and seem piled one over the other anyhow. Right over the town is the ruin of Whitby Abbey. It is a most noble ruin, of immense size and full of beautiful and romantic bits.

In addition to being the manager of Henry Irving, one of the most famous actors of the Victorian era, Stoker was also a writer, and when he arrived in Whitby, he was already thinking about a novel to involve a fiendish Count Dracula, a vampire who lived in Transylvania and preyed upon beautiful young women. Stoker had never been to Transylvania, but chose it for that very reason—nobody else had either.

At Whitby, he found not only the leisure he needed to begin his book, but also real life-and-blood characters and romantic settings to enrich it. He found the prototypes for his two lovely heroines, Lucy and Mina, and for Mrs. Wesentra, in three ladies from Hertford who were staying right there at No. 6 Royal Crescent. A raging storm in the harbor below his apartment window provided the suggestion for Dracula's ghostly ship fleeing its fury.

East and West Cliffs, the swing bridge connecting the two sides of the town, the railway station, and the famous 199 steps of Whitby's historic St. Mary's Church provided other settings. *Dracula,* of course, has become one of the world's best-known tales of terror. People still come to Whitby to see the sites described in it.

There are a number of other things of interest to see there as well. Those 199 steps of St. Mary's are depicted not only in *Dracula* but also in Mrs. Gaskell's *Sylvia,* and a cross commemorating Caedmon stands nearby. The house where Cook was an apprentice, marked by a plaque, is in Grape Lane (originally called "Grope" Lane because it was so dark). Mary Linskill's cottage is in Blackburn's yard, off the church steps. Then there are the ruins of the abbey, which would have to be seen even if Caedmon hadn't been associated with it.

Finally, there's a whole tour called the Whitby Dracula Trail, starting at the Bram Stoker Memorial Seat on West Cliff and ending at the 199 steps at St. Mary's. But don't look for Count Dracula's grave in the churchyard, as some do. He not only didn't die in Whitby—he never got there at all.

DURHAM TO THE BORDER

2

Hadrian's Wall in the Second Century:

> Just when you think you are at the world's end, you see a
> smoke from east to west as far as the eye can turn, and then,
> under it, also as far as the eye can stretch, houses and tem-
> ples, shops and theatres, barracks and granaries, trickling
> along like dice behind—always behind—one long, low, rising
> and falling, and hiding and showing, line of towers. And that
> is the Wall!
>
> Rudyard Kipling, *Puck of Pook's Hill*

> In my judgment, a river flowing through the centre of a
> town, and not too broad to make itself familiar, nor too swift,
> but idling along, as if it loved better to stay there than to go,
> is the pleasantest imaginable piece of scene . . . and this
> river Wear, with its sylvan wilderness, and yet so sweet and
> placable, is the best of all little rivers.
>
> Nathaniel Hawthorne, *English Note-Books*

> Carrying coals to Newcastle
>
> James Melville, *Autobiography*

These quotations from Kipling, Hawthorne, and Melville say much about
England's northeast corner and the four counties that comprise it. Today
all we see of the second-century Hadrian's Wall that Kipling depicts is a
lonely, low, abandoned line of stone running mile after mile through
empty fields. Yet it remains a dramatic testament to the area's antiquity
and strategic location as England's northernmost bastion.

The Romans built it under the Emperor Hadrian between 122 and
128 A.D.—seventy-four miles of wall eight feet thick and twenty high,
going clear across all of what are now Northumberland and Cumbria,
from the mouth of the Tyne and the coast of the North Sea on the east
to the Solway and the waters of the Irish Sea on the west. It was supposed to keep marauding Picts and their successors, the Scots, out. Some-

times it did, sometimes it didn't. The Hotspur of Shakespeare's *Henry IV, Part 1* won his first fame defending Henry from those same Scots twelve centuries later. Hotspur was a Northumbrian.

Hawthorne's paean to the River Wear brings to mind the region's many picturesque rivers and the long stretch of eastern coast they pour into. To the south in Cleveland, near its border with North Yorkshire, there's the Tees with its waterfalls and fine scenery. In the north, where Northumberland gives way to Scotland, there's the Tweed. And between are the Aln and the Tyne, as well as the Wear.

All four counties share the hundred miles or more of eastern coastline between Yorkshire and Scotland. Some parts are low-lying and rocky; some, like the inviting beaches of Alnmouth, are gleaming stretches of sand. And some are marked by forbidding, abrupt cliffs and crashing waves like those of Bamburgh, scene of a notable shipwreck that provoked both Wadsworth and Swinburne into poems that the world might well have done without.[1]

Today's cliché for redundancy, "coals to Newcastle," coined in the seventeenth century by the Scottish diplomat, Sir James Melville, reminds us that to balance the empty middle marshes of Northumberland there are the teeming industrial cities of Tyne and Wear and Cleveland, as well as Newcastle, that were flourishing as far back as the days of James I, thanks to the vast deposits of that same coal.

---

[1]See pp. 227–28.

County Durham and Cleveland

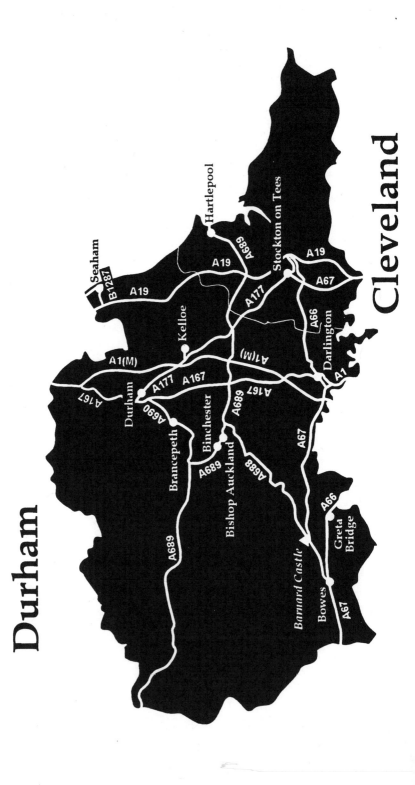

The county of Durham was once populous, but the governmental restructuring of 1974 took away its largest cities, Stockton on Tees going to newly formed Cleveland, Sunderland to Tyne and Wear. Darlington, with 90,000 residents, is now the biggest city. The county seat, Durham, has fewer than 30,000 people.

It's a city, though, that has all you could want as a base for seeing the counties of Durham and Cleveland. Its location is spectacular: high atop a great outcropping of sandstone, with Hawthorne's "sweet and placable" River Wear looping round its feet. Highways like the A(M)1, A 167, and A 177 abound to take you to all points of interest, among them Seaham with Byron and the saga of the mistreated bride, and Bowes with the original of *Nicholas Nickleby's* Mr. Squeers, single eye and all. None is more than twenty-five miles distant, and Durham itself offers much to see, including the final resting place of a renowned peripatetic corpse.

DURHAM

Durham's lofty, rocky perch accounts for both the city's great cathedral and its historic past. On its heights in the year 995 faithful monks at last found sanctuary for the body of their beloved St. Cuthbert, whose corpse they had hauled up and down north England for more than a century to keep it from Danish invaders who sought it relentlessly, not for the hallowed bones, but for the coffin decorated with solid gold.

Cuthbert was a Celtic monk who became bishop on the island of Lindisfarne off the Northumbrian coast, where he died in 687. He must have been a decent sort. His fellow monks decreed him instant sainthood by a unamimous show of hands, and his tomb drew pilgrims from all over England for the next two hundred years. But poor Cuthbert's success proved his undoing.

The pious visitors had so enriched his shrine with their gifts of jewels and gold that the monks feared for its safety, and dug up the body. For the next 120 years the members of their order fled hither and yon with it, often mere miles ahead of the hotly pursuing Danes. Even so, the monks would stop every now and then to assure themselves that their burden was still "incorruptible and sweet-smelling."

Finally in 995 they came to Durham, and safety. Their first simple wooden church to house their saint soon gave way to one of stone, and in 1093 a Norman bishop began building what is now Durham's mighty cathedral. From the start this cathedral was more than a house of worship, and its bishop more than a spiritual leader. It was, as a saying put it, "half church of God, half castle 'gainst the Scot." Durham's bishops were Counts Palatine, bishop-princes with sovereign powers and duties and a palace (the Latin for palace is "palatium") that was really a castle designed to protect the region from northern invaders.[2]

Cuthbert's bier occupied the place of honor behind the cathedral's High Altar until 1540 when it was destroyed during Henry VIII's Dissolution. Then, says Sir Walter Scott in *Marmion* (1808), according to local tradition, the body was spirited away and secretly reburied in a spot known only to "his holiest servants three." Actually, tradition and Sir Walter are more romantic than accurate. St. Cuthbert's corpse was never touched, and rests right where it always did, below the raised site that once held his ornate bier.

Durham Cathedral boasts another distinguished displaced corpse in that of the Venerable Bede, whose *Ecclesiastical History of the English People* (731) has earned him the title of Father of English History. Bede spent his adult life at the monastery at Jarrow and was buried there when he died in 735. But an eleventh-century Durham sacrist, keeper of sacred relics, made a hobby of collecting the remains of the saints. So one night in 1022 he slipped over to Harrow and stole off with the body, which now lies in a simple tomb in the cathedral's Galilee Porch.

One of England's most massive, the cathedral is hardly its handsomest. Writers who have visited it vary in their reaction. In the eighteenth century, Samuel Johnson was struck by its "rocky solidarity" and "majestic vast nave." But the novelist Tobias Smollett, in *Humphry Clinker* (1771), has Mr. Bramble dismiss it as "a huge, gloomy pile" and gives Durham itself equally short shrift: "a confused heap of stones and brick."

Nathaniel Hawthorne, who came to Durham in 1857, was somewhat kinder to both city and cathedral. Although he confessed the building "has not taken hold of my affections," he allowed it "an air of heavy grandeur," and eloquently described the view of it seen from the banks of the Wear—below:

[2]The castle has continued as a residence without pause for more than nine hundred years, and now houses students of Durham University.

We paused upon the bridge, and admired and wondered at the beauty and glory of the scene, with those vast, ancient towers rising out of the green shade and looking as if they were based upon it. The situation of Durham Castle is certainly a noble one.

Among other writers with Durham connections were Christopher Smart, Scott, and Wordsworth. Smart grew up in Durham after his family moved there in 1733 following his father's death. The father had been steward at nearby Raby Castle, and it was through the generosity of the duchess of Cleveland, wife of Raby's Lord Barnard, that Smart was able to attend Cambridge University.

Smart, a good satirist and poet, still known for his *Song to David* (1763), was confined to a madhouse in his later years, but found a stout defender in Dr. Johnson. Said Johnson:

My poor friend Smart showed the disturbance of his mind, by falling upon his knees, and saying his prayers in the street. . . . but his infirmities were not noxious to society . . . and I'd as lief pray with Kit Smart as anyone else. Another charge was, that he did not love clean linen; and I have no passion for it.

Scott was a visitor to Durham in 1827 and shared toasts with the duke of Wellington at a grand dinner staged for the duke at Bishop's Castle. And Wordsworth was honored in 1838 when Durham University, then new, gave him an honorary degree.

Durham remains a city to be seen, much of it still—as it was to Hawthorne—"grand, venerable, and sweet." But the sweetest sight of all may well be the carpark at the top by the Palace Green. That great outcropping of rock which Cuthbert's monks toiled up in 995 still offers a grand view, but there's no sense making it an athletic event if you no longer have to.

KELLOE—BRANCEPETH—AND BISHOP AUCKLAND

Kelloe, Brancepeth, and Bishop Auckland are all within easy distance of Durham. Kelloe is five miles southeast off the A 177, Brancepeth five miles southwest on the A 690, and Bishop Auckland ten miles southwest on the A 689. Each has a tie with a literary figure of prominence— Bishop Auckland with Lewis Carroll, Brancepeth with Tennyson, and Kelloe with Elizabeth Barrett Browning.

Kelloe   If Elizabeth Barrett Browning could visit Kelloe today she might be pleased to see a tablet in the church commemorating her birth. But she probably wouldn't be especially delighted with what's become of the village itself.

When she was born there in 1806 Kelloe was a charming little place, and her parents' house a grand one. Called Coxhoe Hall, it was a handsome eighteenth-century mansion, three storeys high and castellated, sitting amidst one thousand beautifully wooded acres.

But during WWII the hall served as a detention camp for prisoners of war, and then fell into utter disrepair. Now the neighborhood is just another patch of look-alike brick houses in just another so-so village. Today only that plaque in Kelloe's church serves to signify that here once lived the "great poetess, noble woman, and devoted wife" who was Elizabeth Barrett Browning.

Brancepeth   In the nineteenth century Alfred Tennyson knew the old Norman castle at Brancepeth well, for it belonged to his Aunt Elizabeth and her husband, Major Matthew Russell. But he would have liked the castle anyway, for Tennyson loved history, and Brancepeth had history to spare. For centuries it had belonged to the Nevilles, among the most powerful of northern barons. Little of great consequence to England during the Middle Ages occurred without one Neville or another being involved in some way.

Shakespeare uses Nevilles in a number of his plays—*Henry IV, Henry V, Henry VI* (all three parts), and *Richard III*—and in two of these a Neville provides occasion for some of the playwright's' more memorable lines. In *Henry V* it is Ralph Neville, Earl of Westmoreland, who joins Henry before the battle at Agincourt and laments that the king has brought so few soldiers with him to fight in France:

> . . . O that we now had here
> But one ten thousand of those men in England
> That do no work today!

This, of course, allows Henry to respond resoundingly:

> The fewer men, the greater share of honour . . .
> We few, we happy few, we band of brothers;
> For he today that sheds his blood with me
> Shall be my brother.

What makes these lines all the more remarkable is that in real life Westmoreland wasn't in France at all, let alone at Agincourt. Instead, while Henry was off playing hero, Westmoreland stayed comfortably at home, more than content to go right on being virtual ruler of all north England.

In *Richard III* it is Anne, daughter of Richard Neville, earl of Warwick, who sparks the rhetoric. During the Wars of the Roses between the Yorks and the Lancasters, Warwick has Anne, while yet a girl, betrothed to Edward, young heir to the Lancasters' King Henry VI. (In Shakespeare's version, the young couple are actually married). But the Yorks kill both Henry and Edward and install their own Edward IV as king. Soon this Edward's younger brother, Richard, is plotting to gain the throne for himself, and has determined to marry Anne to add legitimacy to his claim.

Shakespeare's play opens at this point, with Richard accosting Anne as she bears Henry's corpse to its grave. Then and there, though he himself was the leader in the murder of Anne's husband (as Shakespeare has it) and her father-in-law Henry, and though Henry's coffin stands before them at that very moment, Richard proceeds to woo the Lady Anne. What's more, he wins her—in a scene so incredible Richard can only murmur at its end:

> Was ever woman in this humour woo'd!
> Was ever woman in this humour won?

Major Russell and Tennyson's Aunt Elizabeth loved Brancepeth Castle and spent huge sums on its restoration. They could afford to, for the major was reputed to be one of the richest commoners in England, thanks to a father who had made a fortune in mining. Tennyson was Elizabeth's favorite nephew. She was the first to recognize the poet's genius, and from his eighteenth birthday on regularly sent him money. When Tennyson married Emily Sellwood in 1850, Elizabeth offered Brancepeth to the couple for their honeymoon. Tennyson turned down the invitation, but was happy to receive it. Tucked inside the envelope was a note for £50.

Brancepeth Castle survives, but don't plan on seeing it. It's on private ground.

Bishop Auckland   One of the sights to see in Bishop Auckland, a town of about 35,000 people, is Auckland Castle. Set in the Bishop's

Park off the market square, the castle and its courtyards and gardens cover five acres of the park, marked off by a fifteenth-century gate.

As far back as the Norman era there has been a manor house on the site, around which in the thirteenth century the original castle was built. For more than six hundred years thereafter, Auckland was, and still is today, the seat of the bishops of Durham. Various bishops added to the castle, and among its distinguished visitors was Charles I, first as a guest in 1633, later as a prisoner in 1647.

However, very little of that castle remains today. In 1647 its owner, a Sir Arthur Hastlerigg, decided to reverse history and convert the fortress that had begun life as a mansion back into its former state. In the process he destroyed much of the original castle.

A nineteenth-century bishop of Durham was an old friend of Lewis Carroll's parents, and the writer was a welcome guest, especially since he kept the bishop's daughter and nieces entertained with stories. In one of these, written in 1857, Carroll made the castle itself the subject. Part prose and part verse, it's called *The Legend of Scotland*—the family's name for the castle because it was so cold and drafty. A typical section was titled "Ladye's History" and began:

> Yn the Auckland Castell cellar,
> Long, long ago
> I was shut—a brisk young feller—
> Woe, woe, ah woe!

BINCHESTER—BARNARD CASTLE—BOWES—AND GRETA BRIDGE

Binchester   Carroll had several other ties with this area, one of them of particular interest. By coincidence the dean of his college at Oxford, Christ Church, was Dr. H. G. Liddell, who was born at Binchester, a village just above Bishop Auckland, and Dr. Liddell had a daughter named Alice, whom Carroll took for a boat ride one day. And he told her a story about a little girl called Alice. The story, of course, became *Alice's Adventures in Wonderland* (1865).

Barnard Castle   The castle, situated on the left bank of the Tees, on the A 688 and the A 67 was begun about the start of the twelfth century by Bernard de Balliol, and thereafter passed through a number of hands. One of them was John Balliol, who in 1291 was crowned king of

Scotland and had to forfeit all his English possessions, including the castle, to England's Edward I. Thereupon the bishops of Durham claimed it and even moved in briefly, but Edward took it back and gave it to the earl of Warwick. Even as late as the reign of Elizabeth I the castle was a source of contention, taken over by northern barons who rebelled against her.

By the time Lewis Carroll stopped to take a look at it, the castle was in ruins, but it provided the writer and his party with a hilarious time nonetheless. They were shown round by a guide who had committed all of Barnard's convoluted history to memory and doggedly persisted in spewing it out by rote. On and on and on he went, allowing his listeners no chance for questions, or even reaction, until they could scarcely contain themselves. Free of him at last, Carroll reported in his diary, they fled to the grounds outside and fell to the grass, shaking with helpless laughter—to the astonishment of other visitors just entering.

Dickens and Hablôt Browne, who as "Phiz" had illustrated the *Pickwick Papers* (1837), came to Barnard Castle in 1838 while doing research on Yorkshire's private schools for *Nicholas Nickleby*. They lodged at the King's Head in the town of Barnard Castle, and Dickens liked the inn enough to give it a boost when he wrote the novel. Says Newman Noggs, eccentric clerk of Ralph Nickleby, in a letter that Nicholas receives shortly after he arrives at Dotheboys Hall: "If you should go near Barnard Castle, there is good ale at the King's Head. Say you know me, and I am sure they will not charge you for it."

Dickens also took special note of another of the town's institutions, a clock maker's shop opposite the King's Head operated by a man named Humphrey. He used the shop for the framework for the miscellany he began in 1840, *Master Humphrey's Clock,* and Master Humphrey himself is the narrator of the first few chapters. And though the structure as such was abandoned fairly early on, Dickens retained the core idea and published the result separately in 1841 in what proved to be one of his most wildly popular novels, *The Old Curiosity Shop* of Little Nell.

The King's Head still operates in the market place, a small but comfortable family-run two-star hotel. And Newman Noggs's cachet holds true: the ale is still good.

Bowes   In 1856 Lewis Carroll stopped by Barnard Castle and Bowes (down the A 67 from the castle) on his way home to Croft in Yorkshire after a summer holiday in the Lake District. His diary's account of what he saw in Bowes is graphic:

We set out by coach for Barnard Castle at about seven, and passed over about forty miles of the dreariest hill country I ever saw; the climax of wretchedness was reached at Bowes where yet stands the original of "Dotheboys Hall"; it has long since ceased to be used as a school and is falling into ruin, in which the whole place seems to be following its example—the roofs are falling in, and the windows broken or barricaded— the whole town looks plague stricken.

The courtyard of the inn we stopped at was grown over with weeds, and a mouthing idiot lolled against the corner of the house, like the evil genius of the spot. Next to a prison or a lunatic asylum, preserve me from living at Bowes!

Dickens found models for Dotheboys Hall and both Wackford Squeers and poor half-witted Smike at Bowes. Dotheboys was not really a hall at all, as Dickens has Squeers admit, but only a "long, cold-looking house, one storey high, with a few straggling outbuildings behind, and a barn and a stable adjoining."

The original of Smike, the tall, lean boy with a lantern in his hand who greets Nicholas at the yard-gate upon his arrival, had been a pupil at the school named after George Ashton Taylor. Taylor died mysteriously at age nineteen in 1822, and was buried in the Bowes churchyard. Recalling Taylor's tombstone, Dickens said later, "I think his ghost put Smike into my head, on the spot."

As for the real-life original of Mr. Squeers, he was a William Shaw, ready-made for Dickens's pen. He had already been hailed into court twice for cruelty to his wards, but continued on his brutal way, apparently unscathed. There's even a memorial window to Shaw in that same church whose graveyard houses the grave of George Ashton Taylor.

Greta Bridge   Greta Bridge is six miles east of Bowes on the A 66, at the junction of the rivers Tees and Greta. Dickens went there in 1838 on the same trip that took him to Bowes, staying at what is now the Morritt Arms Inn, but was originally the George.

Morritt was a well-known name in the area. The Morritts owned the fine old eighteenth-century mansion called Rokeby House, and J. B. Morritt had been a member of Parliament as well as a scholar of classics. Rokeby was made famous in its own right by Turner in his painting, *Meeting of the Greta and the Tees,* and by Sir Walter Scott.

Scott was a friend of J. B. Morritt, and visited him at the mansion in both 1809 and 1812. Out of this came Scott's long poem about the Civil War, *Rokeby* (1813), which includes descriptions of the countryside around Greta Bridge and such appealing songs as "Brignal Banks" (on the River Greta) and "A weary lot is thine, fair maid."

It's pleasant to know that the Morritt Arms today manages to retain some of its old-time coaching inn, Dickensian flavor while earning a two-star rating.

Darlington—Stockton on Tees—and Hartlepool

Darlington, Stockton on Tees, and Hartlepool are all about eighteen miles from Durham, fanning out to the south and east. Darlington, in County Durham, is due south on the M 1 or the A 66. Stockton and Hartlepool, both in what is now Cleveland, are to the southeast, Stockton on the A 177, the A 66 and the A 19, and Hartlepool on the A 689.

Darlington   Darlington's contribution to literature was Ralph Hodgson, who was born there in 1871. Hodgson is one of those poets whose output and reputation are both less than they should be. He scorned commercial publication, preferring to issue his verse himself, sometimes in casual broadsides of one or several poems with handsome illustrations. He was equally off-hand about his career, swinging from journalism and editorial jobs in London to lecturing on English literature in Japan to farming in Canton, Ohio.

When his *Collected Poems* was published in 1961 it contained only eighty-five poems in all. Anthologies keep his name alive with frequent reprinting of the few he is best known for, like "Time, You Old Gipsy Man" and "Eve." But more typical of his fresh lyricism and deceptively simple diction, perhaps, and more evocative of County Durham itself, is the charming "I Love a Hill," beginning:

> I love a hill for in its hands—
> If it's a friendly hill—
> I can get back to magic lands
> Of boyhood when I will

Stockton on Tees   Stockton was the birthplace in 1792 of Thomas Jefferson Hogg. He attended school in Durham, where his grandfather was one of the town's wealthiest men, before going on to Oxford. It was at Oxford, of course, that Hogg won his footnote in literary history. For at Oxford he met Shelley, became his closest friend, and shared with him expulsion from school for their joint publication in 1811 of the poet's *The Necessity of Atheism.*

Their meeting had been memorable. Shelley was having his first dinner at the college dining hall and struck up a conversation with the cool, self-assured fellow student next to him—Hogg. Soon they were animatedly debating the relative merits of Italian vs. German literature, oblivious when dons began leaving the high table and students departed the hall. Not until the servants started to clear their own table did Shelley and Hogg realize they were the only ones left.

Adjourning then to Hogg's room the pair confessed: neither knew the first thing about the foreign literatures they had been so vigorously championing. So they turned to other topics of more interest—science (Shelley was a chemistry fanatic), morality, metaphysics, electricity, the new art of ballooning, and slavery. Shelley took a short break for a lecture, but returned for tea and stayed on for dinner. Finally, with the fire gone out and the candles guttering, they called it a night. That first talk-fest had lasted eight hours.

Their friendship proved life-long, surviving even Hogg's attempt to seduce Shelley's wife, Harriet. By profession Hogg was a lawyer, not a writer, but he did try his hand at writing, including a novel called *Prince Alexy Haimatoff.* His important work is his two-volume biography of Shelley published in 1858. Although Shelley's family didn't like it, it remains a useful source not only on Shelley, but on such friends as Byron, Keats, and Leigh Hunt.

Hartlepool   The novelist Sir Compton Mackenzie gives Hartlepool ("HART-li-pool") such literary significance as it has, and even then he barely made it. He was born there in 1883 of actor-parents who just happened to be playing at the town's Gaiety Theatre at the time. His was a long and active career as a writer, beginning with *Carnival* in 1912, continuing on through works such as the six volumes of *The Four Winds of Love* (1937–1945), and through *Whiskey Galore* (1947), which Americans will recognize (both the book and subsequent movie) as *Tight Little Island.*

SEAHAM

Seaham is in the very northeast corner of County Durham, within a mile or two of its border with Tyne and Wear. For a final word on this literary tour of the county, you couldn't ask for a more dramatic story than the one Seaham provides.

Located fourteen miles northeast of Durham on the B 1287 and fronting the North Sea, Seaham grew from an old Saxon village to a prosperous seaport, shipping coal from the Durham mines. There, in the last years of the eighteenth century Anne Isabella (Annabella) Milbanke grew up in the seclusion of Seaham Hall, a grand house on the bleak limestone cliffs above the harbor.[3]

And there in 1814, at age twenty-two, Annabella brought home for inspection the prize catch of London's highest society—George Gordon, Lord Byron. The wedding was still two months off, but she was already beginning to have misgivings—as well she might.

There was no disputing that Byron was London's most eligible bachelor. He was young, he was titled, he was handsome, and irresistibly charming when he wanted to be. The instantaneous success of *Child Harold* had made him a literary lion at only twenty-four. And now his *Corsair,* just out, had sold ten thousand copies the first day of publication.

But Annabella was no slight catch herself. Her father was Sir Ralph Milbanke, Bart. Her mother was the daughter of Lord Wentworth. Annabella was already an heiress and in line for a peerage in her own right. In addition, she was a beauty, and noted for her perfect figure. But even all this boded ill. Byron had confided to a friend before his first proposal to Annabella, "I should like her more if she were less perfect."

Annabella had rejected Byron's first proposal, and a second that followed, which may well be why they were now, two years later, getting married. For Byron was no man to accept refusal, though it is doubtful that he ever loved her. For her part, Annabella had convinced herself that her cruelty had broken the poet's heart and that he had become a changed man.

Byron arrived at Seaham Hall on November 2, 1814, and stayed for two weeks. His private comments on his bride-to-be and the impending nuptials were sardonic and foreboding: "She is the most *silent* woman I have ever encountered. . . . I like them to talk, because then they *think* less." However, he added, "the die is cast; neither party can recede . . . and I presume, the parchment once scribbled, I shall become Lord Annabella."

And so on January 2, 1815, as he reported in his diary, "the little bells

---

[3]Seaham Hall still stands, now serving as a hospital.

of Seaham church struck up . . . half a dozen fired muskets in front of the house," and Byron and Annabella were wed.

Byron denied to a friend that he married Lady Byron out of spite, because she had refused him twice, or that he had once said in a carriage on the way to Durham that he had wanted to break off the marriage and should have done so. But he added ominously that now she was in his power he "should make her feel it." That he did, promptly and brutally.

The ceremony at Seaham over, the newlyweds drove at once to Halnaby Hall, the Milbanke country estate at Croft, twenty-five miles to the south. Thomas Moore, Byron's biographer and friend, citing what the poet himself had written in his diary, reported what happened immediately upon the couple's arrival at Halnaby. The words are as callous as the deed: "Byron had Lady Byron on the sofa before dinner on the day of their marriage."

With such a beginning, only one significant detail of this marriage could remain to be answered: when it would end. The dates tell how soon it was, starting just eleven months later:

December 10, 1815: their daughter, Augusta Ada, is born.
January 16, 1816: Annabella goes back to her parents, taking the baby with her.
February 1: Byron is informed that Annabella will not return.
April 21: Byron signs a deed of amicable separation.

Byron's very success had bred an ever-growing array of enemies—high placed politicians he had attacked, moralists he had mocked, critics he'd disdained, people everywhere stirred by dark rumors of his relations with his half-sister, Augusta Leigh. Now all rose against him as one.

April 24, London: Hounded by press and public alike, Byron decides to quit the country. So high is sentiment against him, his coachman awaits him outside his house, cocked pistols in hand.
April 25, Dover: Still-adoring young ladies, disguised as chambermaids, throng the hall of his Dover hotel for one last look at "their Byron." But at the dock, he boards his boat between a line of citizens on either side—jeering and shaking their fists.

Then he is gone from England forever.

Northumberland
and Tyne and Wear

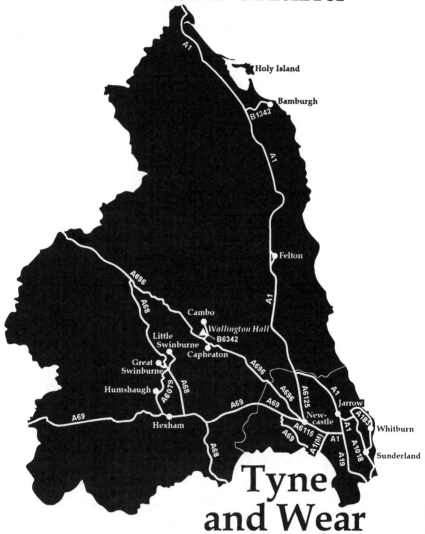

Northumberland

Holy Island

Bamburgh

B1342

A1

A1

Felton

A1

A696

A68

Cambo

Wallington Hall

Little
Swinburne

B6342

Capheaton

Great
Swinburne

A696

A6079

A68

Humshaugh

A69

A69

A696

A6125

A1

Jarrow

A69

Hexham

A6115

New-
castle

A163

A68

A69

A1(M)

A1

A1018

Whitburn

A19

Sunderland

Tyne
and Wear

Even more than the duo of County Durham and Cleveland, Northumberland and Tyne and Wear emerged from the county restructuring of 1974 as studies in contrast—one vast and rural, one compact and urban. Big as it is in territory, Northumberland has only one town of even 10,000, Hexham. Little Tyne and Wear, on the other hand, seems almost one continuous city, stretching from Newcastle upon Tyne to Sunderland.

As a result, you can't just pick some nice, handy spot in the center of the two counties from which to explore them. If you did, you'd find yourself camping out in the wilds of Northumberland's Harwood Forest. For comfort and convenience, Newcastle upon Tyne is probably your best bet, especially if you're coming up from Durham, only fifteen miles to the south.

Newcastle is on all three of the major highways that dominate the entire area: the A 1, A 69, and A 696. Moreover, you'll find the widest possible range of lodgings at your disposal, including several truly elegant hotels. If you'd prefer something cozier and more intimate, however, you'll like Hexham, just twenty miles to the west.

NEWCASTLE UPON TYNE

When James Melville first wrote "carrying coals to Newcastle" in his seventeenth-century *Autobiography,* instead of creating an instant cliché he may have been merely giving a new turn to words of an old Roman poet. Sixteen hundred years earlier, Horace in his *Satires* (30 B.C.) had observed that it was rather silly to "carry timber into the woods." There is no disputing that Melville's version was fitting, however. To give the saying yet another twist, it was centuries of carrying coal *from* Newcastle that did so much to make today's city, with 200,000 people, the industrial and commercial capital of northeast England.

Newcastle indirectly owes its name to the Romans, too; a new castle was built there eight hundred years ago on the site of a Roman fortress near the terminal of Hadrian's Wall. In fact, the easternmost surviving fragment of that wall is at Denton Burn on Newcastle's eastern fringe. Newcastle's contiguous neighbor, the actual eastern terminal is called—what else?—Wallsend.

Folks along the Tyne call Newcastle "canny Newcassel" (their spelling), canny meaning well-ordered and attractive. Well they might, for by careful planning in the years between 1825 and 1840, when much of England was launching into a mad pursuit of nouveau gothic and planned ugliness, Newcastle was constructing a town centre of grace and charm, faithful to a more classic style.

Along the way, Newcastle produced a few writers; Mark Akenside, John Forster, and Hugh S. Scott were born there. Akenside, born in 1721 and son of a Newcastle butcher, became a physician of prominence as well as the author of poems such as *The Pleasures of the Imagination* (1757), in which he remembers his Northumberland youth fondly.

John Forster, Charles Dickens's devoted friend, was born in 1812 and attended Newcastle Grammar School where he showed talent as early as age sixteen with a play called *Charles at Tunbridge*. An editor of several important periodicals, Forster also wrote biographies of Oliver Goldsmith, Walter Savage Landor, and Jonathan Swift, as well as his life of Dickens.

Hugh Stowell Scott, born there in 1862, was a true son of Newcastle. His father had made his money as a local shipowner, and Scott himself early felt the lure of the sea, both traveling and living abroad extensively. Writing under the pen name, Henry Seton Merriman, he enjoyed a considerable vogue with exotically titled novels like *The Slave of the Lamp* (1892) and *In Kedar's Tents* (1897).

Another Scott, William Bell Scott, attracted a pair of writers more gifted than any of the above: Dante Gabriel Rossetti and Charles Algernon Swinburne. Born in Scotland in 1811, this Scott had sought careers as both a poet and a painter, without any great success in either. By 1847 he had drifted to Newcastle as a teacher at the government art school there, and published a five-volume poetic work called *The Year of the World* (1846). The unanimous verdict of the critics can be summed up in a single word: dismal.

Nevertheless the work caught the eye of a Londoner who also wanted to be both a poet and a painter—Rossetti, who fired off a wildly enthusiastic letter insisting that Scott must come to London at once so they could meet. Rossetti can be forgiven. He was only nineteen at the time.

Scott did go to London and the two became great friends. In June of 1853 Rossetti returned the favor, courtesy of his Aunt Charlotte. "Continuing illness," he had assured her, made it imperative that he have the benefits of sea air and bathing. Newcastle, of course, happened to have both. So off Rossetti went, with not only £12 of Aunt Charlotte's money, but also her carpet bag.

A couple of days of Newcastle, however, proved all that he could take. "A rather dreary place," he wrote his mother. The weather, he said, was not very good, and he added, "I find the general stagnation too like the spirit of Banquo." After just two days he set off with Scott on a painting trip, the need for sea air and bathing apparently forgotten.

That was the same year Scott first met a promising sixteen-year-old named Swinburne while decorating a mansion near the boy's grandfather's estate at Capheaton. In later years, the two were drawn to each other and Swinburne visited Scott at Newcastle several times. Scott thought the poet an odd little fellow, overly idle—yet with his pockets invariably stuffed with manuscripts. Even so, he found Swinburne irresistible. "Like champagne," Scott said of him, "or a ray of sunlight."

By the way, should you decide to make Newcastle your headquarters for a tour of the two counties, you're in for a special treat—if you like bagpipes, that is. In Black Gate, once part of the "new" castle, the city has the world's only bagpipe museum.

JARROW—WHITBURN—AND SUNDERLAND

Stringing out from Newcastle to the east and southeast in Tyne and Wear are Jarrow, Whitburn, and Sunderland. Jarrow, six miles east of Newcastle and just beyond Wallsend, is on the A 1. Whitburn, a small coastal town on the A 183, is five miles below Jarrow. And Sunderland, also on the coast, is another four miles south of Whitburn on the A 1018 and the A 183.

Jarrow   Jarrow today is a Tyneside town of 30,000 whose shipbuilders have long been favored by the Royal Navy. The battleship "Resolution," renowned in both WWI and WWII, was built in Jarrow. The parish church of St. Paul, like much of Jarrow, sits amidst the litter of industry, but serves still as a reminder that Jarrow once claimed, in the person of the Venerable Bede, a pioneer of Christianity and the first historian of the English people.

St. Paul stands by the site of the monastery where Bede lived and died in the late seventh and early eighth centuries. It was there that he wrote his *Ecclesiastical History of the English People* (731). And it was there that he lay buried from his death in 735 until 1022 when the zealous sacrist of Durham whisked him off one night to what the sacrist, at least, presumed were more prestigious quarters at Durham Cathedral. Part of today's St. Paul's dates from Bede's time, and inside there's a Saxon chair that legend says was his.

Whitburn   The major credit for Lewis Carroll's "Jabberwocky," according to his nephew Stuart Dodgson Collingwood, belongs to Whitburn. The first four lines had been written at Croft, when Carroll was home on vacation in 1855, and inserted in the home-spun magazine *Mischmasch* that he produced to entertain his family.

Some time later, Collingwood says in his *Life and Letters of Lewis Carroll* (1898) Carroll was visiting the Collingwoods and other kin at Whitburn. There at a party one night, to liven things up, everyone was challenged to a game of impromptu verse. On the spot Carroll dashed off the rest of "Jabberwocky."

Sunderland   Sunderland, too, may have a claim to Lewis Carroll, as well as to James Herriot. While on visits to his Whitburn relatives, Carroll would stroll into nearby Sunderland now and again. And there in Sunderland, so some say, he ran into the chief characters in "The Walrus and the Carpenter." Carpenters, after all, were all over the place, sawing and hammering away for Sunderland's shipbuilders. As for the walrus— well, go take a look for yourself. To this day he's right there on display at the local museum.

James Herriot is the lovable Scotsman who became world-famous writing about his experiences as a Yorkshire veterinarian.[4] But it is generally known he isn't really "James Herriot" at all. Truth is, he isn't really a Scotsman either, despite his charming accent. He was born Alf Wight in 1916—at Sunderland.

The accent? The Wights moved to Glasgow just three weeks after his birth, after which, of course, he learned to talk. And the pen name? Says the author himself, "I was writing in front of the TV, watching a football match, and there was the Scottish International Jim Herriot playing in goal for Birmingham City. He had such a good game that I borrowed it."

---

[4]See pp. 177–78.

HEXHAM

The year 1974 was a very special one in the long history of Hexham, and brought a record number of visitors to the town. That was the year Hexham Abbey celebrated the thirteen-hundredth anniversary of its founding by St. Wilfrid. The church that Wilfrid built there in 674 on a bit of land given him by Queen Etheldreda has given way over the centuries to the imposing building that you see today. But the original crypt survives, and inside the abbey you can see St. Wilfrid's chair, on which the kings of Northumbria once were crowned.

Visitors are no novelty to Hexham. It is perhaps the best single vantage point for examining Hadrian's Wall, which is so near you can see it off in the fields to the north of your car as you come into town along the A 69.

Dante Gabriel Rossetti and William Bell Scott were visitors in Hexham in 1853 on their painting trip out of Newcastle. "Hexham especially delighted me," Rossetti wrote home. He recalled later their happy stop at the old, half-timbered White Horse Inn there,[5] and the beauty of the quiet little town from their window seat as he and Scott "sat and looked at the market place from the deep window of an inn some centuries old and talked of friends for one pleasant hour, while sun and air seemed whispering together and the 'hovering pigeons' touched the street."

In Hexham, Scott and Rossetti were in the home territory of their mutual friend, Charles Algernon Swinburne, for the Swinburnes were an ancient and distinguished family throughout the region. Five miles or so north of Hexham, outside the village of Humshaugh off the A 6079 is Haughton Castle, which belonged in the middle ages to the Swinburnes.[6] A mile east of the castle is Chollerton, whose lord in the reign of Henry II was a William de Swinburne. His little Saxon church still stands. A couple of miles north of Chollerton there's even a handful of houses grandiosely called Great Swinburne, followed by Little Swinburne.

---

[5]The kind folks at the Tynedale council told me "The inn hasn't been with us for about a century now."

[6]Restored and much altered in the nineteenth century, the castle is on private ground and not open to the public.

CAPHEATON—AND WALLINGTON HALL AND CAMBO

Only a few miles to the northeast of Great and Little Swinburne you come to Capheaton, Wallington Hall, and Cambo, all with direct connections to the poet himself. Capheaton is just below the A 696, Wallington Hall and Cambo, both on the B 6342, a bit above it.

Capheaton   Capheaton's great house is Capheaton Hall, acquired by Sir Adam de Swinburne in 1274 and still the family seat. The present structure was built soon after the Restoration by John Swinburne, whose earlier support of the ill-fated Charles I had looked like a bad choice, but gained him a baronetcy when that monarch's son, Charles II, was back on the throne.

In the late eighteenth century, title and mansion were inherited by Sir John Swinburne, the poet's grandfather. It was a grand old place, provincial in style, entered through a magnificent lane of ancient trees. From boyhood on, the poet loved it and visited often. He adored his grandfather, too, even though neighbors declared of Sir John, "the two maddest things in all the north country were his horse and himself." Said the grandson: "I don't think his horse can have been the madder."

In his unfinished novel, *Lesbia Brandon*, Swinburne recalls those visits. Capheaton becomes the book's Ensdon and the poet himself is Herbert Seyton. Swinburne, who had especially enjoyed his grandfather's library, has his hero devour its great collection of books with "miscellaneous voracity," just as he himself had done.

Among literary visitors to Capheaton during those years were John Ruskin and D. G. Rossetti. Ruskin came over in 1857, while staying at nearby Wallington Hall, to see Sir John's collection of paintings by Turner. It was during these stays at Wallington that Ruskin and Swinburne first met. They were to become fast friends, though Ruskin always thought a good deal more of Swinburne's poetry than his morals. Rossetti, recognized leader of the so-called Pre-Raphaelite group of artists and writers to which both Ruskin and Swinburne were attached, visited Capheaton in 1860 and thereafter took to introducing Swinburne to his London circle as "my little Northumbrian friend."

Wallington Hall and Cambo   In July of 1853, at sixteen, Swinburne was removed from Eton to live with his grandfather at Capheaton while preparing for Oxford under the tutelage of the Rev. John Wilkinson, Sir

John's vicar. Though there was no denying his charge's brilliance, Wilkinson was less than enchanted with him as a pupil: "too clever by half," Wilkinson said. The boy never would study, the vicar groused, but instead spent most of his time swimming in the chilly sea or riding about the moors on his long-tailed pony.

Among Swinburne's favorite destinations was the fine old seventeenth-century mansion called Wallington Hall, which he'd pass on his way to Cambo. It was the family home of Sir Walter and Lady Pauline Trevelyan, and Swinburne soon was stopping in as often as he could, a pack of books from his grandfather's library strapped to his pony saddle. Lady Trevelyan was intellectual and high-spirited, with a lively sense of humor. Swinburne delighted in sitting under a hawthorne tree on the lawn, reading books like the novels of Victor Hugo to her, or reciting some poem he had just written.

The boy's relationship with Sir Walter was considerably more restrained. Sir Walter, though a talented amateur geologist and antiquarian, was not only taciturn and humorless, but also a rigid Puritan and teetotaler. Once, spotting a novel by Balzac that Swinburne had just finished reading to Lady Trevelyan, Sir Walter seized it and hurled it in the fire. Infuriated, Swinburne stalked from the house. He got even years later by making Trevelyan the Ernest Radworth of *Love's Cross Currents* (1901).

Lady Trevelyan became a second mother to Swinburne, and he continued to visit her almost to the end of her life. Several times he was the stellar attraction at one of the literary fêtes she staged, all four feet, five inches of him standing there in Wallington's great salon, declaiming for her guests in his high, piping voice, his back rigid but his hands all a-flutter. Once his target was Napoleon III of France. Still in existence is a delicious watercolor caricature Lady Trevelyan did of him. Called "Algernon goes to the guillotine," it shows him standing on the scaffold denouncing the emperor even as he awaits execution.

In 1866, as Swinburne neared the publication of his first major collection of verse, *Poems and Ballads*, Lady Trevelyan begged him to tone down some of the pieces she felt would offend the British public. Please, she entreated, make it "a book that can really be loved and learned by heart." She said he had, "sailed near enough to the wind. Don't give people a handle against you now."

But he did just that, providing critics with an excuse for savage attacks that culminated in the vicious broadside titled "The Fleshly School of Poetry" levelled at both Swinburne and Rossetti. Fortunately, Lady

Trevelyan knew none of this. She died shortly before *Poems and Ballads* appeared.

It was through Wallington Hall that Swinburne was introduced to William Bell Scott, the poet-painter, as well as to John Ruskin. Scott, then an art teacher at Newcastle, was at Wallington in 1853 to redecorate the central hall. Scott's first view of Swinburne was a glimpse of the sixteen-year-old standing at the front door.

Ruskin, too, was at the hall in 1853. An old friend of Lady Trevelyan, he had in tow, along with his wife Effie (Euphemia Gray), the Millais brothers, Robert and John. This was the same John Everett Millais, famous painter and co-founder with Rossetti and Holman Hunt of the Pre-Raphaelite Brotherhood, who was to entice Effie from Ruskin and marry her himself.

On a later visit to Wallington in 1857, Ruskin applied himself to the decorations that Scott had left unfinished, contributing some floral panels that can still be seen. By chance, Ruskin was at Lady Trevelyan's bedside when she died, and wrote later that her very last thoughts were of Swinburne, full of concern for how he would fare.

Wallington Hall now belongs to the National Trust. The grounds are open year-round during daylight hours. The house is open April through September, afternoons daily except for Tuesdays.

FELTON—BAMBURGH—AND HOLY ISLAND AND NORHAM CASTLE

For travelers going north from the Newcastle-Hexham area to the northern-most tip of Northumberland and all England, where the county's northeast corner meets the border with Scotland, four final points of literary interest remain: Felton, Bamburgh, and Holy Island and Norham Castle. Felton is just off the A 1, twenty miles north of Newcastle. Bamburgh, on the coast, is twenty-five miles north of Felton, on the B 1342 four miles east of the A 1. Holy Island, off the coast, is five miles above Bamburgh.

Felton   The novelist E. M. Forster supplies Felton's literary link. His Uncle Willie and Aunt Emily Forster lived in Felton's Acton House, and from the late 1890s on the writer spent a number of summer holidays with them. Uncle Willie, he thought, was "intelligent, handsome, amusing," but also "slightly crazy." Among his eccentricities was a demand that his wife always have a notebook by his dinner plate so he could register in detail his complaints about each meal.

Even so, Forster liked being there. He learned to enjoy hunting otters, oddly enough, and picked up bits of background for his novels. Aunt Emily, for instance, is recognizable in both the Mrs. Failing of *The Longest Journey* (1907) and the Charlotte of *A Room with a View* (1908).

Bamburgh   The unpretentious little seaside resort of Bamburgh is proof enough, were any needed, that long before the days of television a simple event could be blown up overnight into a national epic. The basics of what happened here one day are interesting, but hardly Homeric. On Sept. 7, 1838, a luxury steamer, the "Forfarshire," came to grief off the Farne Islands near Bamburgh. Nine aboard survived.

The reporter who came up from Newcastle at first gave the shipwreck routine treatment. But then it dawned on him that the real story lay not in the wreck or the rescued, but in the two rescuers. One of them, the stalwart old keeper of Longstone Lighthouse, was good copy. The other was sensational. First, she was a woman, the old man's daughter. Second, she was a pretty lass, twenty-two and buxom. Third, her name was, of all things, Grace Darling. And last and best of all, she had actually stripped off her *petticoats* the better to ply the oars.

Within days Grace was known throughout England. Newsmen came from all over the kingdom. Artists queued up to paint her portrait. Locks of her hair in seemingly endless supply sold on Newcastle streets for weeks. Ballads of her exploit were sung on London stages, handbills told her tale. Grace was even offered £10 a week to appear at London's Adelphi Theatre herself, but she sensibly refused.

Poets and would-be poets vied to immortalize her, not only the likes of someone called William McGonegall, but also William Wordsworth and Algernon Swinburne, both of whom should have known better. Swinburne's forté is hardly women like Grace Darling, and Wordsworth turns the poor girl into a "guardian Spirit sent from pitying Heaven in woman's shape":

> As if the tumult, by the Almighty's will
> Were, in the conscious sea, roused and prolonged
> That woman's fortitude—so tried, so proved—
> May brighten more and more!

Soon tourists were crowding aboard sightseeing boats to sail up from Newcastle, lured by advertisements like:

A VISIT TO THE HEROINE
GRACE DARLING
The public are respectfully informed The Tweedside will leave Folly Warf, Newcastle, on Whit-Monday at 8 o'clock, having on board an experienced Holy Island Pilot, to conduct the party to that interesting Family whose Names are now Immortalized.
FARE THERE AND BACK, FIVE SHILLINGS

The good people of Bamburgh still look out for tourists. You can see Grace's tomb in St. Aiden's churchyard and visit the Grace Darling Museum on Radcliffe Road, open daily from 11 A.M. on, April through mid-October. If you like, you also can go out for a closer look at the lighthouse. Restored and extended, it still has the rooms that Grace and her family lived in and the tower from which she watched. The lighthouse, in fact, still functions as such. But the crew no longer keep their families with them. Instead, they're relieved of duty every four weeks— by helicopter.

Holy Island and Norham Castle   At Lindisfarne on Holy Island off the wild Northumberland coast are the ruins of the Benedictine priory from whence the monks, in the seventh century, began their long hegira up and down northeastern England with the corpse of their beloved St. Cuthbert. From the time of his death in 687 until then, Cuthbert's shrine at Lindisfarne had been among the most popular in England. But the jewels and treasure left there by the stream of pilgrims, as well as the saint's gold-sheathed coffin, began to attract pillaging Danes in 875. Not until 995 did the guardians of his remains find final sanctuary for them in Durham Cathedral.

Sir Walter Scott sets the second canto of *Marmion* (1808) amid the priory ruins, and his first canto involves Norham Castle, on the B 6470 fifteen miles northwest of Holy Island. Norham was once the most important castle in this section of Durham palatinate, and from the early twelfth century until as late as 1513 played a role in a number of significant episodes in English history.

Norham Castle's interesting ruins are open to view all year long during daylight hours. Lindisfarne Priory can be seen most days of the year, too. And although Lindisfarne is on an island, you can get there in your car via a narrow causeway. But only at low tide, so be sure to check the time of high and low tides in the local newspaper before you set out.

THE NORTHWEST

III

CHESHIRE
TO LANCASHIRE

The ocean, the [steamer] Persia, Captain Judkins, and Mr.
G. P. R. James, the most distinguished passenger, vanished
one Sunday morning in a furious gale in the Mersey, to make
place for the drearier picture of a Liverpool Street as seen
from the Adelphi coffee-room in November murk, followed
by the passionate delights of Chester and the romance of
red-sandstone architecture.

Henry Adams, *The Education of Henry Adams*

Knutsford itself is a little town of many oak beams and
solid brick walls; there are so many slanting gables left, and
lattices and corners, that the High Street has something of
the look of a medieval street. "'Tis an old ancient place," said
the shopwoman, standing by her slanting counter, where
Shakespeare himself might have purchased hardware.

Anne Thackeray Richie, preface to *Cranford*

The aspect of the country was quiet and pastoral. Woodley
stood among fields; and there was an old-fashioned garden
where roses and currant bushes touched each other, and where
the feathery asparagus formed a pretty background to the
pinks and gilly-flowers. . . .

I begged to look about the garden. My request evidently
pleased the old gentleman, who took me all round the place,
and showed me his six and twenty cows, named after the different letters of the alphabet.

Mrs. Gaskell, *Cranford*

"Cheshire takes a lot of beating."

Pat and Leo Bent of Knutsford

Cheshire and Merseyside provided the American writer and historian
Henry Adams with his first glimpse of England. Adams was the scion of
one of his country's most distinguished families, descendent of two of its

233

first presidents. But in 1858 he was also only a bright, impressionable young twenty-year old, overwhelmed by a world so different from his native Massachusetts and by its violent contrasts.

Those contrasts remain—the murk of Merseyside's Liverpool, the romance of Cheshire's Chester—though less than twenty miles separate the two cities. Merseyside has only been a separate county since 1974, formed of a slender little quarter-moon of land sliced from the coast of old Lancashire, plus a snippet of Cheshire's Wirral peninsula. There is water all about Merseyside; nowhere are you as much as fifteen miles from either the sea or the estuaries of the Dee and the Mersey. And people everywhere—a million or more of them huddled in and about Liverpool. And shipping and docks, too—seven miles of docks in Liverpool itself.

Cheshire, on the other hand, offers variety. It has plenty of water of its own, of course. The estuaries of both the Dee and the Mersey that lead to the sea have their origins in Cheshire. But there is so much more besides.

CHESHIRE

Cheshire

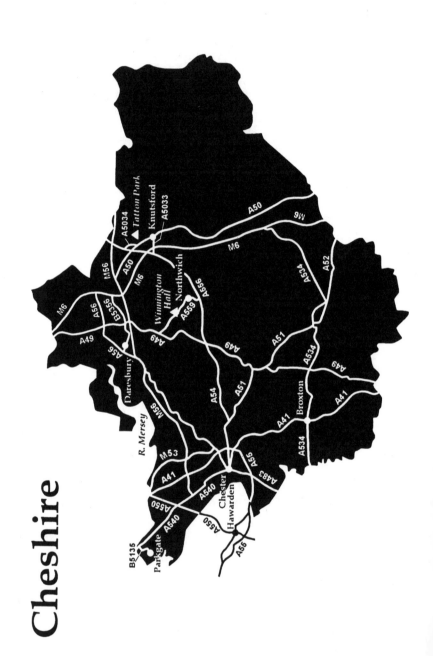

On the west, near Cheshire's border with Wales, is Chester, the best preserved walled city in England. In the east near the Derbyshire line fifty miles away at most are the touches of the wild and picturesque in the valleys of the Dane and the Goyt, and the first hills of the high-rising Pennines. Nearby, too, is Knutsford, the "Cranford" of Mrs. Gaskell's novel of that name.

Central Cheshire is mainly flat, with just such dairy farms as the one Miss Matty's Woodley friend with the alphabetically named cows owned in *Cranford*. From these farms still comes the Cheshire cheese famed for centuries.[1] That same Cheshire cheese apparently gave birth to the Cheshire Cat and his celebrated grin. At one time Cheshire cheeses were molded in the shape of a cat. Would Lewis Carroll have known about this? Yes, indeed. Carroll was born in Cheshire.

There's a neatness, an orderliness, and pride about Cheshire that is irresistible. Scattered here and there are trim little towns with a distinctive black-and-white style of architecture called magpie. And now and then, great mansions like Little Moreton Hall, Tatton Park, and Bramhall Hall. And everywhere are those gardens Mrs. Gaskell so loved, where roses and currant bushes touch each other and form a pretty background.

CHESTER

A wonderful aid to anyone, natives and foreigners alike, touring England in the early part of the twentieth century was Findlay Muirhead's *Blue Guide to England.* Says Muirhead of Chester's unique charms:

> Chester, the county town of Cheshire, with its well-preserved walls, its famous "rows," its quaint timber houses and its fine cathedral, is the most medieval-looking town in England, and should be omitted by no traveller.

Today, as we near the end of the century, his words ring as true as ever.

Chester has been attracting such attention from writers for centuries upon centuries. As far back as the twelfth century, William of Malmes-

---

[1] In the eighteenth century, you'll remember, Dr. Johnson's favorite London tavern was the Cheshire Cheese on Fleet Street. Still thriving, it still serves Cheshire cheese.

bury, an authoritative and lively chronicler born about 1090, was writing of the city's founding by Roman legions in 60 A.D., and explaining that in his own day its citizens "greatly enjoy milk and butter," but "those who are richer live on meat." The late seventeenth and early eighteenth century's most intrepid and vivacious lady traveler, Celia Fiennes, gave Chester its due in her famous *Journal,* which didn't see publication until 1888 under the title *Through England on a Side Saddle in the Time of William and Mary.* Daniel Defoe, too, was a Chester enthusiast in his delightful *Tour through the Whole Island of Great Britain* (1724-27).

Nineteenth-century American writers wrote of Chester in terms as glowing as Muirhead's. Says Nathaniel Hawthorne in his *English Notebooks* (1870), "It is quite an indescribable old town, and I feel at last as if I had had a glimpse of old England." And in his autobiographical *The Education of Henry Adams* (1907), Adams writes similarly, saying of his visit to historic Eaton Hall outside Chester, "the romance was a reality, not a picture."

> Aristocracy was real. So was the England of Dickens. Oliver Twist and Little Nell lurked in every churchyard shadow, not a shadow but alive. Even Charles the First was not very shadowy, standing on the tower to see his army defeated.[2]

Long before William of Malmesbury, Chester was outstanding, as William himself and the very name of the city attest. Those first Roman legions built their settlement on a sandstone spur on the north bank of the River Dee and called it "Castra Devana"—Castra (camp or fortress) on the Dee. Later, as William explains, it also came to be known as Castra Legionis, City of the Legions, because of the veterans of the Julian legions who had settled there.

In their turn, the Saxons of a later date shortened the name to Ceaster, whence ultimately "Chester" and today's nickname for the people, "Cestrians." That original Castra Devana must have been quite a place. Among the sights to see when you're in Chester are the ruins of the largest Roman amphitheatre ever uncovered in England.

From the withdrawal of the Romans in the late third century on, Chester has shared in most of England's historic past. In succession, the British, the Saxons, and the Danes held sway there. In 1070, the Norman William the Conqueror subdued it and gave it to his nephew, Hugh

---

[2]King Charles' Tower is on the northeast corner of Chester's walls.

Lupus. In 1237, Henry III added it to the Crown's own possessions. And in 1301, Edward I went a step further, creating the earldom of Chester as a gift to his son. Ever since, male heirs to England's throne have born the title. Charles, son of Elizabeth II, is earl of Chester as well as Prince of Wales.

Chester's location makes it an ideal base for the visitor to Cheshire and Merseyside. The port of Liverpool, the international airport at Manchester, and the great railway hub at Crewe are all within easy reach. The M 56 and M 53 intersect just north of Chester's city limits, and A-roads come in to it from north, south, east, and west. There's so much to see in Chester itself you'd ordinarily be hard pressed to know where to begin. But happily the city has solved the problem for you. Historic Chester is perforce contained within the narrow confines of its ancient city walls.

Forming an irregular triangle approximately two-thirds of a mile at its deepest, a third of a mile or so wide, and varying in height from twelve to forty feet, the walls are a mere seven hundred years old, built of red sandstone in the fourteenth century on a foundation laid down earlier by the Normans. But for the most part they do follow the same line as the walls the Romans built two thousand years ago. Henry James, so taken with Chester that he incorporated it into his novel *The Ambassadors* (1903), gives a graphic picture of what you can still see today:

> The tortuous wall—girdle, long since snapped, of the little swollen city, half held in place by careful civic hands—wanders, in narrow file, between parapets smoothed by peaceful generations, pausing here and there for a dismantled gate or a bridge gap, with rises and drops, steps up and steps down, queer twists, queer contacts, peeps into homely streets and under the brows of gables, views of cathedral tower and waterside fields, of huddled English town and ordered English country.

Among those "steps up and steps down" of James none are more interesting than the ones at the southeast angle of the wall at Lower Bridge Street called the Wishing Steps. Six short flights of stone steps that lead to the street below, they are officially known as the Recorder Steps, erected, according to a tablet dated 1700, "for the convenience of Roger Comberback, Recorder," as he made his rounds of the city.

But Wishing Steps remain their popular name, and if you'd like to test their efficiency for yourself, all you have to do is make a wish and run from the street to the top, back to the bottom, and back to the top— without taking a breath.

Chester's literary credentials are long, running, as the preceding quotations indicate, all the way from William of Malmesbury in the eleventh century to Henry James in the twentieth. Evidence is strong that among Chester's literary claims is no less than the unknown author of the long fourteenth-century poem *Gawain and the Green Knight*—one of England's first great poets who rivals in skill and sophistication even his contemporary, Chaucer. A delightful put-down of King Arthur and his knights of the Round Table, the poem shows convincingly that its creator not only knew the region about Chester, but also may well have been a Chester man himself. He writes in the Northwest Midland dialect of the Cheshire area, for instance, not in the courtly language of Chaucer's London. And his detailed knowledge of the area around Chester is remarkable, especially when you compare it with the vagueness of his usual geographic references. We can only infer that Arthur's Camelot is somewhere or other in southwest England, for instance. And the early stages are located in only the most general way. But then, suddenly, as Gawain gets to Anglesey off the northwest coast of Wales, within sixty miles of Chester, he begins to handle the terrain from there on with a precision and familiarity possible only to a man who knew the land personally.

Writes the poet:

> Alone went the Knight, through woods and high hills . . .
> Until he had traveled nigh unto Wales.
> Then keeping the Anglesey isles on his left
> He follows the fords that lie on the coast,
> And crosses at Holyhead over the stream
> To Wirral's wild woods, where few could be found
> Who ever loved God, or favored good men.[3]

These last two lines are a sly and decidedly topical commentary on why the Cestrians of the poet's day kept their city walls in such good repair. Those wild Wirral woods outside Chester teemed with criminals and outlaws.

At the very time the poet was writing *Gawain*, Chester had yet another sign of early literary achievement; the notable series of religious plays now called the Chester Cycle were in full flower. Better known as

---

[3]In translating the poet's language into modern English I've tried to retain the flavor of the alliteration he substituted for rhyme. For more of Gawain's quest after he leaves Cheshire, see page 60.

mystery or miracle plays, they were short dramatic presentations of episodes from the Bible or saints' lives. Members of different Chester guilds vied with each other in staging them, each mounting its particular play in the cycle on a huge cart and hauling the cast on selected feast days to various stops within the city walls.

Revived in the twentieth century, the plays are once again being put on by the citizens of Chester at five-year intervals. Each time a different site is selected for the presentation, but it is always still within the city walls.

It was from Chester in 1637 that a young man named Edward King set off for a voyage to Ireland, only to be wrecked and drowned off the Welsh coast. In doing so, however, he gained a measure of immortality. He was the subject of Milton's elegy, *Lycidas,* written that same year, a work that signalled that England was about to have its greatest poet since Shakespeare.

King and Milton had been students together at Christ's College, Cambridge, but there is no evidence they were ever close friends. And certainly the poem's carefully crafted language and involved imagery hardly suggest that Milton was consumed by sorrow as he wrote. As Dr. Johnson said of the poem in his *Life of Milton* (included in his *Lives of the Poets* [1779–81]) "where there is leisure for fiction there is little grief." However, there is no denying its artistry.

Two other writers who stopped at Chester en route to Ireland—both, in fact, did so often—were Jonathan Swift and Thomas Parnell. It was at Chester's Yacht Inn[4] in 1710, indeed, that Swift began writing to his devoted young friend (some say his secret wife), Esther Johnson, the series of intimate letters that were published as *Journal to Stella* (the complete journal was edited by Harold Williams and published in 1948).

Parnell, friend of Swift's and fellow Irishman and clergyman, was a satirist too, as well as author of poems like "Night Piece on Death" and "Hymn to Contentment," good enough to be published posthumously by Alexander Pope. Parnell died in Chester in 1718 while on one of his trips home to Dublin, and is buried at Chester's Holy Trinity Church.

The Restoration playwright Sir John Vanbrugh grew up in Chester, and other eighteenth-century writers with Chester connections were Laurence Sterne and Samuel Johnson. Sterne owed the beginning of his

---

[4]The inn no longer exists but you can have a pint at the pub that has replaced it, the Axe Tavern.

career as a clergyman to Chester, for it was at the Bishop's Chapel there, on August 20, 1738, that he was ordained in a special service arranged through the influence of his Uncle Jaques, a high ranking clergyman.

Johnson was in Chester in July of 1774 on a trip with his friends Henry and Hester Thrale. Mrs. Thrale had inherited property in Wales, and enticed Johnson to join them for a look at it. While at Chester Johnson frightened Mrs. Thrale no end by taking her young daughter, Queenie (his pet name for the child), for a walk atop the walls way past her bedtime, "where," Mrs. Thrale recorded in her diary, "for want of light I apprehended some accident to her—perhaps to him."

During the years 1853–60, when Nathaniel Hawthorne was the United States consul to Liverpool, the author of *The Scarlet Letter* (1850) came to Chester often. It was convenient, of course, but more importantly, as he said in his *English Note-books,* "I love to take every opportunity of going to Chester; it being the one only place, within easy reach of Liverpool, which possesses any old English interest."

On one such visit in 1856 he took along his friend and fellow American, Herman Melville, author of *Moby Dick* (1852), who was on his way to Constantinople. Hawthorne made sure his guest saw all the standard tourist stops, including the walls, the Roman ruins, the cathedral, and the rows.

He made a special point of showing Melville the fine and amusing oak carvings on the cathedral's misericords, those little hinged half-seats on which the monks could semi-sit during the long services. But, as Hawthorne explained to his friend, "if they grew drowsy, so as to fail to balance themselves, the seat was so contrived as to slip down, thus bringing the monk to the floor." No two carvings on the Chester misericords are alike. Among Hawthorne favorites you'll want to search out when you visit are "one representing the first quarrel of a new-married couple . . . Satan, under the guise of a lion devouring a sinner bodily . . . and again, in the figure of a dragon, with a man half-way down his gullet, the legs hanging out."

The "rows" are streets of shops that open onto two-tiered walkways, balustraded and covered, reached by steps from street level. Going back to medieval days, many of the buildings are wonderfully preserved examples of half-timber at its best. Traffic-free, they put modern shopping malls to shame. You'll find them in Watergate, Eastgate, and Bridge Streets. Hawthorne was quite right when he observed almost 150 years ago, "This fashion of Rows does not appear to be going out, and for aught I can see, it may last hundreds of years longer."

Hawthorne and Melville even sought out Jonathan Swift's Yacht Inn in Watergate. "A very old house, in the gabled style," he said, "the timbers and framework are still perfectly sound." Of special interest to the two Americans was the large, comfortable, old-fashioned parlor off a balustraded staircase, on which Swift had eagerly awaited the local clergy he had invited to come and sup with him. They never came. Hawthorne writes of Swift's response, left for posterity:

> . . . on one of the window-panes were two acrid lines, written with the diamond of his ring, satirizing those venerable gentlemen, in revenge for their refusing his invitation.

Thomas De Quincey, Arthur Hugh Clough, and Thomas Hughes had Chester connections, too. De Quincey as a schoolboy, irked by the regimen at Manchester Grammar School, ran away to rejoin his mother in Chester, traveling the whole way on foot with only a penny or two in his pocket. Clough, the son of a Liverpool cotton merchant, attended Chester's King's School before going on to Rugby. Clough has double distinction: he not only wrote fine lyrics himself, such as "Say not the struggle nought availeth," but it was his death in 1861 that moved his friend Matthew Arnold to write the great elegy, *Thyrsis*.

Hughes was a Rugby boy, too, and his famous novel, *Tom Brown's Schooldays* (1857), chronicles the school when Matthew Arnold's father, Dr. Thomas Arnold, was its headmaster. Hughes later became a circuit judge in Chester, and in 1885 built a grand house there in Dee Hills Park overlooking the river which he called Uffington House. Why Uffington? Uffington in Oxfordshire was the village in which Tom Brown—and Hughes himself—grew up.

A Suggested Tour

For a tour of Chester, you can pretty much follow the route Hawthorne and Melville took in 1856, seeing what they saw and adding other sites as you wish.

Beginning at the **Cathedral** (1) at St. Werburgh Street just above Eastgate, for instance, the whole tour can't be more than a mile and a quarter or so, and if the weather is obliging, you couldn't ask for a more delightful walk. And, if the weather *is* fine, take along a picnic lunch. You'll see why later.

From the cathedral, walk down St. Werburgh until you come to East-

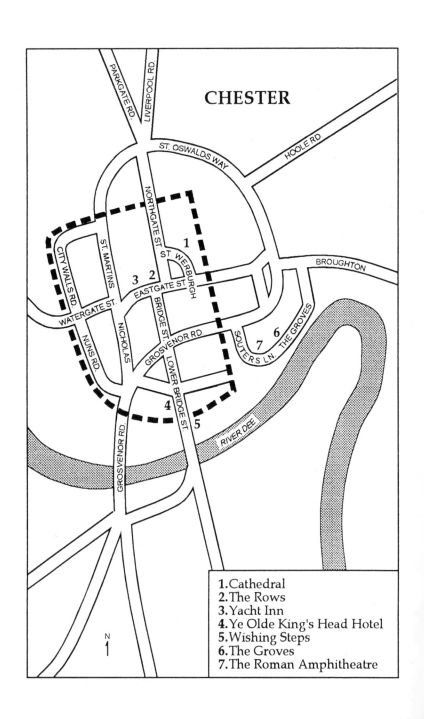

CHESTER

PARKGATE RD.
LIVERPOOL RD.
ST. OSWALDS WAY
HOOLE RD.
BROUGHTON
NORTHGATE ST.
CITY WALLS RD.
ST. MARTINS
ST. WERBURGH
WATERGATE ST.
EASTGATE ST.
NICHOLAS
BRIDGE ST.
GROSVENOR RD.
NUNS RD.
LOWER BRIDGE ST.
SOUTERS LN.
THE GROVES
GROSVENOR RD.
RIVER DEE

N

1. Cathedral
2. The Rows
3. Yacht Inn
4. Ye Olde King's Head Hotel
5. Wishing Steps
6. The Groves
7. The Roman Amphitheatre

gate, then turn right and stroll straight along Eastgate and Watergate until you reach Nicholas Street, stopping and shopping at **The Rows** (2) along the way to your heart's content. At the corner of Nicholas and Watergate is where **Swift's Yacht Inn** (3) used to be. You won't find it now; it has finally succumbed to age and the demands of traffic. But if you'll step into the nearby pub called The Axe, they'll show you photos of Yacht Inn as it used to be, separated from The Axe by a chemist's shop and standing in the space that is now occupied by the widened road.

From The Axe, retrace your steps down Watergate to Bridge Street and turn right. At. No. 50 Lower Bridge Street is **Ye Olde King's Head Hotel** (4), parts of which date back to 1520. It's one-star and small, but there's a historic air about it. It's a three-quartered timbered building where low ceilings call for the caution to "mind your head." A plaque on the wall tells you that the major section was built in 1622 by a Randle Holme, whose grandson, Randle Holme III, was the author of *The Academy of Armoury,* the first book ever printed in Chester.

At the end of Lower Bridge Street, you'll come to the River Dee and, running along its bank, the southern leg of the walls. Here you can mount those **Wishing Steps** (5) for as much of an amble along the wall's paved top as you choose. And, if you feel up to it, you can even race up and down the steps yourself, wishing your wish as you go. Remember, though—hold your breath!

When you're through with the wall, those same steps will take you back down to **The Groves** (6) and a most pleasant stroll eastward through the park along the river, with the ruins of the **Roman Amphitheatre** (7) awaiting you. Finally, ready at last to rest, find a handy bench, take out your picnic lunch, watch the throngs of people as they pass—and think about how happy you are that you came to Chester.

BROXTON—HAWARDEN—PARKGATE—AND WINNINGTON HALL

Broxton, Hawarden, and Parkgate are all near neighbors of Chester. Broxton, nine miles southeast of Chester, where the A 41 and A 534 intersect, briefly but profoundly touched the life of a ten-year-old who, had he lived, might have become one of the great poets of the century. Hawarden, on the A 550, six miles west of Chester, was for sixty years the home of one of Britain's great prime ministers. Parkgate, eleven miles northwest of Chester, off the B 5135, long served as a major port for ships sailing between England and Ireland. As such, it made its mark on a number of writers, the most prominent being John Milton and Jonathan Swift.

Broxton   The poet Broxton affected so powerfully was Wilfred Owen. His idol was a fitting one: John Keats. Like Keats, Owen had a romantic spirit, but controlled by strong self-discipline. Like Keats, his potential was great. And like Keats, his death was all too untimely and tragic. At twenty-five, Owen died on a battlefield in France, one week before the end of WWI.

Owen's brush with Broxton was a fleeting one. Born in 1893 in Oswestry, Shropshire, son of an impoverished railway man, he came to Broxton in 1903 as a ten-year-old on a summer visit while attending the Birkenhead Institute in Liverpool.

The little village utterly delighted him and, boy though he was, he felt himself deeply stirred. Rarely have the pivotal points of time and place in the making of a writer been so clearly marked as Broxton and that summer of 1903 were for Owen. "There," he said later, "my poethood was born."

His *Collected Poems,* of which he said, "the subject of it is War and the pity of War," was published in 1920 by his friend and fellow WWI poet, Siegfried Sassoon. Later editions appeared; the final one edited by C. Day-Lewis in 1963.

Hawarden   Four times prime minister, William Ewart Gladstone lived for sixty years at Hawarden (HAR-den) Castle, an eighteenth-century structure built to replace the original Norman fortress whose ruins can be seen nearby. Gladstone's castle was impressive and its estate a park of singular charm.

Among the guests that Gladstone showed proudly round in 1878 was John Ruskin, then Slade professor of art at Oxford. Theirs was an unlikely friendship. Each man had personal idiosyncracies that called for no little forbearance. And Ruskin's political and economic views—set forth in books like *Unto this Last* (1862), *Sesame and Lilies* (1865), and *The Crown of Wild Olive* (1866)—were usually at odds with those of his host. Nevertheless they got along, and it was a great help that Ruskin was fond of Gladstone's wife and daughter.

Gladstone himself was a writer of some stature. In addition to numerous political works, he was the author of things like *Studies on Homer and the Homeric Age* (1858) and *Juventus Mundi* (1869), and *Translations* by Gladstone and Lord Lyttleton appeared in 1863.

In 1896, two years before his death, he founded Hawarden's St. Deinial's Library, which now houses a Gladstone Museum. The village church has a memorial to Gladstone, too, a stained-glass window designed by the famous Pre-Raphaelite artist, Edward Burne-Jones.

Parkgate   Jonathan Swift was of English heritage, but was born and brought up in Ireland. In adult life he was as much at home there as he was in England. Dublin, in fact, was the center of his career as a clergyman. Beginning in 1699, he was prebend of Dublin's St. Patrick's Cathedral, and from 1713 on, the dean.

As often as he could, however, Swift took himself off to England, and so knew the Dublin-Parkgate crossing well. After one landing in Parkgate, in 1710, he escaped near disaster, thanks to a cooperative horse. He reports it in his *Journal to Stella,* the lively series of letters he addressed to his adoring protege, Esther Johnson. Arriving in Chester, he wrote her, "I got a fall off my horse riding here from Parkgate, but no hurt." The no-hurt, however, was due to the steed, not the rider. "The horse, understanding, falls very well," Swift continued, "and lying [sic] quietly till I got up."

What really won Parkgate its place in literature was not the convenience of the crossing between it and Dublin, but the danger. In a letter to his sister Jane in 1800, the essayist Thomas De Quincey shows he was well aware of this. "We shall sail by the first Parkgate packet," he wrote her from Dublin. "This passage is very dangerous." Violent storms could arise without warning in the Irish sea, and the time of arrival could be highly uncertain. The voyage was "in general not more than three days," De Quincey said, "but sometimes much longer."

Even the waters about Parkgate itself could be treacherous. From time to time great tidal waves would sweep in over the sandy beaches, devastating everything in their way—a phenomenon that moved the novelist Charles Kingsley to write a poem remarkable only for the banality of its title. In *Alton Locke* (1850), his hero, seeking lyrics for a tune that has haunted him, lights upon a painting that shows a girl caught and drowned by such a flood while driving her father's cows home. The title? "Oh, Mary, go and call the cattle home."

Ironically, Parkgate owes its most prominent footnote in literature in no way to one of those great storms De Quincey alluded to. The work in question is John Milton's elegy, *Lycidas,* to his college classmate at Cambridge, Edward King, who drowned en route to Dublin in 1637. As Milton admits in the poem, the weather couldn't have been more ideal:

> The air was calm, and on the level brine
> Sleek Panope [a sea-nymph] with all her sisters played.

What actually happened was all too prosaic. King's ship had departed from Chester and was sailing smoothly along when, barely past Parkgate, it struck a rock and sank.

Winnington Hall   John Ruskin, author, artist, critic, social and economic writer and reformer, was never loath to lend his considerable talents and fortune to the betterment of his fellow man, often with less than the glorious success he imagined. It was this zeal that drew him repeatedly to Winnington where he sensed a kindred soul at work.

Winnington interested him anyway, for as *The Stones of Venice* (1851-53) attests, Ruskin was an architectural scholar, too, and the hall itself was something to see. Located sixteen miles west of Chester, just above Northwich on the A 533, it began 1300 years ago as a hovel a seventh-century Saxon named Wina built there (Wina's "tun," or hut). By the thirteenth century it was a manor of some importance, visited from time to time by no less than the king himself in his capacity as earl of Chester. Thereafter extension followed extension, all sizes and styles, some elaborate and several appalling. By Ruskin's day there had been nine in all, and the hall was an architectural curiosity.

What attracted him most to Winnington, however, was a school established there in 1850 by a Miss Margaret Alexis Bell for the "daughters of the gently born." Miss Bell ran her female academy along lines highly advanced and humane for the Victorian era. Emphasis was as much on pleasure and beauty as on propriety and prayer. "They have morning prayer with only one of the lessons—more beautiful than any ordinary church service," Ruskin wrote his father approvingly on his first visit in 1859, "and [it] must be very good for them, quite different in its effect on their minds from our wretched penance of college chapel."

Evenings everyone gathered for festivities in the drawing room, "a huge octagon—I suppose 40 feet high," he reported, "like the tower of a castle (hung half way up all round with large and beautiful Turner and Raphael engravings) and with a baronial fireplace." Ruskin was entranced: "brightly lighted, with the groups of girls scattered round it, it is a quite beautiful scene in its way." The girls, he added delightedly, "look all healthy and happy as can be, down to the little six-years-old ones, who I find know me by the fairy tale,[5] as the others do by my large books—so I am quite at home."

From 1859 until the school moved elsewhere in 1868 Ruskin returned to Winnington to see his "pets" or "birds" as he called them. He never tired of watching them at their studies, or playing games on the lawn, or at night dancing quadrilles to music by professionals brought in for the occasion. "It was beautiful," he said, "to see the girls' faces round, the eyes all wet with feeling, and the little coral mouths fixed into little half open gaps with utter intensity of astonishment."

Sad to say, even Winnington may not have been as idyllic as Ruskin imagined. At least, not to all its charges. During restoration work years later, a window pane was uncovered with a message scratched upon it: "Mary Summers. My last term. Thank God."

Today Winnington Hall is owned by Imperial Chemical Industries Ltd., and used as a guest house and staff club. But if you'll write in advance and make arrangements with the secretary of Winnington Hall Club, they'll not only show you through, but give you a copy of their interesting brochure, "A History of Winnington Hall."

KNUTSFORD

It's easy to fancy Mrs. Gaskell coming back to see Knutsford today if she could; she portrays it so lovingly in *Cranford* (1853), *Ruth* (1853), "Mr. Harrison's Confessions" (1851), and *Wives and Daughters* (1866). But if she returned via any of our modern approaches to the town, she would grow increasingly dismayed, even apprehensive, as she neared it.

Coming from Chester and Winnington from the west along the A 556 and A 5033, she'd have to cross over the six-lane ribbon of the M 6, filled with vehicles bent on mutual destruction. If she came down from the Lake District and the northwest, or up from London where she was born, she'd wind up on the M 6 itself, desperately looking for the Junction 19 to Knutsford. And if she descended from the northeast and Manchester, where she had lived after her marriage, she'd be on the M 56, equally awash with cars, lorries, and pollutants.

---

[5]The fairy tale was "The King of the Golden River."

But suddenly, as she veered off the M 56 onto the A 50 and reached Knutsford's doorstep, her spirits would begin to lift. For there on the left she'd see, still, great Tatton Park, the "Cumnor Towers" of *Wives and Daughters,* rich in one thousand years of history and magnificent as ever. Once safely in Knutsford, she would rejoice to find so much survives to remind her of her happy childhood there.

Down by the Heath, she'd see, is still the friendly house where she had lived with her Aunt Lumb. Over by the railway tracks, standing and serving yet is the Brook Street Unitarian Chapel where she worshipped and taught Sunday school. And there on Church Hill is St. John the Baptist's Church where, as Elizabeth Stevenson, she married the Rev. William Gaskell. Scattered all about the town are similar souvenirs, immortalized now in her books, that she would recognize with delight.

Time has been kind to Knutsford. It remains essentially as it was when Mrs. Gaskell called it "Dunscombe" in "Mr. Harrison's Confessions" and described it as "a very picturesque place. The houses are anything but regular, they may be mean in their details, but altogether they look well."

Knutsford is principally a two-street town, Kings Street and Princess Street, winding in tandem up a hill and connected by a series of quaint, narrow alleyways. The Danish King Canute (Knute) provided the name when he used its ford to get across Lily Brook on his way north to convince Malcolm of Scotland that paying a bit of homage now and then might not be amiss.

The Domesday Book of 1086 records of "Cunetesford" that it "was and is waste," possibly because its people had given William the Conqueror and his Normans none too warm a welcome. But thereafter it prospered. In the 1790s, a Lord Torrington declared it "a clean and well built, well placed town where the cotton trade brings plenty."

The Industrial Revolution passed it by. Not for Knutsford mills belching smoke and breeding slums. Instead there were simple little cottage industries, making silk buttons and weaving flax, cotton, and silk on hand looms. To this day, such industry as it has is on the light side.

Along the way, Knutsford had its share of notables. Prince Rupert used it as a base in 1644 during the Civil War, and a hundred years later Bonnie Prince Charlie camped there en route to London on his ill-starred attempt to win back the throne for the Stuarts. In the 1730s Clive of India, whose mother was a Gaskell, attended the Allostock School as a boy.

Shortly after Prince Charlie passed through, a citizen of Knutsford made quite a name for himself—or rather, two names. By day he was Edward Higgins, a respected member of the community and a gentleman. But by night, as it turned out, he was "Highwayman Higgins," with a penchant for plunder and murder until the law caught up with him and hanged him in 1767. It was in Knutsford, too, that in 1904 a Charles Rolls met a Henry Royce, with no little consequence to the carmaking industry. During WWII, the American General George Patton, dubbed "Blood and Guts" for his hell-for-leather swashbuckling, made Knutsford his British headquarters and lived at nearby Over Poever Hall.

Colorful as Patton was, he was no more so than two of Knutsford's own: a man known about town as Trumpet Major Smith, who made his small mark on literature, and Richard Harding Watt, who some say left all too much of a mark on the face of Knutsford itself. Smith, a barrel-chested fellow with a grandiose black mustache, was a trumpet major in the army for years. His was the horn that gave the fatal signal to advance at the Battle of Balaclava during the Crimean War, sending his fellow cavalrymen to their slaughter—a military blunder Tennyson managed to glorify in "The Charge of the Light Brigade."

Smith emerged unscathed. After thirty-five years in the military, he retired to Knutsford in 1874, his massive chest now bedecked with six medals and eight additional clasps for valor in battle. The town welcomed him. He became manager of the Gentleman's Club, the town crier, and court crier at the quarter sessions of Chester and Knutsford. His demise was a civic event. Says a recent local history:[6] "He was greatly missed after his tragic death through taking too much laudanum with too much alcohol."

Richard Watt was an amateur architect who became wealthy in the last part of the nineteenth century as a leather merchant in Manchester before establishing himself in Knutsford to put his architectural ideas into practice. And free-wheeling ideas they were, to say the least, filled with exotic touches he'd picked up from abroad. There was the incredible laundry plant that sprawled on and on along Drury Lane, born of a building he'd seen in Damascus and all strewn about with domes, minarets, and towers. And the row of elaborate Italianate houses he built on Legh Road, a wild mélange of circular temples, rustic gateways, turrets, and campaniles that Sir Nikolaus Pevsner in *Buildings of Cheshire* called

<hr />

[6]*Looking Back at Knutsford,* by Kath Goodchild, Pat Ikin, and Joan Leach, which I found useful and interesting.

the "maddest sequence of villas in all England." Of course Watt liked them; he lived on Legh Road himself.

Most controversial of all, surely, is the Gaskell Memorial Tower which in 1907 he set down smack in the middle of King Street. A stark campanile of Portland stone and Cheshire sandstone, it thrusts its way skyward, incongruous amidst the softer, warmer old buildings Mrs. Gaskell loved. Watt wanted to build a new post office alongside the tower, but when the townsfolk demurred, he settled for taking the bas relief of Mrs. Gaskell from the existing post office to join the tower's inscription bearing a list of her works and quotations from Job, Thomas à Kempis, King Alfred, Milton, and Gladstone. In place of a new post office, Watt used the space next to his tower for the Italian-style Kings Coffee House, which became a favorite of visiting artists and literary figures, among them Galsworthy.

Even in their planning stages these buildings in Mrs. Gaskell's honor were not without local detractors. The architect said at the inauguration ceremonies that he hoped they would "forget and forgive" and come to accept his work as a "token of their mutual regard" for the author. But, he went on defiantly, he had found the "best and most unanimous committee was a committee of one"—himself. How anything unanimous could be *more* unanimous, let alone *most* unanimous, Watt never explained.

To stroll through Knutsford today is inescapably to retrace scenes not only from Mrs. Gaskell's own life there, but the lives of the characters she created, as the map for a walking tour at the end of this section shows. Mrs. Gaskell was born Elizabeth Cleghorn Stevenson in London in 1810, daughter of a Unitarian minister. But soon after her first birthday her mother died, and Elizabeth was taken to Knutsford to live with her Aunt Lumb. Mrs. Lumb had been Hanna Holland, and the Hollands were people of consequence in Knutsford. Her house was suitably handsome and spacious, three storeys of Georgian brick. Located on what was then called Heathside (now Gaskell Avenue), it was a delightful place to grow up in. Just across the way was the open heath where Elizabeth could romp and play, and join the throngs at the fairs and festivities held there. In July 1838, as a grown woman, married and living in Manchester, she happened to be back on the heath for one of Knutsford's biggest events ever. "I saw the coronation gaieties [for Queen Victoria]," she wrote a friend, "which I enjoyed because I knew everybody."

Up above Aunt Lumb's house, on Princess Street in the center of town, was where in *Cranford* Miss Matty set up her tea shop in what had been a small dining-parlor in its better days, the boarded floor freshly scoured to a white cleanness and now adorned with a brilliant piece of oil cloth on which customers were to stand as she dispensed her wares from bright green canisters. A very small, discreet sign, "Matilda Jenkyns, licensed to sell tea," was hidden under the lintel of the newly installed glass door. In 1983, after serving for years as a chemist's shop, the building was gutted by fire. But it has been rebuilt and re-opened as offices and a wine shop.

Further down Princess, running off to the left, are Church Hill and Marcliff Grove. St. John the Baptist's, the parish church, is halfway up Church Hill. Elizabeth and William Gaskell were married at St. John's because her own Brook Street Chapel, as a non-conformist church, was not then licensed to perform the ceremony.

Mrs. Gaskell's uncle, Dr. Peter Holland, lived on the corner of Marcliff Grove and Princess in what was then called Church House. His daughters are generally considered the models for the Misses Jenkyns, and he appears as doctor characters in several of his niece's novels. He is the Dr. Gibson of *Wives and Daughters,* for instance, and in *Cranford* he is Mr. Hoggins: "We disliked the name and considered it coarse; but as Miss Jenkyns said, if he changed it to Piggins it would not be much better."

Brook Street Chapel is in the southeast corner of town, across the railway bridge that separates Brook Street from King Street. One glance at the chapel today, and you'll know it's really the one Mrs. Gaskell describes in *Ruth:*

> The chapel had an old and picturesque look, for luckily the congregation had been too poor to rebuild it, or new-face it in George the Third's time. The staircases which led to the galleries were outside, at each end of the building, and the irregular roof and worn stone steps looked grey and stained by time and weather. The grassy hillocks, each with a little upright headstone, were shaded by a grand old wynch-elm.

Sharing those grassy hillocks now are the graves of Mrs. Gaskell, her husband, and two daughters.

Reminders of Mrs. Gaskell are sprinkled all along King Street. Not far above the railway bridge, on the east side of King, is the house of Captain Hill, the prototype of Cranford's Captain Brown. Next, on the other side of the street, come in order Watt's Gaskell Tower and what was originally Kings Coffee House, and then the Royal George Hotel. The George's confirmed credentials go back to the seventeenth century, and its origins may be three hundred years earlier. The "Royal" came from a stay there in 1832 by the then Princess Victoria. Sir Walter Scott stopped there, too.

It was at the George that *Cranford*'s Mr. Peter charmed Miss Matty with a festive luncheon for her friends, Major and Mrs. Gordon, to be followed in the evening by a special program upstairs in the assembly room, where "Signor Brunoni, Magician to the King of Delhi, the Rajah of Oude, and the great Lama of Thibet" etc., etc., according to the great placard Peter had printed, was going to perform in Cranford for one night only.

In her preface to the 1894 edition of the novel, Anne Thackeray Richie, daughter of William Makepeace Thackeray, describes the George as Mrs. Gaskell would have known it, too, except for a picture of Beaconsfield. Disraeli didn't become Lord Beaconsfield until 1876. Says Mrs. Richie of her first visit to the George:

> As we entered the Royal George Hotel out of the dark street, we came upon a delightful broadside of shining oak staircase and panelled wainscott; old oak settles and cupboards stood upon the landings. On the walls hung pictures, and one was of Lord Beaconsfield, one was a fine print of George IV, and others again of that denuded classic school of art which seems to have taken a last refuge in old English Inns. There were Chippendale cabinets, old bits of china, and above all there were the beautiful oak bannisters to admire.

Beyond the George, almost at the end of King Street, is the Angel Hotel. It was at the Angel that the visiting Lord Mauleverer "honoured Cranford with his august presence," and where "his lordship retired to rest, and, let us hope, to refreshing slumbers."

King Street comes to an end at Drury Lane, and there on the corner is the elegant house that was known as the Old Vicarage. Mrs. Gaskell drew on it for one of the pivotal moments in *Cranford*, the scene where Peter's father thrashes him before the crowd that had been watching the boy cavort about in his sister's clothes and pretend to carry a baby. As a result, Peter runs off to India, not to return until the end of the book, when he dramatically reappears to rescue Miss Matty from her financial distress.

After the Old Vicarage, as Mrs. Gaskell says in *Wives and Daughters,* "the little, straggling town faded away into country, on one side close to the entrance lodge of a great park where lived my Lord and Lady Cumnor." In real life, the Cumnors were Lord and Lady Egerton, and their estate, Tatton Park.

Knutsford has several fine, newer hotels, but if you're spending the night and want something literary, either the Angel or the George will do nicely, depending on your style, tastes, and pocketbook. The Angel is small and makes no pretense to elegance, but has retained reminders of Lord Mauleverer's day while adding modern comfort. The Royal George, though larger and grander—it rates three stars—still has an air about it, too.

For high cuisine dining, you might want to try La Belle Epoque Restaurant Français, which took over Watt's Kings Coffee House and added a literary touch of its own. It doubled as Palliard's Restaurant in the televised version of *Brideshead Revisited* that starred Laurence Olivier and John Gielgud.

Either the Angel or the George will do well as a starting point for your walking tour of Knutsford, though the George is more centrally located.

A Suggested Walking Tour

The **Royal George** (1) with its central location makes an excellent starting point for a literary tour, but Knutsford is so compact you can begin anywhere along the way. From The George, go up King to Minshull Street. There on the corner at No. 96 King, on the left, is the **Angel Hotel** (2) where Lord Mauleverer stayed.

Further up King, on the right at the corner with Drury Lane, you come to the **Old Vicarage** (3). Tatton Park (4) begins just above Drury Lane, but you'll probably want to save it for a separate excursion.[7]

From Drury Lane, return down King to Minshull. There turn right and go along Minshull and Canute Place to Princess. **Miss Matty's Tea Shop** (5) was a few steps down Princess to your left, at No. 24.

Now continue on Canute Place to Gaskell Avenue. **Aunt Lumb's house** (6) is half way down Gaskell, and **Highwayman Higgins** (7) lived on the corner where the avenue ends at Stanley Road, though in a smaller house than the one you see now. The current house was built a

[7] See p. 257.

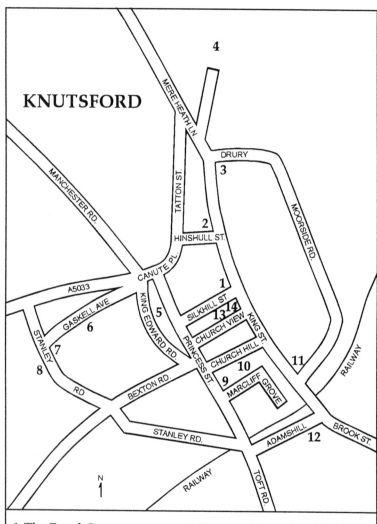

KNUTSFORD

1. The Royal George
2. Angel Hotel
3. The Old Vicarage
4. Tatton Park
5. Miss Matty's Tea Shop
6. Aunt Lumb's House
7. Highwayman Higgins
8. Trumpet Major Smith's Home
9. Dr. Peter Holland's Church House
10. St. John's Church
11. Captain Brown's House
12. Mrs. Gaskell's Chapel
13. Gaskell Memorial Tower
14. King's Coffee House

few years after his death, and Mrs. Gaskell, who had written a short story based on Higgins, knew it well. Her daughters attended the boarding school it housed in her day.

Immediately around the corner on Stanley Road you'll find the home of **Trumpet Major Smith** (8). Now follow Stanley to where it passes Bexton Road. A left turn at this point takes you back up to Princess where, in short order down the right, you'll come to Church Hill and Marcliff Grove. **Dr. Peter Holland's Church House** (9), now known as Hollingford House, is on the corner of Marcliff Grove and Princess, and **St. John's Church** (10) is halfway up Church Hill.

From the church, proceed up Church Hill to King Street, and turn right. At No. 15 King is **Captain Brown's house** (11), which was actually occupied by Captain Hill of the Cheshire Yeomanry. No distance at all below No. 15, King Street ducks under the railway and becomes Brook Street. And there, right where Brook Street begins, is **Mrs. Gaskell's chapel** (12).

With the chapel, the tour is essentially over. Turn around and return up King. Just before you're back at the George, and on the same side of King, are the last two stops: Richard Watt's **Gaskell Memorial Tower** (13) and **King's Coffee House** (14), now La Belle Epoque.

TATTON PARK

Out of Knutsford, to the north above King Street, the A 5034 brings you to the gates of Tatton Park. The grand manor that you see now was new when Mrs. Gaskell used it for "Cumnor Towers" in *Ruth*. Planning for it had begun about 1780 and finishing touches were still being applied in 1811 when she came to live with her Aunt Lumb.

The house is built of local stone, with a sort of "elegant simplicity," in the landscape gardener's words, uncompromisingly classic in design and devoid of fussy ornamentation. The park itself is of vast antiquity. Tattons had owned it in the days of the first Norman kings, and within the grounds are remains of a manor dating from the fifteenth century and the Wars of the Roses during the reign of Henry VI.

The dimensions of the park are enormous, with 2,086 acres in all. It has a drive leading for a mile and a half from the Knutsford entrance to the house, a natural body of water more than a mile long called Tatton Mere, and sixty acres of gardens alone. Sheep roam about at will, and herds of red and fallow dear munch away in their enclosures.

Now owned by the National Trust, Tatton is open to the public and, in addition to the usual complement of stately rooms, fine paintings, and elegant furniture and furnishings, offers facilities for sailing, swimming, riding, and picnics. Both house and gardens can be seen daily at varying hours, April through October. Only the gardens are open during winter months.

DARESBURY

Daresbury is twelve miles northwest of Knutsford on the B 5356. Lewis Carroll was born there in 1832 as Charles Ludwidge Dodgson, third child and eldest boy of what were to be eleven children in all. Their father, the Rev. Charles Dodgson, was vicar of the parish church. But Daresbury was a very poor living, and Mr. Dodgson was hard-pressed to provide for his family. To eke out a livelihood he taught private students and farmed the few acres that went with the parsonage. It was a lonely life, too. The parsonage was two miles from the village and passersby were rare. The children were largely forced to find their own diversions, and early on young Charles began inventing games and telling stories to keep the others entertained.

It must have been a happy day for them all when in 1843, soon after Charles's eleventh birthday, their father acquired the living in Croft, Yorkshire. With it came the magnificent sum of £900 a year, plus a large and lovely house and spacious grounds.

For all its difficulties, however, Lewis Carroll looked back on Daresbury with pleasure. In a poem called "Faces in the Fire," written in 1860, he recalled it most fondly:

> An island-farm, mid seas of corn,
> Swayed by the wandering breath of morn—
> The happy spot where I was born.

And of course there's that other reminder, in *Alice in Wonderland,* of the county in which Carroll was born—he of the famous grin, the Cheshire cat.

******

With Daresbury, you're at the end of Cheshire, with its enchanting old walled city of Chester, quiet little villages, and neatly kept dairy farms. A scant five miles from Daresbury is the county line you cross to the next stage of this tour, Merseyside. And to Liverpool, a modern cacophony, home of the Beatles, seven miles of teeming docks, and a million or more people bustling about.

Brace yourself!

MERSEYSIDE

Merseyside is, in the main, the Liverpool area, the justification for its being separated from Lancashire in 1974 and made into a separate county. Included in the area in addition to Liverpool itself are such immediate neighbors as Wallasey, Birkenhead, Bebington, and Bromborough, all sizable. Knowsley Park, Rock Ferry, and Southport, which rate literary mention of their own, are essentially extensions of Liverpool.

LIVERPOOL

Liverpool owes everything it is—all those people, those unbroken miles upon miles of docks, its position as the country's leading port save for London—to its location on the estuary of the River Mersey, just three miles from the open sea. As early as the first century after Christ there was a settlement on the east bank of the Mersey, near a muddy little puddle, or "lifrug-pool."

To this simple suggestion of how the city's name came about, more colorful details were soon added. Once upon a time, you see, there was supposed to have been a bird called the Liver ("LY-ver") because for reasons known only to himself he liked to wander about with a bit of seaweed called "laver" dangling from his beak. And he adopted the town, or vice versa. Today the legend is official. The city seal bears the liver bird, dangling seaweed and all. A replica of the bird perches three hundred feet up at the top of each of the twin towers of the city's oldest skyscraper, the Royal Liver Building. Citizens of the Liverpool allow themselves to be called Liverpudlians, though the name sounds uncomfortably like something out of *Gulliver's Travels.*

King John got the port going when he built a castle there to facilitate his comings and goings to Ireland and granted the village a charter in 1207. But the real boom began after the seventeenth-century Restoration, with the slave and sugar trade between Africa and the West Indies. After the advent of the steamship in the 1840s it became a terminal for the ocean liners of the Cunard and White Star Lines, and for commerce with all the world.

But Liverpool is not all shipping and docks. It has two of the world's greatest cathedrals, one Anglican, one Roman Catholic, both built in the twentieth century. At the Walker Art Gallery is the finest collection of paintings outside London, especially the works of English painters from the eighteenth to twentieth centuries.

For the well-rounded life, Liverpool also has two of the country's great football teams, with the world's most ferocious fans to boost them. And inevitably, it offers a tribute to its most famous sons, the Beatles. Beatle City is a museum built on the site of the Cavern Club, the night spot where the singers began their meteoric rise to international fame in the 1960s.

For a city of its size and character, Liverpool is remarkable for the number of literary figures associated with it, too. Other great commercial and industrial centers—Manchester and Birmingham, for example—have nothing like such abundance. Some writers were born there. Others came from far and near, for all sorts of reasons and for stays from the briefest to some lasting for years. Matthew Arnold even managed to die there.

Those born in Liverpool included William Roscoe, Felicia Dorothea Hemans, Arthur Hugh Clough and his sister Anne, William Gladstone, and Richard Le Gallienne—none of highest rank, but several of much competence. Roscoe, born in 1753, wrote a widely accepted *Life of Lorenzo de Medici* (1795) and another book on the life and pontificate of Leo X. He was also author of several volumes of verse, one of which, *The Butterfly's Ball and the Grasshopper's Feast* (1807), became a children's classic. Roscoe served as member of Parliament for Liverpool from 1806 to 1808, a seat held two centuries before him by another writer-politician, Francis Bacon, introducer of the essay into English literature, who represented Liverpool from 1588 to 1592.

Arthur Hugh Clough, his sister Anne, and William Gladstone were born on the same street, Rodney Street, notable yet for surviving houses from the eighteenth century that are Georgian architecture at its best. Arthur Clough was born in 1819 and Anne in 1820 at No 9 Rodney (now marked with a plaque); Gladstone was born in 1809 at No. 62. Gladstone showed some skill as a writer in various works on Homer and the Homeric age as well as in his political pieces, but it's hard to think he'd be much remembered now if he had not also happened to be Queen Victoria's prime minister on four occasions. Anne was something of an innovative educator for her day, having the rather startling notion that women were worthy of higher education, and opening a school for them in 1852. She was the first principal of a house for women students at Cambridge. It started in 1871 with five students and evolved into what is now Newnham College.

Arthur Clough, on the other hand, might have earned a prominent place in literature had he taken his writing more seriously. He made his career as an examiner in the education office, and wrote only as the spirit moved. Yet he was capable of bitingly deft satire. He also showed in his first printed poem, and perhaps his best, *The Bothie of Tober-na-Vuolich* (1848) that he could produce highly effective seriocomic verse, and in hexameters, the long six-beat line avoided by most poets. Even in the twenties and thirties of our own century, his *Amours de Voyage,* published posthumously in 1862, was thought avant garde. And his "Say not the struggle naught availeth" will last forever as a tribute to man's indominatability.

Clough is remembered best now as the subject of "Thyrsis," the elegy written after his sudden death at forty-two, in Vienna, by Matthew Arnold, his closest friend and fellow student at Rugby and Oxford. It is the most striking of coincidences, then, that Arnold should have met his death in Liverpool, and in a most bizarre way.

In 1888 Arnold went to Liverpool to welcome his sister, who was returning from the United States. His position as one of the most eminent of Victorian writers, both in poetry and prose, was by then firmly established. At age sixty-six he was still dapper, trim, and nimble. As he hurried toward the docks to meet his sister's ship, a low-lying fence got in his way. He simply leaped over it—and fell dead on the other side.

Richard Le Gallienne was born at No. 55 Prescott Street, Liverpool, in 1866. He enjoyed well-earned success as journalist, critic, and essayist, and was a contributor to that hallmark quarterly of the 1890s, *The Yellow Book.* Among his works were *My Ladies' Sonnets* (1887) and *The Quest of the Golden Girl* (1896). His daughter was the famous actress Eva Le Gallienne.

Liverpool's most engaging native-born writer was Felicia Dorothea Hemans. If her name is unrecognized today, some of the lines she wrote remain memorable. It was one of her poems that made the phrase, "the stately homes of England," a byword. She was born Felicia Dorothea Browne in 1793 at 118 Duke Street (now marked with a plaque). And though the family moved to St. Asaph in Wales while she was still a girl, she returned to Liverpool in 1827 to spend the last years of her life at Wavertree High Street.

At eighteen she had dashed off from St. Asaph in impetuous marriage to a Capt. Alfred Hemans. But within six years she had separated from him and was back there once more. Barely twenty-five, she was still vivacious and pretty, but with debts, five children, and no obvious way to support them. She was courageous and resourceful, however. Other women, she'd heard, had made a living writing verse. She'd give it a try.

She succeeded far beyond her expectations. Poems like "Casabianca," "The Landing of the Pilgrim Fathers," and "The Homes of England" sold well. She was especially popular in America, where schoolboys, who would solemnly avow that Shakespeare lived in the eighteenth century and wrote *David Copperfield,* could recite flawlessly from "Casabianca,"

> The boy stood on the burning deck
> Whence all but he had fled. . . .

Felicia herself was in no way overawed by all this, and said so. She acknowledged that if even a half dozen of her poems were remembered she'd be lucky. She would have been amused, as well as delighted, could she have known that her lines from "The Homes of England"—

> The stately homes of England!
> How beautiful they stand,
> Amidst their tall ancestral trees,
> O'er all the pleasant land

—would come to be parodied by E. V. Knox:

> The stately homes of England,
> How beautiful they stood
> Before their recent owners
> Relinquished them for good.

And that Virginia Woolf would write caustically:

> Those comfortable padded lunatic asylums, which are known euphemistically, as the stately homes of England. . . .

Mrs. Hemans didn't let herself be carried away by the reputations or achievements of others, either. Not even by William Wordsworth, whom she coolly appraised as a "benignant-looking old man." She was the poet's guest at Rydal Mount, his home in the Lake District, in 1830. When Wordsworth, who thought her "totally ignorant of housewifery," sought to steer her toward domestic practicalities by going out of his way to say that his wedding gift to a young lady friend would be a set of kitchen scales, Felicia's response was, "Mr. Wordsworth, how *could* you be so giddy?"

Bully for Felicia Hemans! Anyone who could stand eye to eye with

William Wordsworth, and tell him to his face that he was giddy deserves to be remembered.

With the coming of the transatlantic steamer, people of every sort poured through Liverpool on their way to or from various parts of Britain. They came by the thousands upon thousands from Ireland, Scotland, England itself, driven by hardship and poverty at home, to sail off from Liverpool to Canada, the United States, and Australia for what they hoped would be a fresh start. And in large numbers they sailed into Liverpool from the New World and the Continent en route to their destinations in Britain.

Among Americans who came to Liverpool were writers of some importance, two of whom, Henry Adams and Nathaniel Hawthorne, have left sharply etched impressions of the city as it was when they saw it. Adams, as the earlier quotation from his *The Education of Henry Adams* (1904) indicates, hardly rejoiced at what he saw. But he had barely set foot on shore when he saw it in 1858, his discomforts from a furious gale in the Mersey just vanishing, "to make place for the drearier picture of a Liverpool Street as seen from the Adelphi coffee-room in November murk." The Adelphi should have cheered him up more than it did. Charles Dickens, a connoisseur of hotels who stayed at only the best when he had a choice, had been at the Adelphi in 1842 and thereafter, and liked it.[8]

Hawthorne was kinder, despite saying that "Liverpool, though not very delightful as a place of residence, is a most convenient and admirable point to get away from." But then he knew Liverpool far better than Adams ever could. He was there as American consul for four years, from 1853 to 1857. The post was lucrative, a reward for writing the campaign biography of his Bowdoin College classmate, Franklin Pierce. The book helped make Pierce the fourteenth president of the United States. Hawthorne devotes much space to Liverpool in *Our Old Home* (1863), and even a brief sampling of his observations shows how readable they remain, and how they bring the city to life as it was in Queen Victoria's day.

"The Mersey has the color of a mud-puddle," he wrote, but "is by no

---

[8]Both Dickens and Adams should see the Adelphi today. Now called the Britannia Adelphi, it's elegant, as you can judge for yourself if you're spending the night in Liverpool and in the mood for four-star pampering and the prices that go with it.

means crowded; because the immense multitude of ships are ensconced in the docks, where their masts make an intricate forest for miles up and down the Liverpool shore." The arrival of a transatlantic liner was a great event:

> Once a week comes a Cunard steamer with its red funnel pipe whitened by the salt spray; and, firing off cannon to announce her arrival, she moors to a large iron buoy in the middle of the river. . . . For several hours afterwards, the Cunard lies with the smoke and steam coming out of her, as if she were smoking her pipe after her toilsome passage across the Atlantic.

The city streets teemed with people selling their goods:

> Women and men sit in the streets with a stock of combs and such small things to sell, the women knitting as if they were at a fireside. Cheap crockery is laid out in the street. . . . Stalls of apples are innumerable, but the apples are not fit for a pig. In some streets herring are very abundant, laid out on boards. Coals seem to be for sale by the wheelbarrowful.

There were many plying a trade of quite another kind, too:

> Here beggary is a system, and beggars are a numerous class, and make themselves, in a certain way, respected as such.

A major attraction was the city zoo, with a "bear who climbs a pole to get cake and gingerbread from the spectators . . . lions, wolves, and tigers . . . a colony of monkeys . . . swans and various rare water-fowl swimming on a piece of water [and] a stork parading along the margin, with melancholy strides of its long legs."

It was Hawthorne who occasioned Herman Melville's stopover in Liverpool in 1856 while en route to Constantinople. But actually Melville had been there before, the first time in 1837 as an eighteen-year-old cabin boy on a sailing ship. Now he returned as a man well-known in England for rousing tales of the sea such as *Typee* (1846) and *Redburn* (1849), the latter with a description of that voyage as a cabin boy. This time Melville put up at the White Bear Hotel for ten days, and the two Americans had the happiest of reunions, visiting, talking endlessly of their days together in New England, and seeing the sights round about.[9]

Other American writers of note who came to Liverpool were Wash-

---

[9] For the duo's tour of Chester, see pp. 242–43.

ington Irving, Ralph Waldo Emerson, and Harriet Beecher Stowe—Irving as a literary unknown, but the other two with solid reputations already established. Irving arrived in Liverpool in 1818 to become a partner of his brother, a merchant at the Goree Arcade. But the business failed, for which the world should be grateful. Irving was forced to turn to writing for a livelihood, and out of this came a long and distinguished career, beginning with *The Sketch Book* (1820) and such immortal pieces as "Rip Van Winkle" and "The Legend of Sleepy Hollow." He was the first American to win international recognition as a man of letters.

Such recognition was already Emerson's when in 1847 he presented to Liverpool audiences the series of lectures on great men of the past that was published in 1850 as *Representative Men*.

Nor was Harriet Beecher Stowe unknown when she descended on Liverpool in 1853. Two scant years earlier she had been an obscure former teacher living in Maine. But in 1853, *Uncle Tom's Cabin* had just burst upon the world, demanding the attention of civilized people everywhere, including not a few in Liverpool who had grown rich from the slavery her novel so bitterly decried. From Liverpool Mrs. Stowe moved on to what proved to be a triumphal tour of England, with enthusiastic receptions at every stop, recorded in her *Sunny Memories of Foreign Lands* (1854).

Among English writers who were in Liverpool at one time or another for rather brief stays were Daniel Defoe, William Hazlitt, Thomas De Quincey, John Galsworthy, and William Allingham, as well as Charles Dickens, Alfred Tennyson, and George Orwell. Defoe, in *Tour through the Whole Island of Great Britain* (1724–27) wryly described his unceremonious entry into Liverpool. The waters about his landing point were too shallow for the ferry bringing him from the Wirral peninsula to get close in. And so, Defoe writes:

> You land on the flat shore . . . and must be content to ride thro' the water for some length, not on Horseback, but on the shoulders of some Lancashire Clown, who comes knee-deep to the Boat's side, to truss one up; and then runs away more nimbly than one desires to ride, unless his Trot were easier.

Hazlitt and De Quincey, those fellow essayists and friends of Coleridge and Wordsworth, were in Liverpool within a decade of each other. Hazlitt was there in 1790 and stayed just long enough to have a look around. De Quincey came in 1801 and again in 1803 to visit his mother, who was living there. In 1911 John Galsworthy was there for the staging of his play, *Strife.*

The poet William Allingham came through Liverpool in 1854 on his way from Ireland, where he'd worked at the customs office, to London, where he hoped to find a place for himself in something literary. In Liverpool he stopped by to meet Hawthorne, who described him as "intelligent, dark, pleasing, and not at all John Bullish" in appearance.

A friend of Tennyson, Carlyle, and D. G. Rossetti, Allingham wrote with a pleasing ease and flow, and a few of his songs still turn up now and then in anthologies. But only one of them has enjoyed general exposure in our day, and that came from, of all people, the comedian Danny Kaye. At that, the route was fortuitous.

A leading singer during the early part of this century was an English contralto named Clara Butt, possessed of a voice with remarkable force and range. For years she toured triumphantly, even regally, both at home and throughout the colonies. In her repertoire were songs by William Allingham. And to hear her launch into his "Up the Airy Mountain," a fragile thing at best, with all the power and earnestness at her command, was awesome—as an existing early recording still demonstrates.

Somehow Danny Kaye stumbled upon that recording, and it inspired him to his demonic best. Embroidering upon the soarings and swoopings of Clara's rendition, and punctuating them with a wild assortment of snorts, grunts, and groans, Kaye turned "Up the Airy Mountain" into a comic masterpiece. Poor Allingham.

Charles Dickens was in Liverpool any number of times, starting as early as 1837, when as a mere twenty-five year old he had won overnight success with *The Pickwick Papers* and was just beginning to write *Oliver Twist.* The readings and theatrical performances he put on there sold out, as they did everywhere in England. Hawthorne gives an account of what he calls Dickens's "unweariability" on such occasions, as told him by a friend who'd witnessed one of these Liverpool appearances. In the course of a single evening, Dickens had

> acted in play and farce, spent the rest of the night making speeches, feasting, and drinking at table, and ended at seven o'clock in the morning by jumping leap-frog over the backs of the whole company.

Dickens made huge sums from these performances, true. But he was equally indefatigable in using them for charities and to aid less fortunate fellow writers. Those in Liverpool in 1847 and 1848 were both benefits.

The one in 1848 was for the poet Leigh Hunt, and Dickens not only directed and acted in it, but also persuaded his friend, the novelist Bulwer Lytton, to write a special prologue.

Alfred Tennyson and Arthur Hallam arrived in Liverpool on September 20, 1830, fresh from a perilous and futile attempt to deliver money and dispatches to the rebels in Spain. It was a historic day: the train they were to take would be the world's very first passenger train; their trip from Liverpool to Manchester would be its first run ever. Tennyson was so impressed he used the experience for some lines in "Locksley Hall." Man's progress, he envisioned, would be inevitable and irresistible, like a great locomotive roaring onward:

> Not in vain the distance beacons. Forward, forward let us range,
> Let the great world spin forever down the ringing grooves of change.

"Grooves of change?" The line would be puzzling, were it not for Tennyson himself. The platform had been so crowded that day, you see, and the poet too near-sighted to see exactly what went on. And so, he explained in a note, "when I went by the first train from Liverpool to Manchester, I thought that the wheels ran in grooves."

What brought George Orwell to Liverpool in 1935 was his exploration of workers' living conditions in preparation for *The Road to Wigan Pier* (1937). One could hardly expect Orwell to be delighted with any city of Liverpool's sort. But he was interested in some of its housing estates for workers, and it escaped the vehemence of the castigation he heaped upon cities like Birmingham and Sheffield.

Not a few of Liverpool's literary ties were owing to its educational facilities. Felicia Hemans came back home to live there in 1827 so that her five young sons could take advantage of its schools. The poet Wilfred Owen attended Birkenhead Institute on the other side of the Mersey from 1900 to 1907, at ages seven to fourteen. And beginning at age thirteen, John Masefield was a sea cadet on a training ship from 1891 to 1894. His Liverpool days are reflected in the autobiographical *New Chum* (1944), which has a description of the city, and in poems like "The Valediction" (1902), with his memories of the docks, and "The Wanderer of Liverpool" (1930), an allegory about a four-masted sailing ship.

Liverpool University, established in 1881, drew a trio of distinguished writer-scholars: James G. Frazer, Andrew Cecil Bradley, and Walter Raleigh. Frazer was professor of anthropology there from 1907 to 1922, and author of that vast study of primitive customs and superstitions,

The Golden Bough (1890–1915), which ultimately reached twelve volumes. Bradley served as first professor of literature from 1882 to 1889, and his books on Shakespeare, especially *Shakespearean Tragedy* (1904), brought new insights to lovers of Shakespeare, scholars and students alike, for generations.

Raleigh taught at Liverpool University College before becoming professor of English literature at Oxford in 1904. His works on Shakespeare, Samuel Johnson, Milton, and William Wordsworth won him a knighthood. But bearing the name Sir Walter Raleigh in the twentieth century was often a burden. Everywhere he went he encountered tired witticisms involving his sixteenth-century namesake and the first Queen Elizabeth, especially when he lectured in America, where people tend to be bemused by titles anyway.

For years after Raleigh's visit to Princeton University, they told of how a dignitary sent to meet the guest, not finding him on the station platform, asked the Pullman porter, "Have you seen Sir Walter Raleigh?"

"No sir," said the porter, not about to be taken in, "but Queen Elizabeth's back in the dining car looking for him, too."

While at Liverpool University College, Raleigh taught an eccentric, highly emotional boy named Lytton Strachey, whose arms and legs were so spindly his schoolmates called him "Scraggs." Strachey had been refused admission to Oxford. Now he turned to Raleigh: Could he help him get into Cambridge? Raleigh could and did, praising the boy's extraordinary intelligence, which Strachey certainly had, and his tact, judgment, and gentle temper, which he certainly had not. Thus it was that in 1899 Strachey went to Cambridge, helped found the midnight society there that became the nucleus of the famous Bloomsbury Group, and eventually went on to write his celebrated *Eminent Victorians* (1918).

Gerard Manley Hopkins was a parish priest in Liverpool in 1880, and thoroughly miserable. In one letter to a friend, he wrote:

> I do not think I can be here long. I have been long nowhere yet. I am brought face to face with the deepest poverty and misery in my district.

And in another, he said:

> . . . my Liverpool work is very harassing and makes it hard to write. Tonight I am sitting in my confessional, but the faithful are fewer than usual and I am unexpectedly delivered from a sermon which otherwise I should have had to deliver.

But Hopkins kept a sense of humor, even in Liverpool, and even about the reception of those sermons he had to deliver: "I thought people must be quite touched and that I even saw some wiping their tears. But when the same thing happened next week I perceived that it was hot and that it was sweat that they were wiping away."

KNOWSLEY PARK—ROCK FERRY—AND SOUTHPORT

As is everything in Merseyside, Knowsley Park, Rock Ferry, and Southport are all close to Liverpool. Knowsley is just at the city's eastern edge, on the B 5194. Rock Ferry is across the river and is now a suburb of Birkenhead. Southport is twenty miles up the coast on the A 565. Hawthorne was quite familiar with all three, and commented on them in *Our Old Home.*

Knowsley Park   The present palatial mansion, set in the midst of a great park, is largely seventeenth-to-nineteenth century, but Knowsley goes back well before that. It has long been the country seat of the earls of Derby, and was possibly one of the lordly homes of the area to enjoy a performance by the acting group, the Earl of Leicester's Company, to which Shakespeare had been attached early in his career.

Between 1832 and 1837, Edward Lear was at Knowsley making drawings of the then earl of Derby's menagerie of rare animals and birds. Bored with what Lear called the "uniformly apathetic tone" of the adults there and longing to "giggle heartily and to hop on one leg down the great gallery," he often fled for refuge to the children. It was for them that he began the nonsensical verses and sketches that developed into *A Book of Nonsense* (1846).

Nathaniel Hawthorne visited the park in 1854, gaining admittance through a Knowsley neighbor, Sir Thomas Birch. The mansion, Hawthorne reported, stood off a great distance from the gate,

> in the midst of a very fine prospect, with a tolerably high ridge of hills in the distance. The house itself is exceedingly vast, a front and two wings with suites of rooms, I suppose, interminable. The oldest part, Sir Thomas Birch told us, is a tower of the time of Henry VII.

But Hawthorne was not overly impressed by its appearance:

It stands in my memory rather like a college or a hospital, than as the ancestral residence of a great English noble.

The mansion remains a completely private dwelling and is closed to the public. But there's a safari park on the grounds, with admission daily from the first of March to the end of October.

Rock Ferry   Rock Ferry is about two miles across the river from Liverpool, on the A 41 and is now a suburb of Birkenhead. In the nineteenth century many people preferred to live there and commute to Liverpool on the ferry that ran every half hour. Hawthorne was one of them, living for the first weeks of his consulship, in August of 1853, at the Royal Rock Hotel (demolished some years ago) while looking for more permanent quarters.

On Saturdays Rock Ferry was an especially colorful and crowded place, the boat coming over from Liverpool so packed with people of all classes as to afford scanty standing room. Saturdays were gala days, reminding Hawthorne of Fourth of July celebrations in his own country. Filling the streets to overflowing were solid Liverpool merchants and their wives, charity children on a rare holiday, and working families from mills and factories in the interior, enticed by special low weekend fares on trains and ferries. It was during those early days at Rock Ferry that Hawthorne finished *Tanglewood Tales.*

Southport   Southport owes its existence as a seaside resort to the initiative of one man, William Sutton, who in the late eighteenth century built the first bathing house on its beach. Today it flourishes almost too much for its own good, with a population of some 90,000. But it has charm. Its main thoroughfare, Lord Street, is inviting, a mile-long boulevard of trees and flower gardens, cafes and fine shops.

At one time or another Southport has played host to an assortment of writers, all novelists: Nathaniel Gould, Mary Webb, Michael Arlen, Herman Melville, and Nathaniel Hawthorne. Gould was a student at Southport's Strathmore House School in the 1860s. Generally called Nat Gould, he wrote more than one hundred novels (beginning with *The Double Event*) all about horse racing.

From 1897 to 1899 Mary Webb, author of books set in Shropshire county, like *Gone to Earth* (1917) and *Precious Bane* (1924), attended a school run by a Miss Walmesley. Arlen was born Dikran Kouyoumdjian in Bulgaria in 1895, and came to live in Southport when his parents settled there in 1901. In 1922 he was naturalized as a British subject, changed his name to Michael Arlen, and within two years won resounding success with *The Green Hat*, a best seller.

Melville was in Southport only briefly, coming up to see Hawthorne there during that 1857 stopover in Liverpool on his way to Constantinople. Hawthorne, however, was in Southport for longer than he liked. He found it a large village, almost entirely made up of lodging houses. "Everybody seems to be a transitory guest," he said, "nobody at home." And the streets were jammed with donkey carriages and Bath chairs bearing invalid old ladies; the beach was a thicket of bathing machines.[10]

Entertainment consisted largely of such delights as "a succession of organ-grinders playing interminably under your window; and a man with a bassoon and a monkey . . . and wandering minstrels, with guitar and voice; and a Highland bagpipe, squealing out a tangled skein of discord."

Today, just off the Promenade, there's an inland lake on which yacht, canoe, and dinghy races are held. But in Hawthorne's day the distance from the beginning of the beach to water of any depth was far greater even than Defoe had found below Liverpool when he had to be carried ashore on the back of a flunkie.[11] "In all my experience," Hawthorne grumbled,

> I have never seen the sea, but only an interminable breadth of sands, looking poorly or plashy in some places, and barred across with drier reaches of sand, with no expanse of water. It must be miles and miles, at low water to the veritable sea-shore.

People determined to bathe had to have their bathing machines hauled endlessly by donkeys to reach water even waist high. All in all, Hawthorne concluded.

> Southport is as stupid a place as I ever lived in; and I cannot but bewail our ill fortune to have been compelled to spend so many months on these barren sands, when almost any other square yard of England contains something that would have been historically or poetically interesting.

One exciting event did occur while he was there—a shipwreck within a mile of his window. Bodies of the victims were washed ashore, and

---

[10]Bathing machines were individual bathhouses on wheels, allowing the modest Victorians to walk into the water and enjoy their splash without exposing their bodies.

[11]See p. 269.

they set him to thinking about Edward King, Milton's Cambridge friend, who drowned in the same general area and whom the poet lamented in *Lycidas.* Hawthorne speculated somewhat gruesomely that "it really is not at all improbable that Milton's Lycidas floated hereabouts, in the rise and lapse of the tides, and that his bones may still be whitening among the sands." If so, King's body would have had some floating to do. His ship went down not on the eastern side of the peninsula above Southport, but far off on the western side above the Dee estuary between Cheshire and Wales.

*****

Merseyside ends at Southport. Southport's outskirts touch Merseyside's boundary with Lancashire, and the county line with Greater Manchester is less than a dozen miles to the east. The city of Manchester was Hawthorne's next stop after Southport, the lure being an enormous display of historic paintings and objets d'art that was drawing visitors from all parts of the kingdom. From his lodgings in Manchester Hawthorne wrote in his notebook for July 22, 1857, with considerable glee:

> We left Southport for good on the 20th, and have established ourselves in this place . . . our principal object being to spend a few weeks in the proximity of the Arts Exhibition.

Manchester is our next stop, too. To Manchester in the nineteenth century came some of the greatest names in all Victorian literature. And in Manchester, on August 16, 1819, occurred an event that, as we can now see, ranks with the few truly pivotal moments of history.

GREATER MANCHESTER AND LANCASHIRE

I come from Lancashire,
    From bonnie, bonnie Lancashire
My father and my Uncle Bill
    Go every morning to work in the mill.

I'm going to the barber
    To have my hair cut off,
But I want to tell you before I go—
    I come from Lancashire

                    An old Lancashire song[1]

There are some fields near Manchester, well known to the inhabitants as "Green Heys Fields," through which runs a public footpath to a little village about two miles distant. . . . And here the artisan deafened with the noise of tongues and engines, may come to listen awhile to the delicious sounds of rural life; the lowing of cattle, the milkmaids' call, the clatter and cackle of poultry in the old farmyards.

    Elizabeth Gaskell, *Mary Barton, a Tale of Manchester Life*

What Art was to the ancient world, Science is to the modern. . . . Rightly understood, Manchester is as great a human exploit as Athens.

    Benjamin Disraeli, *Coningsby*

Who shall compute the waste and loss, the obstruction of every sort, that was produced, in the Manchester region by Peterloo alone!. . . . In all hearts that witnessed Peterloo stands written, as in fire-characters, or smoke-characters prompt to become fire again, a legible balance account of grim vengeance.

    Thomas Carlyle, *Past and Present*

---

[1] I learned this song from my older sister, Nona, who told me we sang it as children in our home in Manchester. I was only a baby then, but I did come, you see, from Lancashire.

Coketown[2] . . . was a town of machinery and tall chimneys, out of which interminable serpents of smoke trailed themselves for ever and ever, and never got uncoiled. It had a black canal in it, and a river that ran purple with ill-smelling dye, and vast piles of buildings full of windows where there was a rattling and a trembling all day long, and where the piston of the steam engine worked monotonously up and down, like the head of an elephant in a state of melancholy madness.

Charles Dickens, Hard Times

If they [the people of Manchester] smelled the air along the Cornish cliffs, they would probably declare that it had no taste in it.

George Orwell, The Road to Wigan Pier

The fastest way out of Manchester is a bottle of gin on a Saturday night.

Oft-quoted Victorian saying

When children first sang that song about coming from Lancashire, the county *was* bonnie. There were not only those rural patches of peace and beauty outside the great towns, like the village Mrs. Gaskell described in *Mary Barton,* but also the loveliness of the valleys of the Lune and the Ribble, and the grandeur of the Coniston Water and Lake Windermere that signalled the entrance to the Lake District.

But Lancashire also had its dark side. For Lancashire was those mills of the children's song, too, mills that helped develop vast cities like Liverpool and Manchester. They made Manchester one of the richest cities in the kingdom and one of the most densely populated areas on earth. But to the entire region that was industrial Lancaster, the mills meant Coketowns with their black canals and evil-smelling rivers, and tall chimneys with interminable serpents of smoke.

To the millworkers of Manchester who had to endure all this, the

---

[2] i.e., Preston, Lancashire.

mills brought even worse besides: the Peterloo of Carlyle's grim prediction.

Benjamin Disraeli should have remembered Peterloo when he prattled, in 1844 in *Coningsby,* that Manchester was as great a human exploit as ancient Athens. But Disraeli was a young man when he wrote the novel, a naive romantic indulging in fantasy in his far-off home near London. And he was only reflecting the views of England's ruling class who chose to ignore the foreboding lesson that was Peterloo.

It happened August 16, 1819 at St. Peter's Field (now St. Peter's Square), Manchester. Widespread unemployment and unbearable working conditions had driven 50,000 people to assemble to protest and demand representation in Parliament. Suddenly mounted troops appeared and charged, with sabres flashing, into the crowd. When it was over, eleven lay dead, hundreds wounded. The "Peterloo Massacre," it was called. Waterloo had been four years earlier.

There were some who remembered Peterloo and tried to do something about it. But too often their efforts went unheeded. The Manchester that George Orwell found in 1936 as he trudged through its gloomy streets on his way to Wigan Pier was still too reminiscent of the Manchester that had greeted Mrs. Gaskell when she arrived as a bride in 1832.

And for the workers Orwell talked to, especially when there was no work, the fastest way out of Manchester, often enough, remained a bottle of gin on Saturday night.

GREATER MANCHESTER

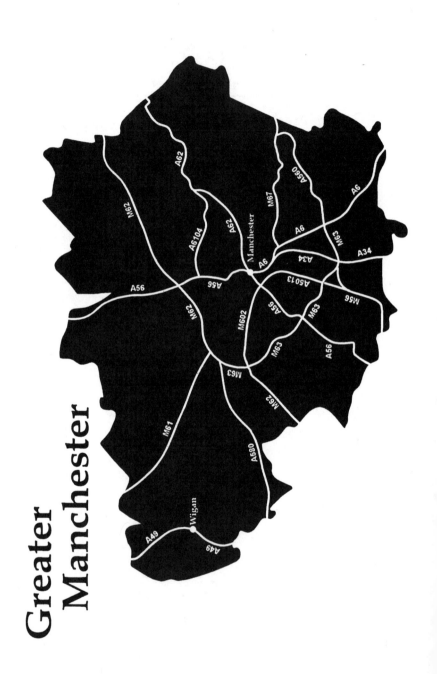

Greater
Manchester

Since Orwell, however, much has happened not only to the city of Manchester, but also to all the region that stretches from Cheshire and the estuary of the Mersey to the beginnings of the Lake District. This, the old Lancashire that was, was totally dismembered by the governmental restructuring of 1974. In the same way that Liverpool with its great port and endless docks was torn off to form the new Merseyside, so the beauties of Coniston Water and Lake Windermere went to help make the new county of Cumbria.

Indeed, the entity that is Lancashire today has been left with little that is distinctive, either of good or of bad. Practically all the other major cities were stripped off in 1974, too, to form yet a third new county called Greater Manchester. As a result, Greater Manchester is almost uninterruptedly urban: from Salford, which merges imperceptibly with Manchester's fringes yet has 100,000 people and is a city in its own right, to Bolton (145,000 people) and Rochdale (95,000, and birthplace of Gracie Fields) in the north, to Wigan (80,000) in the county's west.

THE CITY OF MANCHESTER

You can reach Manchester from any direction via a selection of highways and byways too numerous to show on the map at the front of this section. Among them are the M 56, the M 69, the M 62, the A 6104, the M 34, and on and on and on. Modern changes in the city of Manchester have been mostly for the good. It was first in the nation to establish a "smokeless zone," and the acrid air Orwell complained you could taste has disappeared. Lessening demand for its cotton has forced diversification of industry, giving the city a sounder economic base. It is less crowded, too—the population is down from its peak of three quarters of a million in Orwell's day to 465,000.

The slums have gone, abetted in part by savage Nazi bombing in WWII that simply wiped them out. Pride of the city now is Piccadilly, the great square that rose from the debris. Fine shops and hotels surround it. At its center, lawns and flower beds and walks make a haven of quiet and serenity.

Whatever flavor of the past Manchester retains is largely Victorian. There has been a community of one kind or another there on the banks of the Irwell River for well over two thousand years, but nothing of great consequence happened until the dawn of the nineteenth century. The Celts, who were there before the Christian era began, called it "Mancenium," place of tents—which explains why today's natives are referred to as Mancunians. Then came the usual waves, in succession, of Saxons, Danes, and all the rest.

In the fourteenth century Manchester was introduced to what was to become its major industry by Flemish weavers who began the making of cloth, chiefly woolens and linen. Then, as the nineteenth century neared, Manchester and the Industrial Revolution came together to transform the city into the world center of the cotton trade. Everything was just right to make this happen. The recently invented steam engine had been adapted to machines for spinning and weaving cotton, and the area about the city had plenty of coal to drive them.

The first spinning jennies and spinning mules began operating in Manchester in 1781, and the first steam driven mill in 1798. The moist climate was ideal: the dampness prevented the fine cotton threads from breaking while being spun. Labor was abundant and all too cheap as people poured in looking for work.

By 1819, Manchester was well on its way to winning the title of "Cottonopolis"—and ripe for Peterloo and its bitter, long-lasting aftermath.

Along with its other consequences, Peterloo had a galvanic effect on things literary. It sparked the creation in 1821 of one of the nation's great newspapers, *The Manchester Guardian* (now simply *The Guardian*), to be the voice for radicalism. One of its editors, C. P. Scott, who reigned from 1872 to 1929, was among the best of his era. Two of its long line of outstanding writers were Howard Spring and Alistaire Cooke.

Spring was on *The Guardian* staff from 1915 until 1931, and later won success as a novelist with books like *Fame is the Spur* (1940). Alistaire Cooke, born in Manchester in 1908, is best known to millions of Americans as the erudite and charming host of TV's *Masterpiece Theatre* from its beginnings in 1971 until his retirement in 1993, but his basic career has been as a journalist and author. For twenty-eight years his official position was chief American correspondent of *The Guardian*. His books include *A Generation on Trial* (1950), *One Man's America* (1952), *Talk About America* (1968), *Alistaire Cooke's America* (1973), and *Six Men* (1977).

Most notable of the writers Peterloo stirred directly were Thomas

Carlyle, Charles Dickens, and Mrs. Gaskell. Even Charlotte Brontë, too, felt the impact of the workers' distress, but the setting for her novel *Shirley* (1849) was Yorkshire, and her millhands' protest the Luddite uprisings of 1811–16.

In *Chartism* in 1839 and *Past and Present* in 1843, Carlyle vented his scorn for the theories of contemporary political economists and his disdain for the democratic reforms the workers were looking to for salvation. "The liberty to starve," he proclaimed, "is no liberty." Instead, he called for the ways of the medieval past, when there was a ruling class that really ruled, led by men strong but just, who treated those beneath them firmly but with fairness and consideration.

Charles Dickens had been in Manchester in 1838 and again in 1839. Appalled at the workers' conditions, he promised to "strike a blow" to support them, though he was only twenty-six at the time and his career just beginning. It would be fifteen years before he was able to keep his promise. In January of 1854 he came back to Manchester and then went on to Preston, where a bitter strike was in progress at the cotton mills. There he managed to sit in on one of the strikers' committee meetings, and he praised their moderation and self-discipline.

Upon his return home, he lauded their efforts in an article for his magazine, *Household Words,* and followed this up at once with the novel, *Hard Times,* in which "Coketown" (Preston) is ruled by the Gradgrinds and Bounderbys. Mr. Gradgrind found no need to complicate the human equation with sentiment: "It is a mere question of figures, a case of simple arithmetic." He was always happy to spell things out

> with a rule and a pair of scales, and the multiplication table always in his pocket, sir, ready to weigh and measure any parcel of human nature, and tell you exactly what it comes to.

In 1855 Mrs. Gaskell, with *Mary Barton, a Tale of Manchester Life,* brought to her depictions of the workers' plight an immediacy that Carlyle and Dickens, for all their eloquence, could not match. As a clergyman's wife, she had lived among the factory men and ministered to them. In the guise of her characters she could go to the heart of the matter with stabbing simplicity. When John Barton's friend Wilson suggests that perhaps the mill owners have their problems, too, Barton replies, "Han they ever seen a child o' theirn die for want o' food?"

Manchester itself produced no writers of the stature of Carlyle, Dickens, and Mrs. Gaskell, nor were they as concerned with its problems.

But from among them came two of the best-known titles of the nineteenth century, Thomas De Quincey's *Confessions of an English Opium Eater* (1822) and Frances Hodgson Burnett's *Little Lord Fauntleroy* (1866).

Several other Manchester-born writers had backgrounds of interest. John Byrom, for instance, was born in 1692 in what is now Manchester's most picturesque relic of its medieval past, the Old Wellington Inn. He was a poet whose real talent lay in shorthand, not verse. He invented his own system of shorthand and made his living teaching it in Manchester. However, his attempts at secular poetry, such as a pastoral extolling the charms of Richard Bentley's daughter, are convincing proof that it requires more than ardor to write a good love poem.[3] And his religious verse suggests that piety is no substitute for talent, either. It must be said, though, that his hymn, "Christians, awake! Salute the happy morn," remains a favorite of many.

Thomas De Quincey was born in Manchester in 1785, son of a prosperous merchant. After his father's death, his mother took him off to attend schools in Bath and Wiltshire, but at fifteen he entered Manchester Grammar School to prepare for Oxford. The work proved too easy. Bored, he ran off with only £10 in his pocket, first to his mother in Chester, then to North Wales, and finally to London. There, his money gone, he lived in squalor until his guardians came to the rescue and got him into Oxford. One reminder of his ties to Manchester remains: He wrote "Visions of Sudden Death" in a Manchester tavern.

Another who attended Manchester Grammar School was the novelist William Harrison Ainsworth, born in Manchester in 1805 at No. 57 King Street (now marked with a plaque). He was immediately successful in 1834 with the first novel he wrote, *Rookwood,* and from then on books came profusely. Chiefly historical, they were of a surprisingly good calibre considering that he wrote thirty-nine in all. Some of the best were *Jack Sheppard* (1839), *Guy Fawkes* (1841), *Old St. Paul's* (1841), and *Windsor Castle* (1843). *Merryn Clitheroe* (1857) depicts his days at Manchester Grammar School, and *The Lancashire Witches* (1848) involves much of the countryside about the Ribble valley.

The life of Manchester-born Frances Hodgson Burnett would make a

---

[3]This is the Bentley who took it upon himself to rewrite Milton's *Paradise Lost.*

novel in itself. In the course of her seventy-five years, she went from her rather decent birthplace at 141 York Street (now Cheetham Hill Road) to a run-down section of neighboring Salford, thence to a log cabin in Tennessee, U.S.A., back to England to a grand manor in Kent, and finally to a grandiose villa on New York's Long Island.

Mrs. Burnett's family had been in moderately comfortable circumstances when she was born in 1849. But her father died when she was four, and from then on the family fortunes declined steadily. After even the shabby lodgings in Salford proved more than they could afford, they emigrated to America in 1865 to make a new start, winding up in a log cabin outside Knoxville, Tennessee.

At nineteen, Frances began writing stories for various magazines. In 1877 she had her first really popular success with *That Lass o'Lowries,* a novel of the Lancashire coal mines. But it wasn't until 1886, when she was thirty-seven and had married, raised children, and been divorced, that she wrote the novel that made her rich and famous—and her son miserable for the rest of his life. It wasn't enough that she had named him Vivian, dressed him in a velvet suit and lace collar, and let golden curls cuddle about his neck. Now she made him the model for little Lord Fauntleroy, an identity he was never to escape.

With the proceeds from *Little Lord Fauntleroy* Mrs. Burnett was able to set herself up in style, for a time in America, then back home in England, where in 1898 she established herself at Maytham Hall in Kent. Tiring of it after nine years, however, she returned to the United States to be nearer the excitement of New York City, building a somewhat showy Italianate mansion out on Long Island.

Two other novelists born in Manchester were Nathaniel (Nat) Gould and Louis Golding. Gould, born in 1857, wrote 139 novels, nearly all of them on horse racing. He went off to Australia in 1884 to be a journalist, but returned to live in Liverpool and become a veritable novel-making machine. Golding was born in Manchester in 1895, and Manchester life is featured in both *Magnolia Street* (1931) and *Five Silver Daughters* (1934). But the name he chose for his fictional Manchester was hardly flattering: Doomington.

In discussing writers connected to Manchester by something other than birth, it is interesting to trace the way in which many are linked to one another. Using Dickens as a focal point, for example, one can touch on his association with Harrison Ainsworth, and then move on in unbroken succession from Tennyson to Nathaniel Hawthorne to Mrs.

Gaskell. Turning then to Mrs. Gaskell, you can similarly proceed from her to Carlyle to Harriet Beecher Stowe to Charlotte Brontë and William Makepeace Thackeray.

Dickens first met Ainsworth in Manchester in 1837, and it is through him that Dickens is said to have met a pair of brothers who became the Cherryble Brothers of *Nicholas Nickleby* (1838-39). Alfred Tennyson came to Manchester in 1857 with two purposes in mind: to hear Dickens's public reading of *The Christmas Carol,* and to see the Great Arts' Exhibition. Nathaniel Hawthorne went to Manchester specifically to see that same exhibition, staying well over a month and attending it almost daily. But what stood out in his mind was not any of the great collections of paintings on display, but the day word reached him there that Tennyson himself was just down the hall.

Hawthorne rushed out to see the great man, and was overwhelmed. "Gazing at him with all my eyes," Hawthorne wrote in his notebook, "I like him well, and rejoiced more in him than in all the other wonders of the Exhibition." But the American novelist was shy, even humble, at seeing the poet laureate: "I would most gladly have seen more of this one poet of our day, but forebore to follow him; for I must own that it seemed mean to be dogging him through the saloons, or even to look at him, since it was to be done stealthily, if at all."

Hawthorne gives us a rare picture of Tennyson in his prime:

> He is as un-English as possible; indeed, an Englishman of genius usually lacks the national characteristics, and is great abnormally. . . . Un-English as he was, Tennyson had not, however, an American look. I cannot well describe the difference; but there was something more mellow in him,—softer, sweeter, broader, more simple than we are apt to be.

If Hawthorne wouldn't think of introducing himself to the poet, Mrs. Hawthorne showed no such restraint. Chancing upon one of Tennyson's sons, momentarily separated from his father's group, she grabbed the boy up and, she confessed, "kissed him to my heart's content."

Dickens's links to Mrs. Gaskell were both professional and personal, and the two met a number of times. After the success of *Mary Barton,* Dickens asked Mrs. Gaskell to write for *Household Words.* In 1851 the magazine printed the first of the papers she later republished as *Cranford.*

Elizabeth Gaskell's career as a novelist, however, had begun largely by chance. After she came to Manchester in 1832 as the bride of the Rev.

William Gaskell, she devoted herself to the role of good wife. She assisted him with his duties as minister of Cross Street Chapel. She managed the household, bore and raised the children. First came three daughters, and finally a son. When the boy died at ten months, she was inconsolable. Seeking something to distract her, Mr. Gaskell suggested writing. The result was *Mary Barton* and a whole new life for its author.

The success of *Mary Barton* enabled the Gaskells to buy a commodious house at No. 84 Plymouth Grove, and it became a mecca for distinguished visitors to Manchester. Among writers Mrs. Gaskell entertained there in addition to Dickens were Harriet Beecher Stowe, Thomas Carlyle, Thackeray, and Charlotte Brontë. Carlyle and Mrs. Gaskell shared a common concern for the workers of Manchester, of course, and he was a great admirer of *Mary Barton*. Harriet Beecher Stowe's visit came in 1853 during the tour of England that followed her own triumph with *Uncle Tom's Cabin* (1852) and is described in her *Sunny Memories of Foreign Lands* (1854).

Charlotte Brontë was a guest of Mrs. Gaskell for the first time in June 1851. But she had been in Manchester before, under the cruelest of circumstances. In 1846 her father was approaching blindness and she had to take him to Manchester to have cataracts removed from both eyes. The problems and anxieties she faced were staggering, the courage with which she met them beyond belief.

It was not enough that she had to minister to her father, totally alone among strangers. The Brontës had little money and had to take drab lodgings in one of the dreariest parts of town. Back home at Haworth, her twenty-nine-year-old brother Bramwell, whom she had thought so gifted, was being kept practically a prisoner at the parsonage, his character and body self-destroyed through alcohol and drugs. And the very day of her father's operation she received yet another of the seemingly endless rejection slips that had greeted the manuscript of her first novel, *The Professor*.

To each of her problems Charlotte responded forthrightly. She worried not about her own burdens, but how her sisters, Emily and Anne, were coping with Bramwell at home. Her concern about her Manchester lodgings was not for her personal comfort, but how to feed the nurse who would be there to care for her father. "Papa requires nothing, you know, but plain beef and mutton," she wrote a friend, "but a nurse will probably expect to live much better; give me some hints if you can." As for the rejection of *The Professor*, her reaction was even more resolute.

In those same dreary lodgings, as her father lay in an adjoining dark room, his eyes bandaged, she began writing *Jane Eyre*.

Charlotte had met Mrs. Gaskell through Harriet Martineau, with whom she had stayed in the Lake District in 1850. Mrs. Gaskell had warmly invited Charlotte to come to Manchester for a visit, and she did so in July 1851, at the end of a trip to London. But it was so intensely hot, Mrs. Gaskell says in her *Life of Charlotte Brontë,* "that we did little but sit in-doors, with open windows, and talk." It was however, Charlotte reported later, a cheery break in her journey.

In April 1853 Charlotte was back at the Gaskell's, this time for a more comfortable visit. She was even provoked out of the protective shell she invariably threw about herself when in company. She was acutely sensitive to what she thought was her ugliness. "I notice that after a stranger has once looked at my face," she told Mrs. Gaskell, "he is careful not to let his eyes wander to that part of the room again."

One evening Mrs. Gaskell invited two gentlemen to dinner, hoping Charlotte would find them interesting. But Charlotte drew back from all their advances until at last they abandoned all efforts to engage her and confined their conversation to themselves and Mr. Gaskell. Suddenly, however, she heard them discussing Thackeray and the lectures on writers of the past he had just been delivering in Manchester, and when she heard them mention the one on Henry Fielding, Charlotte's eyes flashed.

She had heard Thackeray's lecture on Fielding and, she said to a friend later, "the hour I spent listening to it was a painful one." She knew Thackeray and esteemed him. He had entertained her in London; his portrait hung on the wall of her parlor back home. She had even dedicated the second edition of *Jane Eyre* to him. But Thackeray's treatment of Fielding in his lecture, especially his amused, light-hearted manner in discussing the weaknesses of character that had destroyed Fielding, she thought dangerously wrong:

> Had Thackeray owned a son, grown, or growing up, and a son, brilliant but reckless—would he have spoken in that light way of courses that lead to disgrace and the grave? . . . If only once the prospect of a promising life blasted on the outset by wild ways had passed close under his eyes, he never *could* have spoken with such levity of what led to its piteous destruction.

With a brother like Bramwell, how could Charlotte Brontë have reacted otherwise?

When Charlotte was next at the Gaskell's, in May of 1854, ahead of her lay a happiness she had never known. She had spent a lifetime caring for others. Now at last she would have someone to care for her. In June she would marry her father's curate, the Rev. Arthur Nicholls—old Mr. Brontë's objection to the match having finally been overcome. She only stayed three days and then was off to Leeds to make various purchases in preparation for the marriage. Mrs. Gaskell went to the wedding, of course, but that was the last time the two met. Ten months later, Charlotte Brontë was dead.

Perhaps Manchester's nearest approach to realizing the prediction in Disraeli's *Coningsby* that science would make it a modern Athens has come from the founding of Owens College. Established in 1851 with money left by John Owens, a Manchester merchant, it rapidly became a center of learning. In 1904 it was the nucleus of the new Manchester University which in this century has provided three Nobel Prize winners in the sciences. Early on, Owens produced in George Gissing and Francis Thompson two writers of much talent, but both were ill-starred.

Gissing entered Owens in 1872, and from the start his brilliance was obvious. But he was caught stealing from schoolmates to finance a shabby love affair, stripped of his honors and prizes, expelled, and sent to prison for a month. There followed a short stint as a clerk in Liverpool, a penniless wandering in America, and a return to London and dank cellar rooms where he was hard put to come up with even the sixpence a day they cost—all this by the time he was twenty-one. If his novels such as *New Grub Street* (1891) rate high marks today for their grim realism and as studies of poverty's deadly effects on creativity, Gissing surely paid for them. He died at forty-six, his health undone by privation.

The career of Francis Thompson was even more tragic. He came to Owens in 1876 to study medicine, but after failing the examinations three times, left without a degree. He fled to London and sank into destitution and drug addiction. There he was befriended by Wilfred Meynell, editor of *Merry England,* and his wife Alice, a poet-critic and essayist. Under their auspices in 1893, Thompson published the collection of verses, called *Poems,* containing his famous "Hound of Heaven." He followed this with several other collections of poems and literary criticism, and made valiant efforts to overcome the drug habit. But he died, not yet fifty, in 1907 of tuberculosis.

Owens College has a link to Mrs. Gaskell through its successor. The University of Manchester now owns her home at 84 Plymouth Grove, a tie most fitting since Mrs. Gaskell lectured at Owens in both history and literature. The university uses the house for its Overseas Centre, and has preserved it beautifully. The room that was Mr. Gaskell's study still has its original bookshelves. The Georgian staircase with its brass banisters remains as lovely as ever. And so does the dining room with its huge bay window, where Mrs. Gaskell liked to sit and do her writing.

In 1842, six years before Mrs. Gaskell began *Mary Barton,* a young German came to Manchester, his arrival largely unnoticed. But he was to become responsible for a climax of global proportions to the problems of Manchester and its workers. He was contemporaneous with Carlyle, Dickens, and Mrs. Gaskell; he anticipated George Orwell by a century; but what his efforts achieved eclipsed them all. It is not too much to say that he truly changed the course of history, not for England but for all the world.

The young man was Frederick Engels. His father was a wealthy German textile manufacturer with considerable holdings outside Germany, and Engels came to Manchester at twenty-two to work in a factory his father owned there. Engels was at once concerned with the workers he saw all about him. When Carlyle's *Past and Present* appeared in 1843, Engels was greatly moved by it. Within a year he wrote an article on it, calling it a "wonderfully beautiful book" and praising its humane spirit. The article, written in German, spread Carlyle's influence widely on the continent. But far more important than that, it brought Engels and Karl Marx together. Marx was a fellow German, ousted from Cologne for his radical views and now editing a magazine. Marx was happy to publish Engel's article.

Thus began an association without which the world might never have heard of Karl Marx. Engels's review of Carlyle became the basis for his own book, *The Condition of the Working Class in England* (1845), and this in turn was one of the foundations upon which Marx built *Das Kapital* (1867). It was Engels's money that subsidized Marx's career. Together the two wrote the *Communist Manifesto.* What is more, when Marx died after finishing only Volume I of *Das Kapital,* Engels himself wrote the other two volumes from Marx's notes.

From *Das Kapital* to Lenin, the overthrow of the Russian monarchy, and the establishment of the U.S.S.R. were but a few short steps. And it all started with Frederick Engels and the days he spent in Manchester.

George Orwell got to Manchester in 1936, ninety-four years after Engels and almost at the end of his trek to Wigan Pier. He stayed with a family called Meade, in one of Manchester's new building estates for workers. "Very decent houses," he said, "with bathrooms and electric lights." He got along well with the Meades, as he did with the other workers he met, but he was annoyed when they insisted on calling him "comrade." It was even worse, however, when they went to the other extreme and called him "sir," and looked askance when he rose when a woman entered the room, offered to help with the washing-up, and so on. "Lads up here expect to be waited on," said Mrs. Meade.

Such quarters as the Meades enjoyed were in short supply for workers, and the general status of the poor was deplorable. Orwell found the city on the whole very depressing. Besides, there was that air, so polluted you could taste it. After a week, he was quite ready to quit Manchester for Wigan.

WIGAN

Wigan, a city of 80,000 people, is eighteen miles west of Manchester on the A 49. The Romans had a fort there in the first century A.D., and it was granted a royal charter as early as 1246. By 1400 Wigan had a thriving weaving industry. But its growth came when the development of the steam engine in the eighteenth century created an enormous demand for its abundant coal. After the opening of a canal from Leeds to Liverpool in 1779 enabled coal barges to stop at Wigan, its coal fueled factories throughout northwest England, including the cotton mills of Lancaster. Its last big colliery didn't close until 1967.

Orwell was surprised to find Wigan was not the absolute nadir he had expected. In fact, he admitted in *The Road to Wigan Pier,* he "liked Wigan very much—the people, not the scenery." In a BBC broadcast in 1943, he elaborated: "Its scenery is not its strong point. The landscape is mostly slag-heaps, looking like the mountains of the moon, and mud and soot and so forth." Yet, though Wigan "has always been picked on as a symbol of the ugliness of industrial areas," he said, "it's not worse than fifty other places."

The conditions of Wigan's workers, however, were abject. Orwell found lodgings with a coal miner who had gone into the pits at thirteen. Now thirty-nine and near-blind in both eyes from coal dust, he had been out of work for nine months. Orwell had to share a room with another lodger, take his meals in the kitchen, and wash at the scullery sink. The son of the house, a boy named Joe, fared even worse. Barely fifteen, he already had been working in the mines for over a year. He left for the mines at nine o'clock at night and didn't return until nearly eight next morning. Once home, he tumbled into a bed just vacated by yet another of his parents' lodgers.

For Orwell personally, Wigan "had only one fault." He wrote in his book that Wigan Pier, which he had set his heart on seeing [had been] demolished, "and even the spot where it used to stand is no longer certain."

On that BBC program in 1943, Orwell was asked about Wigan Pier, and he replied:

> Well, I am afraid I must tell you that Wigan Pier doesn't exist. I made a journey specially to see it in 1936, and I couldn't find it. It did exist once, however, and to judge from the photographs it must have been about twenty feet long.

He went on to say,

> At one time, on one of the muddy little canals that run around the town, there used to be a tumble-down wooden jetty: and by way of a joke someone nicknamed this Wigan Pier. The joke caught on locally, and then the music-comedians got hold of it, and they are the ones who have succeeded in keeping Wigan Pier alive as a byword.

Orwell was wrong on just about all counts. Wigan Pier existed when he was there, and still does, though now deserted. The reason he couldn't find it was that he was looking for the wrong thing. The real Wigan Pier wasn't a tumble-down wooden jetty on a muddy backwash at all. It was a grassy hump on the Leeds-Liverpool Canal where barges pulled up to load on coal.

The joke about it was the deliberate concoction of a native son, a professional comedian named George Formby. When his act was hissed off the stage of Wigan's Hippodrome, Formby retaliated. Since Victorian days, the word pier had come to conjure up in the general public's mind those vast, glamorous structures that stretched out into the water at major sea resorts, all a-glitter with theaters, dance halls, and entertainment. Alongside them, Wigan and its poor little landing place were all too easy to ridicule, and Formby did just that, taking his act to all parts of the kingdom.

Orwell was right about one thing. Thanks to George Formby, Wigan and its pier did become national bywords.

LANCASHIRE

The word "stripped" was used advisedly in describing what happened to the old Lancashire in the county restructuring of 1974. As noted, most of its beauty went to the new county of Cumbria; the major cities, industry, and population to the new counties of Merseyside and Greater Manchester.

The new Lancashire, however, is not totally bereft of beauty. Those lovely spots here and there in the valleys of the Lune and Ribble remain. The Forest of Bowland, which covers much of the county's northern half, has been designated an area of outstanding beauty. There fells rise to well over one thousand feet, the highest being Ward's Stone at 1,836 feet, and they offer splendid views. And on the coast above Lancaster there's Morecambe Bay. Once you get past the large and lively seaside resort that is Morecambe itself, you'll see why its hinterlands were among Mrs. Gaskell's favorite retreats from Manchester.

But of the cities left to the new Lancashire, Blackpool alone, with 150,000 people, has any size. Blackburn has 89,000 people, Preston about 87,000, Burnley 70,000. Lancaster today is just another town of 45,000 with some fine old buildings, its past greatness the merest of memories.

Once, though, Lancaster was the proudest name in England's northwest. Roman invaders provided the name for the town in the first century A.D. when they called their fort on the banks of the River Lune "Lune-castrum (camp)." In time the name was then bestowed upon the whole vast county that became the original Lancashire, and upon one of England's great royal families, the House of Lancaster. Together with the House of York, the Lancasters kept the whole country in tumult for most of the fifteenth century as they fought each other for the throne in the Wars of the Roses, in the process supplying ready-made drama for all of Shakespeare's history plays except *King John*. Once, too, Lancaster was a leading port, greater than Liverpool. Now Lancaster is not even the county town anymore. That honor has gone to Preston.

With all this, it's not surprising that little of Lancashire's once-rich literary heritage remains in what's left of the county. Such as there is centers in the Preston-Whalley area of the southwest and between Morecambe Bay and Cowan Bridge in the north.

PRESTON

Preston is north of Wigan, fifteen miles straight up the A 59. Preston built one of Lancashire's first cotton mills, as well it might. Richard Arkwright, inventor of the spinning frame, was born there in 1732. There's a rather neat balance in the fact that in 1794 Preston was also the birthplace of Joseph Livesay, who saw himself as the savior of men who toiled in those same mills.

The worst of the evils they faced, in Livesay's view, was the Saturday night bottle of gin that provided so many of the mill workers a brief oblivion from the near-slavery to which machinery like Arkwright's had reduced them.[1] So Livesay founded the Temperance Movement, which became worldwide, and published England's first newspaper for abstainers, *The Preston Temperance Advocate.* The word "teetotaler" is said to have been born when a Livesay convert who stammered manfully tackled the official oath and came out with a pledge of "t-t-total abstinence."

Preston is of chief literary interest, of course, as the "Coketown" of Charles Dickens's *Hard Times.*[2] But Dickens was also in Preston while working on *Dombey and Son* (1847–48), and stayed at the Bull on Church Street. Now the Bull and Royal, the hotel is nicely situated in the town centre, and with a three-star rating, it's more than comfortable.

Francis Thompson, the poet of "The Hound of Heaven," was born in Preston in 1859 at No. 7 Winckley Street, but was still a child when his family moved to Ashton-under-Lyme near Manchester.

WHALLEY—HURSTWOOD—AND STONYHURST COLLEGE

Whalley is on the A 59, fourteen miles northeast of Preston; Hurstwood off the A 646, ten miles southeast of Whalley; and Stonyhurst College off the B 6243, four miles or so northwest of Whalley.

Whalley   Whalley is an attractive little place on the River Calder.

---

[1]For details on the traditional bottle of gin, see pp. 280–81.
[2]For Coketown and *Hard Times* see pp. 280 and 287.

In *The Lancashire Witches* (1849) Harrison Ainsworth presents the Whalley Abbey, now in ruins, as it was in its last days before the sixteenth-century Dissolution. Other scenes in the novel round and about Whalley are set in Downham, Pendle Hill, Barley, and Newchurch. (The latter is Ainsworth's "Goldshaw.")

Hurstwood   Still standing in Hurstwood is an old Elizabethan cottage now called "Spenser's House." In the sixteenth century it belonged to Edmund Spenser's grandparents, and the poet himself lived there for several years after his graduation from Cambridge in 1576. He fell in love with a beautiful young lady from somewhere in the area. Her exact identity remains unknown and, besides, she jilted him. Even so, she won a touch of immortality. She is the Rosalind of both *The Shepheards Calendar* (1579) and *Colin Clouts come home againe* (1595).

Stonyhurst College   Stonyhurst College, a Jesuit boys' school whose origins go back to the sixteenth century, came to Stonyhurst in 1794, settling into the Elizabethan mansion that still forms the center for the later buildings clustered about it. Three of its students in the nineteenth century were Alfred Austin, poet laureate from 1896 to 1913; Wilfred Scawen Blunt, author of volumes of poetry like *The Love Sonnets of Proteus* (1880); and Arthur Conan Doyle. Gerard Manley Hopkins was both a student and teacher at Stonyhurst.

Doyle and Hopkins make interesting contrasts. Even as a schoolboy preparing for Edinburgh University and medicine, Doyle already was drifting out of Roman Catholicism. The Jesuits, he thought, "try to rule too much by fear—too little by love or reason." When Hopkins arrived as a student at Stonyhurst in 1870 he had only recently become a Catholic, converted by Cardinal Newman. Doyle eventually abandoned all orthodox religion for spiritualism. Hopkins's devotion to his new faith grew ever stronger.

After practicing medicine for some years, Doyle gave it up for fame and fortune as a writer of short stories and novels. Hopkins lived out his life in obscurity as teacher and priest. Only a handful of his poems were even printed in his lifetime. As creator of Sherlock Holmes, Doyle is known worldwide. As creator of a revolutionary new form of verse called "sprung rhythm," Hopkins remains pretty much "caviar for the general."

SILVERDALE—AND COWAN BRIDGE

Silverdale   Silverdale is located on an unnumbered highway about three miles west of the A 6 almost on the shores of Morecambe Bay. After she became a successful novelist in 1848, Mrs. Gaskell used the village as a treasured escape from what she called the "grey, weary, uniform streets" of Manchester. It is clear that she never really liked Manchester, and never ceased to miss the loveliness of the Knutsford in which she had grown up. Her fictionalized name for Manchester in *Cranford* is "Dumble."

It is easy to hear Mrs. Gaskell's own voice behind the words of old Alice Wilson in *Mary Barton* (1848) when she says to Mary and Margaret,

> Eh, lasses! ye don't know what rocks are in Manchester! Grey pieces o' stone as large as a house, all covered over wi' moss of different colours . . .

And the longing for rural Hampshire that Margaret Hale expresses in *North and South* (1854-55) may have been Mrs. Gaskell's own. In the last year of her life she bought a house in Hampshire, and died there in November 1865 while getting it in shape for use as a second home.[3]

At Silverdale Mrs. Gaskell found unspoiled beauty plus the privacy and freedom she needed as a writer. She stayed at a place now called Gibraltar Tower. From her study at the top, she could watch the sun set gloriously in the west over Morecambe Bay and shut herself off from intrusion as she worked on *Cranford, Ruth,* and *North and South*. "Abermouth" in *Ruth* (1853) is thought to be Silverdale.

The people of Silverdale remembered Mrs. Gaskell warmly. Their village meeting place is now called Gaskell Hall.

Cowan Bridge   In her *Life of Charlotte Brontë*, Mrs. Gaskell says that Charlotte, in her most composed manner, once told her that

> she believed some were appointed beforehand to sorrow and much disappointment . . . that it was well for those who had rougher paths to perceive that such was God's will concerning them, and try to moderate their expectations.

---

[3]Strangely, she had never told Mr. Gaskell about buying this house in Holybourne, Hampshire. Perhaps, as some have suggested, she meant it as a surprise Christmas gift.

Charlotte had more than her share of rougher paths, and Cowan Bridge and Tunstall were two of the earliest and roughest.

In 1824, a School for Clergymen's Daughters was established at Cowan Bridge (on today's A 65) to put a "good female education within the reach of the poorest clergy." Total cost was £14 per pupil per year for clothing, lodging, boarding, and education. There was a £1 entrance fee for books, and £3 for pelisses, frocks, bonnets, etc., so that the girls would all dress alike. The curriculum, unburdened by frills, included "History, Geography, and Use of the Globes, Grammar, Writing, and Arithmetic, all kinds of needlework, and the nicer kinds of household work, such as getting up fine linen, ironing, etc."[4]

The Rev. Patrick Brontë had lost his wife in 1821, leaving him with the care of a son and five daughters. In 1824 his youngest girl, Anne, was only four and too young to go to school. But he sent the four other siblings—Maria, age ten; Elizabeth, nine; Charlotte, eight; and Emily, six— to Cowan Bridge School the year it opened.

The school appears as "Lowood" in *Jane Eyre,* and Charlotte's description of life there is grim. The children were always cold:

> Our clothing was insufficient to protect us from the severe cold: we had no boots, the snow got into our shoes and melted there; our ungloved hands became numb and covered with chilblains.

For the smaller girls, even the warmth of a fireplace was denied. When the pupils came in from the cold,

> each hearth in the schoolroom was immediately surrounded by a double row of great girls, and behind them the younger children crouched in groups, wrapping their starved arms in their pinafores.

Hunger was a constant problem, too, and again hardest on the very small, including Charlotte, eight, and Emily, six. As Charlotte recalls in the novel,

> The scanty supply of food was distressing . . . we had scarcely sufficient to keep alive a delicate invalid. From this deficiency of nourishment resulted an abuse, which pressed hardly on the younger pupils; whenever the famished great girls had an opportunity, they would coax or menace the little ones out of their portion. Many a time I have shared between two claimants the precious morsel of brown bread distributed at tea-time;

---

[4] From the school's official report for 1830.

and after relinquishing to a third, half the contents of my mug of coffee, I have swallowed the remainder with an accompaniment of secret tears, forced from me by the exigency of hunger.

Discipline at the school was of the highest moral order, and therefore relentless. Lowood's director in the novel is Mr. Brocklehurst, based on the real-life Rev. William Carus Wilson, vicar of Tunstall Church and founder of Cowan Bridge School. Mr. Brocklehurst had received admonitions, apparently from the Lord Himself, that he should not supply comfort to his charges at the expense of their immortal souls. Mr. Brocklehurst was not one to ignore divine admonitions.

When Jane Eyre's slate falls and shatters as Mr. Brocklehurst is addressing the students, he makes her stand before them atop a high stool and he thunders:

> "You all see this girl? . . . God has graciously given her the shape that he has given to all of us . . . who would think that the Evil One had already found a servant and an agent in her? Yet such, I grieve to say, is the case. . . .
> "You must be on your guard against her; you must shun her example: if necessary, avoid her company, exclude her from your sports, and shut her out from your converse.

In some ways, Sundays were the worst days of all. The girls had to walk two miles to church to hear their patron hold forth from his pulpit. In Jane Eyre's version, "We set out cold, we arrived at church colder: during the morning service we became almost paralysed." They had to stay for the afternoon service, too. It was dusk when at last they returned over the exposed and hilly road, "where the bitter winter wind, blowing over a range of snowy summits to the north, almost flayed the skin from our bodies."

From Silverdale or Cowan Bridge you can walk, in a matter of minutes, into the next county, final stop on this literary tour of northern England. And what a stop it is! The governmental restructurers may have called it Cumbria when they fashioned it in 1974, but to many it will always be simply "The Lake District," home to Wordsworth and Southey and Coleridge and Ruskin. A land of magic.

CUMBRIA
THE LAKE DISTRICT

3

Cumbria

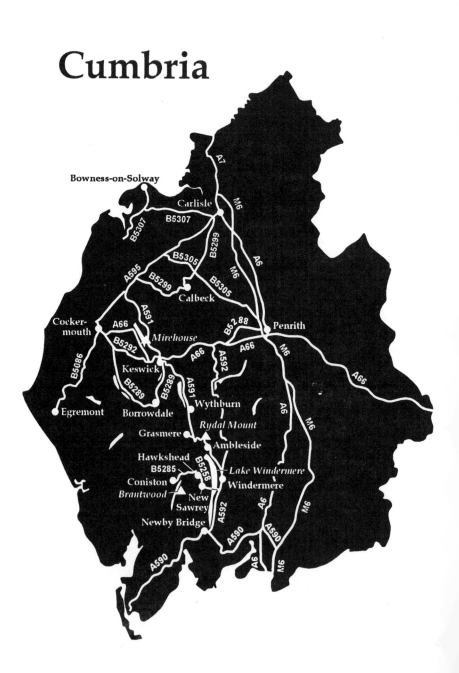

We have clambered up to the top of Skiddaw. . . . Oh, its fine black head, and the bleak air atop of it, with a prospect of mountains all about and about, making you giddy; and then Scotland afar off, and the border countries so famous in song and ballad! It was a day that will stand out, like a mountain, I am sure, in my life.

Charles Lamb in a letter, September 1802

The two views we have had of [Windermere] . . . refine one's sensual vision into a sort of north star which can never cease to be open lidded and stedfast over the wonders of the great Power.

John Keats in a letter to his brother Tom, June 1818

The scenery is, of course, grand; could I have wandered about amongst those hills *alone,* I could have drank in all their beauty.

Charlotte Brontë from Ambleside to Mrs. Gaskell, 1850

Cool farms, with open-lying stores.
Under their burnish'd sycamores
All past! . . .

The red-grouse, springing at our sound
Skims, now and then, the shining ground
No life, save his and ours, intrudes
Upon these breathless solitudes.

Matthew Arnold above Keswick, "Resignation"

. . . all at once I saw a crowd,
A host, of golden daffodils;
Beside the lake, beneath the trees,
Fluttering and dancing in the breeze.
. . . .
[Now] oft, when on my couch I lie
In vacant or in pensive mood,

They flash upon that inward eye
Which is the bliss of solitude;
And then my heart with pleasure fills
And dances with the daffodils.

William Wordsworth at Ullswater,
"I Wandered Lonely as a Cloud," 1802

Lamb, Keats, Brontë, Arnold, Wordsworth—the list of writers and their rhapsodies about the Lake District could go on and on. So could a list of the places they loved: Skiddaw, Windermere, Ambleside, Keswick, Ullswater. Yet none of those rhapsodies seem hyperbole.

Cumbria, created in 1974 from the old counties of Westmoreland and Cumberland and a bit of the top of old Lancashire, is about fifty miles wide (from the Irish Sea to Durham) and sixty-five long (from today's Lancashire to the Scottish border). Of this, practically all the southern half and a bit more comprise the Lake District. Thomas Gray first presented the district to the world at large when he visited it in 1769 and wrote "Journal in the Lakes" (included in *The Poems of Mr. Gray* [1775]). Since then similar books have steadily come along. Writers who interrupted their regular chores to write about the area include Wordsworth, *A Description of the Scenery of the Lakes in the North of England* (1822); Thomas De Quincey, *Recollections of the Lakes and the Lake Poets* (1835–40); and Harriet Martineau, *Complete Guide to the Lakes* (1855).

What makes the Lake District so special is not magnitude or majesty, but sheer beauty. The highest mountains (they call them "fells," from the Scandinavian *fjall*—rock or cliff—of the Norwegian and Danish invaders of the sixth and seventh centuries) are not overpowering. The highest is Scafell Pike, a mere 3,210 feet, but at that it's the highest in England. There are sixteen lakes and numerous small ponds and reservoirs, the biggest being Lake Windermere, ten miles long, again England's largest. And there are spectacular waterfalls, lovely valleys, and wonderfully wooded crags and hills.

All this makes for a beauty unique in its ability to entrance the visitor not on first view alone, but to live on in memory forever. This is the common theme that runs through the quotations that introduce this section: Charles Lamb's Skiddaw, and the day "that will stand out like a mountain, in my life"; Keats's Windermere, a "north star which can never cease"; Wordsworth's daffodils of Ullster Water, oft flashing upon that inward eye "which is the bliss of solitude."

It is impossible to suggest how long you should plan to stay in the Lake District, except, perhaps, to say "as long as you can." Points of particular literary interest divide nicely into three major tours: one in the south, from Newby Bridge to Hawkshead; one in the heart of the district in and around Ambleside and Grasmere; and the third in the north, in and around Keswick, Cockermouth, and Penrith.

You can do all three from a single base in Ambleside, if you like. It has accommodations of every size, style, and price. Or, if you have more time and like variety, you might want to add Keswick, Cockermouth, or Penrith as a second center of operations for the northern sites.

In any case, do your homework before you embark on any excursion. Know exactly how to get to where you are going, and precisely what to look for once you arrive. Above all, don't be too ambitious about how much you want to cover in any one day. Roads are generally good, but many are narrow and often twist and turn abruptly; grades can be steep and frightening. Plan to take time.

THE SOUTH LAKES
NEWBY BRIDGE TO HAWKSHEAD

———————————————————

Newby Bridge is on the A 590, nine miles northwest of Silverdale and the Lancashire border. Hawkshead is only eight miles above Newby Bridge. Between are Near Sawrey, Esthwaite Water, Brantwood, and Coniston.

Newby Bridge   It was Newby Bridge's location just below the southern end of Lake Windermere that made it attractive to Arthur Ransome, purveyor of tales for children. He wrote a number of stories with the lake and its countryside as setting, and stayed at the Newby Bridge Hotel while writing *Scallions and Amazons,* published in 1931.

Nearly a century before Ransome, the American novelist Nathaniel Hawthorne also, found Newby Bridge inviting, stopping there in the 1850s while serving as U.S. counsel at Liverpool. "A very agreeable place," he said, "not striking as to scenery, but with a pleasant, rural aspect." He especially liked his hotel, the Swan, "An old-fashioned inn, where the landlord and his people have a simple and friendly way of dealing with their guests." The Swan isn't all that old-fashioned anymore (it rates three stars now), but the friendly way persists.

Near Sawrey and Esthwaite Water   From Newby Bridge, the A 592 runs northward along the shore of Lake Windermere, and about three and a half miles up you'll come to a ferry that can take you across the lake to the B 5258, Esthwaite Water, and Near Sawrey. It's the same ferry crossing that Wordsworth made in 1799 when on his way to Grasmere to look for a place to live. Wordsworth knew Esthwaite Water well. While yet a child "not nine years old," he tells us in *The Prelude* (published posthumously in 1850), he watched the body of a drowned man "with ghastly face, a spectre shape of terror" being recovered from its depths. Young as he was, however, he assures us he wasn't one bit afraid himself. He had already seen just such sights in visions, "among the shining streams of fairy land." At not quite nine years old!

For a number of years beginning in 1928, Francis Brett Young chose Esthwaite Lodge near the western shore of the lake for his working holidays. Much of *The House under the Water* (1932) was done there.

Hugh Walpole, too, found the lodge ideal for combining work and play. He was a guest of Young's, and his work in hand while there was *Judith Paris,* published in 1931. You, too, can stay at the lodge—if, that is, you are of an appropriate age and if you don't mind a bit of roughing it. The lodge is now a youth hostel.

Beatrix Potter, the creator of Peter Rabbit, was born in London in 1866 yet always hated the city. "My unloved birthplace," she called it. It was not the city alone she disliked, but the oppressively limited life her parents forced her to lead there. Near Sawrey brought salvation.

With her family she holidayed in the neighborhood from childhood on, and loved it. Of Near Sawrey itself she wrote in her journal, "It is as perfect a little place as I ever lived in." By 1905, profits from *The Tale of Peter Rabbit* (1901) had made her financially independent, and when Hill Top Farm in Near Sawrey became available, she bought it. She used it to wean herself from her parents and London with ever-longer and more frequent visits. Here she continued her series of tales. The farmhouse and other parts of Near Sawrey appear in her illustrations for both *Tom Kitten* (1907) and *Jemima Puddle-duck* (1908).

Her emancipation became complete, not only from her parents but from her writing, when in 1913, at age forty-seven, she married William Heelis, her solicitor and a native of the district. They moved across the road from Hill Top to larger quarters in a place called Castle Farms, and Beatrix settled down happily to the life of a lady farmer, overseeing the farming and the raising of livestock, and adding steadily to her land holdings. When she died in 1943 she owned 207 acres, including both Hill Top and Castle Farms, and half the village of Near Sawrey. She left it all to the National Trust.

Hill Top is now open to the public April through October, most days of the week and on Sunday afternoons. On view in the seventeenth-century house are her furniture, china, pictures, and a number of her original drawings. Upstairs, in what were the bedrooms, are museum cases with her letters, manuscripts, and sketchbooks. Portions of the drapes were stitched by Beatrix herself.

BRANTWOOD—CONISTON—AND HAWKSHEAD

From Near Sawrey, a couple of miles' drive up the B 5258 will bring you to Hawkshead, and from there the B 5285 takes you another three miles or so to Brantwood and Coniston. If you want to see all three, it's more expeditious to go right on through Hawkshead and proceed directly to Brantwood and Coniston first, saving a look at Hawkshead for your way back, especially if you plan to push on to Ambleside for the night.

Brantwood   Although he was born in London in 1817, John Ruskin said he couldn't recall a time he didn't know and love the Lake District. The first event of his life he could remember, he said, was being taken as a child to Friar's Crag, where he peered through hollows at the dark lake below with "intense joy mingled with awe." He first visited the Coniston area at five.

In 1871, without ever having seen it, he bought a house and estate, called Brantwood, on the east shore of Coniston Water. The building was a near-shambles, but commanded a view Ruskin termed "on the whole the finest I know in Cumberland or Lancashire." As a wealthy man, he could afford the required extensive repairs, and he made elaborate additions and adorned it with his rich collection of paintings by Titian, Tintoretto, Turner, and the Pre-Raphaelites.

He used the place at first for vacations while Slade professor of art at Oxford (1871-84), and the series of monthly "letters" to the workmen of Britain—published as *Fors Clavigera* (1871-84) was begun there. After Oxford, Brantwood was his permanent residence, and he died there in 1900.

Brantwood is off an unnumbered little road which is off the B 5285 and narrow and more zig-zag than you'll like. But it's well worth a visit. It's open Good Friday through October daily except Saturdays. It's now owned by the Education Trust and used as an adult residential center. But you can see Ruskin's study and drawing room; the small bedroom he first used, with a turret he added; and the large dining room he had specially built to provide the best possible view of the lake. You can have lunch in his original, smaller dining room. Also on display is Ruskin's boat, the Jumping Jenny, and the fine coach he designed for a tour he took in 1875.

And Brantwood offers another treat: you can see it from the lake while riding in a gondola! Not your everyday, plain vanilla Venetian gondola, either, but a seventy-foot beauty, opulent as the Victorian period in which it was built and when it was enjoyed by the likes of Ruskin, Arthur Ransome, and Thomas Carlyle. Named simply "The Gondola," it was restored in 1980 by the National Trust. The interior is elegant red velvet and polished mahogany, with two saloons. On deck and inside the boat seats eighty-five.

During the summer, rides begin at the Coniston Pier, take an hour to go to the end of the lake and return, and offer en route a grand view of Ruskin's home, one of the few built on the beautiful wooded heights of the eastern shore. On a pleasant day you're in for a sparkling experience.

Coniston   Ruskin is buried in the Coniston churchyard, and the village has a Ruskin museum. It's a modest little thing, one room at the rear of the Coniston Institute, offspring of the Mechanics Institute of which Ruskin had been an honorary member and vice president. But there are several good exhibits: some sketches and reproductions, a few paintings and letters, and samples of his wide-ranging interests—the lace-making he once looked into as a possible local industry, mineral collecting, wood chopping, and pottery making. There's even a stone dulcimer.

The museum is open from Easter to the end of October. But don't be surprised if there's no one there to greet you. There often isn't. Just put a coin in the turnstile and go on in.

In 1850, Alfred Tennyson brought his new wife, Emily, to Coniston on their honeymoon. They stayed with his old friends, the James Marshalls, who had an estate called Tent Lodge overlooking Coniston Water. The Marshalls were very rich and given to patronizing writers. Among guests invited to come stay, or at least to drop in and meet Tennyson's new bride, were Thomas Carlyle, the Irish poet Aubrey de Vere, Thomas Woolner, Coventry Patmore, Edward Lear, and Matthew Arnold.

One day Tennyson and Patmore climbed the Old Man of Coniston, a mountain 2,631 feet high with magnificent views on every side. They found the going up more than arduous, and the whole outing took over five hours, but fortified, they said, by frequent nips of the bottle. They thought the whole expedition "rather glorious," and raced down six times faster than they had come up.

Tennyson had begun working on a new section of *The Princess* (1847), and often went for walks outside Tent Lodge to block out lines for the poem as he strode along. But he'd get so absorbed in his composing that on his return he'd pass right by the house without noticing it. So Emily had the gate-post painted white to warn him of its approach.

In 1857 Tent Lodge had another visitor of note. The Tennysons were there again, and Emily asked a Mr. Dodgson, lecturer in mathematics and something of a photographer, to come take pictures of her two sons. For a week Dodgson dutifully fulfilled his assignment and between times walked with Tennyson and listened to the poet recite *Maud* aloud.

Dodgson, of course, was Lewis Carroll.

Hawkshead   From 1779 to 1787 William Wordsworth attended Hawkshead's Free Grammar School before going to Cambridge. The school was founded in 1585 by Archbishop Edwin Sandys and, though free to local boys, charged outsiders like the Wordsworths a moderate fee. William and his brother Richard lodged with a Mrs. Ann Tyson who, with her husband, had kept a little shop in the village during the 1760s, but in 1779 began to take in boys from the school as boarders. The Wordsworths were among the first. Two houses lay claim to being the one William salutes in *The Prelude* as "friendly to studious or to festive hours." One house is on Vicarage Lane in town, the other on the outskirts at Colthouse. Most likely he lived in both. Both still stand, but remain in private hands. You can, however, see them from the outside.

The school is now a museum, open Easter through October daily except Wednesdays. It's a small, two-storey building with the heavy slate roof typical of Hawkshead, and a sundial over the canopied door. Still in the classroom on the ground floor are the desks of Wordsworth's day, one with his fully carved name now protected by a glass cover. There's not too much else to see, but on one of the beams in the ceiling there's a pulley, said to have been used to pull recalcitrant students into just the right position for a birching.

BETWEEN THE LAKES
WINDERMERE TO GRASMERE

———————————————

The four best-known of all the Lake District's famous literary sites are within five miles of each other—the two lakes called Windermere and Grasmere and, between, Ambleside and Rydal Mount. Except for London the roster of leading writers associated with the four is unrivaled. As starters, for instance, how about: Arnold, Matthew; Brontë, Charlotte; Coleridge, S. T.; De Quincey, Thomas; and Eliot, George?

The ten-mile length of Lake Windermere is both figuratively and literally a highway from the Lancashire border to the heart of the Lake District. The A 592 runs along its eastern shore and takes you to the town called Windermere, large by Lake District standards with 8,600 people nine miles northeast of Hawkshead. Then take the A 591 to Ambleside, Rydal Mount, and Grasmere.

LAKE WINDERMERE

The old Saxon word for lake was "mere," and the Saxon's name for Lake Windermere describes it well: "Winander-mere," the winding lake. That original name, indeed, must have persisted even in Keat's day, for in a letter to his brother Tom on a visit there in 1818, he speaks of seeing "the Lake and the Mountain of Winander." Nowhere is the lake more than a mile and a quarter wide, and at one point it narrows to a quarter of a mile, little more than a river. Ultimately it does become a river, the Leven, which flows through Lancashire and empties into Morecambe Bay.

There is a neatness, a kemptness about Windermere that Nathaniel Hawthorne remarked on when he saw it in 1955. "The banks are everywhere beautiful," he said. "I have seen no wilderness; everything is perfectly subdued and polished and imbued with human taste, except, indeed, the outlines of the hills, which continue very much the same as God made them."

Sailing upon Windermere was one of Wordsworth's delights, and in *A Guide to the Lakes* he urged it upon visitors: "One bright, unruffled, evening must, if possible, be set aside, for the splendour, the stillness, the solemnity of a three hours' voyage upon the higher division of the Lake." One Wordsworth convert to this was Sir Walter Scott, who, as Wordsworth's guest in 1825, had a regatta staged on the lake in honor of his fifty-fourth birthday.

Wordsworth himself, of course, became a major lure for visitors to the area. But once Thomas Gray had introduced the lake to the kingdom (in his *Journal* of 1775), they would have come anyway, and in ever-growing numbers. The lake and the views it afforded were, after all, the north star that drew John Keats. That same letter to his brother Tom tells why: "I cannot describe them—they surpass my expectation—beautiful water—shores and islands green to the marge—mountains all around to the clouds."

Charlotte Brontë was equally lyrical when she saw the lake in 1850. "The Lake country is a glorious region," she wrote a friend, "of which I had only seen the similitude in dreams, waking or sleeping." George Eliot, who was there in 1852, singled out Windermere for special praise, along with Derwent Water. And it was as a child, holidaying with her parents at Wray Castle on Windermere's western shore, that Beatrix Potter formed her lifelong attachment to the district.

In consequence of its charm, Windermere in season suffers from that annoying characteristic of all great tourist attractions: people other than yourself insist on going there, too, as Keats discovered way back in 1818. He denounced the crowds of tourists he saw as the "disfigurement of the Lake." The "miasma of London," he called them, "contaminated with bucks and soldiers, and women of fashion—and hatband ignorance." So, if you go to Windermere in July, be prepared for somebody on your jam-packed sightseeing boat elbowing you aside and grabbing that seat on the aft-deck that is rightfully yours. There's not much you can do about it, except to fulminate as Keats did—under your breath.

Unless, that is, you can manage to do what some of the natives do: stay away from Windermere entirely until the summer hordes have gone. That's what that most independent of writers, Harriet Martineau, did. "She always leaves her house at Ambleside during the Lake season," Charlotte Brontë told Mrs. Gaskell, "to avoid the influx of visitors to which she would otherwise be subjected."

Charlotte Brontë should know. She had visited Miss Martineau—but in December, mind you.

AMBLESIDE

With only 2,600 year-round inhabitants, Ambleside is hardly more than a village. But at the peak of the tourist season, as all those visitors try to squeeze by each other on its narrow and crooked little streets, it has the air of a much bigger place.

Nathaniel Hawthorne's description, written in 1855, is even more fitting today. Ambleside "is a little town," he said, but "built on a very uneven hillside, and with very irregular streets and lanes, which bewilder the stranger as much as those of a larger city." Since Hawthorne's day all the shops and facilities that have sprung up to accommodate the many more strangers that come today only heighten the impression.

Ambleside is a funnel through which most travelers going north still pass to see the rest of the Lake District. As such it has shared the comings and goings of just about all the literary elite associated with the Lakes. William Wordsworth paved the way in 1799, the year after he and Coleridge published *Lyrical Ballads*. His lease of Alfoxden House in Somerset had run out, and now he was looking for a permanent place to live.

He found exactly what he wanted at Grasmere, two miles up the road from Ambleside. Thereafter, he lived in the area the rest of his life, and one way or another is connected to most of the writers who came that way. Coleridge and his children stayed with the Wordsworths for extended periods during the early years. Later came Sir Walter Scott, William Hazlitt, and Thomas De Quincey.

Wordsworth was in and out of Ambleside regularly. It was a jumping-off point for his trips to London and elsewhere. He walked in often to see friends. And the only real job he ever had in his life was at Ambleside. In 1813 he was appointed stamp distributor for Westmoreland through the patronage of his friend Lord Lonsdale. His duties were to receive the government stamps required for various documents from London and distribute them to sub-offices throughout the county. At first it took a fair amount of his time. But of the £300 annual stipend, Wordsworth was able to clear £200, a tidy sum. His rent for Dove Cottage in Grasmere for a whole year was £8.

Keats and Shelley were two of the writers who passed through Ambleside about this time, but for quite different reasons. Keats was there in 1818 mainly to begin his tour of the lakes, but also to see Wordsworth.

He made a particular point of seeing Ambleside waterfall and was struck by "the thunder and the freshness," and the more than fifty feet of its three-level plunge,

> . . . the first darting down the slate-rock like an arrow; the second spreading out like a fan—the third dashed into a mist.

Keats was profoundly affected. "I shall learn poetry here," he said, "and shall henceforth write more than ever."

Shelley's presence in Ambleside in October of 1813 was due to what had become a sadly familiar routine. Once again he was fleeing creditors who threatened to jail him for debt. This time he was fleeing from Bracknell in Berkshire. In typical fashion, the penniless Shelley bought his own coach for the trip so he could go in style, paying for it with money borrowed at exorbitant rates against the fortune he would inherit one day. He did need a conveyance of size, however. With him went his wife Harriet, their newly born daughter Ianthe, Harriet's sister Eliza, and Shelley's friend, the poet Thomas Love Peacock.

Shelley chose for their initial lodgings Lowwood (or Low-wood) Inn, outside Ambleside at Lake Windermere's northern edge, because it had the same name and location as a hotel in a novel by another of his friends (and later father-in-law), William Godwin. Shelley intended to rent a furnished house in Ambleside and remain until spring, but none could be found. By the middle of October Shelley and his party were in Edinburgh.

Hawthorne stayed at Lowwood Inn, too, in 1855, and didn't like it one bit. It was, he said, "an extensive hotel, covering a good deal of ground; but low and rather village-inn-like than lofty." In sum, "a scrambling, ill-ordered hotel, with insufficient attendance."

That certainly doesn't fit the hotel that awaits you now. Low Wood, as it is spelled today, enjoys a three-star rating. Spacious lawns and gardens run down to the edge of the lake, and views of both lake and mountains are superb.

Alfred Tennyson was at Ambleside in May 1835, along with Edward FitzGerald and James Spedding. Friends from their days together at Cambridge, they were young then, just twenty-six, with their careers as writers yet to come. FitzGerald's *Rubaiyat of Omar Khayyám* would not appear until 1850, Spedding's first works on Francis Bacon not until 1857. Tennyson had already published, but his *Poems Chiefly Lyrical*

(1830) had been attacked by critics, and the *Poems* of 1832 had fared little better.

Spedding tried to get the other two to go out to see Wordsworth, who by then was living at Rydal Mount, but Tennyson's son, Hallam, says his father refused because "he did not wish to obtrude himself on the great man at Rydal." Hallam must have been mistaken, however. The guest book the Wordsworths kept for visitors to sign has an entry for May 1835: "Mr. J. Spedding, Mirehouse and Mr. A. Tennyson, London."

They had far more right to call on Wordsworth than ordinary visitors. The Speddings and the Wordsworths were old family friends. And the poet's brother, Christopher Wordsworth, was master at Trinity College, the college all three had attended at Cambridge. What's more, Wordsworth himself was aware of the little volume of verse Tennyson and his brother Frederick had published in 1827 called *Poems by Two Brothers,* and he thought well of it. He had come across it while visiting Christopher at Trinity in 1830 and had written a friend, "We have a respectable show of blossom in poetry. Two brothers of the name of Tennyson, in particular, are not a little promising." Wordsworth was prescient. In 1850 Alfred Tennyson succeeded Wordsworth as poet laureate.

Following Wordsworth's lead, other writers came to live in the Ambleside-Grasmere area. Among them was Felicia Hemans, the engaging young poet discussed earlier in the section on Liverpool.[1] She was the one who had no delusions about her talents, and frankly admitted she wrote only because she needed the money to support her five sons. Even so, she left us such lines as "the boy stood on the burning deck," from "Casabianca," and "the stately homes of England" from "The Homes of England."

Between 1829 and 1831 Mrs. Hemans had a home called Dove Nest overlooking Lake Windermere near the Lowwood Hotel, and once was a guest of Wordsworth at Rydal Mount for two weeks. Wordsworth's wife Mary and her sister Sarah thought the stay "long," but perhaps they were miffed with their guest. This was the visit on which Hemans called Wordsworth to his face "giddy."

In 1834 Dr. Thomas Arnold, headmaster of Rugby School and father of Matthew Arnold, built the house known as Fox How as a summer home. It was on the Clappergate Road only minutes from Rydal Mount,

---

[1]See pp. 265–67.

and Wordsworth had not only helped in arrangements to buy the land, but also had a hand in the building plans. It was an inviting, comfortable house, nestled among gardens and trees, and young Matthew loved spending his holidays from school there.[2]

Queen of Ambleside's literati was Harriet Martineau, author of novels like *Deerbrook* (1839), stories for young people, and books and articles of all kinds, often written to wage uncompromising war for her less than conventional ideas about social reforms. In 1845 she built a house called The Knoll on a little hill off Rydal Road and proceeded to take charge of things. Some of the gentry resented her, but lesser folk held her in high esteem. The Knoll was an agreeable place, and hospitable. "Her house is very pleasant, both within and without; arranged at all points with admirable neatness and comfort," wrote Charlotte Brontë during an 1850 visit. Miss Martineau was a most considerate hostess. "Her visitors enjoy the most perfect liberty," Charlotte said, "what she claims for herself she allows them."

Miss Martineau regularly rose at five and was at her desk by seven. Guests, however, could rise when they chose, breakfast at will, and be totally free until two o'clock when the hostess would make herself available for whatever diversions they desired. George Eliot found this true when she visited The Knoll in 1852, and declared her hostess "utterly charming in her own home."

Nathaniel Hawthorne includes The Knoll in his account of his 1855 visit to Ambleside:

> We saw Miss Martineau's residence, called "The Knoll," standing up on a hillock and having at its foot a Methodist chapel, for which, or whatever place of Christian worship, this good lady can have no occasion.

Perhaps the lady's reputation for unorthodoxy intimidated Hawthorne. He continues,

> We stopped a moment in the street below her house, and deliberated a little whether to call on her: but concluded we would not.[3]

Charlotte Brontë said of Harriet Martineau: "She is both hard and warmhearted, abrupt and affectionate, liberal and despotic. I believe that

---

[2]Fox How remains in private hands, and isn't visible from the road.

[3]The Knoll has been preserved as a historic monument and is now part of an educational training school.

she is not at all conscious of her own absolutism. When I tell her of it, she denies the charge warmly; then I laugh at her. I believe she almost rules Ambleside."

Miss Martineau's subjects included even Wordsworth. He had encouraged her to build The Knoll, saying it would double in value within ten years. He helped her plan her gardens and wrote the motto for her sundial: "Come, Light! Visit me!" She repaid him with a mixture of friendship and independence, even derision. She would fuss at his odd ways behind his back, yet until his death in 1850 at eighty, she would charge over to Rydal Mount now and then to see how he was getting along.

Another of the elite who had a home in the Ambleside area was Sir James P. Kay-Shuttleworth, doctor and educationist, with an interest in things literary. He became personally involved in an effort to publish Charlotte Brontë's *The Professor* after her death in 1855. His house, used as a summer place, was Briery Close, overlooking Lake Windermere at Lowwood in the same vicinity as the hotel where Shelley and Hawthorne stayed and Felicia Hemans had her house.

The Kay-Shuttleworth estate was Gawthorpe Hall, a dozen miles from Haworth in Yorkshire where the Brontës lived. Charlotte Brontë's *Shirley* was published in 1849, and in March of 1850, wishing to know more about its author, Sir James and his wife drove over to Haworth to meet her. A bit reluctantly she accepted their invitation to visit Gawthorpe. Abnormally shy though she was, Charlotte rather enjoyed it. When in August they asked her to Briery Close, she agreed to come.

As it happened, Lady Kay-Shuttleworth was a friend of Elizabeth Gaskell and invited her to be a guest that same week. When Mrs. Gaskell arrived it was late afternoon. Awaiting her in the drawing room, along with her host and hostess, she found a little lady in black silk who came up to her at once and shook hands. But after Mrs. Gaskell had gone up to her room to unbonnet and come down again for tea, she reported in a long letter to her friend Katie Winkworth, "The little lady worked away [on her needlework] and hardly spoke."

The little lady was, of course, Charlotte Brontë, and Mrs. Gaskell's impressions at this first encounter are vividly set down:

> She is, (as she calls herself) underdeveloped; thin and more than ½ a head shorter than I, soft brown hair not so dark as mine; eyes (very good and expressive looking straight & open at you) of the same colour, a reddish face; large mouth & many teeth gone; altogether plain; the forehead square,

broad and <u>rather</u> overhanging. She has a very sweet voice, rather hesitates when choosing her expressions, but when chosen they seem without effort, <u>admirable</u> and <u>just</u> befitting the occasion.

But Mrs. Gaskell was a kindly person, and during the week penetrated Charlotte's reserve enough to enable her to talk about her dreadful experiences at the Cowan Bridge School, where as a six-year-old she had watched two older sisters, not yet in their teens, dying of the typhus contracted there. She even managed to get Miss Brontë to argue with her. Mrs. Gaskell said:

> She and I quarrelled & differed about almost everything,—she calls me a democrat, & can not bear Tennyson—but we like each other heartily (I think) & I hope we shall ripen into friends.

As we know, they did indeed become friends. The most intimate picture we have of Charlotte Brontë remains Mrs. Gaskell's *Life of Charlotte Brontë*.

GRASMERE AND ENVIRONS

Grasmere, the lake or mere with grassy banks, is a lovely, level spot ringed by mountains. The lake itself is one of the district's smallest—a mile long and a half-mile wide, but eighty feet deep. Today's resident population is 1,000 or so. In season, needless to say, the streets bulge with visitors, and on one day in August each year, it's foolish even to try to get into town.

That's the day people come to see not Mr. Wordsworth's Dove Cottage, but the Grasmere Sports. They're billed as "The Greatest Sports Event in the North," and probably are. Prizes total more than £2,500 for competitions like wrestling, track, and cycle races. But the highlights are the guides' races and the hound trail races. In the former, professional mountain guides race up the steep sides of 966-foot Butter Crag and back. The dogs do even more. After reaching the top of Butter Crag, they race along the ridge of neighboring fells, ten miles in all by the time they return, following a trail scented with paraffin and aniseed. It's a spectacle to behold.

When Wordsworth came to Grasmere in 1799 the house he and his sister Dorothy settled into wasn't named Dove Cottage. It never was in his lifetime. He knew it only as Town End, a name shared with a cluster of houses at the edge of the village. Some years after Wordsworth's death it got the name Dove Cottage by virtue of having once been a seventeenth-century inn called The Dove and Olive-Branch and referred to by Wordsworth in *The Waggoner* (1819):

> For at the bottom of the brow,
> Where once the DOVE and OLIVE-BRANCH
> Offered a greeting of good ale
> . . . a poet harbours now,
> A simple water-drinking Bard.

The cottage was small but sturdy, with strong stone walls, stone chimneys, and a slate roof. Downstairs there were two rooms plus a kitchen and larder; upstairs three rooms, used variously, and a tiny box-room for storage.

From the beginning, William and Dorothy had guests. The very first year there were Mary Hutchinson and her sister Sarah, and Samuel Coleridge. The Wordsworths and the Hutchinson girls had been childhood friends at the same dame school in Penrith. In 1802 Wordsworth married Mary and came along with his sister to live at the cottage.

Coleridge's visit was the first of many he was to make. He felt free to drop in whenever he chose, and stay as long as he liked. At times his wife and children were there, too. Other times the Coleridges would simply dump the children on the Wordsworths and go their own way. As the years passed the Wordsworth cottage became unbelievably crowded. By 1806 there were eight in the regular household alone: William and his wife; his sister Dorothy and Mary's sister Sarah; and the three Wordsworth children who were born in the cottage—John in 1803, Dorothy (Dora) in 1804, and Thomas in 1806; and a servant.

And the guests kept coming, one of the most dramatic arrivals being that of William Hazlitt. He turned up at the Wordsworth's door without warning one day in December 1803—exhausted, distraught, and desperate for refuge. He had been staying with Coleridge and Robert Southey at Greta Hall in Keswick, where he'd barely escaped the clutches of an angry mob for the near-rape of a local girl. (Hazlitt said he'd merely spanked her for her less than cooperative attitude.) The Wordsworths not only took him in, but also gave him money and clothes, and helped him get back home.

Somehow the Wordsworths were able to accommodate everybody who showed up for a number of years, though when you see Dove Cottage you'll wonder how. When Thomas De Quincey stayed there in 1807, he had to share quarters with a ménage that had risen to ten on a more or less regular basis: the four adults, three Wordsworth children, two Coleridge children, and the maid.

As an eighteen-year-old student De Quincey had written Wordsworth an ecstatic letter about a new edition of *Lyrical Ballads,* recently published in two volumes. The pleasure he had derived "from eight or nine other poets since the world began," De Quincey said, "falls infinitely short of what these two enchanting volumes have singly afforded me." In 1807 he got himself introduced to Coleridge in Somerset, and when he learned that Mrs. Coleridge planned to visit the Wordsworths in Grasmere, offered to escort her. He was so excited when his offer was accepted that he said in *The Confessions of an English Opium Eater* (1822), "I did tremble."

He was a great success in Grasmere. He was attentive to the ladies, played with the children, and idolized his host, though privately he could be quite objective about him. "He is not a well-made man," he observed. Wordsworth skating on ice, he remarked on a later occasion, was "like a cow dancing a cotillion." When the Wordsworths finally moved out of Dove Cottage, De Quincey took over the tenancy, and Dorothy made him new curtains.

The Wordsworths did leave the cottage the very next year, though they hated to. They moved into a house called Allan Bank at the northern edge of the village. It had recently been built for a Liverpool attorney named Crump, and Wordsworth had watched it go up with anger. "When you next enter the sweet Paradise of Grasmere," he wrote a friend, "you will see staring you in the face upon that beautiful ridge that elbows out into the vale beyond the church, and far above its steeple, a temple of abomination in which are to be enshrined Mr. and Mrs. Crump."

But the Wordsworths had no choice. Allan Bank was the only large enough house available. The Crumps had offered it for rent on the understanding that they could reclaim it at any time they wished. It was a handsome house with extensive grounds. The Wordsworths needed every inch of space it provided. Another daughter, Catherine, was born not long after they moved in. Now, without beginning to provide for the guests who dropped in, the Wordsworths needed quarters for a minimum of fifteen on a constant basis. There were themselves, their four children, and their two sisters; Coleridge, who lived with them for eighteen months almost without interruption; Coleridge's sons Hartley and Derwent, there every weekend; Mrs. Coleridge and daughter Sarah, on frequent stays of a week or more; and two servants.

Wordsworth gave Coleridge a room of his own at Allan Bank, and Coleridge began to work on plans for *The Friend,* which he announced would be a "Literary, Moral, and Political Weekly Paper." The first issue appeared in June 1809, the last the following March. Meanwhile, Coleridge gradually destroyed the tranquility of the entire household. His old addiction to alcohol and opium returned. He was often ill, and sometimes took to his bed all day. He had wild delusions and accused everybody of being his enemy.

By February of 1810, Mrs. Coleridge had had enough and departed. In October, Coleridge himself left for London, where he told anyone who would listen how his dearest friends had secretly hated him. So "deep and wrankling [sic]" was the wound he had received from Wordsworth, he declared, that "I cannot return to Grasmere or its vicinity."

In 1811 the Crumps reclaimed Allan Bank and the Wordsworths moved yet again, this time to the village rectory (often called the parsonage), vacant because the rector had found quarters he liked better elsewhere. The three years the Wordsworths spent at the rectory began dismally and ended in the most devastating months of their lives. Everything seemed wrong about the place. The chimneys smoked, and since the house fronted east with no sitting room facing the west, they lost the sun early each day. The field outside was very wet and could not be drained; after playing the children came in dirty and wet.

Then in 1812 came the worst of blows. Their daughter Catherine, now three, died of convulsions in June; before the year was out, their son, Thomas, age six, died of pneumonia. The Wordsworths could no longer bear to live at the rectory where the graves of the two children in the opposite churchyard daily reminded them of their loss. As Dorothy said in her journal: "They only reminded me of desolate gloom, emptiness, and cheerless silence." The Wordsworths began at once to look for somewhere else to live. By May 1813 they found what they wanted at Rydal Mount, two miles down the road.

Before you start your Grasmere explorations, a general warning: parking places in Grasmere at the best of times are limited. In season they seem to vanish entirely. If you're staying at one of the hotels you can leave your car there. Everything's within walking distance. If you're just in town for the day, your best bet is to plan to have lunch at one of the hotels, which will entitle you to the use of its car park, and walk from there to the various sites before and after lunch.

Dove Cottage   The cottage is well furnished with pieces and memorabilia from the various homes Wordsworth lived in during his fifty years in and around Grasmere. On the ground floor you'll see the kitchen-parlor immediately to the left of the front door. On either side beyond it are the kitchen proper, the little panelled, stone-floored room used variously as Dorothy's bedroom and William and Mary's bedroom, and the larder, where food was kept fresh by a tiny stream running beneath the stone-slab floor.

Upstairs over the kitchen-parlor you'll see what was the main sitting room. In the poet's time the buildings that now obstruct the view had not been built, and he had a clear view of the lake. The years at Dove Cottage rounded off Wordsworth's best creative period, producing such things as "Intimations Ode," "The Rainbow," "I Wandered Lonely As a Cloud," "Michael," some of his best sonnets, "Ode to Duty," and parts of *The Prelude*. Wordsworth preferred to compose outdoors, but when the weather was inclement, this was the room he wrote in.

Opening off the sitting room are the three other upstairs rooms: the chief bedroom—the "sort of lumber room," as Dorothy called it, used mainly for the items needed for breakfasts and evening meals served in the sitting room, and a very small room off the latter which began as a box-room for storage. But in later years it, too, was pressed into use as a bedroom, and Dorothy papered it with newspapers for insulation. Outside the cottage is William and Dorothy's beloved garden, restored to look as it was when they tended it.

Less than fifty yards from Dove Cottage, and on the same side of the road, is the building used as a coach house by the Prince of Wales, the hotel built across the road after Wordsworth's death. It's been bought by the trustees of Dove Cottage and now houses an excellent museum. On the ground floor are exhibits of Grasmere and the area, and their past. Above the rooms devoted to Wordsworth's life and works, and much about Coleridge, including individual bays on works like *Rime of the Ancient Mariner*, "Kubla Khan," and "Dejection."

Normally the cottage and museum are open daily March through October, except—and mark this well—that day in August when the Grasmere Sports are held.

Allan Bank   Allan Bank is now owned by the National Trust, but is rented out to a private family and not on display. You can see the house and grounds, however, from a public footpath.

The Rectory   The rectory is not open to visitors, either. It remains the residence of the village rector. But you can see his church, St. Oswald's, which the Wordsworths attended, and where De Quincey got married. It looks much as it did then, and you can still see the exposed "naked rafters intricately crossed" described in "The Excursion" (1814). Also on view at St. Oswald's are Wordsworth's prayer book, Thomas Woolner's medallion portrait of him, and a memorial to the poet Arthur Clough, whose mother was a member of the church.

In the churchyard are eight yew trees planted by Wordsworth. Beneath one of them are his grave and those of his wife Mary, three of their children (Dora, Catherine and Thomas), and Dorothy Wordsworth. Nearby are buried Clough's mother and, by special request of Wordsworth, Coleridge's son Hartley. Wordsworth felt deeply attached to Hartley, and had made him the "six years' Darling of a pygmy size" in the "Intimations Ode."

The Swan   The Swan Hotel is up the road from Dove Cottage. It's a fair-sized place now, and comfortable (three stars). But when Hawthorne saw it in 1855, it was "a small, white-washed house, with an addition in the rear that seems to have been built since Scott's time. On the door is the painted sign of a swan, and the name 'Scott's Swan Hotel.'"

The reference to Sir Walter Scott was intended apparently to cash in on the novelist's popularity. As Hawthorne remembered, poor Scott had to trudge daily to the Swan for his sustaining potion of whiskey whenever he stayed with Wordsworth. His host believed a draught of water stout enough libation for any guest.

Wordsworth speaks of the Swan's sign in *The Waggoner:*

> Who does not know the famous SWAN,
> Object uncouth! and yet our boast
> For it was painted by the Host.

There's a bit of serendipity for you at the Swan. If you're lounging about in the parlor and notice one of the chairs has a little brass plate, get up and give it a look. The plate reads: "William Wordsworth's chair—from Rydal Mount." But you've got to spot it yourself. It just sits there unheralded and unprotected, like any other old chair set out for the comfort of guests.

Nab Cottage   You might also want to have a look at Nab Cottage, on the highway midway between Dove Cottage and Rydal Mount. In 1816 it was the home of a farmer named John Simpson, whose daughter, Margaret, Thomas De Quincey got pregnant—upsetting Dorothy Wordsworth to no end. It wasn't because he'd made the girl pregnant, but because he promptly married her. Gentry didn't marry low-class women, Dorothy said.

Nevertheless, the marriage was a happy one, and despite his in-laws being only a modest farm family, De Quincey enjoyed a fine relationship with them. In 1829 he bought Nab Farm and the cottage from Mr. Simpson and lived there until 1833 when he couldn't keep up his payments and was forced to move. But Nab Cottage hadn't seen the last of its literary figures. Samuel Coleridge's eldest son, Hartley, made it his home from 1840 until his death in 1849.

If you'd like to sleep and dine relatively inexpensively under the same roof as did De Quincey and Coleridge, you can. Today Nab Cottage is an attractive and welcoming guest house that's open Easter through November.

Fox Ghyll and Fox How   If you're really into remote dwellings of the not-quite-great, you can cross the Rothay River on an unmarked road between Rydal Mount and Ambleside, go over a tiny hump bridge and down the narrowest of "please-God-don't-let-a-car-come-along" lanes. There, you'll get a glimpse of Fox Ghyll, rented by De Quincey from 1820 until 1825, and pass by (you can't see it from the road) Fox How, built by Dr. Thomas Arnold for his family when Matthew was a boy. But neither experience is worth the dodgy drive.

Rydal Mount   The last thirty-seven years of Wordsworth's life, from 1813 until his death in 1850, were spent at Rydal Mount. You can visit this large and gracious home just down the A 591 from Nab Cottage, and almost feel that you are one of the hundreds (literally) of visitors who flocked to see the great man in residence. The furnishings (some reproductions, many of the originals having been siphoned off to Dove Cottage and Cockermouth) and structure are virtually unchanged, and you can look out the study window to the gardens the poet planned and loved and find them altered mainly by the growth of some of the trees he planted.

The Rydal Mount years were ones of productivity, serenity and recognition. Although some critics have questioned the quality of his later work, there is no doubt that Wordsworth was prolific during those years. The ultimate in recognition came when he was named poet laureate in 1843. Serenity was achieved when the family acquired a regular income with Wordsworth's appointment as distributor of stamps, a sort of local tax man for what was then the County of Westmoreland.[4]

The financial security allowed the Wordsworths to enjoy an expanded social life, and the poet's growing fame attracted a steady stream of visitors, both invited and uninvited. Harriet Martineau, a neighbor and frequent visitor herself, estimated five hundred people a year appeared without invitation and usually were received personally by Wordsworth, who rather enjoyed being lionized.

The invited guests participated in events such as those described in one of Wordsworth's letters: "In the room where I am dictating we had three days ago a dance, forty Beaus and Belles besides Matrons, Spinsters and Greybeards . . . tomorrow in this same room we are to muster for a venison feast."

The room was the drawing room where the wall shared with the library was later knocked down to make one large room. It is in this room that today's visitors can see, above the fireplace, the only known portrait of Dorothy. It was painted by one S. Crosthwaite when Dorothy was 61 years old, and pleased her brother enough for him to comment: "He has done wonders with Dorothy." There are other family portraits, cases of mementoes, first editions of the poetry, clothing and other stuff of museums, plus the original or reproduced furnishings to be seen in this room and throughout the house.

Among those guests who were invited to parties or for longer visits were Matthew Arnold, neighbor Martineau, the lawyer and diarist Henry Crabb Robinson, Sir Walter Scott, Ralph Waldo Emerson, and Nathaniel Hawthorne. Queen Adelaide, widow of William IV, was a visitor, and eleven-year-old Charles Algernon Swinburne burst into tears when he had to leave. But then, Swinburne always did cry easily.

---

[4]See p. 323.

Rydal Mount, now owned by a great-great-great-granddaughter of the poet, is open 9:30 A.M.-5:00 P.M. March through October. From November through February the hours are 10 A.M.-4 P.M. It is closed on Tuesdays.

And don't worry if your only language is Swahili. There are hand-held guides in thirty languages.

Serendipities   If you are going to Rydal Mount, Rydal Church at the foot of its hill is worth a brief look. The Wordsworths worshipped there from its beginnings in 1824 and William himself helped to select the site.

And you can't help but see Dora's Fields as the land on the slope between the church and the house is called. In 1826 when his landlady was considering renting Rydal Mount to a relative, Wordsworth bought the property with the idea of building on it if the family were forced to move. When that fear was over he gave the property to his daughter[5] and it became known as Dora's Fields. It eventually went to Wordsworth's grandson, Gordon, who gave it to the National Trust in 1935. It is something to see in April! Wordsworth might be inspired to write still more about those daffodils.

Wythburn   A student of mine once said, with some sort of convoluted logic, of the tiny hamlet in which he lived, "If it wasn't there, you'd go right by it." The same could be said of Wythburn ("WYTHE"—rhymes with "lithe"—burn). But if you're heading north on the A 591 and want to pause just where Lake Thirlmere begins, you can see Wythburn's tiny church, which dates from 1640 (there was a chapel there in 1554), and about which Wordsworth, Coleridge and Matthew Arnold wrote briefly. A long-gone inn, The Cherry Tree, was once across from the church and was the scene of the "Merry Night" in Wordsworth's *The Waggoner.*

On a rock nearby, Wordsworth and Coleridge once carved their names, and for some years, the "Rock of Names," as it was called, was an attraction for tourists. There are several local versions of why it is no longer by the church. An amalgam of them all produces a credible explanation: A century or so ago the rock was badly damaged by the company making

---

[5]Dora died in 1841 at Rydal Mount. Her father never really quite got over the loss of his beloved daughter.

a reservoir of Lake Thirlmere. The conscientious company restored the rock in the form of a cairn and replaced it in its original location, where it stayed for nearly a hundred years (one version has it being moved at one point to the property of an exploitive neighborhood hotel keeper) until there was a movement to protect it from possible vandalism. In any case, it was moved and can now be seen behind the Wordsworth Museum at Dove Cottage.

Immediately north of the church is a stone tablet reading:

> A Record of the Two Walks from hence
> Over the Amboth Fells
> July 1833–43
> Which inspired Matthew Arnold's poem
> Resignation
> And in memory of the Poet
> Born 24 Dec., 1822
> Died 18 April, 1888

NORTHERN CUMBRIA

Keswick   Keswick ("KEZ"—rhymes with "fez"—ick) is eight miles north of Wythburn on the A 591. Its beautiful location, at the foot of Skiddaw and Cat Bells and on the Greta River, just north of Derwent Water, draws sightseers, fell-walkers, and holidayers from all parts of the island, as well as a goodly number of non-Britons. And for the literary buff there are many associations with the town and its area. Young Shelley, who took his bride Harriet Westbrook to live in what is now known as Shelley's Cottage on Chestnut Hill, and wrote, "The mountains are now capped with snow. The lake as I see it here is glossy and calm. Snow vapours tinted by the loveliest refractions pass far below the summit of these gigantic rocks. The scene even in winter is inexpressibly lovely. The clouds assume shapes which seem peculiar to these regions . . . Oh! give me a little cottage in *that* scene, let all live in peaceful little houses, let temples and palaces rot with their perishing masters."

To enjoy some of the views that Shelley did, and to see reminders of other writers, find a spot in a car park if you can. You'll be better off to park and walk—even some distances—to most of the places you'll want to see, especially if you're there on a summer Saturday when market crowds swell the throngs of tourists in the narrow streets.

You'll want to have a glance at the sixteenth-century Moot Hall[1] with its famous one-handed clock. And from there you can walk down St. John's Street (which becomes Ambleside Road) to St. John's Church, where Sir Hugh Walpole's grave is perched on a cliff in the northeast corner behind the church, the stone reading:

In loving memory of
Hugh Walpole
1884–1941
Man of Letters
Lover of Cumberland
Friend of his Fellowman

Along the way look for the Royal Oak Hotel. Catty-cornered across the Market Place from Moot Hall and through Pack Horse Court, it also

---

[1]Location of the Tourist Information Centre.

341

can be reached from Station Road and the other entrance of the court. It was frequented by Wordsworth, S. T. and Hartley Coleridge, Scott, Tennyson, Robert Louis Stevenson, Shelley, De Quincey, Christopher North and other notables, including Queen Elizabeth I from whom it acquired its "Royal." Walter Scott wrote much of his *Bridal of Triermain* while a guest of the hotel. It's still an inn (two-star) and you can stay there if you like, but by all means see the large and lovely windows located in what used to be the hotel's dining room. It is now a National Trust memorial to Beatrix Potter. Each of three walls contains stained-glass portraits of John Peel, S. T. Coleridge, Southey, John Ruskin, Wordsworth, Shelley, Hartley Coleridge, and De Quincey.

And you'll surely want to go to the Fitz-Park Museum where, if you're lucky, you can happen en route upon the quintessentially English scene of bowlers on the green and cricketers in white playing in the park across the way. Inside the museum there are letters and mementoes of Southey, Wordsworth, De Quincey, Ruskin, and others. There's an Epstein bust of Sir Hugh Walpole, and a room-sized scale model of the Lake District, done in ceramics over a hundred years ago, which gives you a remarkable overview of the entire area.

You may want to get back in your car for a look at Crosthwaite Church at the end of Church Lane on the north side of town. In 553 St. Kentigern, to whom the church is dedicated, set up his cross in a clearing (thwaite), and there has been a place of worship on this spot ever since. Nothing remains of the first church, but portions of the 1181 one survive. The present church dates from 1523. Southey is buried in its graveyard, and there is a marble effigy of the poet, reclining with an open book in his hand, in the south aisle. A plaque near the front honors H. Drummond Rawnsley, vicar of the church from 1883 to 1917. Canon Rawnsley was a cofounder of the National Trust.

Greta Hall   In the last years of the eighteenth century, one William Jackson selected a site on the northwest side of town and built a Georgian-style, three-storey house that was destined to be a literary magnet for the next fifty years. In 1800, when only half the west wing was finished, Samuel Coleridge moved in with his large family. By 1803 he had begun the various periods of absence which became a pattern after his estrangement from Wordsworth and also from his wife.

But he returned frequently and, coincidental or not, it was also in 1803 that Coleridge's in-laws, the Robert Southey family, arrived, and

Greta Hall became Southey's home until his death in 1843. Various members of the Coleridge family remained in residence and Coleridge himself was there often enough to participate in the life of the household and to do some of his best-known work, including "Christobel" and "Dejection." Southey, of course, did almost all of his major work at Greta Hall.

With Coleridge's absence, Southey assumed responsibility for both families, and the dinner table often sat upwards of fifteen people, prompting Southey to remark, "Greta Hall is an ant hill. Everybody is someone's aunt."

In addition to the family, guests abounded. Charles and Mary Lamb arrived one day in 1808 without notice, but received a welcome hospitable enough to encourage them to stay three weeks. Lamb describes the "comfortable study . . . blazing fire . . . a large, antique, ill-shaped room with an old fashioned organ, never played upon, big enough for a church, shelves of scattered folios, an AEolian harp, an old sofa, half bed, etc. Here we stayed three full weeks."

William Wilberforce, however, was not as welcome a guest when he arrived in 1818 with a coach and retinue. Southey wrote, "He was longer a'*going, going, going* than a bale of goods at an auction, and even when he began to go he brought to at the bookcase on the staircase and again in the parlour."

Friction, apparently, was not unknown in the house. Young Percy Bysshe Shelley, bringing his bride Harriet to call when they were staying at nearby Greystoke Castle, shocked Southey by displaying the same kind of radicalism that had been Southey's own twenty years earlier. Said Southey, "He (Shelley) acts upon me as my own ghost would do." And the younger man felt betrayed, saying of his former idol, "He has *lost* my good opinion, [his] conversation has lost its charm, except it be the charm of horror at so hateful a prostitution of his talents." Even the women of the household came in for criticism from Shelley. He wrote, "I am not sure that S. is uninfluenced by venality. His wife is very stupied [sic]—Mrs. Coleridge is worse."

The numbers and tales of other visitors would take a separate book.[2] They included, in addition to those already mentioned, William Hazlitt,

---

[2]In fact it has been written: H. W. Howe and Robert Woof's charming *Greta Hall*, Daedalus Press, 1977.

De Quincey, Walter Savage Landor, Sir Walter Scott, John Constable, Dr. Thomas Arnold with young Matthew, and Henry Crabb Robinson. Plus, a rather disappointed twelve-year-old John Ruskin, who wrote:

> Now hurried we home and while taking our tea
> We thought Mr. Southey at church we might see!
> Next morning the Church how we wished to be reaching
> I'm afraid 'twas as much for the poet as preaching.
> His hair was no color at all, by the way,
> For half o't was black slightly scattered with grey.
> His nose in the midst took a small outward bend,
> Rather hooked like an eagle's and sharp at the end!

Greta Hall is now part of a girls' school and not open to viewers, but you may want to stroll up into the grounds of the large three-storey stucco house with rounded wings on either side. And on either side of the portico-pillared front door you will see a plaque—the one on the left reading, "Samuel Taylor Coleridge 1800-1803," and the one on the right, "Robert Southey 1803-1843." A later, unknown occupant is remembered by a small tombstone to the left of the driveway just before you reach the house. It reads simply, "Peter, 1900-1920."

And, if it means anything to you, just around the corner from Greta Hall you can see the world's first pencil factory, opened in 1566 and still going strong.

WINDEBROWE—BORROWDALE—AND MIREHOUSE

Windebrowe   The Calverts of Windebrowe can be indirectly credited with a large contribution to British poetry, but not through any creativity of their own. Windebrowe was the successful farm of the Calvert family who befriended Dorothy and William Wordsworth early on. When Raisley Calvert died in 1795 he left William £900, an amount large enough in those days to enable the poet to devote his time to writing.

Dorothy, William, and Mary Wordsworth occasionally visited the Calverts, and the rooms they used can be seen before or after a special weekly dinner-theatre performance (during season) of "The Life and Times of William Wordsworth," or at other times by special arrangement with the Calvert Trust, which owns and operates the building.

Borrowdale   Before heading north toward Wordsworth's birthplace at Cockermouth, you might want to take a beautiful ride down the B 5289 in the Borrowdale Valley. Sir Hugh Walpole lived there off and on from 1924 to 1941 at Brackenburn, still spending much of his time at his Polperro, Cornwall, home. Borrowdale became the setting for his historical novels, *Rogue Herries* (1930), *Judith Paris* (1931), and *The Fortress* (1933). Tiny Watendlath, just above Borrowdale, is the home of the fictional Judith Paris. But the fact of the fiction hasn't stopped several claimants to her quite imaginary house from trying to profit from the non-existent heroine and offering paid tours of "her home." Walpole placed Adam Paris in a Cat Bells cottage, and his description of Adam's view from its window was that of his own windows at Brackenburn. Not claiming anything but privacy, today's residents of Brackenburn do not open it to the public, although twice a year, dates varying, they generously open their grounds.

And while you're at the foot of Cat Bells, you might enjoy slipping back into your childhood and thinking of Beatrix Potter's Mrs. Tiggy-Winkle going about her many adventures right there.

Mirehouse   Four miles north of Keswick, still on the A 591, is Mirehouse, home of the Spedding family whose members had connections to literary folk, including the Wordsworths, Alfred Tennyson, and Edward FitzGerald. And one Spedding is noted for his own work. James Spedding published an edition of Francis Bacon's *Works* (1857-59) followed by his *Life and Letters* (1871-74). James's father John and his sisters Marcia and Margaret had initiated a friendship with William and Dorothy Wordsworth; and Christopher Wordsworth (master of Cambridge's Trinity College and William's brother) befriended young James when he was a student at the university. During that period James invited both Tennyson and FitzGerald to be his guests at Mirehouse and made sure that they visited the Wordsworths, by then in residence at Rydal Mount.[3]

Dorothy wrote of the Spedding sisters: "[They are] women whose acquaintance I am much desirous of cultivating. They have read much and are amiable and engaging in their manners. They live in the most beautiful place that was ever beheld."

---

[3]See pp. 324-25.

You can behold that place Wednesdays, Sundays, or Bank Holiday Mondays from 2 to 5 P.M., April through October.

EGREMONT AND COCKERMOUTH

Egremont   Remember the old story about the farmer who was asked by a lost motorist how to get to a nearby village? After several attempts to give a direct route, the farmer looked baffled and gave up with, "I reckon there ain't no way to get there from here." So it is with Egremont, about fifteen miles due west of Borrowdale with no road at all connecting them. But if you're a big fan of historical ballads, or writing a dissertation on undistinguished Wordsworth poems, you might want to go on over to Egremont via Cockermouth, about ten to twelve miles up the B 5289 until it joins the B 5292 into town. Then drive about fourteen more miles south and west on the A 5086 to Egremont.

What you'll be rewarded with when you get there are the ruins of Egremont Castle started in 1130 by one William de Meschines and made ever so modestly famous in 1807 with the publication of Wordsworth's *The Horn of Egremont Castle* which tells the grisly story of two brothers, Eustace and Hubert, of the House of Lucie. They departed the castle together during the Crusades, but dastardly Hubert arranged (he thought!) with some wicked Saracens to have poor Eustace done in while in the Holy Lands. The plan was for Hubert to come home and claim the castle and

> "—live in glee
> Months and years went smilingly;
> With plenty was his table spread;
> And bright the Lady is who shares his bed."

But somehow gallant Eustace escaped the evil Saracens and back home he galloped. Upon arrival he grabbed the horn that hung by the castle gate and that would respond to no blow but the one given it by the true heir to Egremont. So—

> A blast was uttered from the Horn
> Where by the Castle-gate it hung forlorn.
> 'Tis the breath of good Sir Eustace!
> He is come to claim his right!

Eustace eventually forgave Hubert and

> Lived with honour on his lands
> Sons he had, saw sons of theirs;
> And through the ages, heirs of heirs.
> A long posterity renowned,
> Sounded the Horn which they alone could sound.

If you do go out of your way to see the fourteenth-century gatehouse and what other buildings are still standing, you'll have to see what you can from the road. The castle is in private hands and is not open to the public. The fate of the horn is not known.

Cockermouth   Whether or not you opt for Egremont, this north-west corner of Cumbria is going to require some doubling back and re-tracing steps on your literary tour. But from whatever direction you approach, or reapproach, Cockermouth (via the A 66, A 595, the A 5086, or the B 5292), you'll surely want to make the birthplace of William Wordsworth a stopping off point, particularly since the house in which he was born has been restored to excellent condition and you can see a great deal both outside and inside.

Situated at the west end of Main Street, next to the three-star Trout Hotel, the house has a Georgian front, a back garden that extends down to the River Derwent, and an interior that is much as it may have been when the Wordsworths lived in it when William was born in 1770, with the original panelling, staircase, and fireplaces. Some of the furnishings are of a slightly later period, some pieces having belonged to the poet himself, and there are paintings that were his as well as portraits of him and his contemporaries.

The house, built in 1745, was one of the perks that went with John Wordsworth's (William's father) job as steward to the wealthy and powerful Sir James Lowther.

Before your tour of the inside of the house you may want to go through the garden to what used to be the barn to see the twelve-minute slide/tape presentation (shown every fifteen minutes) which, although it is not state-of-the-art video perfection, can give you a good sense of the area and the poet's place in it. And after your tour you'll probably enjoy a stop in the kitchen-turned-teashop where home-baked goodies and other refreshments await you.

Wordsworth's birthplace is owned by the National Trust and is open

April through November weekdays (except Thursday) 11 A.M. - 5 P.M.; Sundays 2 - 5 P.M.; and November through March open daily (except Thursdays and Sundays) 10 A.M. - 5 P.M. But it is closed entirely during the week after Christmas.

Before you get back on the highway you may want to find All Saints Church on Kirkgate off Market Place. There's a Wordsworth memorial stained-glass window, but maybe the church's greater distinction is that some of its schoolrooms are built over the ground where once stood the school that the little boy Wordsworth attended with the little boy Fletcher Christian. And if you're groping for just who HE was, remember that mutiny on the Bounty?

IN AND AROUND PENRITH

If not *THE*—as claimed by its devotees—Penrith is certainly *A* Gateway to the Lake District, and a very good one. At the junction of the A 6 and the A 66 and just off the M 6, it is a fine place to settle in to explore the surrounding beautiful countryside, rich in historic and literary connections. Many points of interest are available with a short drive—or a long walk—and there is a good selection of accommodations at various price and comfort levels.

To the south are poetically familiar crags, waterfalls, and the setting for those daffodils; to the west, a sanctuary for a down-on-their-luck eloping couple; to the north, a call to arms; and to the east, the home of a novel-writing mother of a novel-writing son.

Yanwath   Heading south from Penrith on the B 5320, before you get to Ullswater and that poetically familiar scenery, is Yanwath. And here, over a tiny, tiny bridge and off on a tiny, tiny unmarked road, is The Grotto, home of Wordsworth's friend, the Quaker poet, Thomas Wilkinson. Wordsworth was a frequent visitor, and among other notables of his day who enjoyed The Grotto's hospitality were Thomas De Quincey, Sir Walter Scott, and Samuel Coleridge.

Ullswater and its Shores   Farther south and east of Penrith is Ullswater, one of the most beautiful of the lakes. The lake and the fells and parklands surrounding it have figured in British history at least since Roman times, and poetry lovers—Wordsworthians in particular—will find the settings for some of the loveliest of his poetic descriptions and images.

Aira Force[4] is the waterfall that "stays the wanderer's steps and soothes his thoughts" in Wordsworth's "Airy-Force Valley"; Stybarrow Crag is very probably the "craggy ridge" referred to in the opening book of *The Prelude.* Lyulph's Tower, of the opening line of "The Somnambulist," is a small private shooting lodge, the name of which is supposed to go back to the same Baron L'ulf who gave his name to the lake: Ulfo's water. And those daffodils? Here is what Dorothy Wordsworth wrote in her journal one April day in 1802 after she and her brother had taken a walk through Gowbarrow Park:

> When we were in the woods beyond Gowbarrow park we saw a few daffodils close to the waterside. We fancied that the lake had floated the woods ashore and that the little colony had so sprung up. But as we went along there were more and yet more and at last under the boughs of the trees we saw that there was a long belt of them along the shore, about the breadth of a country turnpike road. I never saw daffodils so beautiful they grew among the mossy stones about and about them, some rested their heads upon those stones as a pillow for weariness and the rest tossed and reeled and danced and seemed as if they verily laughed at the wind that blew upon them over the lake, they looked so gay ever glancing ever changing.

Three years later William published "I Wandered Lonely As a Cloud" (sometimes called "The Daffodils").

Greystoke Castle   Three or four miles west of Penrith on the B 5288 is Greystoke Castle, dating to 1129 and home for the last several centuries of a branch of the far-flung Howard family. One of them, the then duke of Norfolk, gave refuge in 1811 to newlyweds Percy Bysshe and Harriet Westbrook Shelley. The Shelleys had left Scotland broke and at odds with their families after their elopement to Edinburgh. They were given a temporary home at Greystoke until they could mend their monetary and family troubles. The property is still in private hands and not open to the public, but if you're passing by you can see the gates.

---

[4]Force is the word used in the Lake District for a waterfall. Wordsworth's "Airy Force" is spelled differently from the place name.

Penrith Beacon   Immediately northeast of the town is Penrith Beacon, off the main road and reached only by a footpath, but with some of the finest views in all of the Lake District. On clear days you can see as far as the Pennines to the south and the mountains of Scotland to the north. Atop the 937-foot hill is a beacon light used historically to warn of danger. It was built in 1588, one of a series of beacons erected to warn of a possible attack by the Spanish Armada. In 1804, when Sir Walter Scott was visiting in Penrith, the light flashed. It was during the Napoleonic Wars and Sir Walter was a member of Scotland's Regiment of Volunteers. He promptly returned home to join his regiment.

Carleton Hill and Brougham Castle   Just to the east of town are Carleton and Brougham Castle. At Carleton is Carleton Hill, a mansion on Alston Road. It was built by Frances Trollope, whose failure to make a go of her Cincinnati, Ohio, dry-goods store sent her back to England desperate enough about her family's livelihood and critical enough of America to write the controversial *Domestic Manners of the Americans* (1832). Later she supported her family with fifty or more novels such as *The Vicar of Wrexhill* (1837) and *The Widow Barnaby* (1838) and an assortment of travel books. In 1841 she built Carleton Hill and lived in it until 1843. Her son Anthony visited often. He, of course, was one of the most successful of nineteenth-century authors with such well-known novels (still read and made into television dramas) as *Barchester Towers* (1857) and *The Eustace Diamonds* (1873).

Further east on the A 66 are the ghostly, crumbling ruins of Brougham Castle, where Dorothy and William Wordsworth had played as small children visiting their Penrith family. There is enough of the castle left to get some idea of what it may have been like in the Middle Ages, when knights left from it for the Holy Lands, but it has been allowed to molder since its final abandonment early in the eighteenth century. As you park your car and walk up the cobblestone road to the entrance, grateful for your thick-soled walking shoes, you not only will wonder how those stones might have felt to the thin-clad feet of the little Wordsworths, but also how it would have felt to have ridden over them in a cart with wooden wheels and no inner-springs. The castle is open year-round, but hours and days change with the seasons. And, while William and Dorothy doubtless got in for free, you'd better have your 50 p. ready.

Penrith   An ancient town of some 12,500 people, Penrith was the home of both parents of William Wordsworth and also of his wife. Ann and William Cookson were the maternal grandparents of William and Dorothy Wordsworth, who often came over from Cockermouth to visit them. The Cooksons lived over their drapery shop, facing Devonshire Street, and at one period in their young lives, Dorothy and William lived there while they attended Dame Birkett's School. A fellow pupil was Mary Hutchinson, William's future wife. The school building was built in 1563, a little red sandstone building on King Street. It's still there, and you're welcome to go in. It's now part of the Tudor Restaurant and Coffee Room.

After their mother died in 1778 their Penrith family tried to raise the Wordsworth children, but William, rebellious and unhappy, was sent to Hawkshead to school and Dorothy went to live with relatives in Yorkshire. She came back as a teenager to live again with her grandparents, and to help in the shop. It was here that she and William were reunited after their separation—rarely to be parted ever again. The site of the Cookson shop is now the shop of Arnison's Drapers, and it still faces Devonshire Street.

Although it has no particular literary association, St. Andrew's Church is a charming one and well worth a visit. It is thought that religious worship has taken place at that very spot for over 1,500 years, and it is known that the church was active and functioning in the early twelfth century. In one of the windows in the north side is a portrait said to be either of Richard II or Richard III, and the window on the south side contains portraits of Richard Duke of York and Cecily Neville, parents of King Edward IV and King Richard III.

If you'd like to sit where royalty sat, go into the Gloucester Arms for a drink or a meal. It's in the Town Centre, facing Great Dockray, dates to 1471, and was once home to Richard III.

CALDBECK

If you're heading to or from Penrith on the M 6, a detour of just two or three miles south off the B 5305 onto the B 5299 will take you to Caldbeck, a tiny village of 700 people, where you may or may not ken that John Peel lived there from his birth in 1776 until 1854 when, the story goes, he fell from his hunting horse and was fatally injured—at seventy-eight perhaps not a bad way to go. He is buried in the graveyard of the charming twelfth-century St. Kentigern's Church.

During his active life as a local huntsman, John Peel was so well-known in the area that whenever his distinctive horn was sounded crowds would gather to join the hunt. And the revelry afterwards often was so rowdy that an inebriated John did not make it home to Mrs. Peel, their thirteen children, and his neglected farm.

The words to the popular old song 'D'ye ken John Peel?" were written in 1829 by John Woodcock Graves, a fellow hunter, who worked at the woolen mill where the cloth was made for "the coat so grey." They were, first sung by Graves to the then familiar Scottish border tune of "Bonnie Annie" at The Oddfellows Arms, a village pub. The song did not become famous, however, until 1869 when the music was arranged and printed by William Metcalfe, organist at Carlisle Cathedral.

Whether or not the man or the music appeal to you, the village itself is worth a stopover just to relish the church in whose graveyard Peel is buried; the stone footbridge over the stream which gives the village its name;[5] and the cluster of storybook quaint cottages with their Cumberland slate roofs.

CARLISLE

Although there is not much of interest to attract the literary-minded traveler to Carlisle, the town cannot go unmentioned. Straight up from Penrith off the M 6 and on the A 6, Carlisle is now chiefly an industrial and transportation center, but its history goes back at least two thousand years when Hadrian placed the western end of his wall just north of the town.

And its cathedral, although one of England's smaller ones, is lovely. It has the literary distinction of having seen within its walls the wedding of native daughter Charlotte Charpentier to Sir Walter Scott in 1797.

Also in the town is Carlisle Castle, with a good deal left to see despite endless battles over the centuries for it and its surrounding lands. For instance, you can see the dungeons with carvings on the walls that are

---

[5]Caldbeck means cold stream in Old Norse.

attributed to Scottish prisoners confined there after the rebellion of 1745. In addition to the real prisoners there was Walter Scott's fictional Fergus MacIvor of *Waverly* (1814). And what's left of Queen Mary's Tower gives you some idea of where Mary Queen of Scots was imprisoned for two months in 1568.

BOWNESS-ON-SOLWAY AND SOLWAY FIRTH

The northwestern tip of England is an appropriate place to end a literary tour of the country. Bowness-on-Solway (on an unmarked road off the B 5307), with its face to the Irish Sea, is that place. The sea's treacherous Solway Firth provided an atmosphere sufficiently haunting to suggest to Willkie Collins the setting for his *The Woman in White* (1860), in which Mr. Fairlie's home looks out on the distant coast of Scotland. Earlier a trip through the Lake District with his good friend Charles Dickens had introduced Collins to the area. In fact, the mishaps of that trip resulted in a comic collaboration of the two writers: *The Lazy Tour of Two Idle Apprentices* (1857).

Bowness is also the choice of Sir Walter Scott for the setting of his *Redgauntlet* (1824). With the dangerous tides of the firth in mind, Scott has Darsie Latimer warned, "He who dreams in the bed of the Solway will wake up in the next world."

A far more fitting quotation with which to end this book—if you are closing it and the end of your British literary journey anywhere other than in that "very green and pleasant land"—is the one that will come into your mind and heart and surge throughout your being. It is, of course, Robert Browning's poignant, yearning: "Oh, to be in England!"

Key To The Index

1. AUTHORS are in all capital letters
2. *Titles* are in italics
3. Churches: are included if they are
   a. actual (not fictional)
   b. extant
   c. of enough interest to warrant a visit
4. Hotels, Inns, Restaurants, and Pubs: are included only if they are
   a. actual (not fictional)
   b. of literary interest
   c. still serving the public

   A separate listing of such places appears at the end of this index, arranged by cities and with the page numbers where they are discussed.

INDEX

Aaron's Rod, 93
Abbeydale Industrial Hamlet, 146
Abdon-under-Clee, 8
Aberdeen, 80, 83, 84
Abraham Lincoln, 80
Absentee, The, 39
Absolem and Achitophel, 174
Academy of Armoury, The, 245
Adam Bede, 49, 56, 60, 62, 69, 105
Adam, Robert, 71
Adams, Charles Francis, 175
ADAMS, HENRY BROOKS, 16, 17,
  21, 22, 175, 176, 233, 238, 267
ADDISON, JOSEPH, 37, 40
Adelaide, Queen, 335
Adelphi Hotel (Liverpool), see
  Britannia Adelphi
Adieu, The, 85
Aeschylus, 10
Africa, 263
Aftermath, 166
Agincourt, 208, 209
Agnes Grey, 130, 134
AINSWORTH, WILLIAM HAR-
  RISON, 154, 165, 288, 289, 301
Aira Force, 349
Airy Force Valley, 349
AKENSIDE, MARK, 220
ALCUIN (EALWHINE), 162
Alexander, William, 165
Alfoxden, 179
Alfoxden House, 323
Alfred, King, 252
Algernon goes to the guillotine, 225
Alice's Adventures in Wonderland,
  154, 186, 190, 210, 258
Alistaire Cooke's America, 286

All Creatures Great and Small, 157,
  172, 191
All Things Bright and Beautiful, 172
Allen Bank, 330, 331, 333
ALLINGHAM, WILLIAM, 269, 270
Aln River, 202
Alnmouth, 202
Alton Locke, 176, 247
Ambassadors, The, 239
Ambleside, 307, 308, 309, 315, 321,
  322, 323–28, 334
Ambleside Waterfall, 324
Amboth Fells, 337
America, 289, 293, 350
Amours de Voyage, 265
ANACREON, 97
Angel and Royal, The (Grantham),
  106
Angel Hotel (Knutsford), 254, 255
Angel Hotel (Ludlow), 17
Angel Croft Hotel (Lichfield), 46
Angel Pavement, 130
Anglesey, 240
Annesley Hall, 87–88
Appleby, 41
Appleton Roebuck, 173–74
Apollo, 53
Apostles, The, 175
Arabian Nights, 176
Arcadia, 10
Arkwright, Richard, 300
ARLEN, MICHAEL, 274, 275
Arnold Bennet Literary Society, 35
Arnold Bennett Museum, 35
ARNOLD, MATTHEW, 136, 174,
  243, 264, 265, 307, 308, 316, 321,
  325, 334, 335, 336, 344

ARNOLD, DR. THOMAS, 243, 325, 334, 344

Arthur, King, 240

Ashbourne, 30, 42, 49, 50, 55–59, 60, 62, 64, 66, 70

ASHMOLE, ELIAS, 37, 40

Ashmolean Museum, 37

Ashton-under-Lyme, 300

Astrophel and Stella, 10

Athens, 279, 281, 293

AUDEN, WYSTAN HUGH, 15

AUSTEN, JANE, 53, 64

AUSTIN, ALFRED, 301

Australia, 267

Authoress of The Odyssey, The, 11

Autobiography (James Melville), 201, 219

Axe Edge, 55

AYCKBOURNE, ALAN, 193, 194

Aykroyd, Tabatha, 132, 134, 135

BACON, FRANCIS, 264, 324, 345

Bag Enderby, 112

Bailey, Philip James, 79

Bakewell, 53, 54, 63

Ballad of Burdens, The, 176

Balliol, John, 210

BALZAC, HONORÉ, 225

Bamburgh, 202, 226, 227–28

Barchester Towers, 350

Barden Woods, 184

Baring, Rosa, 110, 111, 118

Barley, 301

Barnard Castle, 210–11

Barnard, William Vane, Viscount, 207

Barnsley, 145, 146

Bath, 9, 163, 288

Battle of Balaclava, 251

Battle of Bosworth Field, 12

Battlefield, 9, 12–13

BAXTER, RICHARD, 24

BAYLY, ADA, see Edna Lyall

Bayons Manor, 118

Beatles, The, 259, 264

BEAUMONT, FRANCIS, 19

Beauvale Priory, 93

Beaux's Stratagem, The, xvi, 37

Bebington, 263

Becket, 82

BEDE, 194, 195, 206, 222

Belinda, 39

BELL, CURRER, see Charlotte Brontë

Bell, Margaret Alexis, 248

BENNETT (ENOCH) ARNOLD, 33, 34, 35, 36

Bennett, Enoch, 36

Bennett, Frank, 36

Bennett, Justice Gervase, 69

Bent, Pat and Leo, 233

Bentinck-Scott, William, 5th duke of Portland, 93

BENTLEY, PHYLLIS, 139

BENTLEY, RICHARD, 288

Beresford Dale, 61

Beresford Hall, 61

Berkshire, 324

Bess of Hardwick, see Lady Elizabeth Cavendish

BETJEMAN, SIR JOHN, 115, 140, 142

Betrothed, The, 20

Betty's Cafe and Tea Shop (Harrogate), xvi, 178

Beverley, 151, 154

Beverley Arms, The (Beverley), 154

Bible, The, 151

Bight, 84

Binchester, 210

Birch, Sir Thomas, 273

Birkenhead, 263, 273, 274

Birmingham, 29, 37, 41, 222

Birmingham Repertory Theatre, 80

Birstall, 137–38

Bishop Auckland, 207, 209–10

Black Bull Inn, The (Haworth), 134

Blackburn, 299

Blackpool, 299
BLAIR, ROBERT, 190
BLAKE, WILLIAM, 175
Bloomsbury Group, 272
Blue Guide to England, 237
BLUNT, WILFRED SCAWEN, 301
Bolton, 285
Bolton Abbey, 157, 178, 182, 183, 184, 185
Bombay School of Arts, 34
Bonduca, 20
Bonnell, Henry Houston, 135
Bonnie Annie, 352
Book of Martyrs, 108
Book of Nonsense, A, 273
Boots Chemists, 81
Boroughbridge, 178
BORROW, GEORGE, 31, 109
Borrowdale, 344, 345, 346
Boscobel, 17
Boston, 78, 105, 107–09
Boston, Massachusetts, 107, 108
BOSWELL, JAMES, 29, 37, 38, 42, 43, 48, 57, 58, 59, 66, 70, 71, 111
Bosworth Field, 79
Botanic Garden, The, 38
Bothie of Tobu-na-Vuolich, The, 265
Bowdoin College, 267
Bowes, 205, 210, 212
Bowland, Forest of, 299
Bowness-on-Solway, 353
Boyle, Richard, 3rd earl of Burlington, 163
Boy's Adventures in the Wilds of Australia, A, 80
Brackenburn, 345
Bracknell, 324
Bradford, 128, 129, 130, 131, 137, 139
BRADLEY, ANDREW CECIL, 271, 272
Bradshaw's Railway Guide, 187
BRADSTREET, ANNE, 108
Bramhall Hall, 237

Brancepeth, 207, 208–9
Brantwood, 313, 315
Branwell, Elizabeth, 132, 136
Branwell, Maria, see Mrs. Patrick Brontë
Break, Break, Break, 114, 117
Brewster, William, 107
Bride of Triermain, The, 342
Brideshead Revisited, 191, 255
Bridgnorth, 23–24
Bridlington, 151, 153–54
Briery Close, 327
Brigantes, 127
Brignal Banks, 273
Bristol, 179
Britannia Adelphi Hotel (Liverpool), 267
British Museum, 24, 39
BRITTAIN, VERA, 34
Bromborough, 263
Brompton, 178, 179, 180, 181–82
BRONTË, ANNE, 129, 132, 133, 134, 135, 136, 137, 153, 193, 194, 291, 303
Brontë (Patrick) Branwell, 129, 132, 133, 134, 139, 291, 292
BRONTË, CHARLOTTE, 54, 67, 68, 123, 128, 129, 130, 131, 132, 133, 134, 135, 136, 137, 138, 139, 153, 166, 193, 194, 287, 290, 291, 292, 293, 302, 307, 308, 321, 322, 326, 327, 328
Brontë, Elizabeth, 132, 303
BRONTË, EMILY, 123, 129, 131, 132, 133, 134, 135, 136, 137, 139, 153, 291, 303
Brontë Family, 193, 291, 327
Brontë, Jane, 132
Brontë, Maria, 132, 303
Brontë Parsonage Museum, The, 134
Brontë, The Reverend Patrick, 129, 131, 132, 133, 135, 136, 291, 292, 293, 303

Brontë, Mrs. Patrick, 129, 132
Brontë Society, The, 134
Brookside, The, 175
Brougham Castle, 350
Brown, Lancelot ("Capability"), 34
Brown, Martha, 134
Browne, Hablôt Knight ("Phiz"), 12, 106, 211
BROWNING, ELIZABETH BARRETT, 208
BROWNING, ROBERT, 353
Broxton, 246
Brussels, 133
Buffalo Inn (Clun), 20
Buildings of Cheshire, 251
Bulgaria, 274
Bull and Royal (Preston), 300
BULWER-LYTTON, EDWARD GEORGE EARLE LYTTON, 1st Baron Lytton, 166, 271
Burne-Jones, Sir Edward Coley, 247
BURNETT, FRANCES HODGSON, 288, 289
Burnley, 299
BURNS, ROBERT, 88
Burslem, 29, 33, 34, 36
Burslem Endowed School, 34
BURTON, SIR RICHARD FRANCIS, 176
Burton, Robert, 112, 114
BUTLER, SAMUEL ("Erewhon Butler"), 8, 10
BUTLER, SAMUEL ("Hudibras Butler"), 8, 16, 17
Butler, Dr. Samuel, 10
Butt, Clara, 270
Butter Crag, 328
Butterfly's Ball and the Grasshopper's Feast, The, 264
Buxton, 54, 55
Byrom, John, 287
Byron, Anne Isabella Milbanke, 86, 88, 189, 215, 216

Byron, Augusta Ada, 216
Byron, Augusta Leigh, 85, 192, 216
Byron, Mrs. Catherine Gordon, 80, 83, 84, 95
BYRON, GEORGE GORDON, 6th baron, xvi, 50, 60, 77, 78, 79, 80, 81, 82, 83, 84, 85, 86, 87, 88, 94, 95, 96, 97, 98, 189, 192, 205, 214, 215, 216
Byron, John, 1st baron, 82, 83
Byron, John ("Mad Jack"—the poet's father), 84
Byron, William, 4th baron, 84
Byron, William ("The Wicked Lord") 5th baron, 83, 87, 96

CAEDMON, 194, 196
Cahn, Sir Julian, 86
Caldbeck, 351–52
Calder River, 301
Calvert Family, 344
Calvert, Raisley, 344
Calvert Trust, 344
Cambo, 224–26
Cambridge, 19
Cambridge History of English Literature, 38
Cambridge University, 8, 40, 47, 83n, 84, 86, 88, 95, 109, 115, 116, 131, 162, 175, 178, 181, 207, 248, 272, 276, 301, 317, 324, 325, 345
Cambridgeshire, 102
Camelot, 240
Canada, 267
Cannock Chase, 29
Canterbury, 9n, 82, 158
Canterbury Tales, The, 104, 123, 152
Canton, Ohio, 213
Canute, King, 250
Capheaton, 221, 224
Caractacus, 19
Caractacus (Elgar), 20
Caractacus (Mason), 20
Carleton Hill, 350

Carlisle, 352-53
Carlisle, Isabella, 192
CARLYLE, THOMAS, 39, 270, 279, 281, 286-87, 290, 291, 294, 315, 316
Carnival, 214
CARROLL, LEWIS, 154, 185, 186, 187, 188, 189, 190, 207, 210, 211, 222, 237, 258, 317
Carthage, 152
Casabianca, 266, 325
Castle of Otranto, 83
Castle Howard, 191-92
Castle Rockrent, 39
Cat Bells, 341, 345
Cat-in-the-Manger, 140
Cavendish, Lady Elizabeth, 63
Cavendish, Georgiana Spencer, duchess of Devonshire, 64
Cavendish, Kathleen Kennedy, 66
Cavendish, William, 1st duke of, Devonshire, 64, 79
Cavendish, William, 5th duke of Devonshire, 65
Cavendish, Sir William, 63
Cavendish, William George Spencer, 6th Duke of Devonshire, 65
Cavendish-Bentinck, Ottoline, see Lady Ottoline Morrell
Cavendish-Bentinck, William, 6th duke of Portland, 93
Celts, 286
Chambers, Jessie, 93
Charge of the Light Brigade, 15, 251
Charlemagne, 162
Charles at Tunbridge, 220
Charles I, 16, 30, 79, 83, 93, 96, 173, 224, 238
Charles II, 17, 64, 153, 224
Charles Cotton, The (Hartington), 61
Charles, Prince of Wales, 239
Chartism, 287
Chateau d'Amour, 103
Chatsworth, 53, 54, 63-66, 67, 71

CHAUCER, GEOFFREY, 104, 115, 123, 128, 145, 152, 153, 240
Chaworth, Mary, 87, 88
Chaworth, William, 83, 87
Cheshire, 9, 16, 29, 33, 186, 233-59, 285
Cheshire Cat, The, 237, 258
Chester, 141n, 234, 237-45, 247, 248, 249, 251, 258, 269n, 288
Chetel, 63
Childe Harold, 85
Chollerton, 223
Christ College (Oxford), 151, 210
Christ's College (Cambridge), 241
Christian, Fletcher, 348
Christians awake! Salute the happy morn, 288
Christmas Carol, The, 290
Christobel, 343
Cincinnati, Ohio, 350
Claudius, Emperor, 127
Clayhanger, 35, 36
Clayhanger Trilogy, 33
Clee Hill, 16
Clergy Daughter's School, 132
Cleveland, 128, 193, 202, 205-16, 219
Cleveland, Henrietta, duchess of, 207
CLEVELAND, JOHN, 97
Cleveland Way Walk, 193
Clifton Grove and Other Poems, 79
Clinton Arms (Newark upon Trent), 97
Clive, Robert (Clive of India), 250
Clough, Anne, 264
CLOUGH, ARTHUR HUGH, 243, 264, 265, 333
Clun, 7, 8, 15, 19-20
Clunbury, 7, 8, 19
Clungunford, 7, 19
Clunton, 7, 19
Cockermouth, 309, 334, 345, 346, 347-48, 351
Coleridge, Derwent, 331

Coleridge Family, 329, 330
Coleridge Hartley, 331, 333, 334, 342
COLERIDGE, SAMUEL TAYLOR,
 11, 14, 39, 81, 98, 179, 182, 269,
 304, 321, 323, 329, 330, 331, 332,
 334, 336, 342, 343, 344, 348
Coleridge, Mrs. Samuel, 330, 331, 342,
 343
Coleridge, Sarah, 331
Collected Poems (Hodgson), 213
Collected Poems (Owen), 246
COLLINGWOOD, STUART
 DODGSON, 222
COLLINS, WILKIE, 195, 353
Colin Clouts come home againe, 301
Cologne, 294
Comberback, Roger, 239
Compleat Angler, The, 32, 56, 60, 61
Compleat Bachelor, The, 130
Complete Guide to the Lakes, 308
*Composed after a Journey Across the
 Hambleton Hills, Yorkshire,* 180n
Comus, 8, 16, 17
*Condition of the Working Class in
 England, The,* 294
Confessions (Rousseau), 50
*Confessions of an English Opium
 Eater, The,* 288, 330
CONGREVE, WILLIAM, 50, 59
Coningsby, 279, 281, 293
Conisbrough Castle, 145, 146–47
Coniston, 313, 314, 316–17
Coniston Pier, 316
Coniston Water, xvi, 280, 285, 315,
 316
Constable, John, 344
Constantine the Great, 127
Constantinople, 242, 268, 275
Constantius, 127
Cook, Captain James, 195, 196
COOKE, ALISTAIRE, 286
Cookson, Ann, 351
Cookson, William, 351
CORBETT, RICHARD, 97

Cornlaw Rhymes, 145
Cornwall, 62, 132, 345
Corve River, 16
Cotton, Charles, 55, 61, 79
Count Hannibal, 11
Coventry, 141n, 146
Cowan Bridge, 132, 302–4
Coxwold, 170–72
Cracroft Family, 109
CRAIK, DINAH MARIA MULOCK,
 34
Cranford, 233, 237, 249, 253, 254, 290,
 302
Crazy Tales, 169
Crewe, 239
Crimean War, 173, 251
Critic, The, 31
Croft-on-Tees, 185–89, 190, 211, 216,
 222, 258
Croft Spa Hotel (Croft-on-Tees), 189
Croft, Stephen, 168, 170
Cromwell, Mary, 173
Cromwell, Oliver, 79, 162, 173, 174
Crosthwaite, S., 335
Crown of Wild Olives, The, 246
Crystal Palace, 66
Cumberland, 308, 315, 341
CUMBERLAND, RICHARD, 95
Cumbria, 201, 285, 299, 304, 305–53
Cunard Lines, 263, 268
Curzon Family, 70

Daffodils, The, see *I Wandered Lonely
 as a Cloud*
Damascus, 251
Dame Birkett's School, 351
Dame Oliver's School, 40, 46
Dane Valley, 237
Danes, 238, 286, 308
Dangerous Corner, 130
Daresbury, 186, 258
Darling, Grace, 228
Darlington, 186, 205, 213

DARWIN, CHARLES ROBERT, 8, 10, 38

DARWIN, ERASMUS, 37, 38, 42, 46

Das Kapital, 294

David Copperfield, 266

DAVIDSON, LAWRENCE H., see D. H. Lawrence

DAY, THOMAS, 39

DAY-LEWIS, CECIL, 15, 246

de Balliol, Bernard, 210

de Meschines, William, 346

De Quincey, Jane, 247

DE QUINCEY, THOMAS, xv, 243, 247, 269, 288, 308, 321, 323, 330, 333, 334, 342, 344, 348

de Romilly, Lady Alice, 183, 184

de Swinburne, Sir Adam, 224

de Swinburne, William, 223

DE VERE, AUBREY THOMAS, 316

Deadlock in Darwinism, 11

Decline and Fall of the Roman Empire, 63

Dee River, 234, 238, 245, 276

Deerbrook, 326

DEFOE, DANIEL, 139, 153, 158, 238, 269, 275

Dejection Ode, The, 332, 343

Denton Burn, 219

Derby, 54, 55, 57, 69-70, 78, 89

Derbyshire, xvi, 9, 29, 42, 49, 50, 53-71, 77, 237

Derwent River, 54, 66, 347

Derwent Water, 322, 341

Derwent Valley, 67

DICKENS, CHARLES, 12, 23, 24, 25, 31, 32, 106, 158, 162, 193, 195, 211, 212, 220, 238, 267, 269, 270, 271, 280, 287, 289, 290, 291, 294, 300, 353

Dictionary of the English Language, 41

DISRAELI, BENJAMIN, 1st earl of Beaconsfield, 279, 281, 293

DODGSON, CHARLES LUDWIDGE, see Lewis Carroll

Dodgson, the Rev. Charles, 189, 190, 258

Dombey and Son, 300

Domesday Book, 250

Domestic Manners of the Americans, 350

Don Juan, 77, 82 86

Don River, 145

Donovan, 104

Dora's Fields, 336

Dorset, 179

Double Event, The, 274

Dove Cottage, xv, 179, 323, 328, 329, 330, 332, 334, 337

Dove Nest, 325

Dove River, 50, 54, 55, 60, 61

Dovedale Valley, 29, 50, 53, 54, 55, 57, 60-61

Doveholes, 61

Dover, 85

Down County (Ireland), 131

Downham, 301

DOYLE, SIR ARTHUR CONAN, 301

DOYLE, SIR FRANCIS HASTINGS, 174

Dracula, 158, 196, 197

DRINKWATER, JOHN, 80, 81

Drury Lane Theatre, 31

DRYDEN, JOHN, 173, 174

DU MAURIER, DAPHNE, 196

DU MAURIER, GEORGE, 193, 196

Dublin, 31, 241, 247

Duenna, The, 31

Duesbury, William, 70

Durham (city), 127, 205-7, 213, 219, 222

Durham (county), 186, 201-16, 219, 308

Durham University, 206n, 207

Earl of Leicester's Company, 273

East Riding, 128

Easton Farm, 153
Eastwood, 77, 78, 81, 88–93
Eastwood Board School, 90
Eboracum, 127
Ecclesiastical History of the English People, 194, 206, 221
Eden, Admiral Arthur, 110
Edensor, 63, 65, 66–67
EDGEWORTH, MARIA, 38, 39, 69
EDGEWORTH, RICHARD LOVELL, 38, 39
EDGEWORTH, MRS. RICHARD LOVELL, 39
Edial, 41, 47
Edinburgh, 9n, 15, 95, 324, 349
Edinburgh Review, 98
Edinburgh University, 301
Education of Henry Adams, 17, 21, 175, 233, 238, 267
Edward I, 96, 152, 211, 239
Edward III, 79, 96, 161
Edward IV, 79, 209, 351
Edward VI, 10
Edward VII, 107
Edward, Prince of Wales (later Duke of Windsor), 58
Edward, Prince of Wales (heir to Henry VI), 209
Edwin, King, 161
Edwinstowe, 78
Egerton, John, earl of Bridgewater, 16
Egerton, Lord and Lady (of Tatton Park), 255
Egremont, 346–47
Egremont Castle, 346–47
Elegy on Newstead Abbey, 86, 97
Elgar, Sir Edward William, 20
Eliot, Charles William, 22
ELIOT, GEORGE, 49, 50, 56, 58, 60, 62, 69, 105, 166, 193, 194, 321, 322, 326
ELIOT, THOMAS STEARNS, 82
Elizabeth I, 10, 16, 55, 161, 183, 211, 272, 342

Elizabeth II, 69, 239
Ellastone, 49–50
ELLIOT, EBENEZER, 145
Embsay, 183
EMERSON, RALPH WALDO, 39, 142, 175, 269, 335
Emile, 38
Eminent Victorians, 272
ENGELS, FREDERICK, 294
English Bards and Scotch Reviewers, 86, 98, 192
English Note-Books, 201, 238, 242
Environment, 140
Epistle to Dr. Arbuthnot, 46
Epping Forest, 114
Epstein, Sir Jacob, 342
Epworth, xvi, 151–52
Erewhon, 10
Esk River, 194
Essays (Montaigne), 61
Esthwaite Lodge (Near Sawrey), 313
Esthwaite Water, 313–14
Etheldreda, Queen, 223
Eton, 68, 224
Euclid and his Modern Rivals, 185, 186
Eugene Aram, 166
Eustace Diamonds, The, 166, 350
Evans, Elizabeth, 62
EVANS, MARY ANN, see George Eliot
Evans, Robert, 49, 62
Eve, 213
Excursion, The, 333
Eyam, 54, 67
Eyre Family, 68

FABER, FREDERICK WILLIAM, 10
Faces in the Fire, 258
Fairfax, Mary, 173, 174
Fairfax, Thomas, 3rd Baron, 162, 173, 174
Fairfax, Thomas, 6th Baron, 168
Falstaff, Sir John, 13

Fame is the Spur, 286
Farewell to Ayreshire, 88
Farne Islands, 227
FARQUHAR, GEORGE, xvi, 11, 37, 45
Father's Revenge, The, 192
Fauconberg Arms, The (Coxwold), 173
Fauconberg, Thomas Belasye, 1st earl of Newburgh, 170
Faustine, 176
Feathers, The (Ludlow), 19
Felley Mill Farm, 93
Felton, 226–27
Fenton, 33, 35
Festus, 79
FIELDING, HENRY, 292
Fields, Gracie, 285
FIENNES, CELIA, 238
Filey, 193
FITZGERALD, EDWARD, 101, 324, 345
Five Silver Daughters, 289
FLETCHER, JOHN, 20
Fleshly School of Poetry, The, 225
Florence, 60
Flower in a Crannied Wall, 104
Fockbury, 8, 21
Force of Prayer, The, 183, 184
Ford, Cornelius, 40
Forest Minstrell and Other Poems, 80
Forever with the Lord, 145
Formby, George, 296
Fors Clavigera, 53, 315
FORSTER, EDWARD MORGAN, 7, 8, 10, 11, 16, 19, 20, 93, 177, 226
Forster, Emily, 226
FORSTER, JOHN, 220
Forster, William, 226
Fortress, The, 345
Foss River, 165
Four Winds of Love, 214
FOX, GEORGE, 69
Fox Ghyll, 334

Fox How, 325, 334
FOXE, JOHN, 108
Fragment of Stained Glass, A, 93
France, 15, 83, 93, 106, 181, 209, 225, 246
FRAZER, JAMES G., 271
Friar's Crag, 315
Friend, The, 331
From Greenland's Icy Mountain, 14, 24
Fugitive Pieces, 95, 97

Gainsborough, 9n, 105
Galsworthy, John, 35, 252, 269, 270
Ganges River, 123, 152
Garden, The, 174
GARNETT, RICHARD, 39
GARRICK, DAVID, 40, 41, 42, 46, 47, 170, 172
Garrick, George, 47
Garrick, Peter, 42
Garsington Manor, 94
GASKELL, ELIZABETH GLEGHORN STEVENSON, 56, 134, 136, 193, 195, 233, 249, 250, 252, 253, 254, 257, 279, 280, 281, 287, 289–90, 291, 292, 293, 294, 299, 302, 307, 322, 327, 328
Gaskell, James Milnes, 22
Gaskell, Mrs. James Milnes, 22
Gaskell, The Rev. William, 250, 253, 290–91, 292, 293, 294, 302n
Guardian, The, 286
Gawain, 50, 60, 240
Gawain and the Green Knight, 60, 240
Gawthorpe Hall, 327
Generation on Trial, A., 286
Gentlemen of France, The, 11
George III, 55, 70, 170
George IV, 254
George VI, 159
George, The (Grantham), 106, 107
George, The (Lichfield), xvi, 45, 46

Germany, 81, 294
Getting On, 90
GIBBON, EDWARD, 63
Gibraltar Point, 117
Gielgud, Sir John, 255
GILCHRIST, ALEXANDER, 175
GISSING, GEORGE, 140, 293
GLADSTONE, WILLIAM EWART, 97n, 247, 252, 264
Glasgow, 222
Gloucester Arms (Penrith), 351
GODWIN, WILLIAM, 324
Golden Bough, The, 272
Golden Fleece, The (Thirsk), 180
GOLDING, LOUIS, 289
GOLDSMITH, OLIVER, 140, 171, 220
Gomersal, 137, 138-39
Gondola, The, 315-16
Gone to Earth, 20, 274
Good Companions, The, 130
GOODCHILD, KATH, 251n
GOULD, NATHANIEL, 274, 289
Gowbarrow Park, 349
Goyt Valley, 237
Grantham, 105, 106-7
Grantham Grammar School, 136
Grasmere, 179, 182, 309, 313, 323, 328-32
Grasmere Rectory, 331, 333
Grasmere Sports, 328, 332
Graves, John Woodcock, 352
GRAVES, ROBERT, 15
Gray, Euphemia, 226
Gray, May, 84
GRAY, THOMAS, 20, 308, 322
Great Bridgeford, 33
Great Cubley, 55
Great Glasstown Confederacy, 129
Great Swinburne, 223
Great Grimsby, 112, 118
Greater Manchester, 276, 279-95, 299
Greece, 60, 85, 86

Green Hat, The, 275
Green Knight, The, 50
Green Man and Black's Head Hotel (Ashbourne), 58-59
Greta Bridge, 210, 212-13
Greta Hall, xv, 329, 341, 342-44
Greta Hall, 343n
Greta River, 212, 341
GREVILLE, SIR FULKE, 1st baron Brooke, 10
Grey de Ruthyn, Lord, 84
Greystoke Castle, 343, 349
GROSSETESTE, ROBERT, 103, 104
Grotto, The, 348
Guide Through the Lakes, A, 308, 321
Guide to Tennyson's Lincolnshire, 116
Guildford, 244n
Gulliver's Travels, 263
Guy Fawkes, 288

Haddon Hall, 54
Hadrian, 127, 201, 352
Hadrian's Wall, 201, 219, 223, 352
Haggs Farm, 93
Hagworthingham, 110
Hal, Prince (later Henry V), 154
Halifax, 139-40
Halifax Gibbet, 139
Hallam, Arthur, 109, 115, 175, 271
Hall-Stevenson, John, 169
Halnaby Hall, 216
Hambleton Hills, 157, 179, 180
Hamlet, 171
Hampshire, 302
Hanley, 29, 33, 35
Hard Times, 280, 287, 300
Hardwick Hall, 54, 63
Hark, the Herald Angels Sing, 152
Harold, 127
Harrington, 109, 110-11, 112, 118
Harrogate, xvi, 128, 176-78

Harrow, 84, 86, 87, 95, 97
Harry and Lucy, 39
Hartington, 60, 61
Hartlepool, 213, 214
Hartshead, 131, 132
Harvard University, 22, 242n
Harwood Forest, 219
Hastings, Battle of, 127
Hastings, Warren, 31
Hastlerigg, Sir Arthur, 210
Hathersage, 54, 67–68
Haughton Castle, 223
Haven under the Hill, 195
Hawarden, 245, 246–47
Hawkins, Humphrey, 40
Hawkshead, 309, 313, 314, 317, 321, 351
Hawkshead, Free Grammar School, 317
Haworth, 129, 131–36, 137, 291, 327
Haworth Churchyard: April, 1855, 136
HAWTHORNE, NATHANIEL, 7, 8, 11, 43, 47, 48, 85, 102, 107, 108, 159, 161, 201, 202, 205, 206, 207, 238, 242, 243, 267, 268, 270, 273, 274, 275, 276, 290, 313, 321, 323, 324, 326, 327, 333, 335
Hazlitt, The Rev. William, 14
HAZLITT, WILLIAM, 8, 11, 14, 269, 329, 343
HEBER, REGINALD, 13, 24
Heckmondwike, 137
Heelis, William, 314
Hegar, Constantin, 133
Heights of Abraham, 54
Heir of Wast-Wayland, The, 80
Helmsley, 193
Hemans, Capt. Alfred, 265
HEMANS, FELICIA DOROTHEA, 264, 265, 266–67, 271, 325, 327
Henry II, 20, 78, 82, 146, 223
Henry III, 96, 239
Henry IV, 12, 13, 142, 154

Henry IV, Part 1, 9, 12, 154, 164, 202, 208
Henry V, 208, 209
Henry V, 208
Henry VI, 209, 257
Henry VI (Parts 1, 2, and 3), 208
Henry VII, 12, 273
Henry VIII, 10, 82, 96, 101, 157, 173, 183, 206
Henry of Richmond, 12
Hereford, 9
HERRIOT, JAMES, xvi, 157, 172, 177, 178, 191, 194, 222
Hertford, 196
Hertfordshire, 154
Hexham, 219, 223
Higgins, Edward (Highwayman Higgins), 251, 255
High Beach, 114
High Tide on the Coast of Lincolnshire, The, 108
Highlands, The, 53, 54
Hill Top Farm, 314
History of Sandford and Merton, 39
History of Staffordshire, 59
History of the Old and New Testament in Verse, 151
History of Winnington Hall, A, 249
HOBBES, THOMAS, 64
HODGSON, RALPH, 213
Hodnet, 13–14, 24
Hodent Hall, 14
HOGG, THOMAS JEFFERSON, 164, 213, 214
Holland, 30, 107
Holland (Lincolnshire), 102
Holland, Dr. Peter, 253, 257
Holme, Randle, 245
HOLME, RANDLE III, 245
Holmes, Sherlock, 166, 301
Holy, Holy, Holy, 14, 24
Holy Island, 226, 228
Holybourne, 382n

Holyhead, 240
HOMER, 11
Homes of England, The, 266, 325
HOPKINS, GERARD MANLEY,
   272, 273, 301
HORACE, 43, 219
Horn of Egremont Castle, The,
   346-47
Horncastle, 109-10, 118
Hotspur, 154, 202
Hound of Heaven, The, 293, 379
Hours of Idleness, 97
House of Commons, 31
House of Lords, 80
House under the Water, The, 313
Household Words, The, 32, 287, 290
HOUSMAN, ALFRED EDWARD, 7,
   8, 10, 15, 16, 18, 19, 20, 21, 22, 23,
   53, 54, 108
HOUSMAN, LAURENCE, 23
Howard, Charles, 3rd earl of Carlisle,
   192
Howards End, 20
Howard Family, 191
HOWARD, FREDERICK, 5th earl of
   Carlisle, 192
HOWE, H. W., 344n
HOWITT, MARY, 80
HOWITT, WILLIAM, 80
Hudson Family, 153
Hugh Lupus, 238-39
Hugh of Lincoln, 104
HUGHES, THOMAS, 243
Hughley, 8, 16, 21, 22-23
HUGO, VICTOR, 225
Hull, 128
Hull River, 152
Humber River, 102, 123, 128, 151,
   152, 153
Humberside, 30, 102, 128, 145,
   151-54, 193
Humphry Clinker, 161, 163, 177, 194,
   206

Humshaugh, 223
Hunt, Holman, 186
HUNT, LEIGH, 214, 271
Hunter, John, 37, 40
Hurstwood, 300, 301
Hutchinson Family, 329
Hutchinson, Sarah, 178, 182, 325, 329
Hutchinson, Thomas, 178, 179, 185
Hymn to Contentment, 241

I Have Been Here Before, 130
I Love a Hill, 213
I Wandered Lonely as a Cloud, 307-8,
   332, 349
IKIN, PAT, 251n
Ilam, 50, 54, 55, 59, 60
Ilam Hall, 57, 59, 60
Ilam Park, 60
Ilam Rock, 61
Imperial Chemical Industries, LTD,
   249
In Accordance with the Evidence, 130
In Kedar's Tents, 220
In Memoriam, 101, 109, 115
India, 152
INGELOW, JEAN, 108
Intimations Ode, 332, 333
Ireland, 131, 162, 241, 247, 270
Irish Sea, 128, 201, 247, 308, 353
Irving, Sir Henry, 196
IRVING, WASHINGTON, 269
Italy, 85
Iter Boreale, 97
Ivanhoe, 146, 162, 165
Izaak Walton, The (Thorpe Cloud), 61

Jabberwocky, 188, 222
Jack Sheppard, 288
Jackson, William, 342
James I, 202
James II, 64
JAMES, HENRY, 239
James Herriot's Yorkshire, 157, 191

Jane Eyre, 54, 130, 133, 137, 139, 154, 292, 303
Japan, 213
Jarrow, 206, 221
Jeffrey, Francis, 98
Jemimia Puddle-Duck, 314
Jesus Christ is Risen Today, 152
Jesus, Lover of my Soul, 151-52
Jew's Daughter, The, 104
Job, 252
John Halifax, Gentleman, 34
John, King, 96, 107, 263
Johnson, Esther, 241, 247
Johnson, Michael, 39, 43, 48, 49, 55n
JOHNSON, SAMUEL, 9, 25, 29, 37, 39, 40, 41, 42, 43, 45, 46, 47, 48, 50, 53, 54, 55, 56, 57, 59, 60, 64, 66, 69, 70, 71, 111, 112, 171, 192, 206, 237n, 241, 242, 272
Johnson, Mrs. Samuel, 41, 57, 70
Johnson, Sarah, 39
Johnson, the Life of Samuel, 29, 57, 66, 111
JONSON, BENJAMIN, 17, 93
Journal (John Wesley), 151
Journal (Dorothy Wordsworth), 180
Journal in the Lakes, 308, 322
Journal to Stella, 241, 247
Judith Paris, 314, 345
Juvenus Mundi, 247

Kay-Shuttleworth, Sir James P., 327
Kaye, Danny, 270
KEATS, JOHN, 114, 142, 175, 214, 246, 307, 308, 309, 322
Keats, Tom, 307, 322, 323, 324
Kedleston Hall, 57, 70-71
Kelloe, 207, 208
Kennedy, Kathleen, see Kathleen Kennedy Cavendish
Kennedy, John F., 87
Kent, 289
Kesleven, 102

Keswick, 307-8, 309, 329, 341-42, 345
Kidderminster, 24
King, Edward, 241, 248, 276
King Edward VI Grammar School, 115, 116
King John, 299
King of the Golden River, 249n
King's Head, The (Barnard Castle), 211
KINGSLEY, CHARLES, 173, 176, 247
Kingsley Upon Hull, 151, 152-53
Kipling, Mr. and Mrs. John Lockwood, 34
KIPLING, RUDYARD, 34, 201
Kipps, 166
Knoll, The, 326
KNOWLES, HERBERT, 190
Knowlsey Park, 263, 273-74
KNOX, E. V., 266
Knoxville, 289
Knutsford, 233, 237, 249-58, 302
Kouyoumdjian, Dikran, see Michael Arlen
Kraken, The, 114
Kubla Khan, 332

La Belle Epoque Restaurant François (Knutsford), 255, 257
La Guida di Bragia, 187
Lady Chatterley's Lover, 69, 93
Lady of Shalott, The, 114
Lake District, xv, 9, 164, 179, 211, 249, 266, 280, 292, 386, 307-53
Lallah Rookh, 50
LAMB, CHARLES, 61, 105, 182, 307, 308, 343
LAMB, MARY, 343
Lancashire, 128, 132, 182, 233, 263, 269, 276, 279-81, 285, 289, 299-304, 308, 315, 321
Lancashire Witches, The, 288, 301
Lancaster, 280, 295, 299
Lancaster, House of, 209, 299

Lancelot, Sir, 103
Land Beyond the Sea, The, 11
Landing of the Pilgrim Fathers, The, 266
LANDOR, WALTER SAVAGE, 220, 344
Langton (Lincolnshire), 110, 111–12
Langton (Staffordshire), 33
Langton, Bennet, 111, 112
Langton Hall, 111
Langton, Stephen, 111
L'Anson, Frances, 191
Last Tournament, The, 117
Laurence Sterne Trust, The, 172, 173
Law Hill, 139
Lawes, Henry, 16
Lawrence, Ada, 62, 68
Lawrence, Arthur, 90, 91
Lawrence, Mrs. Arthur, 89, 90, 91
LAWRENCE, DAVID HERBERT, xvi, 20, 62, 63, 68, 77, 78, 79, 80, 88, 89, 90, 91, 93, 94, 95, 103
Lawrence, Frieda von Richtofen, 81, 93
Lays of Ancient Rome, 188
Lays of Sorrow, 188
Lazy Tour of Two Idle Apprentices, 353
LEACH, JOAN, 320n
LEAR, EDWARD, 273, 316
Leeds, 128, 129, 131, 132, 140, 295
Leeds-Liverpool Canal, 296
Leek, 58
Leen River, 82
Left Hand, Right Hand, 68
Le Gallienne, Eva, 265
LE GALLIENNE, RICHARD, 264, 265
Legend of Scotland, 210
Legend of Sleepy Hollow, 269
Leicestershire, 41, 54
Leighton, 20
Lenin, Nikolai, 294

Leo X, 264
Lesbia Brandon, 224
Levant, The, 85
Leven River, 321
Leviathan, The, 64
Lewes, George, 194
LEWIS, CECIL DAY, see Cecil Day-Lewis
Lichfield, xvi, 29, 36–46, 47, 55
Lichfield Grammar School, 40
Licorice Fields at Pontefract, The, 142
Liddell, Alice, 210
Liddell, Dr. H. G., 210
Life and Letters (of Francis Bacon, edited by James Spedding), 345
Life and Letters of Lewis Carroll, 222
Life and Times of William Wordsworth, 344
Life of Charlotte Brontë, 292, 328
Life of Christ in Verse, 151
Life of Keats, 175
Life of Lorenzo de Medici, 264
Life of Milton, 241
Life's Morning, A, 140
Lincoln, 102–4, 106, 107, 108, 109
Lincoln's Inn, 79
Lincolnshire, 9, 78, 101–18, 128
Lindisfarne, 205, 228
Lindsey, 101–2
LINSKILL, MARY, 195, 196
Lion Hotel (Shrewsbury), 11, 12
Little John, 54
Little Lord Fauntleroy, 289
Little Moreton Hall, 237
Little Nell, 3, 24n
Little Swinburne, 223
Liverpool, 15, 234, 239, 242, 243, 246, 259, 263–72, 274, 275, 280, 285, 293, 295, 299, 313, 325, 330
Liverpool University, 271, 272
Lives of the Poets, 241
Livesay, Joseph, 300
Locksley Hall, 111, 114, 271

London, 7, 9, 31, 35, 41, 43, 47, 54, 79, 84, 85, 93, 94, 111, 114, 153, 154, 170, 171, 172, 182, 213, 215, 216, 220, 224, 227, 240, 292, 293, 314, 321, 322, 323, 325, 331
London University, 15
Long Island, 289
Longest Journey, The, 227
Lonsdale, William Lowther, Lord, 323
Looking Back at Knutsford, 251n
Lord Nelson Inn (Halifax), 139
Loss of the Birkenhead, The, 174
Lotus Eaters, The, 114
Louth, 115-16
Louvre, The, 63
Love, 145
Love Sonnets of Proteus, 301
LOVELACE, RICHARD, 79
Love's Cross Currents, 225
Love's Welcome, 93
Low Wood Inn (Ambleside), 324, 325
Lowther, Sir James, 347
Lucas, Richard Cockle, 43
Luddenden Foot, 139
LUCIAN, 61
Luddite, 133, 287
Ludlow, 8, 15, 16-19, 21
Ludlow Castle, 16, 17, 19
L'ulf, Baron, 349
Lumb, Hanna Holland, 252, 255, 257
Lune River, 299
Lune Valley, 280, 299
LYALL, EDNA, 104
Lycidas, 241, 248, 276
Lyrical Ballads, 179, 323, 330
LYTTLETON, GEORGE WILLIAM, 247
Lyulph's Tower, 349

Mablethorpe, 115, 116-18
Mablethorpe, 117
MACAULAY, THOMAS BABING- TON, 1st baron Macaulay, 188

MACKENZIE, SIR COMPTON, 214
Magna Carta, 96
Magnolia Street, 289
Maine, 269
Malcolm of Scotland, 318
Malton, 191
Man From the North, A, 35
Manchester, 239, 249, 251, 252, 264, 271, 276, 281, 285-95, 299, 300, 302
Manchester Grammar School, 288
Manchester University, 294
Manifold, The, 29, 55, 59-60
Mansfield, 89
MAP (OR MAPES), WALTER, 103
Marches, The, 16
Mariana, 114
Market Bosworth, 41, 47
Market Rasen, 118
MARKHAM, MRS., see Elizabeth Penrose
Marlborough, John Churchill, 1st duke of, 37
Marmion, 206
Marshall, Mr. and Mrs. James, 316
Marston Moor, 173
MARTINEAU, HARRIET, 136, 292, 308, 322, 326, 327, 335
MARVELL, ANDREW, 123, 128, 152, 153, 173, 174
MARX, KARL, 294
Mary Barton, A Tale of Manchester Life, 279, 280, 287, 290, 294, 302
Mary Queen of Scots, 353
MASEFIELD, JOHN, 271
MASON, WILLIAM, 20
Massachusetts, 234
Massachusetts Bay Company, 107, 108
Master Humphrey's Clock, 211
Masterpiece Theatre, 286
Matlock, 53, 54
Matthews, Charles Skinner, 85
Maud, 111
Maurice, 177

Mayfield, 49, 50, 56, 58
Mayflower, The, 107
Meade Family, 295
Meaux Abbey, 152
Meeting of the Greta and the Tees, 212
MELVILLE, HERMAN, 195, 201, 242, 243, 268, 275
MELVILLE, SIR JAMES, 202, 219
MERRIMAN, Henry Seton, see Hugh Stowell Scott
Merry England, 293
Merryn Clitheroe, 288
Mersey River, 234, 263, 267, 268, 271, 285
Merseyside, 234, 259, 263–73, 285, 299
Metcalfe, William, 352
Methodist Church, xvi, 151
MEYNELL, ALICE, 293
Meynell, Wilfred, 293
Michael, 332
Middlesborough, 128
Middleton, 62–63
Midlands, 63
Milbanke, Judith Noel Wentworth, 215
Milbanke, Sir Ralph, 215
Milford Haven, 106
Mill on the Floss, The, 24, 105, 166
Millais, John Everett, 226
Millais, Robert, 226
Milldale, 61
Miller's Daughter, The, 110
MILNES, RICHARD MONCKTON, 1st baron Houghton, 140, 142, 175, 176
MILTON, JOHN, 8, 16, 17, 39, 173, 174, 241, 246, 248, 252, 272, 276, 288n
Miracle Plays, The, 141, 241
Mirehouse, 325, 344, 345
Mirfield Moor, 137
Mischmasch, The, 188, 222

Miss Margaret Wooler's Seminary for Young Ladies, 137
Miss Patchett's School, 139
Mr. Harrison's Confessions, 249, 250
Mrs. Tiggy-Winkle, 345
Mitchell, Reginald, 35
Mitford sisters, 65
Moby Dick, 195, 242
Monk Fryston, 173, 175–76
Monk Fryston Hall, 142, 175–76
Monk Fryston Hall Hotel (Monk Fryston), 176
Monkmon, Julia and Kenneth, 172
MONTAGU, LADY MARY WORTLEY, 46
MONTAIGNE, MICHEL EYQUEM DE, 61
MONTGOMERY, JAMES, 145
Monthly Mirror, The, 97
MOORE, THOMAS, 50, 56, 58, 60, 95, 216
Moorgreen Reservoir, 93
Morecambe, 299
Morecambe Bay, 299, 302, 321
Morrell, Lady Ottoline, 93, 94
Morritt Arms Inn (Greta Bridge), 212, 213
Morritt, J. B., 212
Mortimer, Roger, 1st earl of March, 79
Mount Pisgah, 8
Movements in European History, 63
Mower, The, 174
Much Wenlock, 16, 20, 21
MUIRHEAD, FINDLAY, 237
Murder in the Cathedral, 82
Mustapha, 10
My Ladies' Sonnets, 265
McGONEGALL, WILLIAM, 227
McNally, Leonard, 191

Nab Cottage (Grasmere), xv, 334
Napoleon III, 225
Narrative of a Journey, A, 14

Naseby, 173
Nathaniel, George 1st marquis of
   Kedelston, 71
National Trust, The, 60, 258, 291, 314,
   315, 333, 336, 342, 347
Near Sawrey, 313-14
Necessity of Atheism, The, 164
Nelson, Horatio, Viscount, 19, 132
Nether Stowey, 14
Neville, Anne (Queen of Richard III),
   209
Neville, Cecily, 351
Neville Family, 208
Neville, Ralph, earl of Westmoreland,
   208, 209
Neville, Richard, earl of Warwick, 209
New Chum, 271
New Grub Street, 293
New Mexico, 93
New Rector, The, 18
New York City, 289
Newark upon Trent, 77, 97-98, 102,
   106
Newburgh Priory, 172
Newby Bridge, 309, 313
Newcastle-under-Lyme, 30, 34
Newcastle-under-Lyme Middle School,
   34
Newcastle upon Tyne, 202, 219-21,
   226, 227
Newchurch, 301
NEWMAN, JOHN HENRY
   (CARDINAL), 11, 301
Newnham College (Cambridge), 264
Newstead Abbey, xvi, 80, 82-87, 88,
   95, 96
Newstead Abbey, 86
NEWTON, SIR ISAAC, 106
Nicholas Nickleby, 106, 158, 205, 211,
   290
Nicholls, The Rev. Arthur Bell, 133,
   135, 136, 137, 139, 293
Night Piece on Death, 241

Norham Castle, 226, 228
Normans, 239, 250, 257
North Allerton, 229n
North and South, 302
North, Christoper, 342
NORTH, FREDERICK, 2nd earl of
   Guildford, 192
North Sea, 9, 30, 102, 128, 157, 158,
   193, 201, 215
North Yorkshire, 115, 128, 157-97,
   202
Northumberland, 201, 202, 219-28
Northumbria, 201
Northwich, 248
Norton, Lady Emily, 183
Norton, Francis, 183
Norton, Richard, 183
Norwegians, 308
Nottingham, xvi, 77, 78-82, 89, 94, 95
Nottingham Castle, 78, 81
Nottingham High School, 81, 90
Nottinghamshire, 9, 69, 77-98, 101,
   105, 162
Nun Appleton House, 173-74
Nussey, Ellen, 67, 137, 153
Nussey, The Rev. Henry, 67, 138, 153

O for a Heart to Praise my God, 152
Oakwell Hall, 138
Ode to Duty, 332
Ode to Memory, 116
Oenone, 114
Oft in Danger, Oft in Woe, 79
Oh Mary, go and call the cattle home,
   247
Ohio, 350
Old Bachelor, The, 59
Old Benchers of the Inner Temple,
   105
Old Curiosity Shop, The, 23, 24, 211
Old Man of Coniston, The, 316
Old St. Paul's, 288
Old Wellington Inn (Manchester), 288

Old Wives Tale, The, 33, 35, 36
Oldcoates, 63
OLIPHANT, LAURENCE, 176
Oliver Twist, 270
Olivier, Sir Laurence, 255
On Leaving Newstead Abbey, 83n, 86
On the General Fairfax at the Seige of Colchester, 174
One Man's America, 286
ONIONS, OLIVER, 130
Ormond, 39
ORWELL, GEORGE, 29, 31, 32, 33, 129, 135, 146, 269, 271, 280, 281, 285, 294, 295, 296
Oswestry, 13, 14–15, 246
Our Old Home, 7, 43, 48, 159, 267, 273
Ouse River, 127
Outlook, The, 11
OVID, 63
OWEN, WILFRED, 8, 14, 15, 246, 271
Owens College, 293, 294
Owens, John, 293
Oxford, 9, 94
Oxford University, 16, 37, 40, 41, 68, 104, 111, 151, 164, 174, 185, 188, 190, 210, 213, 224, 246, 265, 272, 288, 315
Oxfordshire, 15, 243

Paganini, Nicolo, 12
Palace of Art, The, 114
Paradise Lost, 362n
Parker, C and Co., 116, 117
Parkgate, 245, 247
PARNELL, THOMAS, 241
Past and Present, 279, 287, 294
PATMORE, COVENTRY, 316
Patton, General George, 251
Paxton, Joseph, 66
PEACOCK, THOMAS LOVE, 324

Peak District, 54
Peel, John, 341, 352
Peel, Mrs. John, 352
Peele, Sir Robert, 12
Pendle Hill, 301
PENN, WILLIAM, 69
Pennines, The, 128, 157, 237
Penrith, 178, 309, 329, 351, 352
Penrith Beacon, 350
PENROSE, ELIZABETH, 104
PEPYS, SAMUEL, 17
Percy Family Tomb, 154
Percy Folio, 24
Percy, Henry, 12
PERCY, THOMAS, 24, 183
Peter Rabbit, 314
Peterloo Massacre, 279, 281, 286
PEVSNER, SIR NIKOLAUS, 252
Philadelphia, 135
Phoenix, 77
Piccadilly, 176
Pickwick Papers, The, 211, 270
Picts, 201
Piece Hall, 139
Pierce, Franklin, 267
Pigot, Elizabeth, 95, 97
Pigot Family, 95
Pigot, John, 95
Pilgrims, 107
Pilgrims of the Night, 11
Pitt, Humphrey, 24
Plantagenet, Hamelin, 146
Plantagenets, 127
Plas Wilmot, 14
Pleasure reconciled to Vertue, 17
Pleasures of the Imagination, The, 220
Plot, Robert, 59
Plymouth Colony, 107
Poem to an Oak, 86, 87
Poems (Tennyson), 117, 325
Poems (Thompson), 293
Poems and Ballads (Swinburne), 176, 225

Poems by Currer, Ellis and Acton Bell, 133
Poems by Two Brothers, 114, 116, 325
Poems, Chiefly Lyrical, 114, 325
Poems of Mr. Gray, The, 308
Poems of Terence Hearsay, The, 8
Poems on Various Occasions, 97
Poet, The, 114
Poetic Works (Milnes), 175
Poet's Mind, The, 114
Polidori, Charlotte, 220
POLLARD, ALFRED WILLIAM, 8
Polperro, 345
Pomfret Castle, 142
Ponden Hall, 136
Pontefract, 140, 142, 175
POPE, ALEXANDER, 46, 241
Porter, Elizabeth, see Mrs. Samuel Johnson
Porter, Lucy, 42
Porter, Harry, 47
Portugal, 85
POTTER, BEATRIX, 314, 322, 342, 345
Practical View of the Prevailing Religious System of Professed Christians, A, 153
Pre-Raphaelite Brotherhood, 224, 226, 315
Precious Bane, 20, 274
Prelude, The, 313, 317, 332, 349
Preston, 280n, 287, 300
Preston Temperance Advocate, The, 300
Pride and Prejudice, 53, 54, 64
PRIESTLY, JOHN BOYNTON, 130
Prince Alexy Haimatoff, 214
Prince Regent, The (later George IV), 50
Prince William of Hatfield, 161
Princess, The, 117
Princeton University, 272
Professor, The, 68, 133, 139, 291, 327

Provok'd Wife, The, 191
Prussian Officer, The, 94
Puck of Pook's Hill, 201

Quakers, 69
Quarterly, The, 114
Queen Mother, The, 176
Queensborough, 153
Quest of the Golden Girl, The, 265

Raby Castle, 207
Rae, Gordon, 178
Railwaymans Arms (Bridgnorth), 23
Rainbow, The (D. H. Lawrence), 62, 63, 81, 93, 103
Rainbow, The (Wordsworth), 164
RALEIGH, SIR WALTER, 272
Rambler, The, 111
RANSOME, ARTHUR, 313, 315
Raphael, 248
Rasselas, 41, 42, 50
Raven Inn (Shrewsbury), 11
Rawnsley, Canon H. Drummond, 342
Rebecca, 196
Recollections of the Lakes and the Lake Poets, 308
Recruiting Officer, The, 11
Rectory Umbrella, The, 188
Red House, The, 138, 139
Red Thread of Honour, The, 74
Redburn, 268
Redgauntlet, 353
Reeve's Tale, The, 123
Relapse, The, 194
Reliques of Ancient English Poetry, 24, 104, 183
Remigius, 103
Reminiscences and Opinions, 174
Remorse, 114
Renishaw, 67, 68–69
Renishaw Hall, xvi, 68, 69

Representative Men, 269
Resignation, 307, 337
Return to Bestwood, 88
Ribble Valley, 280, 288, 299
Riceyman Steps, 35
Richard I (The Lion-Hearted), 96, 146
Richard II, 96, 142, 351
Richard II, 96, 140, 142
Richard III, 12, 79, 106, 209, 351
Richard III, 106, 208-9
RICHARDSON, SAMUEL, 171
Richie, Anne Thackeray, 254
Richmond, 187, 190-91
Rievaulx Abbey, 178, 179, 180-81
Rime of the Ancient Mariner, The,
    179, 332
Rip Van Winkle, 269
Ripley, 62
Rivals, The, 31
Road to Wigan Pier, 146, 271, 280,
    295
Roberts, Sir James, 134
Robin Hood, 54, 67, 78, 81
Robin Hood's Bay, 193
Robinson Crusoe, 139, 158
ROBINSON, HENRY CRABB, 335,
    344
Rochdale, 285
Rock Ferry, 263, 273, 274
Rock of Names, 336-37
Roe Head, 137
Rogue Herries, 345
Rokeby, 212, 213
Rokeby House, 212
Rolls, Charles, 251
Romans, 127, 159, 201, 219, 238, 239,
    295, 299
Romany Rye, The, 31, 109
Rome, 127
Rookwood, 154, 165, 288
Room with a View, A, 227
Rosemund, 176
ROSCOE, WILLIAM, 264

Rose and Crown Inn (Halifax), 139
ROSSETTI, DANTE GABRIEL, 220,
    221, 223, 224, 225, 270
Rossetti Family, 175, 186
Rothay River, 334
Rotherham, 145, 146
ROUSSEAU, JEAN-JAQUES, 38, 49,
    50
Royal Crown Derby China, 70
Royal George Hotel (Knutsford), 254,
    255, 257
Royal Oak Hotel (Keswick), 341, 342
Royal Shrovetide Football, 55, 56, 58
Royce, Henry, 251
Rubáiyát of Omar Khayyám, 324
Rugby School, 188, 190, 243, 265, 325
Runnymede, 111
Rupert, Prince, 30, 250
RUSKIN, JOHN, xvi, 53, 54, 146,
    186, 224, 246, 248, 249, 304,
    315-16, 342, 344
RUSSELL, BERTRAND, 93, 94
Russell, Elizabeth, 208, 209
Russell, Major Matthew, 208, 209
Ruth, 249, 253, 257, 302
Rydal Church, 336
Rydal Mount, xv, 266, 321, 325-26,
    331, 334-36, 345
Rydings, The, 137-38
Rylstone, 182, 183, 184

St. Asaph, 265
St. Cuthbert, 205, 206, 207, 228
St. Hilda, 194
St. Mawr, 20
St. Wilfred, 223
Saint's Everlasting Rest, The, 24
Salford, 285, 289
Sandys, Archbishop Edwin, 317
Saracen's Head Inn (Southwell), 95,
    97
SASSOON, SIEGFRIED, 15, 166, 246
Satires (Horace), 219

Saxons, 127, 238, 286
Scafell Pike, 308
Scallions and Amazons, 313
Scarborough, 128, 137, 153, 179, 182, 185, 193-94, 195
Scarlet Letter, The, 48n, 242
Scarsdale, Lord, 70
Scenes of Clerical Life, 105
School for Scandal, The, 31
Scotland, 66, 80, 84, 202, 211, 220, 267, 349, 350, 353
Scots, 201, 202
Scott, C. P., 286
SCOTT, HUGH STOWELL, 220
Scott, Charlotte Charpentier, 352
SCOTT, SIR WALTER, 20, 24, 38, 39, 98, 146, 162, 165, 183, 206, 207, 212, 213, 228, 254, 322, 323, 333, 335, 342, 344, 348, 350, 353
SCOTT, WILLIAM BELL, 220, 221, 223, 226
Seaham, 205, 214-16
Second Shepherd's Play, The, 141
See the Conquering Hero, 20
Sellwood, Emily, see Lady Emily Tennyson
Sellwood, Louisa, 109
Sellwood, the Rev. Henry, 109
Sentimental Journey, A, 171
Sermons of Mr. Yorick, 171
Servius, 127
Sesame and Lillies, 246
Severn River, 8, 21, 23
SEWARD, ANNA, 37, 38, 40, 46, 67
Seward, Canon Thomas, 37
SHAKESPEARE, WILLIAM, 9, 12, 13, 93, 96, 106, 140, 142, 164, 171, 202, 208-9, 233, 241, 266, 272, 273, 299
Shakespearian Tragedy, 272
Shallowford, 30, 32-33
Shandy Hall, 170-73
Shaw, William, 212

Sheaf River, 145
Sheffield, 123, 127, 128, 129, 145-46, 271
Sheffield Iris, The, 145
Shelley, Harriet Westbrook, 164, 214, 324, 341, 343, 349
Shelley, Ianthe, 324
SHELLEY, PERCY BYSSHE, 163, 164, 213, 214, 323, 324, 327, 341, 342, 343, 349
Shepheards Calendar, The, 301
SHERIDAN, RICHARD BRINSLEY, 30, 31, 194
Sheriff of Nottingham, 81, 82
Sherwood Forest, 78, 82
Sherwood Forest Visitors Center, 78
Shibden Hall, 139
Shifnal, 23, 24
Shirley, 133, 138-39, 154, 166, 287, 327
Shrewsbury, 7, 8, 9-12, 14, 15, 16, 20, 21, 30
Shrewsbury Grammar School, 10, 16, 18
Shropshire, 7-25, 246, 274
Shropshire Lad, A, 7, 8, 18, 21
Sidney, Sir Henry, 16
SIDNEY, SIR PHILIP, 8, 10, 16
Silverdale, 302, 304
Simpson, John, 334
Simpson, Margaret, 334
Sitwell family, xvi, 68, 69, 193, 194
SITWELL, DAME EDITH, 68, 194
Sitwell, Sir George, xvi, 68
SITWELL, SIR OSBERT, 15, 68, 194
Sitwell, Lady Penelope, 69
Sitwell, Sir Reresby, 69
SITWELL, SIR SACHEVERELL, 68, 194
Six Men, 286
Skegness, 115, 116-17
Skelton, 167, 169
Sketch Book, The, 269

Sketch of Modern and Ancient Geography, A, 10

Skiddaw, 307, 308-9, 341

Sladen Beck, 135

Slave of the Lamp, The, 220

Sleep in Peace, 140

SMART, CHRISTOPHER, 207

Smith, Trumpet Major, 251, 256

SMOLLETT, TOBIAS GEORGE, 161, 163, 177, 193, 194, 206

Society of Friends, 69

Sockburn-on-Tees, 179, 182, 185

Solitude, 189

Solway, 201

Solway Firth, 353

Somersby, xvi, 102, 109, 110, 112-15, 116, 118

Somerset, 14, 20, 179, 323, 330

Somnambulist, The, 349

Son of God Goes Forth to War, The, 14

Songs of Praise the Angels Sing, 145

Sons and Lovers, 78, 90, 91, 93, 94, 95

South Yorkshire, 128, 145-54

Southey family, 343

SOUTHEY, ROBERT, xv, 79, 98, 145, 191, 304, 329, 342, 343, 344

Southport, 263, 273, 274-76

Southwell, 80, 87, 88, 94-97

Spain, 85, 271

Spanish Armada, 350

Spectator, The, 37

Spedding family, 345

SPEDDING, JAMES, 324, 325, 345

Spedding, John, 345

Spedding, Marcia, 345

Spedding, Margaret, 345

SPENCER, HERBERT, 69

SPENDER, STEPHEN, 15

SPENSER, EDMUND, 301

SPRING, HOWARD, 286

Stafford, 30-32, 33, 36, 48

Staffordshire, 9, 25, 29-50, 55, 59

Staithes, 193

Stamford, 106

Stamford Bridge, 127

Stanzas in Richmond Churchyard, The, 190, 191

Stepmother, The, 192

Sterne, Elizabeth Lumley, 167, 168

Sterne, Dr. Jaques, 167, 242

STERNE, LAURENCE, 139, 157, 162, 167, 168, 169, 170, 171, 172, 173, 241, 242

Sterne, Lydia, 171, 172

STERNE, DR. RICHARD, 162

STEVENSON, ROBERT LOUIS, 342

Stillington, 167, 168-69

Stillington Hall, 168

Stockton on Tees, 205, 213-14

Stoke, 33

Stoke-on-Trent, 29, 30, 33-36

STOKER, BRAM, 158, 193, 196, 197

Stokesay, 17

Stones of Venice, The, 248

Stonyhurst College, 300, 301

Stourbridge, 21, 40

STOWE, HARRIET BEECHER, 269, 290, 291

STRACHEY, LYTTON, 93, 272

Strangers Yet, 175

Stratford-upon-Avon, 9, 131

Strathallan, 178

Strid, The, 185

Strife, 270

Stuart, Charles (Bonnie Prince Charlie), 250

Stuarts, The, 250

Studies on Homer and the Homeric Age, 246, 247

Stybarrow Crag, 349

Sun, The (Clun), 20

Sunderland, 205, 219, 221, 222

Sunny Memories of Foreign Lands, 269, 291

Surrey, 189n

Sutton-on-the-Forest, 167–68, 169, 170

Sutton, William, 274

Swan, The (Grasmere), 333, 334

Swan, The (Lichfield), xvi, 45, 46

Swan, The (Newby Bridge), 313

Swan, The (Stafford), 31, 32

Swayle River, 190

Sweet Lass of Richmond Hill, The, 191

SWIFT, JONATHON, 77, 220, 241, 243, 246, 247

SWINBURNE, ALGERNON CHARLES, 142, 173, 175, 176, 202, 220, 221, 224, 226, 227, 335

Swinburne, John, 224

Switzerland, 60

Sylvia's Lovers, 195, 196

Tale of Peter Rabbit, The, 314

Tales of a Far Riding, 130

Tales of Orris, 108

Talk About America, 286

Tanglewood Tales, 274

Tatler, The, 37

Tatton Hall and Park, 237, 250, 255, 257–58

Tatton Mere, 257

Taylor, George Ashton, 212

TAYLOR, JEREMY, 14

TAYLOR, JOHN, 153

Taylor, Dr. John, 42, 50, 55, 56, 57, 58, 64, 70

Taylor, Joshua, 138

Taylor, Martha, 137, 138

Taylor, Mary, 137, 138

Tealby, 115, 118

Tees Estuary, 128

Tees River, 127, 187, 202, 210, 212

Teme River, 16

Temperance Hotel (Stafford), 32

Temperance Movement, 300

Tenant of Wildfell Hall, The, 134

Tennessee, 289

Tenniel, Sir John, 154

TENNYSON, ALFRED, first baron Tennyson, xvi, 15, 82, 101, 102, 104, 105, 109, 110, 111, 112, 113, 114, 115, 116, 117, 142, 173, 175, 186, 195, 207, 208, 251, 269, 270, 271, 290, 316–17, 324–25, 328, 342, 345

Tennyson, Charles (the poet's uncle), 112, 113, 118

Tennyson, Elizabeth Fytcher, 113, 115, 116

Tennyson, Emily, 109

Tennyson, Lady Emily Sellwood, 109, 110, 111, 118, 209, 316

Tennyson, Frederick, 114, 115, 116, 325

Tennyson, George (the poet's grandfather), 112, 113, 118

Tennyson, the Rev. George Clayton (the poet's father), 112, 113, 114, 115, 118

Tennyson, Hallam, 325

Tennyson, Mary, 113, 115, 116

Tennyson-Turner, Charles (the poet's brother), 109, 113, 114, 115, 116

Terry, Ellen, 186

Testament of Youth, 34

THACKERAY, WILLIAM MAKEPEACE, 142, 175, 254, 290, 291, 292

That Lass o'Lowries, 289

Thirlmere Lake, 336, 337

Thirsk, 178, 179–80

3,600 Faults in our Printed Bibles, 162

Thomas à Becket, 82

THOMAS À KEMPIS, 252

THOMAS, DYLAN, 15

THOMPSON, FRANCIS, 293, 300

Thornton, 129, 130–31

Thorpe Cloud, 60, 61

Thor's Cave, 55, 59, 60

Those Evening Bells, 56, 58

Thrace, 63

Thrale, Henry, 42, 45, 50, 242

THRALE, HESTER LYNCH, xvi, 42, 45, 50, 57, 242

Thrale, Queenie, 242

Three Crowns Inn (Lichfield), 45

Three Tabernacles, The, 190, 191

Three Tuns Inn (Eastwood), 90, 91

Three Tuns, The (Thirsk), 180

Through England on a Side Saddle in the Time of William and Mary, 238.

Through the Looking Glass, 188, 190

Thyrsis, 243, 265

Tight Little Island, 214

Time and the Conways, 130

Time, You Old Gipsy Man, 213

Tintern Abbey, 179

Tintoretto, Jacopo Robusti, 315

Tithonous, 114

Titian, Tiziano Vecelli, 315

To His Coy Mistress, 123, 152, 174

To Mary, 97

Tom Kitten, 314

Tong, 23, 25, 30

Tono-Bungay, 166

Top Withens, 136

Tour through the Whole Island of Great Britain, 158, 238, 269

Tower of London, 79

Tragedy of King John, The, 187

Translations (Gladstone and Lyttleton), 247

Trent Polytechnic, 81

Trent River, 29-30, 55, 102, 103, 105

Trentham Lake, 34

Trevelyan, Lady Pauline, 225-26

Trevelyan, Sir Walter, 225

Trilby, 196

Trinity College (Cambridge), 8, 325, 345

Trip to Scarborough, A, 194

Tristram Shandy, 157, 167, 168, 169, 170, 171

Triumph of Philamore and Amoret, The, 79

TROLLOPE, ANTHONY, 154, 166, 350

TROLLOPE, FRANCES, 350

Trout Hotel (Cockermouth), 347

Tudor Restaurant and Coffee Room (Penrith), 351

Tunstall, 33

Turner, Joseph Mallord William, 212, 224, 248, 315

Turpin, Dick, 154, 165, 165n, 166

Tussaud, Mme Marie, 12

Tweed River, 202

Two Plays (Swinburne), 176

Twopenny Post Bag, The, 50

Tyne and Wear, 202, 205, 214, 219-28

Tyne River, 201, 202

Typee, 268

Tyson, Mrs. Ann, 317

Uffington, 243

Ullswater (Ullster Water), 308, 309

Ulysses, 114, 117

Uncle Tom's Cabin, 269

United States of America, 267, 271

United Union of Soviet Republics, 294

University College (London), 7

University College (Nottingham), 81

The Unknown, 190

Unto this Last, 246

Up the Airy Mountain, 270

Upon Appleton House, To My Lord Fairfax, 174

Uricon, 21

Uriconium, 21

Useful and Instructive Poetry, 188

Uttoxeter, 47-49

Valediction, The, 271

VANBRUGH, SIR JOHN, 191, 194, 241

Vaughan, Richard, 17
Vence, 93
Versailles, 63
Viator Bridge, 61
Vicar of Wakefield, The, 140
Vicar of Wrexhill, The, 350
Victoria, Queen, 66, 110, 117, 161,
    185, 252, 254, 264, 267
Vienna, 265
Vikings, 127, 159
Village Patriarch, The, 145
Villette, 133
Villiers, George, 2nd duke of
    Buckingham, 174
Vine Hotel (Skegness), 117
VIRGIL, 61, 97
Visions of Sudden Death, 288

Waggoner, The, 329, 333, 336
Waite, The Rev. J., 115–16
Wakefield, xvi, 140–41, 145, 162
Wales, 9, 11, 19, 21, 106, 179, 237,
    240, 242, 265, 276, 288
Wallasey, 263
Wallington Hall, 224–26
Wallsend, 219, 221
Walmesley, Gilbert, 40, 42, 46
WALMSEY, LEO, 193
WALPOLE, HORACE, 83, 145, 146,
    171, 192
WALPOLE, SIR HUGH, 35, 314, 341,
    342, 345
Walrus and the Carpenter, The, 222
Waltham Cross, 154
WALTON, IZAAC, 30, 32, 50, 54, 56,
    58, 60, 61, 79
Wanderer of Liverpool, The, 271
Wanderer of Switzerland, The, 145
Ward's Stone, 299
Wars of the Roses, 12, 209, 257, 299
Warwickshire, 9, 40, 49, 105
Wash, The, 9, 102, 107
Washington, George, 161
Watendlath, 345

Waterloo, Battle of, 281
Watt, Richard Harding, 251, 257
Watts, George, 104
WAUGH, EVELYN, 191
Waverley, 353
Way of All Flesh, The, 11
We Two, 104
Wear River, 202, 205, 206
WEBB, MARY, 20, 274
Wedgwood, Josiah, 33
Wedgwood, Thomas, 11
Weekley, Ernest, 81
Welbeck Abbey, 93–94
Wellington, 19
Wellington, Arthur Wellesley, 1st
    duke of, 97n, 207
WELLS, HERBERT GEORGE, 35,
    166
Wem, 8, 11, 13, 14
Wenlock, 8, 21, 22
Wenlock Abbey, 22
Wenlock Edge, 8, 15, 16, 20, 21, 22
Wenlocks, The, 15, 20–22
Wentworth, Edward Noel, 1st
    viscount, 215
WESLEY, CHARLES, xvi, 151
WESLEY, JOHN, xvi, 151
WESLEY, SAMUEL, 151
West Africa, 129
West Country, 9
West Indies, 263
West Midlands, 29
West Riding, 128, 133
West Yorkshire, 54, 127–47, 175
Westbrook, Eliza, 324
Westmoreland, 308, 323, 335
Weston-super-Mare, 20
Westward Ho!, 176
WEYMAN, STANLEY JOHN, 10, 16,
    17–18
Whalley, 300–1
Wharf River, 183, 184, 185
Wheel of Fortune, 95
Whiskey Galore, 214

Whitburn, 222

Whitby, 193, 194–97

White Doe of Rylstone, 157, 178, 183, 184–85

White Hart Hotel (Uttoxeter), 48n, 49

WHITE, HENRY KIRK, 79

White Peacock, The, 90, 93

White Rabbit, The, 154

White Star Lines, 263

Widdershins, 130

Widener Library, 187n

Widow Barnaby, The, 350

Wigan, 32, 146, 285, 295–96, 300

Wigan Pier, 29, 281, 294, 296

WIGHT, ALF, see James Herriot

Wilberforce Museum, 153

WILBERFORCE, WILLIAM, 153, 343

WILDE, OSCAR FINGAL O'FLAHERTIE WILLS, 25n

Wildman, Col. Thomas, 86

Wilkinson, the Rev. John, 224

WILKINSON, THOMAS, 348

William III and Mary, 64

William IV, 335

WILLIAM OF MALMESBURY, 237, 238, 240

William the Conqueror, 63, 83, 103, 127, 238, 250

Williams, Harold, 241

Wilson, Harold, 130

Wilson, the Rev. William Carus, 304

Wiltshire, 37, 288

Wina, 248

Windebrowe, 344

Windermere Lake, 280, 285, 307, 308, 309, 313, 321–22, 324, 325, 327

Windermere (town), 321

Windsor Castle, 288

Winestead, 152

Winkworth, Katie, 327

Winnington Hall, 245, 248–49

Winthrop, John, 107

Wirksworth, 62, 68

Wirral Peninsula, 234, 240

Witham River, 102, 103, 107

Wives and Daughters, 249, 253, 254

Wolds, The, 102

Woman Magazine, 35

Woman in White, 353

Wombell, Sir George, 173

Women in Love, 93, 94

WOOF, ROBERT, 343n

WOOLF, VIRGINIA, 93, 266

WOOLNER, THOMAS, 316, 333

Wootton, 49–50

Worcester, 9

Worcestershire, 7, 8, 21

Wordsworth, Catherine, 330, 331, 333

Wordsworth, Christopher, 325, 345

WORDSWORTH, DOROTHY, 139, 178, 179, 180, 181, 182, 328, 329, 330, 331, 332, 333, 335, 344, 345, 349, 350, 351

Wordsworth (Dorothy) Dora, 329, 333, 336n

Wordsworth family, 329, 330, 331, 335, 336, 345

Wordsworth, Gordon, 336

Wordsworth, John (the poet's father), 347

Wordsworth, John (the poet's son), 329

Wordsworth, Mary Hutchinson, 178, 179, 180, 182, 185, 325, 329, 332, 333, 344, 351

Wordsworth Museum, 332, 337

Wordsworth, Richard, 317

Wordsworth, Thomas, 329, 331, 331

WORDSWORTH, WILLIAM, xv, 65, 98, 139, 157, 178, 179, 180, 181, 182, 183, 184, 185, 202, 207, 227, 266, 267, 269, 272, 304, 308, 309, 313, 317, 321, 328, 329, 330, 331, 332, 333, 334, 335, 336, 342, 344, 345, 346, 347, 348, 349, 350, 351

Works (Francis Bacon, edited by James Spedding), 345
World War I, 166
Wray Castle, 322
Wreckin, The, 15, 17, 19, 20, 21
Wroxeter, 21
Wuthering Heights, 123, 130, 133, 136, 139
WYCHERLEY, WILLIAM, 8
Wythburn, 336

Yanwath, 348–49
Ye Olde King's Head Hotel (Chester), 245
Ye Olde Trip to Jerusalem (Nottingham), 82

Year of the World, The, 220
Yellow Book, The, 265
York, xvi, 13, 123, 127, 141n, 154, 158, 159–67, 170, 173, 179, 182, 186, 190, 191, 193
York, Edward Augustus, duke of, 170
York, House of, 209, 299
York Minster, 158, 159–62, 163, 173
Yorkshire, 106, 115, 123, 136, 211, 258, 287, 327, 351
YOUNG, EDWARD, 190
YOUNG, FRANCIS BRETT, 313

Zennor, 62
Zoonomia, 38

Hotels, Inns, Restaurants and Pubs

(Although every effort has been made to insure that this list is as current as possible, these kinds of establishments can change their names or go out of business even as type goes to press. So please check before visiting.)

Ambleside: Low Wood Inn, 324, 325
Ashbourne: Green Man and Black's Head Hotel, 58–59
Barnard Castle: The King's Head, 211
Beverley: The Beverley Arms, 154
Bridgnorth: Railwaymans Arms, 23
Chester: Ye Olde King's Head Hotel, 245
Clun: Buffalo Inn, 20; The Sun, 20
Cockermouth: Trout Hotel, 347
Coxwold: The Fauconberg Arms, 173
Croft-on-Tees: Croft Spa Hotel, 189
Eastwood: Three Tuns Inn, 90, 91
Grantham: The Angel and Royal, 106; The George, 106, 107
Grasmere: Nab Cottage, xv, 334; The Swan, 333, 334
Greta Bridge: Morritt Arms Inn, 212, 213
Halifax: Lord Nelson Inn, 139; Rose and Crown Inn, 139
Harrogate: Betty's Cafe and Tea Shop, xvi, 178
Hartington: The Charles Cotton, 61
Haworth: The Black Bull Inn, 134
Keswick: Royal Oak Hotel, 341, 342
Knutsford: Angel Hotel, 254, 255; La Belle Epoque Restaurant Français, 255, 257; Royal George Hotel, 254, 255, 257
Lichfield: Angel Croft Hotel, 46; The George, xvi, 45, 46; The Swan, 45, 46; Three Crowns Inn, 45
Liverpool: Britannia Adelphi Hotel, 267
Ludlow: Angel Hotel, 17; The Feathers, 19
Manchester: Old Wellington Inn, 288
Monk Fryston: Monk Fryston Hall Hotel, 176
Near Sawrey: Esthwaite Lodge, 313
Newby Bridge: The Swan, 313
Nottingham: Ye Olde Trip to Jerusalem, 82
Penrith: Gloucester Arms, 351; Tudor Restaurant and Coffee Room, 351
Preston: Bull and Royal, 300
Shrewsbury: Lion Hotel, 11, 12; Raven Inn, 11
Skegness: Vine Hotel, 117
Southwell: Saracen's Head Inn, 95, 97
Stafford: The Swan, 31, 32
Thirsk: The Golden Fleece, 180
Thorpe Cloud: The Izaak Walton, 61
Uttoxeter: White Hart Hotel, 48n, 49